From the Somme to Victory

From the Somme to Victory

The British Army's Experience on the Western Front 1916–1918

Peter Simkins

Foreword by Gary Sheffield

First published in Great Britain in 2014 by
The Praetorian Press
an imprint of
Pen & Sword Books Ltd
47 Church Street
Barnsley
South Yorkshire
S70 2AS

ISBN 978 1 78159 312 7

A CIP catalogue record for this book is available from the British Library

Typeset in Ehrhardt by
Mac Style Ltd, Bridlington, East Yorkshire
Printed and bound in the UK by CPI Group (UK) Ltd, Croydon,
CRO 4YY

Pen & Sword Books Ltd incorporates the imprints of Pen & Sword
Archaeology, Atlas, Aviation, Battleground, Discovery, Family History,
History, Maritime, Military, Naval, Politics, Railways, Select, Transport,
True Crime, and Fiction, Frontline Books, Leo Cooper, Praetorian Press,
Seaforth Publishing and Wharncliffe.

For a complete list of Pen & Sword titles please contact
PEN & SWORD BOOKS LIMITED
47 Church Street, Barnsley, South Yorkshire, S70 2AS, England
E-mail: enquiries@pen–and–sword.co.uk
Website: www.pen–and–sword.co.uk

Contents

Foreword

Professor Peter Simkins MBE is one of the most significant historians of the First World War that Britain has produced. His reputation rests on his achievements not in one or two fields, but in many. As an author, lecturer, museum curator, battlefield tour guide, teacher, mentor and leading figure in the Western Front Association he has had, and continues to have, a central role in the world-wide community of scholars investigating the British army of 1914–1918. In this book he correctly observes that over the last fifty or so years, military history has become increasingly academically respectable, and that the study of British military history of the First World War has been transformed. In my view, Peter has played a quietly important role in both these processes, through his impeccable scholarship and his role as a public historian.

Undoubtedly, Peter's magnum opus is *Kitchener's Army*.[1] First published in 1988 and since republished, this is a magisterial study of the creation and organisation of the 'New Army' and Territorial units and formations at the beginning of the First World War. Rereading the book over quarter of a century since its first appearance, several things strike me. First is the breadth of the coverage. This is not just military history, but also political, social and economic history of a very high order. The second is Peter's mastery of such a vast range of primary and secondary sources. Third, *Kitchener's Army* has stood the test of time remarkably well. If a second edition ever came out, a great deal of scholarship that has appeared after its initial publication would need to be incorporated (much of it influenced by Peter's work), but this would certainly not invalidate the conclusions of the original book. I am wary of using the word 'definitive', but I can safely say that it will be a very long time indeed before *Kitchener's Army* is supplanted as the essential book on the raising of the New Armies. Finally, it is worth reflecting on the extent to which *Kitchener's Army* has acted as a foundation upon which many other books, articles and dissertations have been built. To have written such a seminal work is a very fine achievement.

Following the writing of *Kitchener's Army*, Peter Simkins' main scholarly focus has been on the operational history of the British Expeditionary Force (BEF) – a natural progression from the raising of the New Armies to their employment on the battlefield. The chapters in this book give ample testimony to his impressive command of both primary sources and the secondary literature. He has produced a number of scholarly articles and book chapters, some of which appear in this book, but I would also mention three important pieces on the command of the BEF which readers of this volume should seek out. The first is 'Haig and the Army

Commanders', published in 1999.[2] This is a seminal piece which examines the often complex relations between Haig as Commander-in-Chief and his principal subordinates. I found myself turning to it again and again when writing my biography of Douglas Haig, *The Chief* (2011). As my current project is concerned with General Sir Henry Rawlinson, commander of Fourth Army on the Somme and in the Hundred Days, I can see Peter's 'For Better or Worse: Sir Henry Rawlinson and his Allies in 1916 and 1918' being equally influential.[3] The third piece is a discussion of Herbert Plumer, who was commander of Second Army for much of the war. The absence of personal papers makes Plumer a particularly tricky subject, but Peter made highly effective use of a range of primary sources to produce a masterly, 'must-read' study.

Peter Simkins has had two careers, as a museum professional and as an academic military historian. His work at the Imperial War Museum, where he rose to become Senior Historian, was important not least for his role in presenting the history of Britain in the two world wars to the public. This was a busy and demanding job, and after retiring from the IWM he has been able to devote more time to research and writing on the Great War. Peter has also, to the great benefit of the subject, became one of the UK's foremost public historians of the First World War. In particular, he is a favourite on the Western Front Association lecture circuit.

Not every great scholar also has communication skills, but Peter is a wonderfully engaging and inspiring teacher. I had the privilege of working with him at the University of Birmingham and latterly at the University of Wolverhampton, and have sat on panels with him at many conferences and seminars, and shared guiding duties with him on a number of battlefield tours. Sparing his blushes, wherever he speaks he adds to his fan club, and he has been hugely influential in the community of First World War scholarship that has grown up in the UK over the last few years. He succeeded Corelli ('Bill') Barnett as President of the Western Front Association, and has been a great success in this role. One of the reasons for Peter's popularity is that he wears his learning lightly. Always friendly and accessible, he has what Denis Healey called a 'hinterland', in this case love of jazz and sport. Among other things, Peter is a talented jazz pianist, and a devoted follower of Ipswich Town FC.

My association with Peter Simkins began in 1981, when as a 20-year-old undergraduate at the University of Leeds I went to visit him at the IWM to ask his advice on a topic for a dissertation on the raising of a Kitchener battalion. Typically, he was kindness itself, gave me some very good advice, and several years later he acted as the eternal examiner of my MA thesis. He has been a hugely positive influence on my career as a mentor, supporter and friend, and I am delighted that he has joined the new military history set-up at the University of Wolverhampton, where he will be playing an active role in the new MA in the History of Britain and the First World War.

Of all the historians who have helped over the last few decades to transform our understanding of the British army in the Great War, I have no hesitation in singling out Peter Simkins as one of the most important. This book is a showcase of the work of a military historian at the very top of his game, and it is an honour to be write the foreword.

Gary Sheffield
Professor of War Studies
University of Wolverhampton
May 2014

List of Illustrations

List of Maps

Abbreviations

AA&QMG	Assistant Adjutant and Quartermaster-General
ADC	Aide de Camp
ADMS	Assistant Director of Medical Services
AEF	American Expeditionary Force
AFA	Army Field Artillery
AG	Adjutant General
AIF	Australian Imperial Force
AOH	Australian Official History
AWM	Australian War Memorial
BEF	British Expeditionary Force
BGGS	Brigadier-General, General Staff
BGRA	Brigadier-General, Royal Artillery
Bt	Baronet
CAB	Cabinet
CB	Companion of the Bath
CBSO	Counter-Battery Staff Officer
CCC	Churchill College, Cambridge
CEF	Canadian Expeditionary Force
CGS	Chief of the General Staff
CHA	Commander, Heavy Artillery
CIGS	Chief of the Imperial General Staff
C-in-C	Commander-in-Chief
CO	Commanding Officer
CoS	Chief of Staff
CRA	Commander, Royal Artillery
CRE	Commander, Royal Engineers
CSM	Company Sergeant-Major
DAAG	Deputy Assistant Adjutant General
DAA&QMG	Deputy Assistant Adjutant and Quartermaster-General
DCM	Distinguished Conduct Medal
DGT	Director-General of Training
DLI	Durham Light Infantry
DMO	Director of Military Operations
DSD	Director of Staff Duties
DSO	Distinguished Service Order
EEF	Egyptian Expeditionary Force

FGCM	Field General Court Martial
FSR	*Field Service Regulations*
GAF	Groupe d'Armées des Flandres
GAN	Groupe d'Armées du Nord
GAR	Groupe d'Armées de Réserve
GHQ	General Headquarters
GOC	General Officer Commanding
GOCRA	General Officer Commanding, Royal Artillery
GS	General Staff
GSO1	General Staff Officer (1st Grade)
GSO2	General Staff Officer (2nd Grade)
GSO3	General Staff Officer (3rd Grade)
HE	High Explosive
HLI	Highland Light Infantry
HQ	Headquarters
IGT	Inspector-General of Training
IWM	Imperial War Museum
JSCSC	Joint Services Command and Staff College
KCL	King's College, London
KOYLI	King's Own Yorkshire Light Infantry
KRRC	King's Royal Rifle Corps
LHCMA	Liddell Hart Centre for Military Archives
MC	Military Cross
MEF	Mediterranean Expeditionary Force
MGC	Machine Gun Corps
MGGS	Major-General, General Staff
MGRA	Major-General, Royal Artillery
MM	Military Medal
NAM	National Army Museum
NCO	Non-Commissioned Officer
NLS	National Library of Scotland
OH	Official History
RAI	Royal Artillery Institution
RE	Royal Engineers
RFA	Royal Field Artillery
RGA	Royal Garrison Artillery
RUSI	Royal United Services Institute for Defence Studies
SS	Stationery Service
TF	Territorial Force
TNA	The National Archives
VC	Victoria Cross
WFA	Western Front Association
WO	War Office

Introduction and Acknowledgements

Advancing years and major surgery – particularly in combination – have an uncomfortable habit of reminding one of one's own mortality and causing one to pause and reflect on remaining ambitions and unfulfilled tasks. A serious illness and a subsequent operation in 2012 certainly made me realise that I still had a fair amount of historical writing 'in the bank' in the form of unpublished historical essays and lectures on topics which have long been of interest to me. With the centenary of the Great War upon us, I felt that these pieces might possibly be of some interest to others and, thanks to Pen and Sword, I am now able to share my thoughts with a wider readership.

The essays that make up this book were written over a period of fifteen or more years, although they have been updated, where appropriate, to take account of fresh evidence and new research and writing on the First World War. While it was by no means a deliberate aim when I first wrote them, most of the essays (or chapters) have a number of common themes. One is the combat performance of the Kitchener-raised New Army divisions on the Western Front, and especially in the Somme region, in the years 1916 and 1918. A second thread is the learning process which took place in the British Expeditionary Force (BEF) in France and Flanders during the 1916–1918 period and the extent to which that process was continuous, smooth or uniform amongst its component formations. The third recurrent theme is the increasing devolution of command downwards to divisional, brigade and battalion level as the war progressed. The first two essays, however, are historiographical in content. As I re-emphasise in Chapter 1, the centenary is probably as good a time as any to take stock of recent interpretations of the fighting on the Wetsern Front and the nature of the front-line experience.

Having been centrally involved in the 'revisionist' movement in British First World War studies, and admitting to being at least partly responsible for applying the term 'learning curve' to the process of operational and tactical improvement in the BEF which culminated in the successful all-arms battles of 1918, I find that I am now often hoist with my own petard. As I hope that this book reinforces, the majority of historians of the British army in the Great War are firmly in agreement that the BEF *did* achieve marked improvements in many aspects of its performance even if most would also argue that the so–called 'learning curve' was in fact far from smooth and was subject to periodic mistakes and setbacks. At this juncture, I feel it necessary to point out that, when first used in this connection among British military historians in the early 1990s, the phrase 'learning curve' was mainly employed as a kind of shorthand to signify that one rejected the 'lions led by donkeys' and 'butchers and bunglers' interpretations of the First World War. It also signalled that, based on archival research and analysis of primary sources, one had come to adopt a different, more objective view of the BEF's real achievements and of the various factors which underpinned them. Given the growing consensus on the issue, we should perhaps at last recognise that, at least among serious students of the First World War, this particular battle has now been fought and won and that the term 'learning curve', when used in this connection, should therefore be laid gently to rest, its duty done.

This is not to say that victory in the wider battle has yet been attained. In a recent lecture, Professor Stephen Badsey, of the University of Wolverhampton, remarked that the 'revisionist' view of the BEF on the Western Front has now become 'mainstream'.[1] I would agree with Steve that this is so in academic circles but I would equally argue that the wider public perception of the Great War is still deeply mired in the seemingly bottomless depths of the *Blackadder* approach and 'butchers and bunglers' myths generally (though not universally) peddled by the popular media.

I still find it difficult to swallow the criticism that the work of several 'revisionist' historians, including myself, has been too Anglocentric in scope, content and tone. Speaking personally, I make no apologies for having spent the best part of thirty years working on the history of the BEF on the Western Front. When we set out on the 'revisionist' path, many academic historians and popular writers still followed the 'lions led by donkeys' interpretation. Now, in 2014, we know a great deal more about the organisation, infrastructure, tactical development, command and control, logistics, artillery and engineering effort, brigade and divisional commanders, and the actual operations of the BEF. As a result of a lot of effort, we have moved some way from the basic 'muck and bullets' perception but this position would not have been reached without a considerable amount of dedicated – and unashamedly Anglocentric – research, which simply needed to be done. Much work remains to be carried out on the role of the British and Dominion forces in France and Flanders, particularly on manpower issues, training, the reserve and drafting system, the social and geographical composition of units, casualties and morale and discipline. So long as these gaps in our present knowledge exist, there will be an important role for *British* First World War studies in general. How can we truly place the achievements of Britain's allies in a proper perspective and really understand our relationships with those allies unless we also genuinely understand the nature and experience of the BEF and its component parts?

In the course of fifty years as a military historian, it has been my privilege to work under, and learn from, some of the leading international figures of my profession. First and foremost is the doyen of British military historians, Professor Sir Michael Howard, under whom I studied as an undergraduate and (briefly) as a postgraduate at King's College, London, between 1958 and 1962. It was Michael Howard who, above all, inspired me to follow in his footsteps and, indeed, who was largely instrumental in securing a post for me as archivist and research assistant to the late Sir Basil Liddell Hart – a position which I held from early 1962 until the late summer of the following year. Ironically, I now hold views on the history of the Great War which are almost diametrically opposed to those instilled in me relentlessly by Sir Basil, but I shall never forget his kindness and encouragement to me as a young historian, and the stimulating after-dinner conversations which we had in his study at States House, Medmenham. I am in little doubt that this sort of exposure to Sir Basil's acute intellect helped me to sharpen my historical instincts to a marked degree at a key formative stage in my career. Then, on 3 September 1963 – the anniversary of Britain's declaration of war on Germany twenty-four years earlier – I joined the staff of the Imperial War Museum in London, the Director of the Museum then being Dr Noble Frankland, the distinguished official historian of the 1939–1945 strategic air offensive against Germany. He taught me much, over the next two decades, about the need for rigorous scholarly methodology. My thirty-five years at the IWM presented many challenges which, I sincerely hope, similarly helped my development as a historian. The task of translating historical concepts and ideas into a visual form for museum exhibitions, through the use of artefacts, documents, photographs and audio-visual techniques – something I was frequently called upon to achieve – imposed its own set of exacting demands. Having to summarise the Battle of the Somme in 175 words at the insistence of an exhibition designer was unquestionably a useful discipline to master! A further inspirational figure, whom I first met in Liddell Hart's study half-a-century ago, is my long-time friend Professor Brian Bond, whose own standards of scholarship offer a constant benchmark of excellence to which I have always, if sometimes inadequately, aspired.

I feel similarly blessed to have worked closely with, and to have learned from, a whole company of other scholars, not only of my own generation but also including promising younger members of the profession. Those whose friendship and advice I shall long treasure – and whose work in this field has contributed hugely to the re-emergence of military history as an academic discipline – include, not least, my colleagues at the University of Birmingham over the last decade or so: Dr John Bourne, Professor Gary Sheffield, the late Dr Bob Bushaway and Dr Jonathan Boff. I owe an immense debt to both John Bourne and Gary Sheffield for encouraging me me to remain active in the academic world after my retirement from the Imperial War Museum and for allowing me to play a role in the development of the MA in British First World War Studies at Birmingham. Others whose help I have greatly valued are Professor Martin Alexander, Professor Stephen Badsey, Professor Ian Beckett, Professor Mark Connelly, Dr Adrian Gregory, Professor John Gooch, the late Dr Paddy Griffith, Dr J.P. Harris, Professor Keith Jeffery, John Lee, Dr Nick Lloyd, Dr Sanders Marble, Dr K.W. Mitchinson, Professor William Philpott, Dr Andy Simpson, Professor Sir Hew Strachan and Professor J.M. Winter. Nor should I forget my friends and colleagues in the Commonwealth, particularly Peter Burness, Ashley Ekins, Roger Lee, Peter Pedersen, Robin Prior, Chris Pugsley, Peter Stanley and Trevor Wilson.

I also owe a special debt of gratitude to those colleagues with whom I worked daily at the IWM for so many years and who did as much as anyone to help shape my historical thinking, especially that relating to the First World War. Foremost among these former colleagues in this connection are Peter Hart, Dr Bryn Hammond, Mike Hibberd, Brad King, Chris McCarthy, Laurie Milner, Dr Simon Robbins, Mark Seaman, Nigel Steel, the late Rod Suddaby and Dr Neil Young. Many of the IWM staff members whom I have just named were regular members of the memorable 'Friday Club' – held at the nearby 'Two Eagles' or 'The Ship' – where, over sausage, egg and chips, and a pint or two of IPA, one invariably engaged in lively discussions on historical issues of mutual interest, ranging from the identity of Jack the Ripper to the BEF's tactics in the 'Hundred Days'. It is, I believe, no facile exaggeration to claim that, for a period in the 1990s, the IWM's 'Friday Club' – at which the likes of John Lee, Gary Sheffield and Andy Simpson were frequent participants – made a notable contribution to the then current 'revisionist' debate and thereby reinforced the Museum's growing reputation as a centre of excellence in First World War studies alongside King's College London, the University of Birmingham and the Royal Military Academy Sandhurst.

While acknowledging my indebtedness to so many in our profession, I must not fail to mention two more who have, in different ways, exerted a huge influence on me. One is the late John Terraine who, for so long, swam courageously against the prevailing tide of opinion about the Great War and who, I hope, was belatedly reassured and repaid by the knowledge that younger generations of scholars now shared his views. The second near-legendary figure who made a lasting impact on me was the late Rose Coombs, herself a former colleague of mine at the IWM. It was Rose who first introduced me to, and taught me to cherish, the battlefields of the Western Front. Through her, I became, in the mid-1980s, an enthusiastic participant in the activities of the Western Front Association, little thinking that, in 2011, I would be accorded the massive honour of being elected as the WFA's Honorary President, in succession to John Terraine and Correlli 'Bill' Barnett. To this day, whenever I am in Ypres, I make a point of treading the path of the Rose Coombs Memorial Walk near the Lille Gate and paying a silent but heartfelt tribute to a remarkable lady.

I am, of course, particularly grateful to those institutions and individuals who have allowed me access to the collections in their possession and have granted me permission to use, or quote from, material for which they hold the copyright. They include The National Archives at Kew and the Controller of Her Majesty's Stationery Office; the Trustees of the Imperial War Museum, London; the Trustees of the National Army Museum, London; the Trustees of the Liddell Hart Centre for Military Archives, King's College London; the Master, Fellows, Scholars and Archivist of Churchill College, Cambridge; the Cambridge University Press; the Trustees of the National Library of Scotland, Edinburgh; the Public Record Office of Northern Ireland; the Councillors of the Army Records Society; the Special Collections Department of the Brotherton Library, University of Leeds; the Regimental Museum of the Royal Highland Fusiliers, Glasgow; the Australian War Memorial, Canberra; Earl Haig; and Mr M.A.F. Rawlinson. Every effort has been made to contact the current copyright holders of material cited in this book and sincere apologies are offered to anyone whose copyright has inadvertently been infringed. In such cases I will seek to rectify the matter in future editions.

Apart from those mentioned above, I must also offer my warmest thanks to various people who have, in their different ways, helped to see this book into print. These individuals, in turn, include Gary Sheffield, for writing the Foreword; Duncan Youel, for his splendid work on the maps; Michael Stedman, for his kind assistance with some of the photographs; William Spencer at The National Archives, for his help in locating relevant documents; Jamie Wilson, for passing on to the publishers my original suggestions for the book; Joyce E.M. Steele and Sandy Leishman at the Royal Highland Fusiliers Museum, for finding and supplying the portrait photograph of A.J. McCulloch; and Suzanne Foster, the Archivist of Winchester College, for additional details abour George Gater. On my return visits to my former place of employment, the Imperial War Museum, my path was greatly smoothed by Suzanne Bardgett, Yvonne Oliver, Tony Richards and Alan Wakefield, as well as the aforementioned Simon Robbins and the late Rod Suddaby. For so generously sharing information and material with me, I am deeply grateful to John Bourne, Steve Broomfield, Derek Clayton, Aimée Fox-Godden, Alistair Geddes, Trevor Harvey, Alison Hine, Dr Peter Hodgkinson, Simon Justice, Andy Lonergan, Dave Molineux, Dr Geoffrey Noon, Dr Alun Thomas, Rob Thompson and Berkeley Vincent. Whenever I got into trouble with my computer, which was often, my son-in-law Jonathan Byford invariably solved the problems for me. My commissioning editor at Pen and Sword, Rupert Harding, has likewise been a model of wisdom, patience and sound advice during the preparation of this volume. Alison Miles, my copy editor, has shown both tact and commendable attention to detail in helping me to fine-tune the text. Finally, I must, above all, thank my brothers, Geoff and Michael, my daughter Catherine and my wife Jane for their love and encouragement.

Peter Simkins
May 2014

Chapter One

'Everyman at War' Revisited[1]

In 1991, I contributed an essay to a book – edited by Brian Bond – called *The First World War and British Military History*.[2] The essay bore the title 'Everyman at War: Recent Interpretations of the Front Line Experience'. With the centenary of the Great War now being commemorated, it seemed to me to be an appropriate time to review the even more recent historiography of the First World War – and of the front-line experience in particular – to assess how far this has developed and changed since I wrote my original essay. In 1991, I made various criticisms of what I then saw as an existing imbalance in First World War studies, and I also suggested some potential topics and areas of research which, if explored, might help to remedy that imbalance and improve our *real* understanding of the front-line experience. Today I will also consider how far those issues have actually been addressed by historians and researchers over the past two decades.

When I looked at the situation as it was in 1991, I was encouraged (as I am now) by the continuing and growing interest in the First World War. One of the factors which I then identified as crucial to this trend was the opening for research of the bulk of the British official records of the conflict. This, of course, is now very much an accepted fact and, since 1991, research facilities and opportunities at the major public archives in the UK and the Commonwealth have, in some respects, changed out of all recognition – not least because of stunning advances in technology. For example, one little thought, in 1991, that twenty-three years later one would be able to sit at one's own desk in Oxford, Cheltenham or Dundee and, through the magic of computers and the Internet, download Australian and Canadian divisional, brigade and battalion war diaries. And none of us who are old enough to recall, with a shudder, how making notes at the Public Record Office once involved hours of laborious handwriting with pencils that constantly needed sharpening, will have failed to embrace the advent of the lap-top or the digital camera. The *physical* aspects of research are therefore now much easier than they were, though the process of analysing and digesting the data thus gathered remains as challenging as ever.

A second factor which I identified as important in 1991 was the increasing respectability of military history as an academic discipline. This, I think, has at least been maintained and probably developed over the past twenty years or so. The establishment, in the last decade, of a flourishing Centre for War Studies at the University of Birmingham exemplifies this trend. As part of its activities, the Centre offers a specialist MA course in British First World War Studies which, in the academic year of 2011–2012, attracted over thirty part-time students – a success which is sufficient testimony in itself to the robust present and future health of Great War scholarship in this country. There are, too, excellent individual military historians, or teams of scholars and teachers, to be found at the Universities of Cambridge, Kent, Leeds, Northampton, Oxford and Wolverhampton, as well as at my own *alma mater* King's College London, and at such institutions as the Royal Military Academy Sandhurst and the Joint Services Command and Staff College. Since making my original observations at the beginning of the 1990s, both Birmingham and Cambridge have published admirable *series* of scholarly studies of various aspects of the history of warfare and focusing, in Birmingham's case, on the First World War.

In 1991 I wrote that 'the present tide of popular interest in First World War topics shows no sign of abating. Evidence of the hold which the war continues to exert on scholars and the general public alike may be seen in the growing numbers visiting the battlefields of Flanders and Gallipoli each year ...' Indeed, since making that comment, the numbers of battlefield visitors have increased to a level that even I would not have dared to predict all those years ago. Battlefield touring is now almost an industry. In the late 1980s there was, I think, only one well-known company specialising in battlefield tours. Now there are several, with extensive programmes of tours on offer.

I also saw evidence of rising popular interest in the Great War in the founding of organisations such as the Western Front Association (WFA) – which, in 1991, was just over ten years old. That lusty infant has now grown into a mature and sturdy adult of thirty-three – still relatively young and, one fervently hopes, with a bright and productive future still ahead. The growth of the WFA to its present strength of some 6,000 members in branches both at home and overseas is an achievement to be commended.

One of the principal features of the works published in the UK and in Commonwealth countries in the latter half of the twentieth century was that, collectively, they tended to give far greater prominence than was previously the case to the views and experiences of junior officers and other ranks. This change of emphasis mirrored the corresponding social history boom of that period and certainly owed a lot to political changes and the emergence of a more egalitarian social climate from the 1960s onwards. A key factor which then encouraged the new level of interest in 'everyman's' experience of the First World War – and continues to do so – was the contribution of the mass media, especially television, in creating an increased awareness of the value of historical material. Such awareness, in turn, greatly helped the assembly and growth of major collections of private papers – including diaries, letters and unpublished memoirs – at the Imperial War Museum, the University of Leeds and elsewhere. Since 1991, as I suggested earlier, new technology has almost totally transformed our ability to record history as well as to undertake research. An indication of just how quickly things have changed in this sphere is that, in 1991, I was talking mainly about television and about the new advantages of the portable cassette-tape recorder. The latter had suddenly enabled almost anyone to record the oral testimony of men and women who had seen active service between 1914 and 1918 and to conduct what one might term 'a smash and grab raid on history'. At that time I noted that, between 1972 and the early 1990s, the Imperial War Museum had recorded over 330 interviews with veterans of the Great War. Thanks to the sterling work of Peter Hart and his colleagues, that figure has now grown to over a thousand, though with the death of the last surviving veterans of the Great War, this particular route into history has been firmly closed.

On the other hand, since the early 1990s, the appearance and development of other forms of technology have more than compensated for this. Few of us, in 1991, would have forecast that, one day, we would explore the battlefields with the aid of satellite navigation, the 'Linesman' technology and trench maps on DVD-Rom. And how many of us foresaw the colossal boom in family history research made possible by ancestry websites on the Internet? The latter phenomenon (i.e. the Internet) is, I feel, the most remarkable of all, since it enables us to carry out much of the basic legwork involved in First World War research without moving from the comfort of our own homes.

Following in the footsteps of writers and historians such as Denis Winter, John Ellis, Peter Liddle, Tony Ashworth and Malcolm Brown, some scholars have courageously sought to provide an overview of British and Dominion soldiers on active service rather than examine their experience and attitudes from the perspective of a particular campaign or battle. Perhaps the most outstanding of these works to appear in recent years is *Tommy: The British Soldier on the Western Front, 1914–1918*, a massive 717-page study by the late and much-missed Richard Holmes which appeared in 2004.[3] While acknowledging the undoubted advances and improvements in First World War scholarship, Holmes remained keenly aware that one of the principal problems in trying to write about the conflict is that many people will have read Siegfried Sassoon, Wilfred Owen, Pat Barker and Sebastian Faulks before they become aware of one's own work. By studying the war primarily in terms of literature, Richard argued that 'we do not simply colour our view of the past and make it all but impossible to teach the war as history. We go on to tint our picture of the present and our image of the future too'. Richard similarly pointed out that, for years, it was impossible to attend a military presentation without a clip from *Blackadder Goes Forth* discussing the strategic imperative of moving Haig's drinks cabinet an inch or two closer to Berlin. There was thus a distinct danger of losing sight of the men who *actually* fought the war. Holmes's *Tommy* – which embodies a judicious and skilful mixture of personal experience accounts (from both published and unpublished sources) and balanced scholarly analysis – happily does not suffer from the 'cut and paste' approach evident in some anthologies whereby the historian – if he or she is not careful – can all too easily become, in Holmes's opinion, little more than a 'copytypist'.[4]

Rightly, I think, Richard urged caution about how we use oral history and other non-contemporary evidence. Even survivors of the Great War, he wrote, sometimes become:

Veterans, General Issue, neatly packed with what we wanted to hear, exploding at the touch of a tape-recorder button or the snap of a TV documentarist's clapper-board. Up to my neck in muck and bullets, rats as big as footballs, the sergeant major was a right bastard, all my mates were killed. And sometimes, just sometimes, they tell us this because they have heard it themselves.

Much better, says Richard, to go back to what people thought at the time, not least by looking at the diaries, letters and unpublished memoirs of junior officers and other ranks deposited at the Imperial War Museum and elsewhere. Holmes is not advocating that we ought not to read Sassoon and Graves but he does suggest that 'the closer we get to events the better our chance of finding out how people really felt'.[5]

Scholarly overviews of the front-line experience are not, of course, solely the province of British historians. Desmond Morton's *When Your Number's Up: The Canadian Soldier in the First World War*, published in 1993, is a worthy example of this genre.[6] Moreover, a new generation of First World War scholars has emerged in Canada, including such historians as Tim Cook, David Campbell and Andrew Iarocci. Tim Cook's two-volume work *At the Sharp End: Canadians Fighting the Great War, 1914–1916* and *Shock Troops: Canadians Fighting the Great War, 1917–1918* – published in 2007–2008 – represents a welcome modern overview of the Canadian Corps on the Western Front.[7] In Australia, Peter Pedersen's *The Anzacs: Gallipoli to the Western Front*, which appeared in 2007, builds upon earlier general studies of Australians on active service by Bill Gammage and Patsy Adam-Smith.[8] Fortunately, current Australian scholars are continuing to demythologise the 'Digger' stereotype and, like their Canadian counterparts, are seeking to avoid the narrow and nationalistic 'colonial superman' approach that permeated much Commonwealth writing on the Great War until the mid-1960s. The same might be said of recent work by Glyn Harper – including his *Dark Journey: Three Key New Zealand Battles of the Western Front* (2007) – which enhances our understanding of the motivation, morale, attitudes and achievements of the officers and men of the splendid New Zealand Division in 1917–1918.[9]

Earlier I referred, with Richard Holmes, to the pitfalls of employing the 'cut and paste' or 'copytypist' approach to history. One should observe, however, that a fair number of historians *have* successfully avoided the problems inherent in that approach while *still* mining the rich seams of private papers and personal experience accounts housed at the IWM and in other archives. This applies especially to a succession of writers who have followed the lead of Martin Middlebrook and Lyn Macdonald in providing studies of particular battles or campaigns which remain substantially based upon oral history and the letters and diaries of junior officers and other ranks. Malcolm Brown, whose *The Imperial War Museum Book of the Somme* and *The Imperial War Museum Book of 1918: Year of Victory* – which came out in 1996 and 1998 respectively – has proved one of the most popular of such writers, combining, in his books, well-chosen extracts from documents and oral history with a highly readable narrative.[10]

One of the most encouraging features of the period under review has been the steady flow of books on battles or campaigns which have made excellent use of first-hand accounts. Worthy of mention here, I feel, are Ian Passingham's *Pillars of Fire*, on the Battle of Messines, and Jonathan Walker's *The Blood Tub*, on the Battle of Bullecourt, both of which were published in 1998; Paul Cobb's *Fromelles 1916* (2007); Charles Messenger's *The Day We Won the War: Turning Point at Amiens, 8 August 1918* and Bryn Hammond's *Cambrai 1917: The Myth of the First Great Tank Battle*, both published in 2008; Paul Kendall's *Bullecourt 1917: Breaching the Hindenburg Line* (2010); and three works which appeared in 2011, namely Dale Blair's *The Battle of Bellicourt Tunnel*, Scott Bennett's *Pozières: The Anzac Story* and Chris Baker's *The Battle For Flanders: German Defeat on the Lys, 1918*.[11] The prolific Jack Sheldon deserves a special commendation, I suggest, for preventing us from being totally Anglocentric in outlook and his books on the Imperial German Army at First Ypres, in 1915, and at the Somme, Vimy Ridge, Passchendaele and Cambrai – all published between 2005 and 2010 – have added greatly to our understanding of the front-line experience of the *feldgrauen* across no-man's-land. If nothing else, Jack Sheldon has made it absolutely clear that not all the pain and suffering was felt by one side alone on the Western Front.[12]

The modern master of this type of popular anecdotal history is almost certainly Peter Hart who has, in many respects, inherited the mantle of Martin Middlebrook and Lyn Macdonald. Peter's long career at the IWM has unquestionably given him direct access to its wonderful collections of letters, diaries and oral history interviews, but it still requires extensive subject knowledge, a lot of research and considerable skill and empathy in order to turn such raw material into coherent and compelling accounts of military operations. Not least in his book on 1918, Peter adopts a broadly 'revisionist' stance in noting the importance of the tactics, technology and training that not only helped the BEF to withstand the German onslaught in the spring of 1918 but also enabled it to conduct the all-arms battles which were the foundation of its ultimate victory. Hart is the first to concede that he does not always present detailed operational analysis but instead relies, in his own words, mainly on 'hundreds of personal stories that illustrate the nature of the fighting and how individuals responded to some of the worst fighting of the war'. The veterans' original words, he asserts, 'have a real immediacy and power that can't be beaten' and his message, in his book on 1918, is that war is 'always dirty, murderous and frightening', and rarely in any way glorious or inspiring. One story from among many will offer something of the essential flavour of Peter's work on 1918. Captain Charles Brett, of the 5th Connaught Rangers, relates how on 10 October that year, near Le Cateau, a shell fragment disembowelled one man while another had a leg almost severed below the knee. Brett completed the amputation by cutting the remaining strands of flesh with his own penknife. Later on, while falling back in the face of a German counter-attack, Brett found himself sharing a shell-hole with the same amputated limb. One doesn't get much closer to the reality of the front-line experience than that! What Hart conveys best, perhaps, is the raw courage, doggedness and sheer bloody-mindedness of the junior officers,

NCOs and men of Haig's armies who were called upon to go into action repeatedly in the final months and weeks of the war.[13]

One might reasonably contend that the biggest single growth area in First World War studies since 1991 has been that of new unit histories, especially battalion studies – a field in which the output has been prodigious over the past two decades. Pride of place here should perhaps be given to the series of Pals battalion histories published by Leo Cooper and Pen and Sword since the mid-1980s. Considerations of space preclude one from listing them all individually, but the series has included books on the locally raised Pals battalions from Accrington, Barnsley, Birkenhead, Birmingham, Bradford, Durham, Halifax, Hull, Kensington, Leeds, Liverpool, Manchester, Salford, Sheffield and Tyneside, as well as slightly less localised units such as the Sportsman's Battalion of the Royal Fusiliers and the 16th (Public Schools) Battalion of the Middlesex Regiment. Bill Mitchinson's *Cotton Town Comrades*, on the 24th Manchesters, published in 1993, was one of the few Pals battalion studies *not* originally published by Pen and Sword. Other New Army battalions which fall outside the 'Pals' category have also received detailed attention. One could cite, for example, Matthew Richardson's book *The Tigers* on the 6th, 7th, 8th and 9th Leicesters (2000); Jack Alexander's *McRae's Battalion* on the 16th Royal Scots (2003); Derek Clayton's book on the 9th King's Own Yorkshire Light Infantry (2004); John Stephen Morse's study of the 9th Sherwood Foresters (2007); and Wayne Osborne's ongoing work on the 10th Notts and Derby Regiment, the first volume of which came out in 2009.[14] Local Territorial battalions too have received their share of scrutiny. From this group one could justifiably single out Bill Mitchinson's *Gentlemen and Officers* (1995), which covered the London Rifle Brigade; the late Jill Knight's *All Bloody Gentlemen*, on the Civil Service Rifles (2004); Alec Weir's *Come on Highlanders!* on the 9th Highland Light Infantry (2005); and Derek Bird's *The Spirit of the Troops is Excellent*, on the 6th Seaforth Highlanders (2008). Neither should one overlook Leonard Sellers' work on the Hood Battalion of the Royal Naval Division (1995).[15] Regular battalions have not been ignored, I am pleased to say – as demonstrated by the appearance of John Ashby's *Seek Glory, Now Keep Glory*, on the 1st Royal Warwickshires (2000), and by James W. Taylor's fine books on the 1st and 2nd Royal Irish Rifles in the Great War (2002 and 2005).

While it may be unfair even to consider placing works in any sort of order of merit, one or two, I feel, are models of their kind and possibly provide scholarly templates for future unit studies. In her *Citizen Soldiers* (2005), Helen McCartney examines in depth the wartime experience on the Western Front of two Territorial units – the Liverpool Rifles and the Liverpool Scottish – and the links between the troops of these mainly middle-class battalions and the civilian society from which they came. She argues persuasively that, far from being passive victims of the conflict, officers and men of these units largely retained their civilian outlook throughout the war and used it to modify and influence their experience in the front line. The maintenance of close cultural and personal ties with home buttressed their morale to an appreciable extent. Dr McCartney likewise presents convincing evidence that, despite heavy casualties, conscription and changes in the reserve and drafting system, these battalions at least retained a strong local and county identity up to the Armistice.[16] Dale Blair's stimulating book *Dinkum Diggers* (2001) is an equally penetrating analysis of the 1st Battalion of the Australian Imperial Force (AIF). Apart from providing a fresh look at the causes and effects of the mutiny in that veteran battalion in late September 1918, Blair seeks to identify some of the points at which the reality of the front-line experience on the one hand and the 'Digger' myth on the other may be seen to diverge. He places particular emphasis on the myths of egalitarianism and individualism that have long been synonymous with the Anzac stereotype. He contends that the actual experience of the 1st Battalion reveals significant contradictions to the accepted 'Digger' image and he also has some useful things to say about the degree of anti-British sentiment that contributed to the establishment of that image and to the emerging sense of Australian nationhood.[17] Recently, however, the unit history has been taken to the ultimate extreme by Peter Stanley in his *Men of Mont St Quentin* (2009) – a fascinating microscopic study of the lives, and in some cases the deaths, of a dozen or so members of No. 9 Platoon, 21st Battalion AIF, who were involved in the capture of Mont St Quentin, near Péronne, on 1 September 1918.[18]

Besides continuing to help concentrate a fair amount of attention on the front-line experience of junior officers and other ranks, many of the new battalion histories I have mentioned offer a very useful service to military and family historians alike, in providing detailed rolls of honour and service, lists of decorations and awards, and information as to where the fallen are buried or commemorated. Nevertheless, I remain slightly uneasy about the possibility that the lingering focus on Pals battalions may have distorted our interpretation of the front-line experience and to overrate their achievements – though *not* their sacrifice. My own research into the performance of New Army divisions on the Somme in 1916 appears, for example, to run counter to the original claims and expectations of the raisers of Pals units – i.e. that those who shared a common geographical, social or occupational background would *necessarily* train and fight better than those who did not enjoy such advantages. In fact, I have found that, in general, not only did those divisions which were essentially composed of Pals battalions actually have lower success rates in offensive operations than War Office-raised New Army formations, but also that they tended to have a worse disciplinary record in terms of soldiers who were executed during, or as a result of, operations on the Somme that year.

While the writing of battalion histories has undoubtedly flourished since the early 1990s, the same cannot be said, overall, of divisional histories. Some work, it must be conceded, *has* been done in this field. Kenneth Radley's work on the 1st Canadian Division, published in 2006, is one example that springs to mind, and I have already mentioned, in another context, Glyn Harper's recent writings about the New Zealand Division.[19] To these one might add Mitch Yockelson's *Borrowed Soldiers* (2008) which covers the story of the US 27th and 30th Divisions, under British command, in the summer and autumn of 1918; Mark Ethan Grotelueschen's *The AEF Way of War* (2007), which examines in detail the performance of four other American divisions – the 1st, 2nd, 26th and 77th – in the final Allied offensive; and Leonard Smith's *Between Mutiny and Obedience*, published in 1994, which analyses the experience of the French 5th Infantry Division, a formation with a fine fighting record but which, in 1917, was the most mutinous division in the whole French Army.[20] Smith looks, in particular, at the key role played by junior officers and NCOs who both exerted command authority yet also shared the dangers and privations of the ordinary *poilu*. His argument is that soldiers developed self-determined rules of how they would, or would not, fight and imposed these rules on those above. By altering the parameters of command authority to fit their own perceived interests, soldiers and commanders negotiated a behavioural space between mutiny and obedience (hence the title of the book).[21] Whether or not one agrees with all of Len Smith's conclusions, it is to be regretted that his work generally failed to inspire similar, and new, studies of British divisions. Indeed, some British divisions have no published history at all, let alone a new one, to the best of my knowledge. The 1st, 30th, 31st, 32nd, 37th and 41st Divisions are cases in point at the time of writing. There is, then, still plenty of scope for bright young historians to exercise their talents in this particular area.

That said, the twin topics of the morale and discipline of the front-line soldier – the central themes of Leonard Smith's book – have certainly *not* been overlooked by British historians in the years under review. Far from it. Many of us inevitably became involved in, and swept along by, the heated debate which raged throughout the 1990s and until 2006 over the campaign to pardon the 306 British and Empire soldiers shot at dawn for military offences during the Great War. One could maintain that no other aspect of First World War history generated more hot air or stirred up more hot blood than this subject. Since the pardon was granted in 2006, things have calmed down somewhat but, even when the debate was at its height, a handful of British historians, to their great credit, managed to make contributions to it which were notable for their objectivity as well as their scholarship. In his essay on Capital Courts-Martial, published in *Look to Your Front* in 1999, Dr John Peaty usefully reminded us that a fair proportion of those executed were already under suspended sentences for a previous offence (including some under *two* suspended sentences) or had been previously sentenced to death. One had been sentenced to death for desertion on two previous occasions.[22] Two years later, in their book *Blindfold and Alone* (2001), Cathryn Corns and John Hughes-Wilson not only provided us with a much-needed balanced yet compassionate overview of British military executions in the Great War but also with a number of in-depth case studies which were solidly based upon detailed examination of the original court-martial records.[23]

As in 1991, scholarly surveys of morale and discipline in the BEF as a whole are still comparatively thin on the ground, although *some* outstanding work in this field has been published in the intervening years. Gary Sheffield's excellent *Leadership in the Trenches*, which appeared in 2000, focuses upon officer-man relations as a factor in the maintenance of the British army's morale in the First World War.

Gary argues persuasively that the paternalistic ethos of the pre-war Regular officer infused the wartime officer class and was essential to such maintenance of morale. Deference on the part of the other ranks was similarly accepted as part of an interdependent, reciprocal relationship which worked as long as the officers kept their side of the paternalistic bargain and acted in a way that inspired trust and permitted the socially conservative British working man – who was neither revolutionary nor abjectly submissive – to retain self-respect.[24] In this context one must also mention Timothy Bowman's book, published in 2003, on discipline and morale in Irish regiments in the Great War. Bowman demonstrates that, in fact, discipline and morale varied at the battalion, let alone the brigade or divisional, level. He concedes that, generally, Irish units had worse courts-martial records than their English, Scottish or Welsh counterparts. He also shows that, while there is little evidence to suggest that soldiers in Irish formations felt any real sympathy for the emerging Sinn Fein movement, events in Ireland did cause some mistrust among non-Irish units as well as some concern in the War Office.[25]

The long-neglected subject of the role of the junior infantry officer on the Western Front has similarly, if belatedly, received serious attention from scholarly historians within the past few years. John Lewis-Stempel, in his eminently readable and sometimes moving *Six Weeks* (2010) – sub-titled *The Short and Gallant Life of the British Officer in the First World War* – asserts that the wartime junior officers from public schools and grammar schools brought with them the very values that the country needed. 'After all', he asks, 'who could withstand the highly drilled militarism of the Kaiser's Army – except for a corps of young British men who believed in the qualities of courage, patriotism, selfless service, leadership and character?' He is clearly in no doubt that, in the Great War, Britain helped to overcome a 'right wing military dictatorship' because of the 'thin khaki line of 1914–1918, led by their junior officers'.[26] A similar, if slightly less emotional, stance is adopted by Christopher Moore-Bick in *Playing the Game: The British Junior Officer on the Western Front, 1914–18*, published in 2011. The latter author suggests that junior officers were fortunate in possessing an ability, in the front line, to create and maintain positive conceptions of their work and status by *adapting* familiar practices and ideas. This was due, he writes, 'partly to their elevated status as officers and partly to their backgrounds and educations, despite claims that the public-school ethos was unsuited to conditions on the Western Front ...'. Crucially, he recognises the degree to which faith in the justice of their cause and a traditional belief in honour and self-sacrifice sustained most of them in the most trying conditions, the emergence of disillusionment – as expressed by Sassoon and Owen – notwithstanding. In his view, young officers 'did not merely cling blindly to an outdated creed. As they became increasingly experienced they achieved an understanding of the nature of the Western Front, retaining that conviction in the justice of their cause and subtly (and unconsciously) remoulding their ethos to enhance its relevance'. If the juxtaposition of Victorian concepts of honour and glory with the horrors of the Western Front were strikingly incongruous, many officers were still able to adapt their expectations of soldiering and their sense of military virtue so that 'this dislocation was not insupportably stark'. Moore-Bick rightly emphasises that British soldiers were neither the 'inbred, ineffectual fops of some popular mythology' nor the 'undifferentiated plaster saints created by some commemorative practices'.[27]

One must not forget the thought-provoking comparative approach adopted by Alexander Watson in his important study *Enduring the Great War: Combat, Morale, and Collapse in the British and German Armies, 1914–1918*, which appeared in 2008. The purpose of the book, Watson states, is 'to provide a new understanding of the impressive resilience demonstrated by the British and German armies … by focusing on individual soldiers' psychology'. Concentrating on the Western Front, Watson analyses the impact of attritional trench warfare on the British and German armies and discusses the nature and extent of the physical and mental strains it imposed on front-line soldiers. He then surveys the motives and factors – including unit loyalty, coercion, discipline, comradeship and the need to protect home and family – which persuaded men to endure discomfort and danger and sustained their will to fight. He also looks at the various coping mechanisms, such as fatalism, religious beliefs, superstition and self-deception about chances of survival, that helped most soldiers avoid psychological meltdown and retain some sort of combat motivation. When assessing the role of junior officers in this process, Watson underlines both the similarities and differences between the British and German officer corps, while conceding that inter-rank relations in the German army 'were perhaps never so good' as those in the BEF. He also maintains that it was not 'better nerves' but 'superior supplies and a lower level of exhaustion' that allowed the BEF to survive the trials of 1918 and eventually triumph. In his judgement, hunger, lack of rest and apathy – rather than anger, resentment or revolutionary aims – lay at the root of Germany's military collapse, with this taking the form of an 'ordered surrender' *led* by junior officers whose own morale was eroded.[28]

Perhaps the last word on 1918 should be left to an ordinary British soldier – Geoffrey Husbands, a Derby lad who, between the ages of 18 and 22, served in three different battalions of the Sherwood Foresters. His wonderful 550-page memoir – *Joffrey's War* – was published as recently as 2011. It is one of the very best First World War memoirs of a citizen-soldier that I have read and I have been privileged, with John Bourne and the late Bob Bushaway, to have played a small part in bringing it to public attention. As Geoffrey Husbands wrote of the German March 1918 offensive: 'It was one thing to grouse and contemplate more drastic measures to end a stalemate and an unending state of trench warfare, but to let Jerry walk through without a fight, no fear!'[29]

In several respects, then, scholarship on the front-line experience in the First World War has come a long way since my historiographical survey in 1991. There is now general recognition of the existence of a learning process in the BEF, particularly from 1916 to the Armistice. The debate now is *not* whether there *was* a learning process but, instead, how patchy or uniform that process actually was and how it may have varied – in both depth and speed – in different parts of Haig's forces on the Western Front. Thanks to the acknowledgement of this learning process, the junior officers and ordinary soldiers of the Great War are no longer seen – at least not in scholarly circles or by bodies such as the WFA – simply as passive and helpless victims or as 'lions led by donkeys'. Rather, they are viewed as men, who, to varying degrees, contributed to the learning process by actually applying – and in some cases helping to originate – the improved tactics and techniques that finally broke the trench stalemate in France and Flanders. But quite how far this awareness and recognition extends is another matter entirely, as the popular conception of the front-line experience in the Great War is far more likely to coincide with, or be influenced by, *Blackadder Goes Forth*, *Birdsong* or *Downton Abbey* than by the works of Gary Sheffield or Peter Hart.

Moreover, despite the huge strides made since 1991, we still have a great deal to learn and discover. For example, there are, as yet, no major studies of the role and experience of the NCOs of the BEF. Other questions too await a full scholarly answer. How was it that the soldiers of 1918, many of whom were conscripts, were able to adapt to the new conditions of semi-open warfare and fight a greater succession of both major battles and minor actions than their counterparts in 1916–1917? To what extent were the tactical improvements of those years truly understood and applied by junior officers and other ranks? How and why were they able to keep going over a week or more of constant movement and repeated action? What was the socio-geographical composition of units in 1918 and how far had this altered since 1915–1916? What were the real effects of changes in the reserve and drafting system? What real degree of continuity was there in junior leadership – in other words, how many officers and NCOs survived in each unit long enough to facilitate the victories of 1918 and ensure that there was sufficient experience and expertise, and knowledge of good practice, available to see the young conscripts through the ordeal of battle?

The years 2014–2018 will undoubtedly prompt a veritable torrent of new books on the First World War, as writers and publishers seek to mark the centenary of that conflict. Let us earnestly hope that the high standards attained by much recent scholarship are not totally sacrificed in the scramble to meet the anticipated public demand for fresh books on the subject.

Chapter Two

The Lessons and Legacy of the Somme: Changing Historical Perspectives

Ever since the mid-to-late 1920s, the conduct of the 1916 Somme campaign by the BEF under Sir Douglas Haig has generally received a bad press. On 1 July each year, on the anniversary of the start of the battle, the Somme offensive is presented to the public by the media in predominantly negative terms, with a heavy and repetitive emphasis on words such as 'carnage' and 'incompetence'. Indeed, if people in Britain and the Commonwealth ever pause to reflect upon the 1916 experience, it is highly likely that their thoughts – influenced by a vaguely defined collective folk-memory of the Somme – will have turned towards the slaughter of the Pals battalions, 'lions led by donkeys', 'butchers and bunglers', a 'lost generation', inadequate weapons, misguided strategy and tactics, drawn blinds in countless streets in the industrial North-West, in Belfast and on Tyneside, and, not least, the death of innocence and idealism on the blood-soaked fields of Picardy.

But is that deeply rooted public perception of the Somme wholly justified or, alternatively, did the BEF – from Haig and GHQ down to divisions, brigades, battalions and batteries – actually learn and apply the lessons of the Somme battle? Did the BEF make organisational changes and adopt new tactics and techniques as a result of the Somme experience and, if so, did these changes and new tactics lead to an overall improvement in fighting methods and battlefield performance and thereby contribute significantly to eventual victory in 1918? In other words, can one detect a learning process in the BEF which either started during, or was accelerated by, the Somme offensive? In order to answer some, or all, of these basic questions, it might first be helpful to examine the nature and content of the historical debate on such issues as it was conducted between the early 1920s and the mid-1980s. One will then try to show how, over the last twenty years or so, modern scholarship and archive-based research has not only widened and deepened our knowledge and understanding of the command, operations and infrastructure of the BEF in the First World War but has also simultaneously begun to alter the whole tone of the debate for the better, even if there is still a long road to travel in that direction.

As Ian M. Brown has observed, the literature on the operational aspects of the BEF's performance on the Somme and after can be split into two main groups. One of these groups sees that performance as being primarily influenced by 'internal' factors, while the other group emphasises 'external' considerations. The former, or 'internal' school of thought, tends to focus upon Haig, GHQ and the

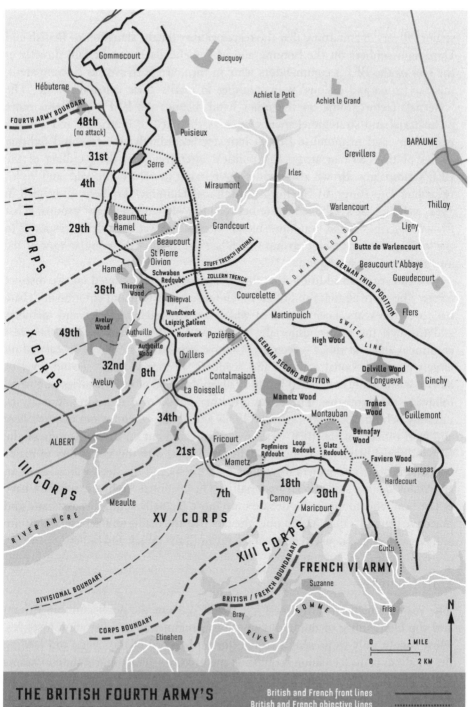

THE BRITISH FOURTH ARMY'S
ZONE OF OPERATIONS, SOMME
OFFENSIVE, 1 JULY 1916

British and French front lines
British and French objective lines ·············
Army boundaries
Corps boundaries – – –
Divisional boundaries
German lines

senior officers, maintaining that the responsibility for the slaughter of British and Dominion soldiers on the Somme and at Passchendaele can be laid directly at the feet of the BEF's commanders who, in turn, are portrayed as 'incompetent, mistake-prone and callous' with 'nothing to rectify their colossal errors'. The 'external' factor group, on the other hand, blames the BEF's problems more on material and strategic elements, such as the need to improvise and equip a mass army and to mobilise British industry accordingly; the size and fighting ability of the German army; and political interference in the handling of the BEF's campaigns. Brown also divides the relevant literature into 'old' and 'new', regarding *Fire-Power*, by Shelford Bidwell and Dominick Graham, published in 1982, as being the symbolic marker between the 'old' and the 'new' groups. What Brown describes as the 'mud-and-blood' view of the war roughly corresponds to the 'old' or 'internal factor' group which 'set the tone for the popular view of the War that remains strong today'.[1]

One can argue, in addition, that the debate has been conducted on two distinct levels. The more audible, and often much more superficial and emotional, debate has, over the years, been waged in widely read popular histories and memoirs and through the media, especially newspapers and television. The other, less emotional and – at times – seemingly almost private debate has been carried on largely by professional soldiers and academic historians. This second level of debate was initially conducted in the 1920s in the flood of unit histories published following the Armistice. There was a further period of discussion and analysis, virtually behind closed doors, in the 1930s and 1940s, when former commanders and staff officers of the BEF were invited to comment on draft chapters of the British official history. Finally, since the late 1960s, with the availability of major collections of private papers in various institutions and the declassification of an enormous quantity of official material in The National Archives, scholars have at last been able to move the debate onto more factually solid, dispassionate and objective ground – notwithstanding the fact that the media and general public are still largely bogged down in no-man's-land amid the 'muck and bullets'.

Unit Histories

The years immediately after the First World War saw the publication, in Britain and the Dominions, of numerous divisional, regimental and battalion histories. Most sought only to present a straightforward record of the deeds and leading personalities of the formation in question and to convey something of the conditions under which its officers and men fought. They therefore tend to be high in factual and narrative content – many being based substantially on the appropriate unit war diaries – and correspondingly low on analysis of operational methods or command and control factors. However, the majority avoid triumphalism and a fair proportion retain a degree of objectivity that, as Gary Sheffield and Dan Todman comment, has stood the test of time.[2] For example, the history of the 34th Division (published in 1921) contains a note by Major-General C.L. Nicholson – who commanded the formation from 25 July 1916 until the Armistice – on the reasons for the division's failure to take Intermediate Trench, to the east of High Wood, in August 1916. He identifies these as being that both the objective and the division's front line were under enfilade observation from High Wood; that the German artillery could therefore bring down enfilade fire on both trenches; and 'last, but not least, the attacks, after that of the 3rd/4th August (owing to circumstances beyond divisional control) were carried out as isolated operations, and never as part of an attack on a wide front'.[3] The history of the 56th (London) Division, which also appeared in 1921, similarly reproduces a report, written in late 1916 by Lieutenant-Colonel A.D. Bayliffe – the commanding officer of the 1/12th London Regiment (Rangers) – on 'Lessons to be Deducted [*sic*] from the Operations on the Somme'. With the experience of the battle fresh in his mind, Bayliffe concluded that objectives should be clear and include well-defined landmarks; that attacks should always be delivered with sufficient weight – and never less than four waves – even against apparently inferior defences; that brigade headquarters should be sited as far forward as possible; that to maintain the efficiency of units, a larger ratio of experienced officers than was customary should be kept out of an attack, since the average replacement officer was 'quite useless' on his first appearance in a modern battle; that assault troops should stick as closely as possible to the creeping barrage; that there was a need for closer liaison between infantry and the heavy artillery; and that improvements must be wrought in the use of Stokes mortars and in tank-infantry co-operation. Tanks, he asserted, should have officers in charge 'who have more experience and knowledge of the methods of infantry and artillery in war'.[4]

In the history of the 5th Division (another 1921 publication), the formation's problems in the July fighting at Longueval are squarely attributed to Fourth Army's tendency at that time to mount piecemeal attacks on a narrow front, enabling the Germans to concentrate most of their artillery fire on relatively small sectors. The authors point out that, on 5 and 25 September 1916, when the division took part in co-ordinated attacks on a broader front, it was much more successful. 'We hoped', they wrote, 'that the lessons of these operations had been learnt'.[5] The 25th Division's history, which was being written even before the war ended, judged that success in the attack on Stuff and Regina Trenches on 21 October 1916 was due to 'careful and thorough preparation', excellent artillery support and 'the increased confidence with which the troops advanced close up under the artillery barrage'.[6] Cyril Falls, in his history of the 36th (Ulster) Division – published in 1922 – states that, on the Somme, the use of artillery 'had not yet reached anything approaching the science of the following year … It was still, however, to cost thousands of lives before the factories could produce sufficient of the latter [i.e. artillery and ammunition], or the higher commands reach the ratio between infantry force and mechanical aids necessary to the prosecution of a given operation'. Falls also perceived, however, that other 'external' factors had caused difficulties. No explanations, he declared, 'that can be found stand without ample tribute to the fighting qualities of the German soldier'.[7] These remarks, nevertheless, indicate that Falls (later one of the official historians) was in little doubt that a learning process had clearly begun on the Somme. The author of the history of the 5th Australian Division shared this view: 'The Somme Battle', he remarked, 'eventually had tactical results of the most far-reaching character – though they were not fully seen until over a year later ...'.[8]

Disenchantment

It must be conceded that, despite the large number of veterans, unit histories had a relatively restricted readership and influence and, from the mid-1920s onwards, they were engulfed by a tide of works which stressed the negative aspects of the war and of the Somme and Passchendaele in particular. Professor Brian Bond has already presented a splendid survey of the so-called 'anti-war' literature of the late 1920s and 1930s in his book *The Unquiet Western Front* (2002).[9] However, a few key points about such works should perhaps be re-emphasised here. Robert Graves's *Goodbye to All That* (1929), Edmund Blunden's *Undertones of War* (1928) and Siegfried Sassoon's *Memoirs of a Fox Hunting Man* (1928) and *Memoirs of an Infantry Officer* (1930), together with other works in this period, all stressed the appalling conditions faced by the front-line soldier and criticised commanders for their bloody-mindedness and remoteness from such conditions. Bond is anxious to highlight the paradox that some of those who appeared to be the angriest anti-war writers were not pacifists or conscientious objectors but brave, efficient and even zealous officers 'who voluntarily returned to the front after recovering from wounds or illness'.[10] Even so, at a time when the euphoria of victory and the headiness of the Jazz Age had largely worn off and the world was suffering from economic depression and the emergence of dictatorships, such works struck a major chord with a public which was now highly receptive to anti-war messages and strongly disinclined to see war in any kind of positive light. Indeed, the receptiveness of the British public to these eminently readable works, combined with the war poetry of Sassoon, Owen and others to encourage a mindset that now regarded the Great War with revulsion, and laid a firm foundation for the 'mud and blood' view of the Western Front. Again Brian Bond sounds a note of caution, venturing to suggest that the 'anti-war' writers have exerted more influence since the 1960s than they actually did in the 1930s. He contends that Owen's poetry was comparatively little known in 1930, whereas Rupert Brooke was still enormously popular. Today, he adds, Owen is widely accepted as the 'voice' of the Western Front while Brooke's poetry is out of fashion.[11]

Even in the late 1920s and early 1930s, some former officers published accounts which offered a different, much less negative, view of the Western Front in general and the Somme in particular. In *A Subaltern's War*, written just after the conflict but not published until 1929, Charles Carrington (who served on the Somme in the 1/5th Royal Warwicks and published his book under the pseudonym of Charles Edmonds) confidently pronounced that the Somme battle raised the morale of the BEF in France and Flanders:

Although we did not win a decisive victory, there was what matters most in war, a definite and growing sense of superiority over the enemy, man to man. The attacks in mid-July were more successful and better managed than those of July 1st. In August and September things went better still. When the tanks made their surprising appearance on September 15th, rejoicing knew no bounds; but the Germans were not yet badly beaten enough nor our skill great enough for us to make the best of our winnings ...

Perhaps more interesting, and to the point, are Charles Carrington's remarks, written many years later, in the Preface to the 1984 edition of his book. He declared:

It can only have been a very stupid, insensitive young man who did not concentrate his mind, sometimes during the long months of military training, on blood and wounds. We were pretty well prepared for the horrors of war by the time we came to face them, and though, for my part, I have never been able to work the Somme out of my mental system, nothing happened to me there which could be described as 'disenchantment' or 'disillusion'. It was what I had bargained for.

He went on to say:

Why and how did the survivors of the Somme and Passchendaele persist in their solidarity, defeat the German onslaught in the spring of 1918 and break the Hindenburg Line in the final advance of hard and bloody fighting? They could not have reached their goal if they had at all resembled the woe-begone weaklings with no confidence in their leaders who were described in the books produced by the school of 'disillusion'.[12]

Official Histories

There were other sub-groups of published sources in the late 1920s and 1930s which, each in their own way, helped to shape our current collective view of the Somme. One of these sub-groups consists of the official histories of the Somme campaign. The first to appear, in 1929, was Volume III of the Australian official history – *The Australian Imperial Force in France, 1916* – by C.E.W. Bean. This is a monumental work, with well over 900 pages of main text. In all the volumes written by Bean on the AIF, his principal purpose was to record for posterity, and to extol, the fighting qualities and the independent spirit of the Australian soldier, leading him to produce highly detailed narratives of operations with much emphasis on the deeds of individual units, officers and men. As Peter Pedersen notes in his Introduction to the 1982 edition of Bean's Somme volume, I Anzac Corps delivered nineteen attacks at Pozières and Mouquet Farm between 23 July and 5 September 1916, at a cost of 23,000 casualties. At home in Australia, Pedersen writes, 'these losses were seized upon by both sides of the conscription debate, fuelling a controversy whose effects have been felt ever since. The strain affected the attitude of the Australian soldier towards the war and many believed that they had been uselessly sacrificed'.[13] As might be expected, Bean, in 1929, was highly critical of the conduct of the operations at Pozières and Mouquet Farm, feeling that the strength and vitality of the Australian divisions had been largely wasted there and suggesting that, if the Australians had instead been kept fresh for the 15 September attack at Flers-Courcelette, the results would almost certainly have been 'infinitely greater'.[14]

Bean roundly condemned the tendency of Gough's Reserve (or Fifth) Army to order successive piecemeal and isolated attacks on a narrow sector, thereby attracting the concentrated weight of hostile artillery fire. In a 1944 letter to John Gellibrand – who had commanded the 6th Australian Brigade on the Somme – Bean described the operations of August–September 1916 as 'springing from an impossible tactical conception – that of forcing a salient gradually behind an enemy salient on a strongly fortified front ... giving a bang with the hammer every day or two to drive the wedge in another fraction of an inch'.[15] Referring to Gough in the 1929 volume, Bean judged that the 'Australian troops, who learned to hate the reiteration of attacks on narrow fronts, not unfairly attributed to him the responsibility, and their aversion to serving under him, which became pronounced the following year, dated from this time'. While acknowledging that Haig, in accordance with *Field Service Regulations* (*FSR*), was more often than not inclined to leave the detailed conduct of operations to the 'man on the spot' – in this case Gough – Bean also attributed blame to Haig as the overall 'author' of the piecemeal tactics which prevailed between 23 July and 15 September, the Commander-in-Chief having informed Gough and Rawlinson (the two army commanders concerned) on the former date that the battle was to be continued with the object of wearing down the enemy by a series of local assaults until conditions favoured a resumption of the wider offensive.[16]

Nor was Bean prepared to swallow the argument – advanced by some of Haig's apologists – that the Somme offensive had primarily been intended to wear down, rather than break through, the enemy. This idea had been fostered, to some extent, by Haig's Despatch of 23 December 1916 in which he called the Somme 'The Opening of the Wearing Out Battle', and by his Final Despatch in 1919, when Haig retrospectively claimed that the victory of 1918 had been made possible by the attritional battles of 1916–1917 and that the fighting on the Western Front had been 'one great and continuous engagement'.[17] Bean maintained, however, that 'Haig looked back upon this battle with different eyes from those with which he had planned it'. Bean admitted it was true that, before the offensive began, Haig had foreseen that his first effort to achieve a breakthrough might not be successful, 'in which case he might attempt to wear down the enemy to a breaking point and then again endeavour to create the break ... The truth appears to be that, although Haig did believe attrition to be necessary, it was, in this battle, merely a subsidiary aim ...' Haig's choice of senior subordinates was 'far from perfect' in Bean's opinion and the 'internal working of the British offensive was from first to last marked by a lack of co-ordination of which the fighting at Mouquet Farm was merely a single instance'.[18] According to Bean, Haig's leadership in 1916 was deficient in 'quick imagination and sure judgement of subordinates'. Yet Bean was happy to praise Haig's capacity to learn from his mistakes and to show 'the moral courage to change his attitude when the need became clear to him'. It was possible, Bean predicted (rightly as it turned out) that history

> will assign him a greater share than is yet recognised in the responsibility for the victories with which the war ended. It is difficult to conceive any factor more ominous to the Germans than the continued presence among their opponents of this resolute, unwavering soldier, deeply skilled in technique, but prevailing by qualities of character more than of intellect; cold and inarticulate, but with the strength to keep the British Government at arm's length; punctiliously loyal to it, to his subordinates, and to his Allies.[19]

In these passages Bean pinpoints both the best and the worst of Haig, although his overall summary of the Somme contains only a very limited and inadequate analysis of the tactical and organisational improvements in the BEF that the 1916 offensive generated.[20]

The two volumes of the British official history which covered the Somme – written by Brigadier-General Sir James Edmonds and Captain Wilfrid Miles – appeared respectively in 1932 and 1938. Edmonds and Miles were much less overtly critical of the high command of the BEF than Bean, although Haig, GHQ and the army commanders do not totally escape censure. In a fine essay on Edmonds, David French suggests that loyalty to friends and contemporaries may partly explain why Edmonds tends to gloss over the shortcomings of the high command, Edmonds having served at GHQ during the war as one of Haig's Deputy Engineers-in-Chief. He may thus have felt it necessary to close ranks with his old comrades in the face of civilian criticism at a time, in the 1930s, when large numbers of polemical and self-justifying books were being written by former participants and politicians, especially Lloyd George.[21] In general, then, Edmonds and Miles emphasise 'external' rather than 'internal' factors when discussing the setbacks and losses suffered by the BEF in 1916. Attrition was inevitable, writes Miles, given the continuous nature of the Western Front, which made manoeuvre impossible, and also the 'character and temper of the German resistance'.[22] Other problems stemmed from the pre-war neglect of the army; the massive expansion of the BEF in 1915–1916, which meant that much had to be improvised and learnt in the field while fighting a skilled and implacable enemy; the inherent difficulties arising from the advent of new technologies (such as the tank); the loss of many experienced instructors and staff officers in battle in 1914–1915; political interference from Whitehall and Paris; and Britain's junior position in the alliance in 1916, relative to the French – a fact which considerably restricted the BEF's strategic choices and freedom of action.[23]

It is true that, in his Preface to the second Somme volume, Edmonds – after mentioning the BEF's shortages of heavy artillery and the inadequate training of the troops – *does* list some 'internal' factors, namely 'the unevenness in the fighting value of the different divisions ... faulty tactics, as exemplified by the terribly heavy losses ... on the first day of the assault; and ... the failure of the commanders of the higher formations to consult, or accept the views when offered of the forward leaders ...'.[24] The differences and disagreements between Haig and Rawlinson before the 1 July, 14 July and 15 September attacks are also discussed although such disputes are never strongly underlined. The main text contains much detailed operational narrative but, unlike Bean's history, has comparatively few comments upon individuals. As an example of how Edmonds and Miles gloss over uncomfortable facts, we now know that, on 24 August 1916, Haig – frustrated by the repeated failures of Fourth Army's narrow-front and insufficiently supported attacks on Guillemont – left Rawlinson in no doubt of his displeasure, sending him what Robin Prior and Trevor Wilson have called a 'boys'-own-guide on how to command an army'. The only oblique reference to this reprimand in the official history reads:

> Conferring with his corps commanders on the morning of the 25th August, General Rawlinson read a GHQ letter, received the previous evening, which emphasised the extreme importance of securing Ginchy, Guillemont and Falfemont Farm without delay. The Commander-in-Chief considered the task well within the power of the troops and artillery available, provided that the higher commanders, bearing in mind the standards of training which existed among the troops and subordinate leaders, gave their personal attention to the details of preparation.[25]

Drafts of each chapter of the official history were sent before publication to hundreds of officers who had participated in the events being discussed, their comments being invited. The resulting correspondence can today be examined in the CAB 45 files at The National Archives. These files are full of interesting views – both critical and adulatory – from the individuals involved about their brother officers or the reasons why particular actions were successful or unsuccessful. One recognises that much of this was anecdotal gossip and that some of the more severe criticisms may perhaps have been unconsciously coloured by the 'anti-war' literature then in vogue, but, while Edmonds undoubtedly used the reminiscences and comments of surviving officers to augment and cross-check the written record, he did not do so with an uncritical eye, recognising that at least some of those who replied to him might be taking advantage of the opportunity to present their own decisions and actions in the best possible light. Whatever its shortcomings, the CAB 45 correspondence, if judiciously approached, still provides meaty pickings for modern historians.

As for the tactical and organisational lessons of the Somme, Miles does note, in the concluding chapter of the second 1916 volume, the growing effectiveness of the creeping barrage; the increasing importance to the artillery of flash-spotting, sound-ranging and the work of the Field Survey units of the Royal Engineers; and the creation of 'army' field artillery brigades to provide a more flexible field artillery reserve. In contrast, he somewhat underplays the potential of the tank, Lewis guns, Stokes mortars and overhead machine-gun barrages, and, characteristically, the crucial appointment of Brigadier-General Arthur Solly-Flood as head of a Training Directorate at GHQ is dealt with in only a footnote.[26] Certainly Miles presents the New Army divisions of 1916 in an unfavourable light when compared with the old professional BEF (see Chapter 3). One should also note that, whereas Bean's works were enormously influential in shaping Australian views of the war, the British official histories – which Edmonds hoped would be 'suitable for general readers and for students at military schools' – failed to reach a wider public. Indeed, as David French reminds us, their appeal was initially so limited that the publishers, Macmillan, had to be subsidised so that they could make a profit from printing them.[27]

Critics and Commentators

A military commentator who had a much greater immediate impact – and a more lasting one – was Basil Liddell Hart, under whom I worked as an archivist and research assistant in 1962 and 1963. Liddell Hart's books *Reputations* (1928), *The Real War* (1930) and *A History of the World War* (1934) did a great deal to set the tone and content of the debate on the Great War until, and beyond, his death in 1970. As a young officer in the 9th King's Own Yorkshire Light Infantry, he was present at Fricourt on the Somme on 1 July 1916 and also saw action at Mametz Wood, where he was badly gassed with phosgene. He later collapsed, was sent home to England and was mainly involved thereafter in training men in minor tactics. Following the Armistice he served under Ivor Maxse in Northern Command, helping to rewrite the *Infantry Training Manual*, but was compelled to leave the army, on health grounds, in 1924. During the First World War itself, Liddell Hart's attitude to the generals had largely been one of near-idolatry. He wrote, after the Somme battle, that 'the British GHQ ... under the Haig régime comprise the most brilliant collection of brains in the world' and he thought that never had 'any military operation been so wonderfully and minutely organised or so brilliantly conducted as this offensive'. In his judgement at the time, Haig had created 'the finest fighting machine the world has ever known', while Archie Montgomery, the MGGS of Fourth Army, was one of 'the brilliant Chiefs of Staff of the two armies on the Somme'.[28] He was similarly proud of having been present at the introduction of the creeping barrage – 'This wonderful wall of bursting shells' – in 1916.[29] As Liddell Hart himself confessed when jotting down some random thoughts in 1936: 'I intensely admired many of my superiors, and even hero-worshipped a number'.[30]

It was on being obliged to leave the profession he cherished that Liddell Hart's views began to undergo an almost complete transformation. 'I loved the Army all the years I was in it, and my perception of its faults had developed subsequently to leaving', he recalled.[31] Influenced by J.F.C. Fuller, he became a champion of mechanisation in the army and particularly of tanks, which he saw as a war-winning weapon that would help save soldiers' lives. As Military Correspondent, first of the *Daily Telegraph* and then, for several years from 1935, of *The Times*, he was frustrated and irritated by those senior officers in the army whom he regarded as obstinately conservative in their attitude to mechanisation and, since a fair proportion of such officers had held important appointments in the First World War, Liddell Hart became, by extension, an increasingly acerbic critic of British generalship between 1914 and 1918. The truth is that he established his own reputation as a military commentator at least partly by criticising Haig and other First World War commanders and, to preserve that reputation, he had to maintain such a stance, thus painting himself intellectually into a corner from which there was no escape.

His opinions on Haig in *Reputations* were still comparatively mild and while he wrote of Haig's serious errors in conducting offensives, he also stated that there had hardly been a finer defensive general. Haig emerges from this book as a skilful and hard-working soldier who unfortunately proved unwilling or unable to adapt to new technology, a stereotype which Haig's detractors have followed enthusiastically, if misguidedly, ever since.[32] *The Real War* and *A History of the World War* presented an even more negative picture of the performance of the generals on the Western Front, though, as Dan Todman and Gary Sheffield have observed, *The Real War* was actually less caustic in its criticisms of the British high command than later recycling of Liddell Hart's works would lead us to believe.[33] Brian Bond suggests that the main thrust of Liddell Hart's arguments is that Britain – thanks to Henry Wilson's machinations as Director of Military Operations between 1910 and 1914 – made a fundamental and tragic mistake in committing the BEF to a mass continental war of attrition and that this original sin was compounded, from December 1915, by an incompetent, unimaginative and stubborn Commander-in-Chief (Haig), backed by an 'excessively loyal and single-minded' Chief of the Imperial General Staff (Sir William Robertson).[34]

The above-mentioned works of Liddell Hart, however, have several glaring weaknesses. Liddell Hart makes no real attempt to convey the experiences of, or the conditions faced by, junior officers and other ranks, and he is never greatly concerned with the wider factors underlying military operations – such as manpower issues, munitions supply and logistics, or morale. The naval element of the war is only covered briefly and superficially and, despite identifying the importance of the Allied naval blockade in the defeat of Imperial Germany, this merely appears as a kind of afterthought in the Conclusion of *The Real War* rather than being analysed at length in the main narrative. Above all, Liddell Hart dwells on the period of attrition and the BEF's setbacks in 1916–1917, then on the desperate defensive battles of March to May 1918, almost ignoring the BEF's outstanding successes in the summer and autumn of that year, on which, as Hew Strachan notes, Haig's 'claim to greatness must rest'. In overlooking the 'culminating battles of the war', Strachan remarks, 'Liddell Hart allowed his portrayal of British generals to assume an easy continuum, from incompetence on the Western Front to conservatism in the 1920s and 1930s'. Professor Strachan has also shrewdly commented that Liddell Hart's criticisms of the high command in the Great War are naïve in that, while he based his analysis of Haig principally on the Somme and Passchendaele, he (Liddell Hart) apparently failed to appreciate that 'the skills demanded in the leadership of mass armies in an industrial age were more managerial than heroic'. Brian Bond – who personally knew Liddell Hart very well – believes it would be pedantic to place so much emphasis on the shortcomings of Liddell Hart's writings on the First World War were it not for the enduring influence 'of the theories based on such faulty foundations' and the fact that 'so much of the British discussion of the First World War still takes place ... under the guidelines which he established ...'[35] Indeed, one only has to listen to, or read, the glib assertions of the media commentators on the Somme each year to realise just how prevalent some of Liddell Hart's ideas and conclusions still are.

Two major works by senior politicians, both published in the inter-war years, left a similar, if not more bitter, legacy. In *The World Crisis*, which first appeared in six volumes between 1923 and 1929, and later in a two–volume edition, Winston Churchill indicted the attrition strategy adopted by the Entente powers in 1916 and 1917 as being wasteful in soldiers' lives and consequently futile and based on false principles. The 1916 campaign, Churchill declared, was, from start to finish, 'a welter of slaughter which ... left the British and French armies weaker in relation to the Germans than when it opened'. He also accused Haig and Foch (the Allied Generalissimo in 1918) of having launched 'with obstinacy and serene confidence' offensives which were subsequently seen 'to have been as hopeless as they were disastrous', though he did admit that, with the restoration of semi–open warfare and more mobile operations in the final months of the war, Haig and Foch 'were vindicated in the end'.[36]

David Lloyd George's *War Memoirs* were published a few years after *The World Crisis* and rank, in David French's opinion, as 'foremost' among the works of self-justification written by former participants.[37] So far as Haig and the high command were concerned, there can be absolutely no doubt about Lloyd George's venomous intent. In 1934 he candidly told Maurice Hankey, the Secretary to the Cabinet, that he was aiming to re-establish his own reputation as the man who won the war. On another occasion he let it be known that he was 'very sick that Haig and Robertson were not alive. He intended to blow their ashes to smithereens ... Unfortunately, he could not get at them personally'.[38] In his original Preface, he claimed that he lamented 'more than words can express' the need to tell 'the bare facts of our bloodstained stagger to victory', and, in the Foreword to an abridged edition of the *War Memoirs*, published in 1938, he wrote that the 'incredible heroism of the common man' had been squandered 'to repair the incompetence of the trained inexperts ... in the narrow, selfish and unimaginative strategy and in the ghastly butchery of a succession of vain and insane offensives'.[39] I dare say that I am probably not alone in detecting a distinct echo of Lloyd George's vindictive, subjective and hypocritical remarks in many of the present-day media's pronouncements on the First World War, but, as Professor Brian Bond has justifiably suggested, it is perhaps 'unnecessary to comment that Lloyd George had been prime minister when the most controversial of these offensives [Passchendaele] had taken place and had the constitutional responsibility to stop it if he deemed it to be failing or too costly in casualties'.[40]

One incidental but important result of Lloyd George's interpretation of the high command's conduct of the war was that it tended to shift the focus of attention and interest away from the Somme and towards Third Ypres (Passchendaele), so that the latter battle rather than the former thenceforth became for many years – in the collective mind of the British public – the quintessential symbol of the horrors of the Western Front. In the unabridged version of his memoirs, and with Liddell Hart's active assistance, Lloyd George devoted over a hundred pages to Passchendaele as against twenty-seven to the battles of the Hundred Days in 1918, when the Allies actually won the war.

Mud and Blood

The Liddell Hart-Lloyd George view of the Western Front still held sway some twenty-five years later when, with the fiftieth anniversary of the Great War looming on the horizon, another generation – mostly born just before, during or shortly after the Second World War – was introduced to the subject through a new wave of books, films and television productions. This latter generation, however, was, in many respects – and quite literally – *radically* different from their parents and grandparents. The late 1950s and 1960s witnessed the growth of the Campaign for Nuclear Disarmament and the Aldermaston marches; the Suez crisis; the end of National Service; the building of the Berlin Wall; the Cuban missile crisis (when the world appeared to teeter on the brink of annihilation); the Profumo scandal; the emergence of an independent youth culture and sexual freedom; and, in particular, the Vietnam War, which served as a catalyst for anti-American, anti-imperial and anti-establishment opinion, culminating in radical student protests and clashes with authority throughout Europe and the United States. It was decidedly *not* a period when it was easy to have an objective debate about the BEF's handling of the Somme offensive, for example, since the youth of the 1960s generally perceived the Great War as yet another case of 'them against us' and the 1914–1918 conflict as representing a betrayal of the ruled by the rulers.

All this was inevitably reflected in contemporaneous writings on the Great War, even if *some* of the authors in question were neither young nor necessarily radical. Leon Wolff's *In Flanders Fields* (1959) not only kept the public gaze fixed firmly on Passchendaele but also kick-started a new round of 'Haig-bashing'. In Wolff's opinion, the fact that the Ypres offensive of 1917 had continued into November of that year was principally the fault of Haig, and his overall conclusion was that the war had 'meant nothing, solved nothing and proved nothing'.[41] Alan Clark was certainly no radical but his book *The Donkeys* (1961) – which concentrated mainly on the battles of 1914–1915 – nevertheless perfectly mirrored the mood of the coming decade. Although he was not yet Commander-in-Chief during the 1914–1915 period, Haig was still depicted as the leading 'donkey' and as a stubborn, ambitious megalomaniac. Clark contended that the courage and devotion to duty of the 'lions' (i.e. the ordinary soldiers) was so great that, after being squandered in successive ill-conceived offensives and losing more men in one day (1 July 1916) than any other army in world history, they achieved victory in spite of the bungling 'donkeys' (Haig and his generals). Michael Howard, then my tutor and supervisor at King's College London, reviewed the book and described it as entertaining but 'worthless' as history.[42] The portrayal of Haig and the senior commanders as callous, incompetent idiots arguably reached its peak in Joan Littlewood's production of *Oh! What a Lovely War* at the Stratford East Theatre Workshop in March 1963. The production (like Richard Attenborough's film adaptation in 1969) presented the First World War from the citizen-soldier's viewpoint, then a largely fresh approach but one which, as Brian Bond observes, has become relatively common ever since, thus giving *Oh! What a Lovely War* considerable historiographical significance.[43]

The Somme *did* receive some renewed attention in the early 1960s. To his credit, the distinguished historian A.J.P. Taylor, in his *The First World War: An Illustrated History* (1963), did not unreservedly accept the 'lions led by donkeys' myth, concluding that 'this character was not confined to the British, or to soldiers. All the peoples were in the same boat. The war was beyond the capacity of generals and statesmen alike'. However, he regarded the Somme as an 'unredeemed defeat' which shaped the lens through which future generations viewed the Great War: 'brave helpless soldiers; blundering obstinate generals; nothing achieved'.[44] Brian Gardner, in *The Big Push* (1961), presented a straightforward account of the 1916 offensive, drawing largely upon already well-known published sources. Gardner tended to dodge the issue as to whether the Somme battle would be judged by posterity to have been a victory or a failure for the Allies although he appeared to lean towards the more negative standpoint.[45]

A much more balanced study was provided in Anthony Farrar-Hockley's *The Somme*, first published in 1964. Farrar-Hockley's book was, for the time, more thoroughly researched than many books on the subject, making use of both published and unpublished sources, discussions with survivors and – here was a novelty – personal visits to the sites of the actions described. And, Farrar-Hockley added, as 'a subsidiary advantage' he had actually had the experience of being shot at in battle. The book clearly benefits from the author's intimate knowledge of the army and its command structures and it contains interesting and thought-provoking coverage of the planning of the offensive, the bloody first day, and the long summer of hard fighting up to 15 September, much of it at the tactical level and from a divisional, brigade or battalion perspective. To give just one example, he describes, at some length, how elements of the 18th Division, led by Lieutenant-Colonel Frank Maxwell VC of the 12th Middlesex, seized Trones Wood on 14 July 1916. He also examines the difficulties involved in finding experienced officers to replace those killed or wounded whilst in command of brigades or battalions; the lessons learned in successive assaults, such as the need for infantry to keep close to the creeping barrage; and the 'enhanced skill of the gunners' as the battle progressed. These were all themes which would be explored in greater detail by later generations of historians. When discussing Haig's reasons for continuing offensive operations after September 1916, Farrar-Hockley argues that, while the Commander-in-Chief may have believed that the German line might suddenly collapse, he was unable to appreciate fully that his own casualties placed such a cumulative strain on the remaining British infantry that it was unlikely that either the Fourth or Fifth Armies 'had units sufficiently vigorous' to exploit the situation. Disappointingly, his concluding analysis of the strategic consequences of the battle is somewhat superficial, there being no investigation, for instance, of the German decisions to withdraw to the Hindenburg Line or to resume unrestricted submarine warfare in 1917. Neither does Farrar-Hockley seek to emphasise the *positive* tactical and organisational lessons of the 1916 offensive and the changes and reforms in the BEF and the French army that these inspired. All the same, in a 1960s context, he is refreshingly fair in his final summation: 'It may be right to attack the military leaders, they held the responsibility... But it is difficult to avoid the suspicion that they have become whipping posts or scapegoats'.[46]

Counter-attack

One historian, above all, swam resolutely against the prevailing current in this decade, and that was John Terraine. When I was working with Liddell Hart in the early 1960s, I was encouraged to regard Terraine (and, by extension, Haig) as the devil incarnate. Now, with the wisdom of hindsight, I am more inclined to regard Terraine as, in many respects, a model of robust common sense. His *Douglas Haig: The Educated Soldier* (1963) unquestionably represents the first major step in the rehabilitation of the Commander-in-Chief, portraying Haig not as a 'butcher' but as a single-minded professional who was driven by an innate sense of duty and was, in fact, reform-oriented and receptive to new technology. Terraine's views, set out in this book, were repeated in several other works over the next twenty years, notably *The Road to Passchendaele* (1977), *To Win a War: 1918, The Year of Victory* (1978), *The Smoke and the Fire: Myths and Anti-Myths of War* (1980) and *White Heat: The New Warfare, 1914–1918* (which appeared in 1982). None of these books concentrated specifically upon the Somme though all contributed in various ways to the modern debate on the battle.

The core of John Terraine's argument was that 'external' factors made the terrible attrition on the Western Front, *and* the problems faced there by the BEF, unavoidable. With the Germans tenaciously occupying large areas of France and Belgium, a decision *had* to be sought there – hence the 'necessity' of the Somme and the 'inevitability' of Passchendaele. However, poor battlefield communications and the dominance of artillery and machine-guns meant that the defensive frequently held sway over the offensive, ruling out brilliant generalship or an easy route to victory. Terraine asserted that, from mid-1916, the task of engaging the main body of the main enemy in a continental war fell increasingly upon the British army, for the only time in its history, and that it carried out that task, at a heavy cost, with ultimately decisive effect. Although he invariably underplayed, or neglected to cover, the 'internal' and often self-inflicted problems faced by the BEF, and was sometimes weak on tactical and organisational detail, he reminded us all that the Allies actually *won* the war and that the British and Dominion forces, under Haig, had played a leading part in that achievement.

For Terraine, the Somme battle was an undeniable Allied victory and mainly a British one, since it 'laid the essential foundation for the final defeat of the Germans in the field'. He believed that even the horrors of 1 July 1916 helped to shape the whole course of the offensive, since the losses and setbacks of that day had played a 'great part' in 'finally disposing of the idea of positional warfare, with geographical prizes, and had forced the recognition that the true objective must, until it was broken, be the German Army itself'. In Terraine's view, measurements of gains on the map had little relevance to the real nature of the Somme victory, 'unless those gains are related to the cost to the enemy of taking that ground from him'.[47] In *The Smoke and the Fire*, Terraine also made the important point that the 'true texture' of the Somme was at least partly determined by the fact that the Germans had launched a minimum of 330, largely unsuccessful, counter-attacks against the BEF during the battle – this having done much to blunt the cutting edge, and wear down the motive power, of the old first-class, peace-trained German infantry. Making this observation a few years after the publication of John Keegan's *The Face of Battle* and Martin Middlebrook's *The First Day on the Somme*, Terraine declared that this was why it was 'utterly pernicious' to dwell constantly on 'the freak' of 1 July. The enduring image of British infantry rising from their trenches to be mown down is, he writes,

> only a true picture of the Battle of the Somme when set beside that of the German infantry rising from their trenches to be mown down. Those military historians of the 1930s who . .. like Captain Liddell Hart, preferred to lend support to the Lloyd-George-Churchill version of the battle did grave disservice to the men who fought on from 2 July ...[48]

Terraine was one of the principal scriptwriters for the ground-breaking, twenty-six-part, BBC TV series *The Great War*, which was first shown on the new BBC2 channel in 1964. Liddell Hart resigned from the BBC's team of consultant historians in protest over John Terraine's script for the Somme episode which, he felt, placed too much emphasis on the inexperience and lack of skill of British troops instead of criticising the shortcomings of Haig and the high command.[49] But if Terraine could claim a minor victory here, his revisionist advance still had a long way to go. While Terraine had put forward a more positive interpretation of Haig's leadership and strategy, and of the BEF's contribution to victory from 1916 onwards, audience research reports indicated that, contrary to Terraine's intentions, viewers had been struck, most of all, by the horrific images of trench warfare and the apparent futility of the First World War.[50] In this respect, the series – at least in the short term – possibly did more to reinforce existing myths and prejudices than to inspire a major reappraisal of the conflict. Nevertheless, as Alex Danchev has noted, Terraine progressively influenced military historians for the next three decades and beyond. 'Terraine's viewpoint', he writes, 'stripped of its rhetorical excess and forfeit of its emotional charge, served to reorient the historian's mental map of the war'.[51]

The View from the Parapet

An important ingredient in the BBC series was the extensive use, by Tony Essex and the production team, of film, letters, photographs and interviews with veterans, providing a powerful impetus to renewed interest in the experiences of the common soldier. Up to this point the attention of historians remained largely focused upon the war of the generals and politico-military relations. However, as observed in the previous chapter, a number of other factors in the late 1960s and 1970s also combined to alter the whole tone and substance of the debate. These included the opening to the public of the official records of the conflict; the increasing acceptance of military history as an academic discipline; the assembly and growing accessibility of superb collections of private papers – rich in diaries, letters and unpublished memoirs – at the Imperial War Museum and elsewhere; and the advent of the portable tape recorder, which made it possible to interview men who had seen active service in the Great War while they were still around in sufficient numbers to make such oral history projects of real value in furnishing comparative evidence.

The first, and possibly most influential, of the fresh crop of books generated by these important developments was Martin Middlebrook's *The First Day on the Somme: 1 July 1916* (published in 1971). It is difficult to overstate the immense impact which this book had – and still has – in stimulating serious study of the First World War. Speaking personally, it almost certainly did more than any other work, academic or otherwise, to rekindle my passion for the subject. John Keegan later dubbed the book 'a truly heroic effort of historical fieldwork'.[52] Middlebrook drew upon the personal experiences of nearly 550 British and German soldiers to produce an account of 1 July 1916 that possesses both power and sensitivity. He also mined newly available archive sources such as unit war diaries at the Public Record Office (now The National Archives) and the Rawlinson diaries at Churchill College, Cambridge. Admittedly, much of Middlebrook's evidence comes from junior officers and other ranks who had a limited perspective and grasp of events on 1 July itself, yet the many individual stories he quotes are skilfully threaded together to yield a much more rounded picture of Britain's citizen-soldiers of 1916 than most previous historians had presented. In addition, he was perceptive enough to question the inaccurate, but lingering, popular impression that the New Army divisions on 1 July were all bands of 'uniformed innocents', as even

John Keegan called them, noting that the 18th, 30th and 36th Divisions – three of the most successful on 1 July – had not conformed blindly to the Fourth Army's Tactical Notes issued as guidance before the battle. He also outlines the weaknesses of the artillery preparation before the assault and of artillery support on the day itself. On the debit side, he appears to have missed the point that three out of the five British corps along the main battlefront employed some form of creeping barrage on 1 July; is seemingly unaware of the extent to which deference to the commander 'on the spot' was often accepted in accordance with *FSR*; and consequently stops short of analysing just how many assaulting battalions on 1 July adopted formations and tactics other than simply walking forward in long lines 'at a steady pace' as Fourth Army had recommended.

The popularity of *The First Day on the Somme* had two main effects in my view. One was to spark a whole succession of new books (and television programmes) of a similar *genre*, particularly around the sixtieth and seventieth anniversaries of the Somme battle. The second was once more to swing the spotlight decisively away from Passchendaele and back to the Somme as the symbol of the First World War in the public mind. Another powerful work, John Keegan's *The Face of Battle* (1976), was only partly about the Somme, but again concentrated on 1 July. As one might have expected from someone who was then still a Senior Lecturer in Military History at Sandhurst, Keegan's study contains a sharper analysis than Middlebrook's of the BEF's tactics and communication problems on 1 July as well as of the motivation of the British divisions in action that day. However, his work tends to support the negative interpretation of the Somme experience rather than underline its positive aspects. He does, though, pay tribute to the standards of junior leadership on the Somme, arguing that this was of higher quality and greater military significance in the First World War, at least in the British army, than before or since.[53] Malcolm Brown's 1976 television documentary *The Battle of the Somme* – memorably presented by actor Leo McKern – provided another extremely moving examination of 1 July and was again enriched by the use of diaries, letters and personal photographs, much of this material finding its way into Brown's subsequent spin-off book *Tommy Goes to War*.[54] A commendable battalion study also appeared during these years – Alex Aiken's *Courage Past: A Duty Done* (1971), which looks at the operations of the 1/9th Highland Light Infantry (Glasgow Highlanders) at High Wood on 14 and 15 July 1916.[55]

These types of study – concentrating on the experiences of 'everyman at war' or on the deeds of particular infantry formations – continued to flourish and grow in popularity in the 1980s. Lyn Macdonald further reawakened interest with her book *Somme* in 1983. Her canvas was broader than Middlebrook's and she proved adept at providing a straightforward narrative framework of the battle within which individual participants were allowed to relate their own experiences or reminiscences.[56] But the problem with this approach lies precisely in its focus on the individual soldier for, as Robin Prior and Trevor Wilson have shrewdly commented, it often fails to give a proper explanation as to why such heroism could be in vain. They point out that when attacks on the Somme proved futile, as they did on 1 July, this has frequently and mistakenly been attributed to 'the faulty tactics imposed on the infantry by their commanders' and not to 'the insufficiency of killing weapons to facilitate such an attack'. In their judgement, only an abundance of shells and guns could foster the conditions whereby the infantry might operate with a genuine prospect of success. They maintain:

> When the guns proved insufficient and were employed inappropriately ... the infantry also failed, with great slaughter. When the guns were employed with sufficient numbers and skill ... foot soldiers were placed in an environment where they could display their skills and gain a modicum of success. None of this may seem glamorous or heroic, but it more nearly represents the reality of 1 July 1916 than any obsessive focus on infantry tactics.[57]

The oral and written memories of ordinary soldiers obviously had – and still have – an immediacy which appealed directly to general readers, who can often identify more readily with the originators of such testimony than with other sources of evidence, but, again, in Lyn Macdonald's *Somme*, questions of tactical evolution, organisational improvements and command and control are almost totally ignored. In these latter respects, a major step forward was taken by Colin Hughes in his book *Mametz: Lloyd George's 'Welsh Army' at the Battle of the Somme*. First published in 1982, this detailed study of the operations of the 38th (Welsh) Division at Mametz Wood between 7 and 12 July 1916 makes extensive and scholarly use of unit war diaries and private papers, enabling Hughes to produce a reasoned and fair assessment of the command weaknesses and difficulties which beset the division at that stage of the offensive. Hughes was, for example, one of the first modern historians to acknowledge the widespread effects of the 'de-skilling' of the BEF following its rapid expansion in 1914–1915. 'Many of the staff were inexperienced and working under great pressure', he maintains.[58] Philip Orr's work on the 36th (Ulster) Division, *The Road to the Somme*, which appeared in 1987, bravely questioned the traditional explanation that the division's achievements on 1 July were the product of unique religious and sectarian fervour and of an intense *esprit de corps*. In reality, Orr insists, there was only one *military* reason which allowed the 36th Division to enter the German trenches at Thiepval in considerable numbers:

> If Middlebrook is right to suggest that the British lost the battle by a matter of seconds (the interval between the lifting of the barrage and the arrival of the first wave at the German parapet where machine-guns were already opening up on their targets), then it becomes clear that the Ulster HQ decision to send the men out into No Man's Land before the barrage lifted was a crucial factor.[59]

These post-Middlebrook years also saw the inauguration in the mid-1980s of the series of books on individual Pals battalions, published by Wharncliffe/ Pen and Sword. Each gives a very detailed picture of the raising and training of the battalion concerned, the fascinating socio-military history thus presented being the outcome of assiduous research on the part of the respective authors. Unfortunately, a number of these works succumbed to the tyrannical hold which 1 July 1916 was by then firmly exerting on British First World War studies – a by-product of the trend-setting works of Middlebrook and Keegan. For example, William Turner's book on the Accrington Pals covers the post-Serre actions of the battalion in just 16 out of over 250 pages, while Philip Orr devotes only 8 pages to the story of the 36th Division after the Somme.[60]

The striking visual images of the Somme battlefields shown in Malcolm Brown's 1976 television documentary coincided with the publication of the late Rose Coombs' guide *Before Endeavours Fade* and I am firmly convinced that both – in the wake of Middlebrook's book – were key factors in inspiring and establishing the present popularity of battlefield tours. Tonie and Valmai Holt – founders of, and leading figures in, the modern battlefield tour industry – once told me that, so far as they were concerned, it was the legendary Rose Coombs who had done most to 'open up' the Western Front to new generations. To these names must be added that of John Giles, whose *The Somme: Then and Now* (1977) similarly helped to persuade many to pay personal visits to the battlefields. Giles saw the book not only as a record of the series of engagements that made up the Battle of the Somme, and a view of the topography, but also as a special tribute to the men of Kitchener's New Armies, 'so many of whom lie beneath the soil of France', and as 'an acknowledgement to the tenacity of an enemy who fought bravely to retain his hold on former territorial gains'.[61] John Giles's greatest achievement, however, was the founding of the Western Front Association (WFA) in 1980. Now over 30 years old, the WFA currently has some 6,000 members and 60 branches and affiliated organisations in Britain and overseas. It also publishes a scholarly journal, *Stand To!*, and plays a very important role in stimulating and maintaining serious public interest in the 1914–1918 period, including the Somme, at all levels from the family historian or hobbyist to the academic.

At this stage in the revival of interest in the Great War, a number of popular books, films and television programmes also sprang from Commonwealth writers, producers and directors. These included Bill Gammage's book *The Broken Years: Australian Soldiers in the Great War* (1974); Patsy Adam-Smith's *The Anzacs* (1978); the film *Gallipoli* (1981); Peter Charlton's *Australians on the Somme: Pozières 1916* (1986); the television series *Anzacs* (1987); and, in Canada, Pierre Berton's *Vimy* (1986). Most of these tended to reinforce stereotypes rather than break new ground, perpetuating the myth of the ruggedly independent 'colonial superman' from the backwoods or outback and invariably portraying British officers as haughty idiots who wasted the precious lives of emerging nations in their futile and badly conducted offensives. In this incarnation, the 'them' (i.e. the establishment) and 'us' (working-class victims) of *Oh! What a Lovely War* were now replaced by the 'them' (Britain and aristocratic British officers) and 'us' (young nations and misunderstood and ill-used Dominion soldier victims) of Peter Weir's film *Gallipoli*. John Laffin's *British Butchers and Bunglers of World War*

One (1988) possibly represents the nadir of this approach. But, as the Australian-based scholars Peter Dennis and Jeffrey Grey had rightly pointed out two or three years before, the 'Digger myth' propagated by Bean is difficult to challenge as it has long been 'a potent force in the development of an Australian consciousness'.[62] Perhaps the best of this group of works is Peter Charlton's book on the fighting at Pozières on the Somme. Highly critical of British command and tactics on the Somme, he differs from Bean in as much as he dates Australian disillusionment with British methods from the summer of 1916 rather than from the ordeal at Anzac Cove a year earlier, but, to be fair to Charlton, he also tries to place the Australian achievement in taking Pozières in the context of a coalition war, stating that 'to treat it as solely an Australian victory is to ignore the very substantial British contribution in this sector of the Somme before 23 July 1916'.[63]

Happily for the future health of First World War studies, archive-based scholarly works were beginning to make their mark by the mid-to-late 1980s. From the standpoint of serious, objective study of the BEF, however, this proved, in some respects, a double-edged sword, for the period witnessed the blossoming, particularly in the United States, of what Chris Pugsley has called 'the Germans did it first and best' school of historians.[64] The pattern was set, in 1981, by Timothy Lupfer in *The Dynamics of Doctrine: Changes in German Tactical Doctrine during the First World War*. Lupfer's book, which examines the corporate effort behind German doctrinal changes in the Great War, undoubtedly overrates the effectiveness of German offensive *and* defensive tactics – and, by implication, denigrates developments in the BEF – but his work had a great deal of influence in American military and historical circles (and on some in Britain). Other recent books with pro-German and anti-British overtones were Bruce Gudmundsson's *Stormtroop Tactics* (1989) and two books by Martin Samuels: *Doctrine and Dogma: German and British Infantry Tactics in the First World War*, published in 1992, followed, in 1995, by *Command or Control?: Command, Training and Tactics in the British and German Armies, 1888–1918*. Samuels claims that the BEF was hamstrung by a rigid approach to battle and that its system of 'restrictive control' lay at the root of the 36th (Ulster) Division's inability to exploit its impressive early gains on 1 July 1916.[65] Yet, in contrasting 1 July – Britain's worst day of the war – with 21 March 1918, one of Germany's best, he is hardly making an objective comparison. Had he, for example, compared the failed German attack at Arras on 28 March 1918 with 8 August 1918, the opening day of the Battle of Amiens, he might just have drawn some different conclusions.

Firepower

Again it was fortunate that an antidote to all this Anglophobic history was already to hand. *Fire-Power: British Army Weapons and Theories of War, 1904–1945*, published in 1982 and written by former gunner officers Shelford Bidwell and Professor Dominick Graham, at long last began to lift the debate up from the emphasis on mud, blood and 'butchers and bunglers' to the more solid ground of reasoned analysis of the BEF's tactical development and operational performance. Andy Simpson recently indicated why Bidwell and Graham's book was so important, namely that virtually everything published before *Fire-Power* was based on the official history narrative, with a leavening of formation histories and a re-working of published biographies, memoirs and diaries, whereas Bidwell and Graham clearly demonstrated that fresh and interesting interpretations could be extracted from the then largely untapped sources in the Public Record Office.[66] With Colin Hughes' *Mametz*, published the same year, *Fire-Power* truly heralded the advent of a new, scholarly, archive-based approach to the study of the First World War.

Bidwell and Graham concentrated primarily upon tactical issues and debates before, during and after the Great War. Their central argument is that, prior to 1914, British officers were largely unaware of the principles of co-operation and had not really grasped how to co-ordinate different branches of the service or how to orchestrate the fire of different weapons. Hence the close interaction between fire and manoeuvre was not fully understood. Artillery was seen simply as an accessory, 'an extra wheel for the coach', and the three main arms – the cavalry, infantry and artillery – 'dined at separate tables'. Consequently, new lessons had to be learned during a long struggle in which many of those best qualified to analyse events became casualties. Even so, the authors go on to emphasise the nature and extent of the BEF's overall achievement in the latter half of the war. It should be borne in mind, they suggest, that the BEF had to overcome a highly organised defensive system, which was protected by firepower of unprecedented intensity and occupied by some of the best and bravest soldiers in history. It also had to cope simultaneously with the flow of new weapons and inventions, fresh methods, the growth of the 'base administrative apparatus' supporting the expanded army, and the problems of training a mass of men who, unlike their adversaries, had no deep-rooted military tradition or experience. It is therefore hardly surprising that costly mistakes were made, they write, yet, by the same token, it is 'truly amazing that the efforts of the staff and fighting soldiers were finally crowned with such an overwhelming success'.[67] These statements almost perfectly encapsulate the views of most 'revisionist' historians of the First World War over the past twenty-five years or so. Moreover, Bidwell and Graham went much further than, say, the official histories, Liddell Hart or Terraine, in actually defining and explaining the improvements that took place in the BEF's infantry and artillery tactics and techniques, as well as all-arms co-operation, from 1915 onwards. They illustrated how a creeping barrage worked, made many of us aware, for the first time, of the positive influence of progressive and clear-sighted infantry commanders, such as R.B. Stephens (of the 5th Division) and Ivor Maxse (of the 18th Division), and also outlined the role and contribution of senior artillery officers such as H.H. Tudor, 'Curly' Birch, Herbert Uniacke and C.E.D. Budworth.

Although it had less general impact on the scholarly community, and almost none on the wider public, when it was first published in 1986, General Sir Martin Farndale's Western Front volume in *The History of the Royal Regiment of Artillery* must be included in any serious historiographical survey covering the lessons of the Somme. Farndale too stressed the importance of the creeping barrage, used 'shakily' in the July fighting of 1916, when 'it was not fully understood', but 'perfected' and employed 'with confidence by October and November'. He noted the introduction of counter-battery staffs and the enormous improvements in 1916 in conducting the counter-battery battle: 'At last the vital importance of silencing the enemy guns was realised by all'. Methods of controlling the fire of guns once an attack had started was also being perfected, Farndale asserts, and there were advances too in the area of artillery command and co-ordination: 'The GOCRA at Corps HQ was shown to be all important and the Heavy Artillery Commander emerged as his subordinate' – a crucial step in Farndale's judgement. He admits that, by the end of the Somme offensive, there was still room for improvement in the quality of ammunition, in passing on information about targets to the guns, in the techniques of flash-spotting and sound-ranging, and in the calibration of guns to ensure greater accuracy, but suggests that things were going in the right direction. Farndale also brings to our attention the pressure exerted by GHQ in late 1916, as a result of the Somme experience, for the creation of Army Field Artillery (AFA) brigades – over and above the existing divisional artillery – in order to provide a more flexible artillery reserve for major operations. Finally, he lists what Major-General Noel 'Curly' Birch – Haig's chief artillery adviser at GHQ – saw as the four key artillery lessons of the Somme: first, army-level headquarters (e.g. Fifth Army headquarters) must lay down from the outset the principles of the artillery plan for a battle; second, every available spare gun and period of time must be utilised for counter-battery work before and during an attack; third, accuracy must be improved; and, fourth, a more thorough artillery intelligence and reporting service was needed.[68] These professional and technical factors may not have a broad public appeal but, in delineating them, Farndale did us all a great service, for they remain vital to our proper understanding of operations on the Somme and thereafter.

The modern, archive-driven approach was even more evident in another important work – *The Killing Ground: The British Army, the Western Front and the Emergence of Modern Warfare 1900–1918* – by the Canadian historian Tim Travers. This book, first published in 1987, contained two thought-provoking chapters on the planning and conduct of the Somme offensive as part of its overall thesis. Because his work was founded on a bedrock of research into primary sources, Travers remains, as John Bourne has remarked, 'an influential critic not only of the army but also of Haig ...'. Travers examines the British army's weaknesses in the Great War chiefly in managerial terms. As a result, writes John Bourne, the 'villain' in the eyes of Travers, is 'not one individual, not even Haig, but the pre-war Regular Army itself'.[69] Travers regards the ethos of the pre-1914 British officer corps as that of an over-personalised and exclusive old-boy network which was rigidly hierarchical and more concerned with the 'dishonest' preservation of individual and collective reputations than with intellectual enquiry. All this meant that, when faced with war on a continental scale, involving large armies, the officers of the BEF were ill-equipped to respond to the challenges they encountered. Initiative and independent judgement were not encouraged and, since intellectual honesty was also largely absent, failure was concealed or tolerated and the historical record manicured. A second problem, as identified by Travers, was that the British army's ethos allowed pre-war ideas and attitudes to persist throughout the 1914–1918 period, fostering a 'human' image of the battlefield rather than prompting useful evaluation of the tactical potential of new technology. The firepower lessons of the Russo-Japanese War were therefore overlooked and, instead, emphasis was placed on a 'human-centred' model of operations in which mass, the concentration of force, morale, the 'offensive spirit' and the concept of 'breakthrough' were all essential ingredients. Hence, Haig and his senior subordinates tended to pursue unwise and inappropriate tactics which were beyond the actual capacity of the weapons and communications systems to hand.[70]

Linked to this was a third problem, which was that the BEF's senior officers – as a result of what they had been taught at Staff College – tended to see battle as an 'ordered' and structured activity. Travers argues that Haig's stiff and aloof character, coupled with his personal views on the role and authority of the Commander-in-Chief, did much to isolate GHQ in 1916 and 1917, giving it 'an unnecessarily authoritarian aspect'. According to Travers, Haig believed that the C-in-C must be 'determined and display singleness of purpose'; that there should be continuity at GHQ; and that the authority of the C-in-C would be undermined by permitting subordinates to promote their own ideas. In general, the C-in-C should lay down the broad strategic objectives of operations but leave the detailed conduct of battle to his subordinates. The army commanders – like Rawlinson and Gough – were therefore often left alone. However, as Travers explains, while Haig was, in principle, committed to setting strategy and leaving the tactics to his army commanders, he often intervened or interfered in matters such as the depth and number of objectives or the length of a bombardment. This unpredictable mixture of the 'hands-off' and 'hands-on' approaches led to confusion and compromise on some occasions, especially in 1916, and created a command vacuum and paralysis at the top on others. The BEF's problems were exacerbated by serious gaps in communication between Haig and his army commanders, because many senior officers were simply afraid of Haig and were not prepared to question him. Many therefore operated in a climate of fear which further isolated Haig and GHQ.[71]

While the arguments propounded by Travers are, without doubt, superficially seductive, they are, in fact, seriously flawed. When one examines his footnotes and source references, one discovers that a fair proportion of the evidence on which his conclusions are based comes from the correspondence between various officers and the official historians in the 1930s or from Liddell Hart's clubland gossip with Edmonds and others in the same period. Andy Simpson has remarked that Travers is too often inclined to accept anecdotal evidence which supports his conclusions, but fails to verify it elsewhere, such as by reference to the General Staff and headquarters war diaries of formations: 'It is important to deal with what can be verified in the documents or corroborated by other, independently recorded anecdotes, rather than simply to relate retrospective tittle-tattle'.[72] My own examination of Haig's relations with his army commanders also suggests a different interpretation to that put forward by Travers concerning the supposed 'isolation' of GHQ. Henry Rawlinson's diary entries for the Somme period by no means wholly support the idea that he was frightened of Haig, and the army commanders met Haig regularly at conferences held at each of their headquarters in turn. Given the difficulties met by the New Armies on the Somme, Haig did not see a 'hands-off' command style on some occasions and close supervision on others as being inconsistent or incompatible. 'It is not "interference" but a legitimate and necessary exercise of the functions of a Commander on whom the ultimate responsibility for success or failure lies', he told Rawlinson in August 1916, during a particularly tough phase of the Somme fighting. Precisely because he *did* carry the ultimate responsibility – and a continuing weight of responsibility at that – it should barely come as a surprise to scholars that Haig sometimes found it desirable or tempting to intervene at a tactical level, however unfortunate the end product of such intervention may have proved.[73] In addition, one can challenge some of the fundamental points underpinning the case presented by Travers regarding the pre-1914 British army. John Bourne has rightly observed that the 'wars of empire' in reality produced an officer corps with vast active and combat experience. Bourne claims that the range of professional opportunities offered by the pre-1914 British army was enormous. He also finds it difficult 'to reconcile the fit, adaptable, energetic, resourceful, pragmatic men who emerge from the pre-war army's multi-biography with the somnolent, dogma-ridden, unprofessional, unreflecting institution depicted by Tim Travers and Martin Samuels'.[74]

By the early 1990s, the 'revisionist' interpretation of the conduct of the war on the Western Front was beginning to gather real momentum, especially in the Commonwealth. Two very influential books appeared in 1992: *Surviving Trench Warfare: Technology and the Canadian Corps, 1914–1918*, by the Canadian historian Bill Rawling, and *Command on the Western Front: The Military Career of Sir Henry Rawlinson, 1914–18*, by the Australian-based Robin Prior and Trevor Wilson. In his very scholarly book, Bill Rawling deals at length with the transformation in the tools and technology of war between 1914 and 1918 and also with the tactics that governed their employment on the battlefield. He clearly shows how the systematic evaluation of after-action reports in the Canadian Corps, particularly from the Somme period onwards, drew out the principal lessons of successive operations and led to improvements in the application of the creeping barrage; in counter-battery fire; in co-operation with tanks and aircraft; in attack formations; in wire-cutting; and in the use of overhead machine-gun barrages, Lewis guns and Stokes mortars in the assault. Rawling was, indeed, one of the first modern historians to highlight the importance of the British manual *SS 143: Instructions for the Training of Platoons for Offensive Action*, which was issued in February 1917 and which heralded a major change in infantry tactics and platoon organisation. In 1915–1916 the platoon had essentially consisted of four sections of riflemen but, from the spring of 1917, it was reorganised into four specialist fighting sections which respectively contained riflemen, rifle grenadiers, bombers and Lewis gunners. In other words, the infantry company now comprised four platoon teams, each capable of waging its own battle in miniature, using a variety of weapons. This is but one of a series of weighty points which Rawling makes to support the view that the Canadian success at Vimy Ridge in April 1917, and in other limited-objective attacks that year, owed a lot to the lessons which the Canadian Corps, and the BEF in general, had learned on the Somme.[75]

Rawling also maintains that some of the most important lessons – particularly in relation to counter-battery fire, flexible attack formations and the structure and weaponry of the infantry platoon – were derived from French experience in 1916 and had been passed on to the Canadian Corps and BEF by Major-General Arthur Currie, then commander of the 1st Canadian Division, who made a special fact-finding visit to the French army at Verdun in January 1917. The impression given by Bill Rawling, if only by omission, is that Currie made this visit to Verdun alone – thus gaining much of the credit for the improvements which it inspired – and this line has been followed by other, though not all, Canadian historians.[76] As will be seen later, recent research has shown that this impression is highly misleading, for Currie's January 1917 trip to Verdun was far from a solo mission. To his credit, however, Bill Rawling does not pretend that these improvements were exclusive to the Canadian Corps and notes that they were simultaneously being effected, albeit somewhat unevenly, throughout the BEF, thanks partly to cross-fertilisation and a steady exchange of information and lessons at corps, divisional and brigade levels.[77]

Prior and Wilson's *Command on the Western Front*, as its title implies, concentrated on the *exercise* of command – in this case mainly at army level – rather than on the minutiae of tactics. It was, and is, a seminal work, chiefly because it provided the first scholarly archive-based examination in modern times of the operational performance of a senior commander in France and Flanders. It was much more even-handed and objective than *The Killing Ground* by Tim Travers, but it is by no means uncritical of Haig or its central figure, Henry Rawlinson, the commander of Fourth Army on the Somme and in 1918. In the view of the authors, Rawlinson had learnt and demonstrated, at Neuve Chapelle in 1915, that artillery was the key to success yet failed to apply this lesson consistently on the Somme, often leaving decisions concerning the use of the creeping barrage, or the weight and intensity of preparatory bombardments, to less experienced lower-order commanders. On the Somme he initially advocated a limited objective 'bite and hold' approach but 'proved sadly amenable to launching, without protest, an unlimited campaign in accordance with the ideas of the high command'. On 16 July 1916, Rawlinson declared that the time for narrow-front attacks was past, but then persisted with exactly that course of action for another two months. He was quick to agree with Haig's instructions to suspend operations on the left flank of Fourth Army while bringing his right flank into line, yet then proceeded to launch twice as many assaults on the left flank as on the right. 'Towards the end of the battle', write Prior and Wilson, 'we find him simultaneously calling for the campaign to be terminated and prosecuting it so unrelentingly as to cause a revolt by one of his corps commanders [Lord Cavan of XIV Corps]'.[78]

The authors conclude that, in Rawlinson's case, there was no 'undeviating advance towards wisdom, and no certain demonstration that at the end of the day Rawlinson was master of his job'. On the other hand, they do generally endorse the idea that a learning process had taken place in the BEF between 1916 and 1918, even if Rawlinson's contribution to it had been marginal. By 1918, they comment, 'expertise in the technical aspects of conducting battles had become so widespread throughout the British army, and supplies of the sorts of weaponry appropriate to this expertise had become so generous, that the importance of command in accomplishing victory had diminished absolutely'. As the BEF became a more complex, sophisticated and specialist organisation, detailed intervention by the C-in-C and army commanders became less relevant. 'Haig's job, like Rawlinson's, was ... diminishing not expanding as the forces under his direction grew in expertise and complexity. And Haig, again like Rawlinson, proved far more effective as a commander once the sphere of his activities began to diminish to an extent that brought them within the limits of his capabilities'.[79] One may disagree with some of Prior and Wilson's conclusions – such as their heavy emphasis on artillery as an almost universal key to success in operations – but one must pay tribute to their major contribution to the ongoing debate, not least in illustrating how far *real* command and control on the Western Front devolved downwards during and after the Somme.

Advance of the Revisionists

As the decade wore on, more books of genuine value appeared. Most of these, in varying degrees, reflected the fact that, at long last, a serious debate about the Somme and the Great War was in progress. Historians at, or associated with, the Imperial War Museum were now starting to make an important contribution to the historiography of the First World War, as were a group of historians based at the Royal Military Academy Sandhurst, and also postgraduate students and researchers working under Professor Brian Bond at King's College London and Dr John Bourne at the University of Birmingham. The increasing co-operation and mutual support of these groups of historians did as much as anything, in my opinion, to place First World War studies – particularly in this country – on a really solid and scholarly footing for the first time. The IWM's team of historians certainly acted as one of the catalysts in this process. A tangible indication of this was provided, in 1993, by Chris McCarthy's *The Somme: The Day-by-Day Account* which, as its title implies, contains a useful and concise daily summary of the BEF's operations on the Somme (including details of the weather and temperature), thereby helping us all to obtain a clearer understanding of the unfolding pattern of the battle.[80]

The following year saw the publication of yet another significant 'revisionist' work, namely *Battle Tactics of the Western Front: The British Army's Art of Attack, 1916–18*, by Dr Paddy Griffith, himself a former Senior Lecturer in War Studies at Sandhurst. In this book, Paddy Griffith examined, in some depth, the evolution of British infantry tactics throughout the war and concluded that, while the BEF's plans and technologies frequently failed during the period of improvisation in the first half of the conflict, Haig's forces gradually improved their methods and their technology from 1916 onwards, thus also gaining greater self-assurance. By the time of its successful sustained offensive in the autumn of 1918, Dr Griffith argues, the BEF was consistently demonstrating a battlefield skill and mobility that would rarely be surpassed, even during the Second World War. He contends that in fields such as the timing and orchestration of all-arms assaults, 'predicted' artillery fire, 'commando-style' trench raiding as a 'schooling' for assault tactics, the use of light machine guns or the indirect barrage fire of heavy machine guns, the BEF led the world, and he suggests that many of these improvements owed a great deal to the lessons learned on the Somme. Griffith undoubtedly tends to underplay the influence of the French in this process and possibly also oversteps the mark in claiming that the British were already masters of 'stormtroop' tactics by the end of 1916, but he does show, quite convincingly, that the BEF as a whole – and not just its Dominion or élite formations – progressed a long way in its battle tactics during the latter half of the war. Furthermore, he was, with Bill Rawling, the first modern historian to make us truly aware of the considerable importance of the SS series of pamphlets published and circulated by GHQ, especially *SS 135 (Instructions for the Training of Divisions for Offensive Action)* and *SS 143*.[81]

These arguments were reiterated in 1996 in *British Fighting Methods in the Great War*, a book edited by Dr Griffith and containing essays by himself and various other authors. One of the contributors was Jonathan Bailey, a serving officer then based at the Staff College, Camberley. Bailey developed some of the points made earlier – by Bidwell and Graham, by Bill Rawling, and by General Sir Martin Farndale – concerning the BEF's advances in artillery techniques. In Bailey's judgement, not only were shells, guns and fuses greatly improved in 1916–1917 but pinpoint accuracy, which had previously been achievable only in optimistic theory, also became daily reality. In 1916, the infantry assault was made more effective by the support of the creeping barrage, and in 1917 the main German response to it, in the form of defensive artillery fire, was increasingly neutralised by counter-battery programmes and techniques that really worked. In Bailey's eyes, this represented a step-change from the linear battles of the nineteenth century. The term 'deep battle' may only date from the NATO debates of the 1980s, but Jonathan Bailey suggests that, in practice, this modern concept was already evident in the artillery tactics of 1916–1918, when technological developments facilitated the employment of effective *indirect* artillery fire which had a devastating impact upon the enemy's morale and organisation.[82]

The new wave of 'revisionist' historians of the Great War did not advance entirely unopposed during this period. When reviewing the book *Facing Armageddon* – an important collection of essays and papers produced for a big First World War conference in Leeds in 1994 – the late Sir John Keegan denigrated 'revisionist' historians in Britain and the Commonwealth, declaring that the BEF learned little or nothing between 1916 and the Armistice and remarking that to claim that there was a 'learning curve' was rather like saying that Dunkirk provided valuable lessons in amphibious operations which were later applied on D-Day. He repeated this criticism in a subsequent book on the First World War, dismissing the work of the 'revisionists' as pointless.[83] However, as soon became evident, Keegan only succeeded here in portraying himself as a latter-day version of King Canute, for the swelling tide of scholarly opinion was now running firmly against him. Indeed, as historians began to look at areas of the BEF's activities other than simply its command and tactics, more and more substance was added to the 'revisionist' arguments.

Ian M. Brown's *British Logistics on the Western Front, 1914–1919*, which was published in 1998, clearly showed that, with Haig's active support, the appointment of the civilian railway expert Sir Eric Geddes as Director-General of Transportation at GHQ in September 1916 transformed the BEF's supply and transport system. Within two years, the BEF had a 'truly superb fighting and administrative organisation' that allowed Haig – in the autumn of 1918 – to mount limited-objective attacks of tremendous power almost at will and to switch their locations at short notice. Ian M. Brown also believes that, in the sphere of relating operational ambitions to logistic necessity, the BEF, in the Hundred Days, displayed a better grasp of the reality of fighting on the Western Front than the much-vaunted German General Staff had in the spring of 1918.[84]

Brown's significant work was followed, in 1999, by Peter Chasseaud's monumental 543-page study *Artillery's Astrologers: A History of British Survey and Mapping on the Western Front, 1914–1918*. The latter work is decidedly not the sort of book that one reads on the train or at bedtime and its size, density and technical subject matter are likely to deter all but the most dedicated students of the Western Front. It will, nevertheless, repay the effort because it *is* – as its dust-jacket blurb claims – the definitive operational history of the British field survey organisation. It covers the work of both the Royal Artillery and the Royal Engineers in survey, sound-ranging and flash-spotting, and all aspects of map production and use in the BEF, as well as drawing comparisons with French, German and American survey and mapping. Chasseaud describes, in huge detail, how the Royal Engineers – with a substantial gunner contribution – helped to make possible the initial British success at Cambrai in November 1917 and the victories of the Hundred Days in 1918. Visionary sappers like Lieutenant-Colonel Harold Winterbotham and gunners like H.H. Tudor played a major part in the development of techniques such as 'predicted fire' – achieving surprise by means of massive bombardments without previous 'registration' – and in the neutralisation of German artillery and machine guns during set-piece assaults.[85]

In retrospect, 1999 can, in fact, be seen as a vintage year for British First World War studies. Sixteen leading historians contributed essays, for example, to *Haig: A Reappraisal 70 Years On*, edited by Brian Bond and Nigel Cave. As the editors admit in their Foreword, the volume is 'pro-Haig' in that

scholarly opinion – with some notable exceptions – is generally moving towards a more favourable interpretation of Haig's achievements – reflecting those of the vast forces he commanded, based on a wider range of sources than those available to earlier polemical writers such as Liddell Hart – and from a more understanding approach derived from a longer perspective and access to a proliferating array of specialist studies.

The 'revisionist' interpretation, in their view, shows that Haig has been wrongly or excessively criticised on specific issues, namely that he supposedly appointed a disproportionate number of cavalry officers to the highest commands; opposed or obstructed technical innovation; was callous or indifferent towards casualties; and remained isolated from the front line. Not only were these criticisms misguided, Bond and Cave observe, but historians have now also come to appreciate the enormous difficulties created by the sudden and colossal expansion of the BEF. Relatively few historians, the editors claim, now question the 'impressive developments in material and war-fighting efficiency embodied in the term "learning curve"'. The debate, they say, has 'moved on to consider the timing and steepness of the "curve" and to assess the level at which improvements were introduced, codified and implemented'.[86] In his contribution to the volume, John Bourne tellingly comments that Haig's name has become synonymous with the huge organisation and complex operations of the BEF for which no single person can realistically be held responsible. 'In future', Bourne predicts, 'there seems little doubt that Haig's reputation will be finally determined, not by studies of the man himself, but of the man in the context of the armies which he commanded, and especially by detailed operational analyses at the army, corps, divisional, brigade and even battalion level'. Though he judged that, in 1999, such a day had not yet arrived, he *did* detect a shift away from 'an increasingly sterile debate' about a handful of political and military leaders towards 'an increasingly fruitful consideration' of the British army as an instrument of war, based largely on contemporary archive sources, including unit war diaries and after-action reports.[87]

Brian Bond also edited another collection of essays which appeared the same year in *Look to Your Front: Studies in the First World War by the British Commission for Military History*. An essay of particular relevance was John Lee's 'Some Lessons of the Somme: The British Infantry in 1917', which covered the reorganisation of British and Dominion infantry platoons in early 1917 as well as the content and influence of the pamphlets *SS 143: Instructions for the Training of Platoons for Offensive Action* and *SS 144: The Normal Formation for the Attack*. This essay powerfully underlined the *positive* trends in British infantry doctrine and tactics which resulted from the experience of the Somme. As John Lee confirms, the 'after action reports themselves show that the army was constantly looking for tactical, organisational and technical lessons to be absorbed and disseminated to improve both future training and battle performance'. In a later essay, Lee explores, in some depth, how these pamphlets, together with *SS 135*, helped in the development of 'standard operational procedures' and also how the principles embodied in such pamphlets were successfully applied in the Battle of the Menin Road Ridge in September 1917.[88]

Gary Sheffield is perhaps the most prolific of the new wave of First World War historians. His balanced and judicious assessments of the 1916 offensive were clearly set out in three works which appeared in the space of just four years: *Forgotten Victory. The First World War: Myths and Realities* (2001); *The Somme* (2003); and *Douglas Haig: War Diaries and Letters, 1914–1918*, which he edited with John Bourne and which was published in 2005. In *Forgotten Victory*, Sheffield cites examples of tactical flair and improvisation displayed, even by New Army divisions, in the early weeks of the battle. One such case was a 'Chinese' (diversionary) bombardment, complete with smoke, delivered against Ovillers on 2 July and intended to cover an assault on neighbouring La Boisselle by two battalions of the 19th Division. Tactical initiative was also shown by the 23rd Royal Fusiliers, a New Army battalion in the Regular 2nd Division, at Delville Wood on 27 July, when their advance was checked by a German strongpoint. After several failed attempts, the position was captured by sending bombers and Lewis gunners to probe around its flanks. This, Sheffield believes, offers 'a graphic example of an inexperienced unit literally learning on the job, groping their way towards effective tactics while actually in contact with the enemy'.[89] The learning process was still far from complete, for not all divisions were as tactically advanced as the best formations. Nonetheless, by November 1916, 'the BEF resembled a coherent weapons system much more closely than it had on 1 July'. Reports on, and analysis of, recent operations emanated from all levels of the BEF, including the pamphlets such as *SS 143* and *SS 144*, which were issued by GHQ. The fruits of this progress were certainly apparent by 9 April 1917 – the first day of the Battle of Arras – when greater density of guns, more plentiful and reliable ammunition, increasingly effective counter-battery work, and better infantry training along the lines laid down in *SS 143* and *SS 144*, all underpinned the tactical successes gained by British and Canadian formations that day. Given the inexperience of the British citizen army only months before, 'the level of tactical and operational development demonstrated at Arras was substantial' and it can be traced back to 'the trial and error days of the Somme'.[90]

Sheffield makes the valid point that, in any consideration of the results of the Somme, the importance of the French operations, to the south of the BEF's sector, 'must not be underrated'. He similarly observes that, up to the year 2001, the impact of the Somme on the German army had been insufficiently examined. In his judgement, large numbers of experienced German officers, NCOs and men were killed on the Somme, casualties which the German army could ill afford. The British, Sheffield estimates, lost 'mostly green soldiers'. Those who survived profited greatly, in a strictly military sense, by *gaining* experience. 'The Somme taught the BEF how to fight, while it degraded the quality of the German army'. Thus, although Haig and others may have underestimated German resilience, the two armies were more evenly matched by 1917. At the beginning of 1916, the Germans had to cope with two major armies, the Russian and the French, but at the end of the year, a third (the British) 'had made its presence felt'. In addition, the benefits of the Somme, in terms of coalition politics, should not be overlooked:

'In four and a half months of bloody fighting, Britain had demonstrated to its allies its willingness to pay the blood tax, to play a leading role in taking on the main enemy in the main theatre of operations'.[91]

Reappraising Haig

In the Introduction to their edition of Haig's war diaries and letters, Sheffield and Bourne remark that, in January 1916, Haig had rejected the idea of a purely attritional battle on the Somme, striving instead for a decisive success. The impact of the Battle of Verdun on Allied strategy obliged Haig to modify that approach somewhat and, by May, he had a more modest view of the likely outcome of the Somme offensive, as a 'wearing-out' battle. In the words of Sheffield and Bourne, the Commander-in-Chief of the BEF now wished to 'dampen down expectations if the battle did turn out to be an attritional affair; but not to exclude the possibility of operations of a more decisive character. Haig's post-Somme despatch, which excluded mention of his hopes of open warfare, was to some extent *ex post facto* rationalisation, but he had certainly anticipated that the battle might be one of attrition and limited gains'.

On the question of the plans for the opening of the battle, Sheffield and Bourne tend to see the proposals presented by Rawlinson, rather than Haig, as being more appropriate to the tactical and technological realities of July 1916. Whereas Haig's ideas were over-ambitious, envisaging that Gough's Reserve Army would exploit initial success by striking north in the direction of Arras, Rawlinson advocated a more cautious 'bite and hold' approach in which the BEF would capture a section of the German trenches, hold it against counter-attack and – when the enemy had exhausted themselves – carry out the process again. He was thus aiming to mount fairly limited attacks that could be properly supported by artillery. Sheffield and Bourne suggest that, in overruling Rawlinson, Haig was turning a blind eye to the fact that the BEF's logistic system was actually incapable of sustaining a significant breakthrough in 1916. Moreover, 'the width of front to be attacked, some 20,000 yards, and Haig's insistence on capturing trenches to an average depth of 2,500 yards, diluted the available firepower. Too few guns were given too much to do. In general, Haig's plan was too ambitious, given the state of training and level of experience of his troops in 1916'.

The editors rightly point out that Haig's command relationships with Rawlinson and Gough during the battle were governed by the concept that the Commander-in-Chief should define the broad objectives but leave the detailed planning to his subordinates. 'Sometimes', they note, 'Haig adhered to this, but on other occasions he intervened, for good or ill'. Haig, they feel, can therefore be reasonably criticised for a lack of control over his senior subordinates: 'Too often Rawlinson and Gough used "penny packets" of troops (and guns) rather than committing the sort of numbers that would make success possible, and failed to co-ordinate actions across formation boundaries. Such actions generally gained a little ground but at a high price'. Haig did, at times, offer Rawlinson advice, or even give him instructions, on how to conduct operations, and occasionally overruled his 'man on the spot', such as during the planning for the 15 September attack at Flers-Courcelette. Overall, the editors conclude, Haig's approach, in this regard, 'lacked consistency and "grip"'. Sheffield and Bourne also confess to being puzzled by the failure on the Somme of both Haig and Rawlinson consistently to apply the lessons of those operations which *were* successful, but they comment that Haig had only been C-in-C of the BEF for just over six months when the offensive commenced. In effect, Haig was serving his apprenticeship as an Army Group commander on the Somme and was himself 'still learning'. However, his persistence in prolonging the offensive when a breakthrough was obviously beyond the bounds of possibility was, Sheffield and Bourne assert, 'the consequence of coalition politics'. Haig was unwilling to allow Joffre, the French Commander-in-Chief, to determine the precise nature and form of his attacks, yet, whatever his personal preferences, he had no real choice other than to continue the offensive.

Sheffield and Bourne accept that the Somme was bloody, wasteful and sometimes badly conducted by the British generals, while shattering the strategic consensus in Britain and seriously undermining relations between Haig and Lloyd George. On the other hand, they maintain that the British and Dominion forces on the Somme in 1916 did help to administer a severe blow to the German army and that, if it was not a 'victory', then the offensive was at least a strategic success:

> German strategy in 1917 was in large part a reaction to the Somme. The Germans abandoned the 1916 battlefield by withdrawing to the Hindenburg Line, and opened unrestricted submarine warfare in an attempt to defeat Britain in the full knowledge that this was likely to bring the USA into the war, with ultimately disastrous consequences for Germany. This is a powerful vindication of Haig's strategy.

Sheffield and Bourne likewise reinforce the now common 'revisionist' argument that, by the end of the Somme, the BEF was a much more effective and experienced force than it had been in July 1916. This was of major importance, for Haig, they state, was much more than a battlefield commander: 'He presided over the BEF's expansion and development, taking a keen interest in diverse matters, including reforming the logistic system, training and minor tactics. Improvements in administration and infrastructure were vital elements in the learning curve that transformed the BEF from the clumsy organisation of July 1916 to the formidable army of 1918'. Although they find it difficult to quantify his influence, Sheffield and Bourne are in no doubt that, as Commander-in-Chief, Haig 'deserves a share of the credit for the transformation of the BEF, just as he deserves a share of the blame for battlefield setbacks'.[92]

As the ninetieth anniversary of the Somme drew near, so the stream of new books about Haig and the battle continued to flow. The American scholar Andrew Wiest produced an articulate, if short, study of Haig's command of the BEF which largely echoed the conclusions presented by Gary Sheffield. Wiest views the reactions of the Germans to the Somme – in the withdrawal to the Hindenburg Line and the resumption of unrestricted submarine warfare – as confirmation of the doubts of the German high command concerning their army's ability to endure another such round of attrition. He therefore supports the argument that the attrition on the Somme 'should be seen as an essential step along the path to eventual overall victory in 1918'. Like Sheffield, Wiest is not uncritical of Haig, suggesting that the latter's command style was variable, that Haig expected too much from several of his major attacks and that he and Rawlinson often failed to grasp the lessons of the artillery's role in the offensive. Yet, if the Somme was not the great victory that ended the war, neither was it 'the fruitless catastrophe of recent historical memory'.[93] The main thrust of Walter Reid's 2006 biography of Haig is implicit in its title – *Architect of Victory* – though Reid frequently reminds us of the colossal price paid by the British army for the policy of 'wearing down' the Germans on the Somme. In Reid's opinion, the BEF's piecemeal attacks on narrow fronts in July and August 1916, including the successive assaults on High Wood, 'cannot be justified even on an attritional basis'. Haig also stands accused of allowing the battle to drag on in the terrible weather conditions of the late autumn of 1916. Reid, in fact, sees much of the value of the Somme offensive as lying in its 'educational function'. At every level of the BEF, he remarks, 'commanders learned lessons and learned them very quickly, though in recognising this one must always remember just how expensive their education was'. Reid too follows Professor Sheffield in highlighting the importance of the training pamphlets *SS 143* and *SS 144*, which appeared eleven months before the so-called German 'stormtrooper's manual *Der Angriff im Stellungskrieg* (*The Attack in Position Warfare*) dating from January 1918. In such official pamphlets, and the thinking that they reflect, lay 'the genesis of the transformation of the British army which would achieve victory two years later'. In the end, Haig's shortcomings were 'not overwhelming. The dreadfulness of the Somme was the fault not of Haig but of modern warfare'. Haig, in essence, was still at the beginning of his own learning curve.[94]

Another biography of Haig, by Gary Mead, followed hot on the heels of Reid's study of the Commander-in-Chief, but, if less pro-Haig than the books by Wiest and Reid, it added little of substance to the debate. In general, Mead recognises Haig's devotion to duty, gritty determination, receptiveness to new technology and utter dedication to his profession, but also stresses his tendency towards obstinacy and dangerous optimism. Mead notes the benefits that Haig and the BEF gained by welcoming the appointment of Sir Eric Geddes as Director-General of Transportation at GHQ. However, he insists that the Somme threw the weaknesses of Haig's personality and the army's traditional *modus operandi* into a harsh light. What Mead fails to explain is precisely how Britain's unskilled citizen army of 1916 developed, under Haig's leadership, into the highly effective and modern all-arms force of August 1918. The inadequacies of this biography are revealed by the fact that Mead allocates less than four pages to the decisive Allied counter-strokes and offensive operations of July to November 1918.[95]

A far more valuable contribution to the historiography of the BEF in the Great War was made by Dr Simon Robbins of the Imperial War Museum, whose *British Generalship on the Western Front, 1914–1918: Defeat into Victory* appeared in 2005. The product of lengthy and painstaking examination of an immense range of archival and published sources, this book adds yet more scholarly weight to the 'revisionist' interpretation of the war on the Western Front, helping to explode the long-established stereotype of a blundering BEF with the perception that the formations fighting under Haig's command became increasingly effective from 1916 onwards. Dr Robbins analyses in great detail the learning process whereby the small, close-knit officer corps of 1914 not only overcame the heavy losses suffered in the opening battles of the war, and also the widespread 'de-skilling' that accompanied the huge expansion of the BEF, but managed to adapt to new technology and to retrain and transform itself into a body capable of planning and winning the victories of 1918. All this, moreover, was done while fighting a skilful and implacable enemy, by officers who were invariably operating at levels of command of which they had no previous experience. In these circumstances, as Simon Robbins illustrates, it is small wonder that there were mistakes and reverses or that the learning process was sometimes irregular. Nevertheless, the formation commanders of the BEF were a younger, fitter and more dynamic group by the end of the war and, having adopted a more managerial approach than hitherto, were able to oversee the introduction, codification and application of key new developments in tactics, staff work, operational planning, training and all-arms co-operation. This was an enormous achievement which, thanks to scholars such as Dr Robbins, is finally receiving the recognition it merits.

Training and Tactics

Robbins reiterates the importance of the improvements in the BEF's artillery techniques which occurred during, or as a result of, the Somme offensive. The employment of the creeping, or rolling, barrage – a moving curtain of fire in front of the advancing infantry – was now becoming standard practice. The introduction of the new 106 fuse, which detonated on immediate impact with the ground, enabled barbed wire to be cut more efficiently without cratering the terrain over which the infantry had to assault. Increasing attention was paid to the calibration of each field gun, and to the amount of wear suffered by individual barrels, as well as to the need to make adjustments to allow for changes in temperature, wind and barometric pressure. All these factors, together with the more precise location of enemy batteries, improved accuracy, helped the gunners to neutralise rather than destroy the enemy defences, and encouraged a shift towards surprise bombardments without registration – thus greatly assisting the battle performance of the British artillery during 1917 and 1918. Robbins similarly re-emphasises the crucial role of Brigadier-General Arthur Solly-Flood as Director-General of Training from early 1917, in recommending and overseeing the changes in the structure of the infantry platoon from four rifle sections to specialist bombing (grenade), rifle, Lewis gun and rifle grenade sections; in disseminating these tactical and organisational reforms through the widespread issue of manuals such as *SS 143* and *SS 144*; and in seeking to standardise and co-ordinate training based on the new tactical principles. The infantry platoon – now being more self-contained – could more successfully exploit the greater firepower it possessed in the form of rifle grenades and Lewis guns and was, at least in theory, more capable of dealing with enemy strongpoints. Within each platoon, the rifle grenadiers and Lewis gunners now acted as the covering fire team while the assault team comprised the rifle and bombing sections. It was, in effect, 'an army in miniature' with its own fire support, though Robbins is overstepping the mark in suggesting that, from 1917, the German machine guns 'ceased to intimidate'.[96]

Two years after the publication of the above work, Alistair Geddes explored, in greater depth, the central part played by Solly-Flood in the reorganisation of the British infantry platoon and of the BEF's subsequent training. Already an advocate of a return to fire and movement tactics during rehearsals for the Somme, when he was GOC of the 35th Brigade in the 12th (Eastern) Division, Solly-Flood was appointed Commandant of the Third Army School in November 1916, apparently at the instigation of General Allenby, then commander of the Third Army, but almost certainly with Haig's knowledge and backing. The research undertaken by Geddes indicates that, at the school, Solly-Flood was expected to experiment with new infantry formations and tactics and that, as part of his brief, he joined a party of British officers who visited the French army at Chalons in late November to study its current practice. The French, as the fighting on the Somme had shown, were clearly more advanced in this sphere than the BEF, having adopted a self-contained platoon organisation, including specialist bombing and automatic rifle sections and riflemen trained as rifle-grenadiers. The British observers swiftly appreciated the potential of these measures and Geddes presents strong evidence that, in offering an 'off-the-shelf' solution to problems with which the BEF had been wrestling on the Somme, the new French platoon tactics were the inspiration for *SS 143*. 'It is not surprising', Geddes states, 'that Solly-Flood should have taken these ideas away with him to Third Army School to experiment with and modify for use by the BEF'.[97]

By early January 1917, Solly-Flood was clearly testing the new platoon organisation, attack formations and tactical methods which were being adapted for British needs and specially tried out by the 7th Norfolks, who had served under Solly-Flood when he was commander of 35th Brigade. Meanwhile, other parties of British and Dominion officers were visiting the French army and drawing similar conclusions. As Geddes argues in his scholarly dissertation, not all senior officers were aware of Solly-Flood's activities, which explains why Lieutenant-General Sir Julian Byng sanctioned Arthur Currie's move to a new platoon organisation and training methods in the Canadian Corps in January 1917. Geddes also notes that the 29th Division successfully employed the 'French method of capturing strong points' by working round them with Lewis guns in an operation on 27 January.[98] However, the final and principal impetus for the changes seems to have come from a demonstration by the 7th Norfolks on 2 February which was attended by Haig and some 200 officers of the Third Army. Shortly afterwards, Haig gave the green light for the appointment of Solly-Flood as head of the Training Directorate, for the adoption of the new platoon organisation and for the production of the relevant training pamphlets. Alistair Geddes suggests that *SS 144* was, in fact, circulated first, on 14 February, followed by *SS 143*, probably in March.[99] He also lays considerable stress on the point that, as a consequence of these developments, Solly-Flood was able to restructure the BEF's training system and to redesign and standardise the schools at each level of the BEF's hierarchy in an effort (not always successful) to meet the demands of the platoon organisation and tactics covered by *SS 143*. In Geddes's view, the BEF's most important publication with regard to training – *SS 152: Instructions for the Training of the British Armies in France* – initially issued in June 1917, has received all too little attention from historians, even though, to standardise training, it prescribed the curriculum of every school and the syllabus of each course. Contrary to previously held opinion, Geddes maintains, it is evident that 'Haig and GHQ did provide leadership by overseeing the development of a sophisticated training organisation which was responsible for the creation of the BEF's tactical doctrine and its uniform application in its schools system'.[100] Both Jim Beach and Dave Molineux have recently underlined that the updating of training pamphlets, continued experiments with the platoon structure and the addition of an Inspectorate of Training under Ivor Maxse, lead one to conclude that, even in the final months of the war, GHQ remained proactive in seeking to adapt training and tactics to the changing circumstances of the Western Front. Since GHQ plainly endeavoured to apply uniform methods of tactics and training, 'the BEF's learning curve in this instance was neither haphazard nor accidental'.[101]

Even more recent doctoral research by Trevor Harvey has revealed that Arthur Currie's visit to the French army at Verdun between 5 and 8 January 1917 was made in the company of twenty other officers. Interestingly, two-thirds of the twenty-one officers in the party were gunners, including such senior figures as 'Curly' Birch (Haig's chief artillery adviser at GHQ) and Herbert Uniacke (MGRA, Fifth Army) and some relatively junior officers such as Major Alan Brooke, then still with the 18th (Eastern) Division. Among the other divisional commanders present on this visit were Cyril Deverell (3rd Division), Reginald Stephens (5th Division), Arthur Scott (12th Division), Victor Couper (14th Division) and Cameron Shute (63rd (Royal Naval) Division). It is notable from these details that nearly all the members of the party were drawn from the First, Third and Fifth Armies, which were to be involved in the offensive at Arras in April 1917, while the combination of influential senior figures and promising junior officers strongly suggests that not only were the participants nominated by GHQ and the appropriate army commanders but also that a degree of 'talent spotting' was being exercised. Trevor Harvey's ongoing research additionally indicates that the subsequent production and publication of the pamphlet *SS 139/3: Counter-Battery Work* may have owed something to the Verdun visit. It could therefore be inferred from this that the simultaneous counter-battery developments, the restructuring of the infantry platoon and the lesson-dissemination process were all parts of one reform and reorganisation movement approved and authorised by a proactive GHQ which bore little resemblance to the remote and isolated body depicted by Tim Travers.[102]

Command and Control

Another major pillar supporting the 'revisionist' arguments was provided by Andy Simpson's book *Directing Operations: British Corps Command on the Western Front 1914–18*. Published in 2006, this is one of the most significant recent studies of the actual mechanics and functioning of command in the Great War. Like Albert Palazzo's *Seeking Victory on the Western Front* (2000), it stresses the importance of *Field Service Regulations Part I (Operations)*, drawn up under Haig's aegis (as Director of Staff Duties) in 1909, and shows how *FSR I*, supplemented by the SS series of pamphlets, helped to shape the ethos of the BEF and was consistently applied and used by commanders throughout the conflict. The principle of deference to 'the man on the spot' was enshrined in *FSR I* and encouraged, where possible, the devolution of command and control downwards. It may be perceived from Simpson's study that this process of decentralisation and devolution was, to some extent, already under way by, and during, the Somme offensive. Simpson describes how, within the framework of the overall strategic plan and objectives agreed by GHQ and the army level of command, the army concerned – e.g. the Fourth Army – would then assign to its corps the resources which it hoped would suffice for the task set. While the general timetable for a big attack would probably come from the army headquarters, corps could make their own arrangements within it. Indeed, as Simpson demonstrates, the role of corps in operations had grown by 1916 in parallel with the increasing importance of artillery and of the need to co-ordinate its activities in battle. Next, according to Simpson, divisions would be informed of their objectives and expected to produce detailed plans of attack for their individual sectors. Thus divisions acted within the parameters defined by corps but did not simply have plans imposed on them. During this planning process there was often discussion and consultation at all levels – even down to brigade and battalion – though the extent to which the ideas of subordinates were listened to, or adopted, in practice frequently depended upon the character, temperament or command style of the corps and army commanders involved.

This latter issue, and the fact that, in 1916, no one in the BEF, including Haig himself, was yet quite sure when, or how, to apply the principles of *FSR I*, helps to explain why there were variations in the attack formations, tactics and artillery plans adopted by the different corps and divisions both on 1 July and throughout the Somme battle. As Simpson detects, the huge changes in the style and techniques of warfare employed by the BEF, coupled with the need to impose a degree of consistency on a number of corps and divisions undreamed of in 1914, led, for a period on the Somme, to a more prescriptive style of command, particularly as exercised by the relatively authoritarian Hubert Gough as the battle progressed. This drift towards prescriptive methods was 'made all the more necessary because the commanders and staffs of corps and divisions had not been trained at these levels of command and consequently lacked the trained judgement required to use *FSR I* effectively'. Poor battlefield communications in 1916 also made it highly tempting to attempt to cover all likely eventualities prior to an attack, in case any variation from the plan threw the 'whole complex machine' out of gear, and the 'vital need for a comprehensive artillery programme to permit any infantry advance exacerbated this'. However, as the BEF in general moved towards a more managerial and consultative style of command, the advance, in Simpson's judgement, 'leaves no doubt' that the Battle of Arras in April–May 1917 'did encapsulate the lessons of the Somme' and that the Battle of Messines in June 'represented a further progression in tactical and operational thought'. Some staffs, by then, had greater experience, 'corps were less prescriptive in their dealings with divisions too, and their respective responsibilities were now clearer. Corps dealt with the general (or operational) and divisions with the local (or tactical)'.[103]

Peter Hart, the Imperial War Museum's Oral Historian, has produced a number of commendable books on Great War topics, all making extensive use of the Museum's rich collections. These works include one called simply *The Somme*, which came out in 2005, the same year as Robin Prior and Trevor Wilson produced a book bearing an identical title. Hart's primary focus is upon the experience of relatively junior officers and other ranks but his final assessments show that he is fully aware of the main trends of the recent historical debate. As he remarks in the concluding part of his study: 'There was a learning curve and the British Army slowly ascended it, though occasional, heart-stopping "big dipper" moments still occurred right to the very end of the war'. He also gives due credit to the 'indomitable defence' mounted by the German army on the Somme. 'Overall', says Hart, 'it was a supreme example of sustained courage in one of the greatest defensive battles ever fought in the history of warfare'.[104]

Ever since the publication, in 1992, of their seminal work *Command on the Western Front*, a more lengthy study of the Somme by Robin Prior and Trevor Wilson had been eagerly awaited by historians. When it finally appeared in 2005, it proved, in some respects, to be a disappointment. On the credit side, it contains much excellent analysis of the realities of operations 'at the sharp end', especially the impact of battle upon individual formations. It reveals, for instance, that the British 1st Division suffered over 10,000 casualties in an 80-day period between July and September 1916 (almost 100 per cent of its infantry strength) without actually taking part in any of the *major* set-piece assaults launched by the BEF during that time. Despite such losses, the 1st Division, like many others, not only survived the bloody ordeal of the Somme but still emerged as an effective fighting formation. The explanation, Prior and Wilson submit, lay not in superior training or skill in manoeuvre but in 'the ability to stick close behind a barrage' and in what Winston Churchill called the 'wonderful tenacity' of the British infantry.[105]

Prior and Wilson reserve their main criticisms, as in earlier books, for Haig and his principal subordinates who, in their eyes, were repeatedly deficient in strategic insight, tactical understanding and organisation. Some corps commanders – such as Pulteney (III Corps), Hunter-Weston (VIII Corps) and Horne (XV Corps) – are similarly castigated for poor decision-making. A handful of divisional and brigade commanders or BGRAs, including H.B. 'Hooky' Walker (1st Australian Division), H.H. Tudor (9th Division), Ivor Maxse (18th Division), Harold Higginson (53rd Brigade) and Thomas Shoubridge (54th Brigade), receive some praise for their tactical flair and innovation, but most brigade and divisional commanders remain shadowy figures at best in this study. The authors justify this by stating that 'it was often not the quality of the brigade or divisional command that led to success but the position in which their troops were placed by decisions made elsewhere'. If adequate fire support was absent, 'a Maxse, Tudor, or Walker could make no difference whatever'.[106]

Most First World War scholars would find it hard to disagree with Prior and Wilson's central criticisms of the British high command on the Somme. There were fatal contradictions, faulty assumptions and misunderstandings in the British planning for the assault on 1 July. As the offensive unfolded, Haig consistently failed to exercise sufficient 'grip' on his subordinates, to co-ordinate their actions, or to control their tendency to persist with small-scale, isolated and narrow-front attacks. In addition, Haig, Gough and Rawlinson seemed unable, at the time, to grasp the full implications of the successes of 14 July and 25 September with regard to the formidable weight of artillery fire which, on those occasions, had been concentrated on every yard of enemy trench attacked. And yet, however well-founded some of these points may be, the almost unrelieved litany of criticism in this book gives the study an unnecessarily negative and sour tone. In their concluding reflections on the Somme, the authors themselves totally fail to mention the *positive* lessons which Haig and GHQ not only drew from the campaign but *acted upon* during the winter of 1916–1917.[107] One has an uncomfortable feeling that the Prior and Wilson approach to the study of the Great War, with its recurrent emphasis on the failings of the most senior commanders and on the cardinal importance of artillery fire as an almost universal solution to all tactical problems, has become just a trifle formulaic. In their largely negative view of the British high command, they are now at variance with the majority of 'revisionist' historians in Britain.

The fact is that, because Prior and Wilson have chosen to focus their critical gaze on a few very senior officers, their view of the BEF's command system is consequently somewhat restricted and, indeed, has been exposed as such by a number of works written by other British and Commonwealth scholars in the last decade or so. Thanks to these, we now have a much more rounded picture of British and Dominion commanders at all levels – and of the *mechanics* of command in the Great War (i.e. how it actually functioned in the field) – than we previously enjoyed. For example, Christopher Pugsley's *The Anzac Experience: New Zealand, Australia and Empire in the First World War* (2004) contains an excellent summary of the process of learning and improvement which occurred in the BEF and its

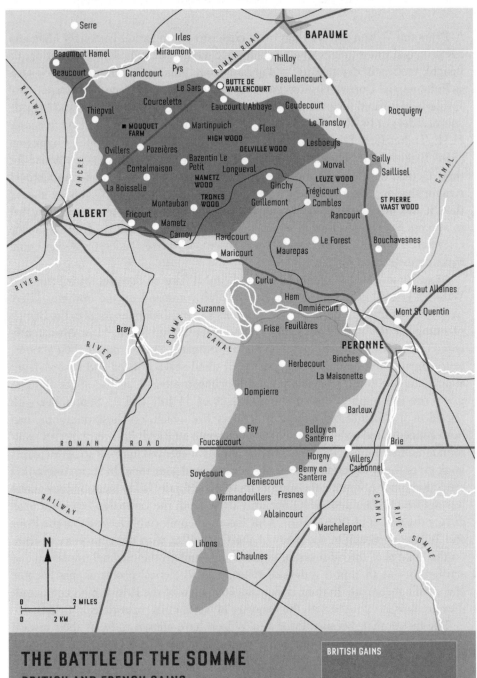

Serre
Irles
Miraumont
Beaumont Hamel
Beaucourt
Grandcourt
Pys
Le Sars
Courcelette
BUTTE DE
WARLENCOURT
Thilloy
Beaullencourt
Thiepval
Eaucourt l'Abbaye
Ceudecourt
Rocquigny
MOUQUET
FARM
Martinpuich
Flers
Le Transloy
HIGH WOOD
Ovillers
Pozeières
Bazentin Le
Petit
DELVILLE WOOD
Lesboeufs
Contalmaison
Longueval
Morval
Sailly
Saillisel
La Boisselle
MAMETZ
WOOD
Ginchy
LEUZE WOOD
ALBERT
Montauban
TRONES
WOOD
Guillemont
Frégicourt
Combles
ST PIERRE
VAAST WOOD
Fricourt
Mametz
Rancourt
Carnoy
Hardcourt
Le Forest
Bouchavesnes
Maricourt
Maurepas
ANCRE
RAILWAY
Curlu
Hem
Haut Allaines
Suzanne
Ommiécourt
Mont St Quentin
Bray
Frise
Feuillères
RIVER
SOMME
CANAL
PERONNE
Herbecourt
Binches
La Maisonette
Dompierre
Barleux
Fay
Belloy en
Santerre
Brie
ROMAN   ROAD
Foucaucourt
Horgny
Villers
Carbonnel
Soyécourt
Deniecourt
Berny en
Santerre
RAILWAY
Vermandovillers
Fresnes
Ablaincourt
CANAL
RIVER
SOMME
Marcheleport
N
Lihons
Chaulnes

BAPAUME
CANAL

0   2 MILES
0   2 KM

THE BATTLE OF THE SOMME
BRITISH AND FRENCH GAINS
JULY TO NOVEMBER 1916

BRITISH GAINS

FRENCH GAINS

Dominion contingents between 1916 and 1918, and shows convincingly how gifted 'middle management' commanders, such as Andrew Russell of the New Zealand Division, could have a genuine and beneficial influence on the planning and conduct of operations.[108] These themes were also developed in *Command and Control on the Western Front: The British Army's Experience, 1914–1918*, a book of essays by eight leading British and American historians, under the editorship of Gary Sheffield and Dan Todman, which appeared towards the end of 2004. The essays in question moved the debate about British generalship in the Great War a significant step forward by examining the *practicalities* of command and control at all levels, from GHQ down to battalion, demonstrating how operational and tactical command really did devolve downwards, particularly in the latter half of the war. Collectively, the essays leave a strong impression that the BEF's command and control system was a good deal more flexible, pragmatic, robust and innovative than many earlier critics would have us believe, and that these qualities help to explain why the British and Dominion formations in France became much more effective in waging modern all-arms warfare by the summer and autumn of 1918.[109]

The Debate Continues

It was perhaps inevitable that the dogged advance of the 'revisionist' First World War scholars would eventually be met by answering fire of varying intensity. The view from the other side of no-man's-land is, for instance, rightly – if belatedly – receiving renewed attention. Jack Sheldon's *The German Army on the Somme, 1914–1916* does for German officers and other ranks what Peter Hart's *The Somme* did for their British counterparts. Sheldon justifiably gives Anglocentric historians a timely reminder that the British army was not the only one learning lessons on the Somme. As was the case for the British army, he observes, the German army was 'endlessly analytical and self-critical' with every unit producing, at the end of each tour of duty, after action reports which were then processed and widely circulated. In this way, the overall lessons drawn from the Somme experience influenced German defensive doctrine and operations for the remainder of the war. Deep dugouts and continuous trench lines gave way to concrete bunkers and strongpoints, surrounded by belts of obstacles and sited so that they could provide mutual support: 'In came flexibility, defence in depth, a huge increase in infantry fire power, streamlined command and control and numerous tactical innovations'.

Sheldon also asserts that to claim that the Somme was a beneficial and necessary stage in the development of the Kitchener divisions is 'a judgement based on hindsight' which, even if true, 'glosses over the dislocation of British national expectations and appalling sense of loss' and is all the more offensive because it 'provides a fig leaf of dignity and respectability to the moral bankruptcy of attrition theory'.[110] With the greatest possible respect to the author, whose work I much admire, these arguments, in turn, seem to me to 'gloss over' two or three important points. The first is that the new German tactics – adopted and developed as a result of the Somme experience – *ultimately* provided no real answer to the superior logistics of the Allies or to the British, French and American all-arms limited-objective attacks. The second point is that, in 1916, the German army still occupied much of Belgium and northern France, not the other way round. The Allies had no genuine option but to try to eject the Germans at the very least and, given the quality of the German army in 1916 and the strength of its defensive positions, this was bound to involve great loss of life and self-sacrifice. The French and British simply had to adopt an offensive stance and to find a way of defeating the German army. It was unthinkable for them to allow the Germans to remain in northern France and Belgium merely on the grounds that it would be difficult and painful to drive them out. A third consideration is that, while the Allies could hardly sit back and assume a strictly defensive posture in July 1916, the BEF, in particular, did not *yet* possess the resources, command and control systems, logistical flexibility or firepower to carry out truly effective offensive operations against a skilful, obdurate and well-entrenched army. However, this situation began to change during the course of the Somme battle and in its immediate aftermath.

The German experience on the Somme – especially from the point of view of those units facing the BEF – is also covered in some depth by Christopher Duffy in *Through German Eyes: The British and the Somme 1916* (2006), a study which, unusually, is based in part on records of the interrogation of British prisoners of war and which examines the enemy's perception of British performance and morale in the course of the offensive. Certainly, at the start of the campaign in July 1916, the Germans found their French opponents more highly trained and more skilful than the British, since they had a better grasp of the tactical situation and were thus able to display greater independence when their leaders fell. Duffy duly acknowledges and traces the developments and improvements in British technology and tactics from July onwards, though he too challenges the idea that there was a *smooth* 'learning curve' in the BEF. The progression, he declares, 'was more of a series of steps, some of which led downwards. It was, if anything, a learning or re-learning process'. All the same, the BEF was feeling its way towards the 'tactical revolution' of 1917, when the platoon became firmly established as the basis for fire and manoeuvre, exploiting the mobile firepower of the Lewis gun. In the long run, Duffy suggests, this was to prove a more promising development than that of the much-vaunted German stormtroops, 'who remained a minority within the German Army, and who in 1918 sucked the unimproved masses of the German infantry forward to be massacred by aircraft and machine guns'. In 1916 itself the BEF's *sustained* effort on the Somme compelled the Germans to scale down and eventually abandon their own offensive at Verdun and, what is less generally appreciated, to call off an intended attack against British forces between Arras and the Somme sector. Hence the Allied offensive on the Somme was, 'if not a victory, at least a costly strategic success that was important to the outcome of the war'.[111]

This general view of the Somme was evidently becoming commonly held by the ninetieth anniversary of the battle. J.P. Harris, in his *Douglas Haig and the First World War* (2008) judged that, although it was one of the most ghastly episodes in modern British history, the Somme offensive 'wrested the initiative on the Western Front from the Germans', helped to save Verdun and 'contributed very largely to the general crisis experienced by the Central Powers' in the summer and autumn of 1916. While, in humanitarian terms, it was 'a catastrophe for all concerned', it was also, in military terms, 'a gruesome kind of limited victory for the Allies'. Haig, however, is subjected to a fair amount of censure from Harris. The latter criticises Haig's operational methods – particularly his failure to adopt a 'step-by-step' approach, as advocated by Rawlinson and others, at the beginning of the battle. Harris also feels that, after mid-July, Haig appeared to lose his grip on the offensive for several weeks and, during the battle as a whole, not only neglected to create an Army Group command to give proper operational direction, co-ordination and control of the Fourth and Reserve (Fifth) Armies but never really performed consistently as an Army Group commander himself: 'GHQ in 1916 and 1917 was not designed, organised and staffed appropriately to function effectively as an Army Group headquarters'. The significance of the various improvements in the BEF's artillery techniques and of Solly-Flood's achievements at the newly established Training Directorate by the spring of 1917 *are* recognised by Harris, who considers that the scale and sophistication of the preparations for the Battle of Arras – launched on 9 April – were, 'for a mass army thrown together in a few years and desperately short of trained staff officers, highly commendable'. Even so, Harris deems that, despite much recent research, it is not clear 'how widely and deeply such new doctrines had yet been disseminated and absorbed' and he doubts whether much of the evolution of the BEF after 1 July 1916 was attributable 'to any personal inspiration' on the part of its Commander-in-Chief.[112] The response to this last point, one could argue, is that, as C-in-C, Haig had at least presided over many of the acknowledged improvements and, if he did not initiate them personally, he should be given credit for encouraging the learning process and allowing it to flourish – rather like a good football manager successfully rebuilding a team which had previously been threatened with relegation.

Of all the studies of the battle which have appeared over the last decade, William Philpott's magisterial *Bloody Victory: The Sacrifice on the Somme and the Making of the Twentieth Century* (2009) offers the most comprehensive survey, analysing in depth the experience of all three major armies on the Somme and discussing the political, social, economic and cultural impact of the struggle in France and Germany as well as in Britain and the Dominions. Like most recent historians of the First World War, Philpott sees the Allied offensive on the Somme in 1916, and the sacrifice it entailed, as a necessary stage in an intense and brutal war of attrition, and as a bloody victory which has become obscured by the myth of tragedy. Although the war was far from over at the end of 1916, 'after the Somme there would be only one ultimate victor'. Philpott also follows recent historiographical trends in tracing the gradual and painful evolution of the BEF from its low point of 1 July 1916 – when it was a 'naïve and partly prepared' citizen army, '"New" in name and limited in expertise, knowledge and experience' – into a much more effective force by late September of that year. The BEF's tactical and organisational changes and reforms are briefly summarised by the author, but he stresses that the learning process was far from smooth or uniform, and that some lessons were ill-absorbed, even if the British army by 1918 was as good as any on the Western Front. The main lessons acknowledged and absorbed related to the use of individual arms on the industrial battlefield and their effective co-ordination into what would today be called a 'weapons system'. These basic principles, Philpott writes, were being grasped for the first time in July and August 1916. Only by a process of trial and error, in a gruelling fight against a skilled and stubborn adversary, 'could the talented rise to the top in the short time available, and the expanded army develop an effective system of devolved operational command'.[113]

The German army at the beginning of 1916 is described as being 'at the height of its morale and physical effectiveness' and as battle-hardened, aggressive and tactically skilled in the field. It would literally have to be ground down and its morale undermined by 'continuous hard pounding' before an Allied victory could be attained. However, as Philpott reveals, the German army was indeed subjected to just such an ordeal: 'In this relentless *Materialschlacht* on the Somme, Germany's once proud and victorious divisions met their Nemesis – a tenacious, determined enemy who, despite no obvious strategic breakthrough, simply would not let go'. Nor is Philpott convinced by those historians who credit the Germans with initiating and developing infantry tactics which were appropriate for the modern industrial battlefield. All armies, he remarks, were confronted by the same challenges and worked out similar solutions. '"Storm-troops", infiltration tactics, combined-arms tactics, heavy support weapons, infantry specialists and small group formations are all identified in the paeans to German military skill. But all were employed by the French army on the Somme in 1916'.[114]

It is in rightly re-emphasising the scale and key importance of the French army's contribution to the Somme offensive that Philpott differs from most British and Commonwealth historians of the Great War. In too many accounts of the campaign, argues Philpott, the French generals concerned are 'relegated to walk-on parts', their successes having been largely ignored and obscured and all but vanishing from history. Bill Philpott's contention is that, by the beginning of the battle, the French army had learned, digested, applied and disseminated the bitter lessons of 1915 and of Verdun, its tactics being far more advanced and sophisticated than those of the BEF at that stage. In his judgement, much of the blame for the comparative neglect of the French contribution can be laid at the door of Haig, whose record, in his diary, of some episodes – such as the French Sixth Army's outstanding success at Bouchavesnes on 12 September – is viewed by Philpott as 'bizarre, erroneous and indeed deceitful ...'. Because British historians have often taken their cue from Haig's account of events, the latter should perhaps 'bear ultimate responsibility for the French army's marginalisation'.[115]

One of Philpott's own principal contributions to the historiography of the battle has been to refocus our attention on the ability and achievements of General Marie-Émile Fayolle, the commander of the French Sixth Army, and his superior, General Ferdinand Foch, commander of the *Groupe des Armées du Nord* (G.A.N.

or Northern Army Group). Fayolle, himself a gunner, is credited with employing methodical and scientific artillery techniques, which were designed to conserve lives, accepted that neutralising counter-battery fire was often more effective than destructive fire, and were founded on meticulous calculations of the number of shells per metre required to overcome the enemy's defences and defenders. Foch, for his part, is seen by Philpott as being the Allied general with probably the clearest understanding of what was needed to ensure genuine progress – rather than short-lived, shallow or narrow gains – on the congested industrial battlefield. By September 1916, certainly, Foch appears to have grasped that, instead of seeking to exploit limited penetrations of the enemy's line in order to secure a bigger 'breakthrough', it might be better to exploit successes *laterally*, spreading one's attacks successively across different sectors in a rolling series of blows, killing more Germans and keeping them off-balance, thereby dislocating and destabilising the defence. This operational method, which Foch termed 'general battle' (*bataille générale*) could be applied along the whole front and, on a wider scale, provided the basis for the overall Allied victory on the Western Front in 1918. According to Philpott, this was 'the most important, if now long forgotten, intangible outcome of the Somme campaign ...'.[116] Such an approach was foreshadowed in September 1916, when the French and British forces launched a succession of blows across the entire Somme front, bringing the defence close to crisis point and causing German resources to become dangerously thin before the weather intervened and the momentum of the Allied offensive slowed once more.

As might have been expected, Philpott's important work did not, in fact, end the debate, though the most recent contributors to it have tended to give general support to the 'revisionist' interpretation. In his scholarly, and not uncritical, biography of Haig – *The Chief: Douglas Haig and the British Army* (2011) – Gary Sheffield broadly maintains the position he occupied earlier in the decade but suggests that, as applied to the Somme, the term 'victory' is 'simply inappropriate for an affair that in the end was aimed at inflicting maximum damage on the enemy'. Sheffield states that the BEF's apprenticeship in 1916 made it a much more formidable machine and that its morale remained largely intact in spite of its ordeal: 'Haig's argument was, in effect, that the Somme had not resulted in a decisive victory because the German army had not yet suffered enough from attrition'.[117] However, Haig's swift recognition of the value of Solly-Flood's tactical, organisational and training reforms of early 1917 is duly underlined by Sheffield and he recounts an interesting conversation in December 1916 between the Commander-in-Chief and Major-General Oliver Nugent (GOC of the 36th (Ulster) Division), which throws revealing light upon Haig himself. When the latter suggested to Nugent that the Ulster Division may not have been given sufficient support at Thiepval on 1 July 1916, Nugent had conceded that 'perhaps we had all been rather optimistic as to what it was possible to do'. Haig's unusually candid response was 'Well, we were all learning'.[118] Just what was learned by British generals in 1916 has also been re-examined in detail by the American historian Sanders Marble, who, in a recently published study of British artillery on the Western Front, expands upon the earlier conclusions reached by Bidwell and Graham, Martin Farndale and Jonathan Bailey – particularly those relating to developments in the creeping barrage and counter-battery fire. 'What is impressive', Marble claims, 'given the reputation of First World War generals for obstinacy, is the eager search for lessons'.[119]

Whatever side one takes, it is pleasing to note that, at least in scholarly circles, the debate is now based firmly on sound archival research and can, if the media allows, be treated – in the words of Brian Bond – 'as history (like earlier wars) rather than being approached emotionally and polemically in terms of "futility", "horror" and "national trauma"'.[120] There can surely now be little doubt that various aspects of the BEF's command, organisation and tactics *did* show a marked improvement during, or as a direct result of, the Somme. By 1917 the creeping barrage had become standard and was better understood and applied; overhead machine-gun barrages were more common; the introduction of the 106 fuse would help artillery to cut enemy wire without cratering the ground; progress was being made towards the location of enemy gun batteries by flash-spotting and sound-ranging, facilitating much more effective counter-battery fire and enhancing understanding of the 'deep battle'; and GHQ's reorganisation of the artillery in late 1916 created Army Field Artillery (AFA) brigades which, in turn, provided a flexible reserve of field artillery to reinforce divisional gunners when required and give the latter more rest by reducing the frequency of calls upon them to assist other divisions.

In addition, the preparation and dissemination of training pamphlets such as *SS 135*, *SS 143* and *SS 144* led to standard operating procedures and more uniform application of tactical lessons, aided by an increase in schools of instruction at GHQ, army, corps and divisional level; the crucial reorganisation of the infantry platoon early in 1917 encouraged more flexible small-unit tactics, with the platoon becoming a miniature all-arms battlefield team capable of providing its own internal fire-support and of maintaining the momentum of an advance for longer periods; there was a renewed emphasis on higher musketry standards and less reliance on the 'cult of the bomb'; unsuitable commanders at all levels were removed and replaced with younger, fitter officers; and command and control continued to devolve downwards in the best corps, divisions and brigades, with more trust in the 'man on the spot' (as *FSR* had advocated) and a more managerial, consultative style of command being adopted. All this, one can argue, *does* strongly indicate the existence of a learning process and the beginning of 're-skilling' the BEF in 1916. As John Bourne has neatly summarised it: 'In some ways, the most important day of the war was 2 July 1916. The British had suffered an appalling reverse, but it was apparent that they were not going away, that their operational method was bound to improve and that the resources available to them from the mobilisation of British industry would make them what they eventually became, a formidable enemy'.[121]

Chapter 3

The Performance of New Army
Divisions on the Somme, 1916

Many of the people making the journey from Britain to the Somme battlefields each year will, on various occasions during their trip, give some thought to the experience of Kitchener's Army in the 1916 offensive. Whether travelling there as individuals, in family groups wishing to see where granddad or great-granddad and his brothers fought, or in organised coach parties, they will assemble in their hundreds (perhaps thousands) at the Memorial to the Missing at Thiepval on the morning of 1 July. A fair proportion will also include, on their itinerary, the other principal sites on the battlefield, such as Newfoundland Park, the Serre Road No. 2 cemetery, Lochnagar Crater and Delville Wood. Some, from Lancashire and Yorkshire, from Northern Ireland and the Irish Republic, and from Wales – or people with a particular interest in their local battalion or formation – will pay special visits to the copses at Serre, the Ulster Tower, Guillemont and Mametz Wood but the majority will, at some stage, probably concentrate their thoughts primarily on the events of 1 July 1916 and, rightly, on the courage and sacrifice of Britain's citizen-soldiers on that bloody day.

No one, least of all myself, should seek to underplay or deny the unprecedented suffering, sacrifice and tragedy which coloured the whole Somme experience in 1916 and which has left such a massive, raw and lasting scar on the national psyche. Moreover, the scar was all the deeper because of the enormous gulf between expectation and reality. As the British official historian put it:

> No braver or more determined men ever faced an enemy than those sons of the British Empire who 'went over the top' on the 1st of July 1916. Never before had the ranks of a British Army on the field of battle contained the finest of all classes of the nation in physique, brains and education. And they were volunteers, not conscripts. If ever a decisive victory was to be won it was to be expected now.[1]

Though historians still argue about the nature and extent of the dilution, and how quickly it actually occurred, there is little doubt that, after its terrible awakening on the morning of 1 July, the unique character of the highly localised BEF of mid-1916 – in which many battalions, batteries and field companies had special links to particular communities – was gone for ever.

Given the scale of the casualties and the suddenness with which so many national illusions were shattered in July 1916, it is therefore hardly surprising that, ever since, a largely negative view of the experience of Britain's New Armies on the Somme has tended to prevail among the general public. It must also be pointed out that this view has been powerfully reinforced over the years by various veterans and historians (see Chapter 2). In *The Imperial War Museum Book of the Somme*, Malcolm Brown quotes from an interview he recorded, in 1976, with George Morgan, who went over the top with the Bradford Pals at Serre on that fateful morning of 1 July 1916. Some sixty years after the event, George was still clearly bitter and disillusioned:

> We were all pals, very happy together; and they were such good people. They were fine young men, the cream of the country. That spirit lasted until 1 July 1916. We had so many casualties that we were all strangers after that. The new men who came were fed up, they were conscripts and they didn't want to come, they didn't want to fight. Things were never the same any more ... After July 1st I hated the generals and the people who were running the country and the war. I felt we'd been sacrificed ... We didn't do anything. We didn't win a thing.[2]

If that is the view of a veteran of the Somme, it is again small wonder that such attitudes have proved so persistent.

The British official historians of the Somme offensive – Brigadier-General Sir James Edmonds and Captain Wilfrid Miles – attribute many of the problems faced by the New Armies in 1916 to what John Bourne has called the widespread 'de-skilling' of the BEF following its huge and rapid expansion in 1914–1915. Certainly in his final chapter in the second volume on the Somme, published in 1938, Miles arrives at a series of conclusions which present the New Armies of 1916 in an unfavourable light when compared with the performance of the old professional BEF. This may be explained by the fact that the decentralisation of tactics to the level of temporary officers and citizen-soldier NCOs was a very unsettling development in the eyes of many Regulars. There is indeed an element of this in Miles's statement that:

> Owing to the dearth of trained officers, the staffs of corps, divisions and brigades included many young Regular and New Army officers who had to learn the duties of their branch in the heat of battle. In some cases over-anxious staff officers 'nursed' inexperienced brigade and battalion commanders too much, thereby curbing and discouraging initiative; on the other hand, proper guidance and help from the staff were not always forthcoming when most needed.

Miles goes on to claim that:

> The perfunctory battle training of the troops was based upon tactical principles sound for the most part, but lacking in some essential details and

in a proper anticipation of the difficulties with which the infantry would have to contend ... Generally speaking, the new British infantry, unlike that of the old Regular Army, had not been taught to combine fire and movement to the best advantage ... it was not well practised in the use of ground; and, whilst inclined to be unduly sensitive as regards to open flanks, did not sufficiently appreciate the necessity of helping adjacent formations ... There remained in the Armies few battalions possessed of the deep grounded knowledge and battle discipline which react instinctively to an unexpected situation and deal with it.[3]

In more recent years, several historians have added their weight to the negative interpretation of the experience and achievements of the New Army divisions on the Somme. Writing in 1991, Denis Winter maintained that the army which Haig sent into battle was 'as badly organised as most people came to suspect in the post-war period. Poorly trained and ill-equipped, supported by staff work of low quality and commanded by generals inadequate to the task, the BEF under Haig was indeed the bluntest of swords'.[4] The American scholar Bruce Gudmundsson asserts, with a staggering degree of certainty, that 'most British officers worked hard to maintain an air of detached amateurism ... This became even more true as the war progressed and those few regular officers who took their profession seriously found themselves concentrated on staffs, leaving small unit leadership to enthusiastic but tactically incompetent schoolboys'.[5] Closer to home, Martin Samuels, in his book *Doctrine and Dogma*, states that the British army in the First World War was characterised by its unsubtle and inflexible approach to battle: 'Having once adopted this approach, it proved virtually impossible to alter it'. Similarly, in a later work, when analysing the performance of New Army formations on 1 July 1916, Samuels declares that, 'since troops could not be trusted to act effectively without direct orders, such orders must be provided in advance ... Commanders made little effort to train their men to make flank attacks, or even to alert them to the potential benefits of such actions'. He adds that, whereas the British units tended to be leaderless and lacking in a natural ability to assess tactical problems, 'the German forces enjoyed leaders at every level who went forward and who were ready to act on their own initiative, according to circumstances'. In his view, the failure to follow up the initial success of the 36th (Ulster) Division on 1 July was largely the product of the British army's 'system of restrictive control'.[6]

All these arguments notwithstanding, my own research, over the years, into the operations of the 18th (Eastern) Division – a typical New Army formation in many ways – has consistently indicated that there is another side to the story and that the truth about the New Armies on the Somme is much more complicated than the above historians would have us believe. I therefore thought that it might be helpful to look afresh at the New Army divisions on the Somme by adopting the same approach as I used in the 1990s when analysing the BEF's performance in the Hundred Days offensive of August to November 1918.[7] What I have done (as I did for the Hundred Days) is to go through the Somme volumes of the British official history and to list, analyse and assess each attacking operation undertaken by all the New Army divisions on the Somme – from the 9th (Scottish) Division to the 41st Division – including those which are either merely mentioned in passing or, alternatively, covered in detail by Edmonds and Miles. The operations involved, which amounted to 281 separate attacks in all, ranged from strong offensive patrols, company or battalion actions, and bombing attacks, to full-scale set-piece assaults by several divisions at a time. If a division's initial assault, on a particular day, failed or was inconclusive and was followed by a second attack the same day with a specific new start-time and a new artillery barrage, then I have classed them as separate operations. Hence the overall figure of 281 does not just include the big operations such as those launched on 1 July, 14 July or 15 September, but also embraces quite minor local affairs and many of the small-scale, isolated, narrow-front attacks on the Fourth Army front in the late summer for which Rawlinson was sternly admonished by Haig on 24 August. It is not, of course, a comprehensive list but I do believe that the sample based on mentions in the official history is sufficiently extensive and thorough to offer some reasonably accurate, significant and instructive conclusions about divisional performance in 1916.

Operations which I classed as 'successful' fell into five main categories, including operations in which all the assigned objectives were taken and consolidated; attacks in which most of the objectives were secured and substantial progress (albeit in relative terms) was achieved; actions in which part of the division or battalion concerned secured part of the objective while other elements made only limited gains or merely secured a foothold; operations in which *only* limited progress was made (e.g. company-strength bombing attacks leading to the seizure of, say, 200 yards of enemy trench and the erection of blocks or barricades to secure the gain); and finally, in a few cases, success against negligible opposition. This latter category does not necessarily denote a 'walk-over' and usually indicates that the Germans had abandoned a village or strongpoint as the result of a series of attacks or cumulative pressure by the New Army formation in question. On the more negative side, I classed as a 'limited success verging on failure' any operation in which a unit had *largely* failed in its assigned task, had done well initially but had subsequently been driven out of *most* of its gains, or had ended the day with only the smallest toehold in the enemy positions to show for its efforts. Inevitably, some operations were *outright* failures. However, even these two latter categories sometimes disguise an operation, such as the 36th (Ulster) Division's assault on the Schwaben Redoubt on 1 July, which might have ended as a major success but for poor command decisions at army or corps level or lack of progress by, or support from, the divisions on either side.

Having established the broad criteria, it might be useful to look first at the overall or collective performance figures for the twenty-five New Army divisions which conducted meaningful and active offensive operations on the Somme between 1 July and 24 November 1916. Of the sample of 281 attacking operations mentioned in the relevant official history volumes, 104 (or 37.01 per cent) achieved all objectives or made substantial progress towards that end; 10 (or 3.55 per cent) saw some elements of the division or battalion involved securing part of the objective while other parts made only limited gains; 43 (or 15.30 per cent) were actions in which *only* limited progress was made; and 3 (or 1.06 per cent) were successes against negligible opposition. Thus, of the 281 attacks considered, *some progress or success* – ranging from limited to substantial – was registered in 160 of them, or 56.93 per cent of the operations under review. On the debit side, I assessed 20 attacks (or 7.11 per cent) as being 'limited successes verging on failure' while 101 (or 35.94 per cent) were complete failures. It is worth noting, at this early stage, that the overall success rate – i.e. with all the categories of success brought together – was over 55 per cent and that the proportion of *total or outright failures* in New Army attacks on the Somme was as low as 35.94 per cent. These figures alone would seem to suggest that the widely held *negative* view of the tactical performance of New Army divisions in 1916 is somewhat ill-deserved.

The figures are even more revealing, and in many ways surprising, if one looks at the overall performance figures for the individual divisions. My examination of the statistics relating to the divisions of the First New Army ('K.1') which fought on the Somme – namely the 9th (Scottish), 11th (Northern), 12th (Eastern) and 14th (Light) Divisions – revealed that the overall success rate (i.e. attacks in which *some* progress was made) was as high as 85.71 per cent for the 11th Division, 70 per cent for the 14th Division, 64. 28 per cent for the 9th Division (despite the bitter struggle at Delville Wood), and 63.63 per cent for the 12th Division. The number of attacks carried out by these divisions ranged from 7 in the case of the 11th Division to 14 in the case of the 9th (Scottish). Collectively, the K.1 or First New Army divisions mounted 41 attacks and achieved an overall success rate of 69.04 per cent – with all 4 engaged attaining a success rate of 63 per cent or more.

The statistics are only slightly less impressive for the divisions of K.2 or the Second New Army, all six of which saw action on the Somme. The lowest success rate here was recorded, in 22 attacks (itself a high number) by the 17th (Northern) Division, at 40.90 per cent. Next, in ascending order, came the 15th (Scottish) with 54.54 per cent in 11 attacks; the 16th (Irish) with 66.66 per cent in 6 attacks; the 19th (Western) with 73.33 per cent in 15 attacks; the 18th (Eastern) with 76.92 per cent in 13 attacks; and, highest, the 20th (Light) Division with 85.71 per cent in 7 attacks (though admittedly over 50 per cent of its successful actions fell into the 'limited progress' category). It may be noted that, apart from the 17th Division, the other 5 had an overall success rate of 54 per cent or more (with 3 of them over 70 per cent). Collectively, they made 74 attacks and achieved some progress in 62.16 per cent of the operations under review.

Four divisions of the Third New Army (K.3) undertook attacks on the Somme – the 21st, 23rd, 24th and 25th Divisions – two of which, the 21st and 24th, had experienced a disastrous baptism of fire at Loos the previous September. The 24th Division's success rate of 38.46 per cent in 13 attacks (with a corresponding outright failure rate of 61.53 per cent) may well suggest that the formation had not yet recovered from the Loos debacle. The 23rd Division achieved an overall success rate of 54.16 per cent in 24 attacks; the 25th Division reached a success rate of 62.49 per cent in 24 attacks; and the 21st Division, in marked contrast to the 24th, registered a highly creditable 80 per cent overall success rate in 10 attacks. All the K.3 divisions, apart from the 24th, achieved a success rate of 54 per cent or more and, collectively, their overall success rate in 71 attacks was 57.74 per cent.

One may pause at this point to consider that, in terms of achieving *some* progress in their attacks on the Somme, the divisions of the First, Second and Third New Armies attained a collective success rate of 62.98 per cent, while the percentage of total failures was between 28.51 per cent (for the First New Army) and 33.8 per cent (for the Third New Army), or an average outright failure rate of 31.6 per cent. I would therefore argue from these figures that, in general, the divisions of the first three New Armies performed at least creditably, and in some cases with great distinction, in their attacks on the Somme. Certainly the figures do not lend any real support to the idea that the Kitchener divisions were largely ineffective in operations in 1916 and were merely bewildered and innocent pawns in the game.

As nearly always occurs in any discussions of the Battle of the Somme, the experience of the Pals or locally raised formations clouds the issue. Indeed, I would go further and assert that many of the negative assessments of the BEF on the Somme seem to stem from the performance of the Fourth and Fifth New Armies – and the Fourth in particular. The 30th, 31st, 32nd, 33rd, 34th and 35th Divisions of the eventual Fourth New Army (K.4) were all involved, at some stage, in the offensive and their figures do compare unfavourably with those of the other four New Armies. Again, in ascending order, the 31st Division had a failure rate of 100 per cent (or a success rate of nil per cent) in 2 attacks; the 35th (Bantam) Division recorded similarly depressing figures in 4 attacks; the 33rd Division's overall success rate was 41.66 per cent in 12 attacks; the 34th Division achieved a success rate of 45.45 per cent in 11 attacks; the 30th Division registered a success rate of 46.15 per cent in 13 attacks; and the 32nd Division had a success rate of 50 per cent in 10 operations (though even here a high proportion of the 50 per cent was made up of attacks which fell into the 'limited progress' category). Thus only 1 of these 6 divisions recorded even a qualified overall success rate of 50 per cent and their *collective* success rate in 52 attacks was only 40.38 per cent.

The figures for the five divisions of the Fifth New Army which fought on the Somme – the 36th (Ulster), 37th, 38th (Welsh), 39th and 41st Divisions – are more varied. The 36th (Ulster) Division had a success rate of nil per cent in its *one* major attack – although this bald statistic in no way reflects its quite outstanding feat – and near-success – in overcoming the formidable Schwaben Redoubt on 1 July. Its 'limited success verging on failure' on that day can be attributed to command failures at corps level and the lack of progress by neighbouring divisions rather than to any serious shortcomings on its own part. The 38th (Welsh) Division too had a low overall success rate (28.57 per cent) in 7 attacks, no doubt largely as a result of its unhappy initial experiences at Mametz Wood. The 37th Division's units attained an overall success rate of 56 per cent in 25 attacks (many of which were undertaken while elements of the formation were attached to other divisions, such as the 34th); the 39th Division's success rate figure was 71.42 per cent in 7 attacks; and the 41st Division achieved some meaningful progress in both its major attacks (100 per cent). In other words, 3 out of these 5 divisions had an overall success rate of over 50 per cent. In all, the 5 divisions representing the Fifth New Army carried out 42 attacks and achieved some progress in 54.76 per cent of them.

One may deduce from all this that the overall success rate of divisions in the Fourth and Fifth New Armies was between 40.38 and 54.76 per cent, giving the K.4 and K.5 divisions together an average overall success rate of 47.57 per cent and an average failure rate – i.e. outright failures – of 43.31 per cent. The only group of New Army divisions with an overall success rate of less than 54 per cent were those constituting the Fourth New Army, which were largely composed of Pals formations.

If broken down into months, the figures are equally instructive. Out of both interest and convenience, I have separated the statistics for 1 July 1916 from those for the rest of that month. In all, I calculated, from the official history, that 11 out of the 281 separate attacks by New Army divisions took place on 1 July, of which 4 (or 36.36 per cent of these 11 attacks) resulted in some progress or success while 7 of the 11 (or 63.63 per cent) fell into the 'limited success verging on failure' or outright failure categories. 111 attacks were mounted in the remainder of July, producing some progress in 57.65 per cent of these operations. If one combines the figures for 1 July and the rest of the month, then one arrives at a total of 122 attacks in July as a whole, of which 68 (or 55.73 per cent) resulted in varying degrees of success or progress, while 54 (or 44.26 per cent) fell into the 'limited success verging on failure' or outright failure categories. Of the sample of 281 attacks by New Army divisions, 45 took place in August, the overall success rate by Kitchener formations that month being 48.88 per cent (22 of the 45 attacks); a further 54 attacks were carried out in September, when some success was achieved in 34 of the operations (62.96 per cent); in October the overall success rate rose as high as 71.87 per cent (i.e. some success in 23 out of 32 attacks, despite the deteriorating conditions); and in November there were 28 attacks, with some success in 17, or 60.71 per cent.

Not surprisingly, the failure rate was high on 1 July 1916, although, even on that bloody day, some progress was made by New Army divisions in approximately 36 per cent of their assaults. It will have been noted, from the above statistics, that the heaviest month of fighting for New Army divisions was July but also that the worst month for them, in terms of performance, was August when, though not so heavily engaged as they had been in July – and would be again in September – their overall success rate dropped to 48.88 per cent. August was, in fact, the only month between 1 July and the end of the offensive in which the overall success rate fell below 50 per cent. This may in part be ascribed to the Fourth Army's tendency that month to deliver unco-ordinated small-scale attacks on narrow local fronts. The overall improvements in September and October – as indicated by the monthly figures – may owe a fair amount to the developments in artillery tactics and techniques, including the widespread adoption in the BEF of the creeping barrage, and also to the greater concentration and density of set-piece bombardments, such as that preceding the 25 September attack towards Morval, Lesboeufs and Gueudecourt. The overall failure rates drop from 63.63 per cent on 1 July and 51.11 per cent in August to 37.03 per cent in September and 28.12 per cent in October. In the same way, the success and failure statistics for November (when the percentage of 'limited progress' attacks was 21.42 per cent, exceeded only by September at 24.07 per cent) remain creditable in poor battlefield conditions and often foul weather. There is little doubt in my mind that, apart from August, the trend was towards improvement rather than any major shortfall in standards of performance. And it should be emphasised that this improvement, as indicated by the performance figures, was achieved in the face of continuing heavy losses, command changes, the terrible strain of the attrition battle and the constant influx of new drafts to replace casualties. If nothing else, the above figures appear to support the existence of a tactical and command learning process in the BEF's New Army divisions in 1916.

One particularly tenacious idea in the general public's perception of Kitchener divisions on the Somme is that they were composed largely of brave and patriotic but, above all, *amateur* citizen-soldiers – using the word 'amateur' in both of its principal accepted meanings. But just how raw and inexperienced were the New Army divisions when the offensive began? The short answer is that, in terms of previous length of service on the Western Front or combat experience, they were by no means as universally raw as many people seem to imagine. Three of the four divisions of the First New Army which fought on the Somme had been in France over a year when the battle started. The only exception here was the 11th (Northern) Division, which did not arrive on the Western Front until July 1916 – *after* the commencement of the battle – but it had gone overseas at the end of June 1915 and had fought on Gallipoli from August until the evacuation of the peninsula. The 9th (Scottish) and 12th (Eastern) Divisions had seen action at Loos the previous autumn, while the 14th (Light) Division had literally undergone its baptism of fire in the German liquid fire attack at Hooge at the end of July 1915, also seeing action at Bellewaarde that September. Five of the six divisions of the Second New Army had been in France for at least a year by July 1916. The 15th (Scottish) had fought at Loos in 1915 and had also taken part in operations on the First Army front, near Hulluch, in April and May 1916; the 17th (Northern) had been engaged at Hooge in August 1915 and in operations at The Bluff, near Ypres, in February–March 1916; the 19th (Western) had taken part in operations subsidiary to the main attack at Loos in September and early October 1915; and the 20th (Light) Division had seen some action at Fromelles in September 1915 and at Mount Sorrel as recently as 2–13 June 1916. The 18th (Eastern) Division had crossed to France in July 1915 and, for the best part of the following twelve months, had served its trench warfare apprenticeship on the Somme front, mainly in the Tambour sector at Fricourt and at Carnoy and La Boisselle. It was therefore very familiar with the Somme, which, even in late July 1915, was not always a 'cushy' sector. The 18th had suffered 1,247 casualties by the end of 1915 but its prolonged period of trench warfare unquestionably helped it to 'shake down' into an effective fighting formation. For a variety of reasons, including lack of equipment and the slow progress of its training, the 16th (Irish) Division had only arrived in France between late September and the end of February yet it had already seen action in the German gas attacks on the Hulluch sector in late April.[8]

The four divisions of the Third New Army which fought on the Somme had all, by then, been on the Western Front for ten to eleven months and two of them – the 21st and 24th – which *were* then truly green, had gone into action, albeit with near-disastrous results, on the second day of the Battle of Loos. In the case of the divisions of the Fourth and Fifth New Armies, containing the bulk of the Pals battalions, five had been on the Western Front for eight months or more (the 37th having been there as long as eleven months); another three had been there for between five and seven months; and three had served in France for four months or less, the 41st Division having arrived as late as May 1916. One may observe, at this juncture, that – with one or two notable exceptions, such as the 17th and 24th Divisions – the formations of the first three New Armies, which had collectively been in France the longest, perhaps not surprisingly recorded higher success rates (54 per cent or more) than most of the later arrivals from K.4 and K.5. Even here, however, two of the least experienced divisions, the 39th and 41st, which crossed to France in March and May 1916 respectively, registered success rates of 71.42 per cent and 100 per cent. On the whole, I am persuaded that, since a significant majority of the New Army divisions had been in France and Belgium for at least eight months by July 1916, they can hardly be described as 'raw' or completely 'amateur' in the ways and conditions of warfare on the Western Front. One should also note that approximately half of the 25 New Army divisions that fought on the Somme had real combat experience before that great battle started.

A related factor which should be taken into account at this point is the 'stiffening' of New Army divisions – mainly after the setbacks at Loos in 1915 – by exchanging one of their brigades for a brigade from a Regular division, presumably to give the New Army divisions in question a leavening of experience and 'professionalism'. Not counting those Kitchener divisions which exchanged brigades with *each other* before and during the Somme battle, or the 9th (Scottish), which received a South African brigade, six of the 25 New Army divisions appear to have been involved in this process, namely the 23rd, 24th, 25th, 30th, 32nd and 33rd. Their success rates were, respectively, 54.54 per cent, 38.46 per cent, 62.49 per cent, 46.15 per cent, 50 per cent and 41.66 per cent. In short, only two of the six had a success rate of 50 per cent or more and the average success rate of these divisions was 48.88 per cent, scarcely a ringing endorsement for the policy. Again, and possibly to the surprise of many, those New Army divisions which retained their original units tended to perform better than those which were 'stiffened' with Regulars, though, of course, there were relatively few survivors from the old 1914 formations by the time of the Battle of the Somme.[9]

Did either the freshness or the resting of units help to improve battlefield performance? The immediate and obvious answer is that indeed it did, as in a lengthy battle of attrition, shattered formations undeniably needed time to reorganise, refit, train and, above all, regenerate their fighting spirit. Yet, here too, the picture is a little more complex than one might initially suppose. If one analyses the number of major operational 'tours' of active offensive duty, or 'battle periods', undertaken by each of the 25 New Army divisions on the Somme, one finds that three – the 18th, 23rd and 39th – had four or more; eleven (or over half of the remainder) had three battle tours; seven had two such tours; and only four had one such tour. However, if one had jumped to the conclusion that combat fatigue might be reflected in the success or failure rates of those divisions with the most battle periods, then one would be wrong. The 23rd Division, with four tours, achieved an overall success rate – i.e. with *some* progress in its attacks – of 54.16 per cent; the 39th, with four tours, had an overall success rate of 71.42 per cent; and the 18th, with five tours and seven major assaults, had a success rate of just under 77 per cent. On the other hand, the 31st Division, with only two tours, had a 100 per cent failure rate.[10] Even the official historian was moved to acknowledge the achievement of the 15th (Scottish) Division which, having been in the line continuously since 8 August, 'attacked with remarkable success' on 15 September and was not relieved until four days later. Despite Chris Pugsley's more recent claims on behalf of the New Zealand Division, this was, in my view, probably the longest continuous operational tour – if only by a narrow margin – of any British or Dominion division on the Somme, and the 15th Division still ended up with an overall success rate of more than 50 per cent.[11]

On the other side of the coin, some divisions were 'tired' even before they had undertaken *major* offensive operations. A case in point was the 35th (Bantam) Division which, it may be recalled, was one of the formations with the highest failure rates on the Somme. On at least three occasions – 20 July, 20 August and 24 August – officers at divisional, brigade and battalion levels registered severe doubts about the ability of their troops to mount an effective attack, despite the fact that the division had so far carried out no *major* assaults to match those of, say, the 18th, 32nd, 34th and 36th Divisions on 1 July or the 9th Division at Longueval-Delville Wood later that month.[12] Therefore, it does not necessarily follow that relatively 'fresh' divisions did well or that there was a corresponding reduction in the fighting capabilities of 'well-used' divisions the more they were employed.

While challenging various Somme shibboleths, let us look at the deep-rooted perception that 1 July was an *unmitigated* catastrophe for the New Army divisions. As I stated earlier, no one should ever seek to underplay the appalling losses and horrors endured by all who fought on the Somme – especially those who went into action on 1 July – but the reverses at Serre and Thiepval aside, the day was not an *unrelieved* disaster for the New Army formations. In this connection, it might be helpful to summarise what progress, if any, was made by the New Army divisions between Montauban and Serre on 1 July.

On the right flank, in the south and next to the French, the 30th and 18th Divisions of XIII Corps – admittedly assisted by French artillery – captured all their objectives, including the village of Montauban. Next, on the XV Corps sector, elements of the 63rd and 64th Brigades of the 21st Division made good progress to the left, or north-west, of Fricourt, advancing 2,000 yards across the top of the Fricourt spur to the sunken Pozières–Fricourt road and Round Wood, although the attached 50th Brigade from the 17th (Northern) Division suffered terribly nearer the village and on the slopes to its immediate left, close to the Tambour. However, their collective efforts paved the way for the occupation of Fricourt the following day.[13] The 34th Division, in III Corps at La Boisselle, suffered heavier losses than any other division that day, while the 102nd (Tyneside Scottish) Brigade and 103rd (Tyneside Irish) Brigade each incurred, according to Martin Middlebrook, more casualties than any other brigade on 1 July. The 21st and 22nd Northumberland Fusiliers (2nd and 3rd Tyneside Scottish) succeeded in taking a section of the German trenches around *Schwaben Höhe* on the northern slopes of Sausage Valley – a gain which Middlebrook estimates at around 20 acres – but, on the right, the 15th and 16th Royal Scots (the two Edinburgh City battalions), with some men of the Tyneside Irish, also made progress astride the Fricourt spur towards Birch Tree Wood, pushing a little beyond their first objective.[14] At Thiepval, in the X Corps sector, the 32nd Division could do no more than secure a foothold in the Leipzig Redoubt, at the tip of the Leipzig Salient. To their left, the 36th (Ulster) Division performed the extraordinary feat of overcoming the formidable defences of the Schwaben Redoubt and even, at one stage, penetrated to within 500 yards of Mouquet Farm. Had they been in greater strength at this critical juncture – or had Morland, the corps commander, not chosen to employ his corps reserve to reinforce failure at Thiepval village rather than success at the Schwaben Redoubt – they might have been able to advance down the Mouquet Switch towards the farm, thereby threatening to take in reverse the entire German position along the Thiepval spur. It is speculation, of course, but the Ulstermen could perhaps have achieved one of the most remarkable successes of the entire campaign but for faulty command decisions and lack of progress on their flanks. As it was, at the end of the day's fighting, only a few small parties remained in the original German front and support lines.[15] Finally, for all the immense courage displayed by the Pals battalions of the 31st Division at Serre, in the VIII Corps sector, they had nothing to show for their efforts and sacrifice by the time darkness fell.[16]

If one excludes, for a moment, the 50th Brigade of the 17th Division at Fricourt, the above summary shows that only one of the seven New Army divisions (the 31st) made no progress at all; two (the 32nd and the 36th) made only minor gains; another two (the 34th and 21st) achieved some progress on at least part of their respective fronts; and the remaining two (the 18th and 30th) captured all their objectives. It is worth noting that, of the four Regular divisions engaged on 1 July, only one – the 7th at Mametz – made significant progress. Some gains made by the 8th Division at Ovillers had been lost by the end of the day; the 29th Division made no lasting progress at Beaumont Hamel; and while the 4th Division won a footing in and near the Quadrilateral, this was abandoned next morning. One might also point out that, of the five divisions which suffered the heaviest casualties on 1 July, *three* were Regular. It could be claimed, therefore, that, even given the scale of the disaster on 1 July, the New Army divisions, overall, performed at least as well as, and in some cases even better than, their Regular counterparts.

Denis Winter has caustically criticised the policy of shuffling British units around from corps to corps 'like cards in a pack'.[17] It cannot be denied that Dominion troops in the Canadian or Anzac (later Australian) Corps gained a great deal from remaining together as formations, which enhanced morale and team spirit, improved confidence and cohesion through familiarity, and made it easier to disseminate battlefield lessons. In contrast, a British division could come under the command of up to four different corps in six months or less. But did this apparently frequent rotation of divisions between different corps invariably have a negative effect on combat performance? My general conclusion is that it did not. Between 1 July and the end of the Somme battle, one of the 25 New Army divisions engaged – i.e. the 12th (Eastern) – served under four different corps; one (the 24th) served under three corps; twelve came under two different corps; and the remaining eleven served in one corps throughout.[18] It is undoubtedly true that some of the divisions which stayed in one corps had high success rates, the 21st Division with 80 per cent and the 11th (Northern) with 85.71 per cent being good examples. Conversely, the 12th Division, rotated through four corps, had a very respectable success rate of 63.63 per cent, while the 34th Division and 38th (Welsh) Division – both of which served under only one corps command – had respective success rates of 45.45 per cent and 28.75 per cent. My belief is that, bearing in mind the various strengths and weaknesses of the corps commanders on the Somme, it mattered more what corps you were in at a given time than how many corps you might pass through in the course of the battle.

Here it might be relevant to review the number of attacks in the sample which were carried out by New Army divisions under different corps and the success rates which resulted. When serving in Jacob's II Corps, New Army divisions had an overall success rate of 68.25 per cent in 63 attacks; in Pulteney's III Corps, 57.69 per cent in 52 attacks; in Edward Fanshawe's V Corps, 62.5 per cent in 16 attacks; in Hunter-Weston's VIII Corps, nil per cent in one attack; in Morland's X Corps, 57.69 per cent in 26 attacks; in Congreve's XIII Corps, 44.82 per cent in 29 attacks; in Cavan's XIV Corps, 61.53 per cent in 26 attacks; and in Horne's XV Corps, 50 per cent in 68 attacks. The figures for Horne's XV Corps, for example, appear to reflect the large number of relatively small-scale attacks carried out around High Wood and Delville Wood in July and August while those for Claud Jacob's II Corps encompass the bitter fighting for Thiepval and the Ancre Heights in September, October and November. Considering that a number of historians have, in recent years, been somewhat critical of Hubert Gough's command of the Reserve (Fifth) Army on the Somme, it is interesting to observe that, in terms of success rates, New Army divisions seem to have fared better in attacks under II and V Corps in the Reserve or Fifth Army than under most of the corps in the Fourth

Army – with the exception of Lord Cavan's XIV Corps. Although the relatively high success rate in the case of II Corps probably owes much to the methodical command style of Claud Jacob, and the presence of good assault divisions such as Ivor Maxse's 18th, this aspect of battlefield performance on the Somme might merit more thought in the future.

Command and Commanders

However much historians such as Tim Travers and Martin Samuels may suggest that the BEF, particularly in 1916, was subject to over-centralisation, restrictive control and a one-way, top-down command system, operating in a climate of fear of GHQ, I would argue that, even by the Somme, there was at least a degree of devolution of tactical decision-making and deference to the 'man on the spot', as advocated by *Field Service Regulations*. I would also contend that the identity and command style of the corps, division or brigade in which one served could, and often did, influence battlefield performance. In some units the decentralisation of command gradually increased during the battle, though the process was never uniform. Even on 1 July there was considerable variation in the attack formations adopted. At La Boisselle, for instance, the 34th Division threw all twelve infantry battalions and all three brigades into the assault, attacking in four 'columns' with each column three battalions deep.[19] 18th Division, at Carnoy-Montauban, also attacked with all three brigades in line, but here the brigades themselves, according to the divisional history, each used two battalions to lead the assault with another in support and the fourth in reserve.[20] Other divisions tended to attack with two brigades 'up' with the third in support or reserve. In addition, a number of divisions, brigades or individual battalions on 1 July – including units of the 21st, 31st, 32nd, 34th and 36th Divisions – sent their troops out into no-man's-land before zero hour, at times which seem to have varied between 7.15 a.m. and 7.27 a.m., in order to rush the German line at zero when the barrage lifted. Robin Prior and Trevor Wilson, among others, have recently been at pains to explode the myth that, on 1 July, the British infantry were simply 'ordered by a doltish command to walk shoulder to shoulder across No Man's Land' at a steady pace. They have calculated that, for the 80 battalions that went over the top in the first assault on 1 July, as many as 53 crept out into no-man's-land close to the German wire before zero, while 10 others rushed the German front line from their own parapets. This leaves 17 battalions, 12 of which *did* advance at a steady pace and 5 for which evidence is difficult to find. Prior and Wilson add that there is a further complicating factor, in that at least some of the battalions which advanced at a steady pace on 1 July 'did so because they were following a creeping barrage. These were some of the most successful units of all on the first day'.[21] Command and control as practised in the BEF in July 1916 did not, then, remove all initiative and decision-making from divisional, brigade and battalion commanders nor necessarily exclude them from participation in the planning process.

As John Bourne has underlined, the 'de-skilling' which accompanied the rapid expansion of the British army applied not only to ordinary soldiers but also to officers at almost every command level. He writes: 'The higher the level of command the less impressive was the degree of relevant experience. During the Somme campaign, the BEF was compelled to undergo a particularly brutal form of on the job training. Some commanders rose to the challenge. Some did not. The result was a considerable turnover'.[22] At this point, and fully acknowledging John Bourne's outstanding work in this field, it may be profitable to look at the experience and performance of the New Army divisional and brigade commanders on the Somme, beginning with those in post on 1 July.

Of the officers commanding the nine New Army divisions in the front line or immediate reserve on 1 July, the longest-serving was T.D. Pilcher of the 17th (Northern) Division. He was also the only one who had commanded his formation in a significant action, at Hooge in 1915, but this did not save him from becoming, as early as 13 July 1916, the third divisional commander to be sent home from the Somme.[23] Two more divisional commanders – David 'Soarer' Campbell of the 21st Division and J.S.M. Shea of the 30th Division – had been in post less than two months by 1 July. Campbell, who had won the 1896 Grand National on a horse called 'Soarer', had proved to be a fine cavalry regimental commander with the 9th Lancers in the opening weeks of the war. Bourne describes him as a 'restless, impatient curt man' who was often unpopular with New Army officers, but there is no doubt that Campbell helped to rebuild his division's fighting reputation after the debacle of Loos and he commanded it with some distinction for the remainder of the war. Shea's 30th Division fought admirably on 1 July, taking all its objectives, and although his career stuttered in 1917, after Allenby, then the Third Army commander, had criticised his performance at Arras, it is noteworthy that Allenby himself subsequently asked for Shea to head the 60th Division in Palestine, where he shone as the best of the EEF's infantry division commanders.[24]

Campbell and Shea, as well as Ivor Maxse (18th Division), R. Wanless O'Gowan (31st Division), E.C. 'Inky Bill' Ingouville-Williams (34th Division) and Oliver Nugent (36th Division) had all led brigades in action, both 'Inky Bill' and Maxse having commanded brigades in the original 1914 BEF. Ingouville-Williams was killed on 22 July but Maxse's 18th Division would soon be recognised as one of the foremost assault formations on the Somme. Maxse was, in fact, the only New Army divisional commander on 1 July who subsequently rose to corps command. Neither Tom Bridges of the 19th Division nor W.H. Rycroft of the 32nd Division had any experience as brigade commanders. Rycroft was unpopular with some of his subordinate officers and was removed shortly before the end of operations on the Somme (see Chapter 5). However, he went on to serve as a competent staff officer in Salonika. Bridges had been a squadron commander in the 4th Hussars, being promoted CO of his regiment in September 1914. Having begun the war as an ageing major, he had become a comparatively youthful major-general, at 44, by December 1915, a swift rise which made him the second youngest of the officers who commanded a division on the Somme in 1916. When his right leg was shattered by a shell in September 1917, he famously ordered hospital staff to feed the leg to the 19th Division's lion mascot.[25]

The New Army brigade commanders on 1 July were predominantly infantrymen, though J.B. Jardine (97th Brigade, 32nd Division) was a cavalryman. One, C.R.J. Griffith (108th Brigade, 36th Division) had begun the war in command of an infantry battalion. A further proportion were former battalion officers, mostly majors, while some had been staff officers. Four of the New Army brigades on 1 July were commanded by 'dug-outs' – men who had retired before the war – the oldest of these being R.B. Fell (51st Brigade, 17th Division), who was 55. The others were W.J.T. Glasgow (50th Brigade, 17th Division), Ferdinand Stanley (89th Brigade, 30th Division) and Trevor Ternan (Tyneside Scottish Brigade, 34th Division). One may note in passing that two of the three brigades in the 17th (Northern) Division on 1 July were commanded by 'dug-outs'. Six of the brigade commanders in New Army divisions on 1 July had been in post less than a month, namely H.R. Headlam (64th Brigade, 21st Division), C.C. Onslow (57th Brigade, 19th Division), Cecil Rawling (62nd Brigade, 21st Division), H.C. Rees (94th Brigade, 31st Division), H.G.M. Rowley (56th Brigade, 19th Division) and O. de L. Williams (92nd Brigade, 31st Division). Again one may observe that, in the 21st Division, the divisional commander and two brigade commanders had been in post for only two months or less on 1 July, and two of the three brigade commanders in the 31st Division had also been appointed less than a month before the start of the battle. As a group, the New Army brigade commanders on 1 July did not flourish. Only two – H.W. Higginson (53rd Brigade) and T.H. Shoubridge (54th Brigade) – later rose to divisional command and both were from the successful 18th Division. Others became casualties, including N.J.G. Cameron (Tyneside Irish Brigade, 34th Division), who was wounded on 1 July; C.J. Sackville-West (21st Brigade, 30th Division), wounded on 30 July; and R.C. Gore (101st Brigade, 34th Division) and Cecil Rawling, both of whom were killed later in the war.[26]

A further sixteen New Army divisions entered the battle *after* 1 July, a quarter of which experienced changes of command at the top during the course of the offensive. These were all from the Fourth and Fifth New Armies and included the 33rd and 35th Divisions, which simply exchanged their commanders (Herman Landon and R.J. Pinney) in mid-September; the 37th Division, where S.W. Scrase-Dickens took over from Lord Gleichen on 21 October and was himself succeeded by Hugh Bruce Williams on 9 November; and the 38th Division, where C.G. Blackader replaced Ivor Philipps on 9 July.[27] A fair proportion of these sixteen additional divisional commanders had previously commanded brigades, some in the original BEF. They included G.J. Cuthbert (39th Division, formerly 13th Brigade); Lord Gleichen (37th Division, formerly 15th Brigade); Herman Landon (35th and 33rd Divisions, formerly 3rd Brigade); Sydney Lawford (41st Division, formerly 22nd Brigade); and F.W.N. McCracken (15th Division, formerly 7th Brigade). Ivor Philipps, who did not last long, was in many respects an odd man out. He had been a Regular, serving in the Indian army for ten years and seeing action in Burma and various expeditions before retiring as a major in 1903. His military service from then on was restricted to the Pembrokeshire Yeomanry, which he eventually commanded from 1908 to 1912, but his main interests lay in business and politics, and he became a Liberal MP in 1910. He owed his command of the 38th (Welsh) Division largely to political patronage, chiefly that of Lloyd George. One of his staff officers, G.P.L. Drake-Brockman, remarked that it was hardly surprising that, as a divisional commander, 'he was ignorant, lacked experience and failed to inspire confidence'. Drake-Brockman criticised Philipps for launching piecemeal attacks at first – one brigade at a time – and for declaring beforehand that he did not wish for attacks to be pressed home in the face of machine-gun fire. In such circumstances, battalions were instructed to return to the start-line until fresh artillery support could be organised. This latter policy might not have been entirely bereft of common sense, but when the division's attempts to capture Mametz Wood faltered, Philipps – portrayed by John Bourne as 'very much a cuckoo in the Regular Army's nest' – was shorn of protection and dismissed on 9 July, the official reason being that he had displayed 'lack of thrust'.[28]

The only cavalryman, and the only other 'dug-out' among these sixteen additional New Army divisional commanders, was Sir James Babington of the 23rd Division, who had retired as a colonel and honorary major-general in 1907. The 24th Division's commander, J.E. Capper (later Director-General of the Tank Corps), was a sapper, while Bill Furse (9th Division) and Arthur Scott (12th Division) were gunners. The remainder were infantrymen. Babington, who was 60, was also the oldest of this group and the longest in post, having commanded 23rd Division since it was raised in September 1914, though Victor Couper (of the 14th (Light) Division) had taken over his formation the following month. At the other end of the scale, Guy Bainbridge had taken over the 25th Division as recently as 4 June, and both Gerald Cuthbert (39th Division) and C.L. Woollcombe (11th Division) were appointed in July 1916, after the start of the battle. The officer succeeded by Gerald Cuthbert was R. Dawson, who had been in command of the 39th Division for just thirty-five days, one of the shortest tenures of all. The highest-ranking of these officers at the outbreak of war was Charles Woollcombe, who had risen to lieutenant-general by 1913 and who, at 59, was one of the oldest officers in the BEF. When Haig had become Commander-in-Chief in December 1915, Woollcombe – whose rank would normally have precluded him from anything less than a corps appointment – asked him for an active command and was happy to accept the chance to take over the 11th Division the following July. The first army commander he served under, Hubert Gough, was thirteen years his junior. Woollcombe was given command of IV Corps at the end of the Somme offensive, but was 'degummed' in 1918 in the aftermath of the German counter-stroke at Cambrai.[29]

Other New Army divisional commanders later promoted to corps were Babington (to XIV Corps in October 1918) and McCracken (to XIII Corps in June 1917). Bill Furse (of the 9th (Scottish) Division) was appointed Master-General of the

Ordnance in December 1916. Two who remained as divisional commanders until the Armistice were R.J. Pinney and Sydney Lawford. Reginald Pinney has had a mixed press. Although he was the second longest-serving divisional commander in the BEF at the time of the Armistice, he is perhaps best remembered as a non-smoking teetotaller and as the GOC who abolished the rum ration in his division. Frank Richards, of the 2nd Royal Welsh Fusiliers, called him a 'bun-punching crank more fitted to be in command of a Church Mission hut at the Base than a division of troops', but Lieutenant-Colonel Graham Seton-Hutchison, in contrast, saw him as 'a soldier's general ... where the men were so was he; how they lived so did he'. Haig himself is reported to have stated: 'When the 33rd Division was there, I could always be sure'.[30] Lawford, a dapper, well-dressed officer whose nickname in the army was 'Swanky Syd', did not lack personal courage and had led 22nd Brigade from the front, and with some distinction, in the critical days of First Ypres. He was also known to be concerned about the welfare of his troops. At the end of the war, Lawford was the longest-serving divisional commander in the BEF.[31]

After 1 July eighty-one infantry brigade commanders of all categories and not just New Army formations joined the Somme battle with their units, with an average age of 44.9 years. The oldest was H.J. Evans of 115th Brigade in the 38th (Welsh) Division, who was 56. He stayed in command until 30 August 1916, his removal ostensibly being on grounds of age, although the initial performance of the division at Mametz Wood and the 'degumming' of the divisional commander can scarcely have helped. Evans had been critical of his superiors for their conduct of operations on 7 July 1916 and had spoken his mind, confiding to Captain Wyn Griffith: 'You mark my words, they'll send me home for this: they want butchers, not brigadiers'. Griffith believed that Evans had, in fact, saved his brigade from annihilation.[32] The majority of officers who entered the battle as brigade commanders after 1 July had no previous experience at that level. The highest rank any of them had held by the outbreak of war was colonel and most had been majors. Some had been in post for three months or less. Two of the three brigade commanders in the 15th (Scottish) Division, for example, had only been in post since mid-April, while in the 19th (Western) Division two of the brigade GOCs (F.G.M. Rowley and C.C. Onslow) had not taken over their formations until mid-June and the third (A.J.W. Dowell) had only been appointed at the end of April.[33] The longest-serving of this group was B.R. Mitford of the 72nd Brigade (24th Division), who had been in his post since September 1914. He not only survived his formation's unhappy baptism of fire at Loos in 1915 but later, in 1917, was promoted to command the 42nd (East Lancashire) Division.[34]

As in the case of the brigade commanders on 1 July, those who took their formations into battle after that date included a number of 'dug-outs'. Some, like W.H.L. Allgood, did well. He had retired as a major in February 1914, yet, having been appointed to lead the 45th Brigade in the 15th (Scottish) Division, retained his command until May 1918. R.C. Browne-Clayton of the 59th Brigade in the 20th (Light) Division had retired as a major in 1909, but succeeded Cameron

Shute in command of 59th Brigade in October 1916 and remained in that post until August 1917.[35] Another officer who had originally retired in 1909 was M.L. Hornby, who led 116th Brigade (39th Division) from 13 April 1916 to 23 March 1918, when he was badly wounded. He then briefly reappeared at the head of 118th Brigade before transferring to 137th Brigade a few days before the Armistice.[36] George Pereira of the 47th Brigade in the 16th (Irish) Division similarly overcame the possible stigma of being a 'dug-out' and won considerable respect as a front-line commander, particularly at Guillemont in September 1916.

Nevertheless, the position of brigade commanders could be tenuous. Tim Travers asserts that Haig once told Edmonds that he had 'degummed' over 100 brigadiers.[37] Examples of the removal of brigade commanders litter the Somme offensive. R.B. Fell, of the 51st Brigade in the 17th (Northern) Division, lasted only until 6 July.[38] R.S. Oxley, of the 24th Brigade (attached to the 23rd Division), was dismissed because of his brigade's failure to hold on to Contalmaison on 7 July.[39] One well-known case, recounted by Malcolm Brown, is that of Frederick Carleton, of the 98th Brigade, 33rd Division, who was replaced following what was perceived to be a disappointing performance at Wood Lane Trench in late August 1916. In a damning report to XV Corps, the divisional commander, Herman Landon, commented that the qualities expected of a brigade commander – 'quick, practical methods of command, and a cheerful outlook which will communicate itself to the troops' – were 'not possessed' by Carleton. The latter subsequently appealed against his dismissal and was given another brigade, but his next posting was to Salonika where his health was fatally undermined and he died in 1922, aged 54.[40] Even being part of a successful division did not guarantee security of tenure. After the capture of Thiepval on 26–27 September, Ivor Maxse was far from impressed by the efforts of the 55th Brigade to clear the Schwaben Redoubt over the following few days. He therefore engineered the removal of the brigade commander, Sir Thomas Jackson, recording that the brigade had not been handled satisfactorily and that the situation should have been more firmly grasped (see Chapter 4).[41] It should be added that the dismissal caused some bitterness in the ranks of the brigade. As John Bourne points out, brigade commanders were convenient scapegoats if things went wrong and, of the twenty-seven divisions of all categories which joined the Somme offensive after 1 July, only five experienced *no* changes at brigade level during or just after the battle.[42]

Not all departures were due to incompetence. Henry Page-Croft, a Territorial officer, who had been elected Unionist MP for Christchurch in 1910 and was promoted to command the 68th Brigade in the 23rd Division in February 1916, aged only 34, resigned his command in August 1916 to concentrate on his parliamentary and political career.[43] Others went sick. One was N.F. Jenkins, a 'dug-out' aged 55, who left the command of the 75th Brigade (25th Division) only a few days after the start of the Somme battle. This group also included G.A. Armytage (74th Brigade, 25th Division) on 17 October 1916; J.W.V. Carroll (17th Brigade, 24th Division) in January 1917; E.H. Finch-Hatton (118th Brigade,

39th Division) on 4 December 1916; R.G. Jelf (73rd Brigade, 24th Division) on 9 November 1916; and the commander of the 61st Brigade in the 20th Division – W.F. Sweny – on 24 July 1916.[44]

A fair number of the changes also resulted from promotion. All three brigade commanders in the 9th (Scottish) Division received divisional appointments during or soon after the battle. H.T. Lukin, of the South African Brigade, took over the division in December 1916 when Bill Furse became Master-General of the Ordnance; A.B. Ritchie of the 26th Brigade became GOC 11th Division on 5 December; and S.W. Scrase-Dickens (27th Brigade) was promoted to command the 37th Division on 22 October.[45] Similarly, R.W.R. Barnes (111th Brigade, 37th Division) replaced Rycroft at the head of 32nd Division in late November 1916, though he was himself soon succeeded by Cameron Shute.[46] P.R. Robertson, of the 19th Brigade, 33rd Division, rose to command the 17th (Northern) Division on 13 July and stayed in that post until the Armistice, despite being classed as a 'dud' by the acerbic J.C. Dunn.[47] In addition to those already mentioned, I calculate that thirteen other New Army brigade commanders, from the group who entered the battle after 1 July, also rose to divisional command later in the war.

There is indeed some evidence to suggest that, even in 1916, the BEF was moving to a more devolved command style and that the 'man on the spot' – certainly down to brigade level – had sufficient powers of decision-making, and room for initiative, to make a difference at a *local* level. In the 21st Division, for instance, H.R. Headlam of the 64th Brigade took personal charge at the forefront of his brigade's operations near Fricourt when the attack ran into problems during the morning of 1 July. Two days later, when German columns were seen from the air to be moving forward from Contalmaison, Cecil Rawling, of 62nd Brigade, anticipated the enemy's intentions and, using the 13th Northumberland Fusiliers from reserve to join in an enveloping movement which was covered by Stokes mortar fire, he took Shelter Wood without too much further trouble.[48] On 10 July, L.A.E. Price-Davies (GOC of 113th Brigade), T.O. Marden (of 114th Brigade) and Lieutenant-Colonel H.E. ap Rhys Price, the GSO1 of the 38th (Welsh) Division, combined to restore impetus to operations at Mametz Wood, ordering a fresh advance involving six battalions in the late afternoon which cleared the wood to within 40 yards of its northern edge.[49] In the 34th Division, R.C. Gore, of 101st Brigade, ordered the commanding officers and headquarters of his four battalions to stay out of the initial assault at La Boisselle on 1 July, thereby keeping them more or less intact and available to reorganise their shattered battalions that night. It must be conceded, however, that a similar policy backfired in the case of the 36th (Ulster) Division when, during the late morning and afternoon of 1 July, no senior battalion officers were present to take advantage of the opportunities offered near Mouquet Farm.[50]

One formation which clearly accepted the concept of the 'man on the spot' was the 18th (Eastern) Division. On two critical occasions – at Trones Wood on 14 July and at Thiepval on 26–27 September – Maxse, the divisional commander, and Thomas Shoubridge, of 54th Brigade, successfully entrusted the actual conduct of the attack 'at the sharp end' to Lieutenant-Colonel Frank Maxwell VC, the redoubtable CO of the 12th Middlesex (see Chapter 4), although it appears to have been Shoubridge's idea for his troops to sweep straight through Trones Wood from south to north on 14 July.[51] Nor was tactical 'grip' and innovation confined to infantry commanders. H.H. Tudor, the BGRA and later GOC of the 9th Division, helped to pioneer the use of high explosive (HE), rather than shrapnel, shells in the preparatory bombardment at Longueval-Delville Wood on 14 July, fitting the HE shells with delayed action fuses so that, even if a tree was hit, the shell would continue on its trajectory. As the divisional historian emphasises:

> During the Somme Battle the use of the creeping barrage became universal by the British Army ... Shrapnel was generally used, but the Ninth Division, having taken to HE, and having found it successful, stuck to it ... In the Ninth the opinion was that the HE barrage had the greater moral effect, was easier to follow, and did not throw such a strain on the artillery that the setting of fuses for a shrapnel barrage necessitated.[52]

I have obviously stressed the *positive* aspects of divisional and brigade command on the Somme, at least partly to counter the widely held *negative* views of New Army performance that I outlined earlier. However, only a blinkered fool would fail to recognise that incompetence, inexperience, inconsistency and inability to learn lessons at different command levels all contributed to making the Somme the long, bloody and frequently frustrating battle that it was for the BEF. It seems extraordinary, for example, that on 8 July the 38th (Welsh) Division, in its first battle, should give the task of securing the southern salient of Mametz Wood, *at night*, to a solitary platoon of the 14th Royal Welsh Fusiliers – the sort of decision which precipitated the removal of Ivor Philipps.[53] Yet the BEF continued to attack with insufficient weight and co-ordination on many other occasions throughout the battle. On 23 July the 21st Brigade of the 30th Division assaulted Guillemont with just two battalions – the 19th Manchesters and the 2nd Green Howards. The Manchesters actually succeeded in entering the village but the survivors were either overwhelmed there or obliged to withdraw. The official historian tartly comments that: 'To some observers it appeared that Guillemont would have been won had the Manchester[s] received support'.[54] An attack on the same village a week later was indeed given greater weight but the end result was no less depressing. Miles, the official historian, remarks about this *second* action:

> It is little matter for surprise that the attack made on the 30th July should have taken almost the exact course of the action of the 23rd: the conditions under which it was delivered were practically the same. After the first experience it seemed to the local commanders that an assault against the Guillemont position from the west – up the exposed shallow trough which marked the termination of Caterpillar Valley – and from the south-west – over a crest and down a slope, both devoid of cover – had little chance of success.[55]

A large share of the responsibility for the failure of such attacks must be borne by the army and corps commanders and their staffs, rather than at division and brigade level. As we observed in Chapter 2, Major-General C.L. Nicholson, 'Inky Bill's' successor as GOC of the 34th Division, made this plain when he later summarised the reasons for the division's inability to take Intermediate Trench, between Bazentin le Petit and High Wood, in the first half of August.[56]

Apart from playing some part in the planning process – if the division in question held regular conferences – a *battalion* commander in battle could also have a local influence which transcended simply leading his troops into action. The role of Frank Maxwell at Trones Wood and Thiepval has already been noted in this regard. A similar case is that of Lieutenant-Colonel W.E.C. Tanner, of the 2nd South African Infantry in the 9th (Scottish) Division, who was entrusted by Brigadier-General Lukin with the execution of the South African Brigade's attack at Delville Wood on 15 July. Again, when the 9th Division reached a critical point in the fighting at Longueval-Delville Wood three days later, on 18 July, Lieutenant-Colonel C.W.E. Gordon of the 8th Black Watch and Lieutenant-Colonel J. Kennedy of the 7th Seaforth Highlanders launched a telling counter-attack in the early evening, supported by Lieutenant-Colonel G.B. Duff and the 5th Cameron Highlanders. Having driven the Germans back from the village, Gordon and Kennedy wisely restrained their men from following the enemy into the western side of the wood, where control and cohesion would have been lost, and then rallied and re-formed the survivors of their units. Duff was severely wounded in the action, but Kennedy subsequently succeeded A.B. Ritchie in command of the 26th Brigade – a promotion from within the brigade – while Gordon commanded the 123rd Brigade in Lawford's 41st Division from 23 September 1916 until he was killed by a shell in Belgium in July 1917.[57]

These are, of course, just two or three examples from among many, but such leadership came at a price. In his list of senior officer casualties on 1 July 1916, including *acting* battalion commanders, Martin Middlebrook names twenty-four such officers from the New Army divisions alone. Of these, seven (or over a quarter) were from the 34th Division, thus underlining the wisdom of Brigadier-General Gore's decision to keep the battalion commanders of 101st Brigade out of the initial assault at La Boisselle. A further six (25 per cent) were from the 21st Division, and another five (20.83 per cent) from the 31st Division.[58] This means that approximately three-quarters of the senior officer losses suffered by battalions in New Army divisions on 1 July were concentrated in only three divisions. However, while the 21st Division recovered to record an overall success rate of 80 per cent in the battle as a whole, the 31st and 34th Divisions both fell below the 50 per cent mark. Unhappily for the New Army divisions, senior officer losses on this scale were not limited to 1 July. I estimate that, at Mametz Wood between 5 and 12 July, the 38th Division lost seven out of its twelve infantry battalion commanders killed or wounded and, even in its successful first action, at Flers on 15 September, the 41st Division lost six, or half, of its infantry battalion commanders, four of whom died in action.[59] Under such circumstances it was no easy task to maintain real continuity of command at battalion level, particularly if one also takes into account officers such as Maxwell, Gordon and Kennedy, who were promoted to brigades during or soon after the battle.

Reorganising and Rebuilding Units

Whichever way one looks at them, the casualty figures for the New Army divisions on the Somme are appalling and need little or no amplification. A few, almost random, examples will perhaps suffice to remind us of their scale and of their likely impact on individual formations. Jonathan Nicholls points out that the *daily* casualty rate on the Somme was 2,953, this being the equivalent of losing nearly 3 whole infantry battalions every 24 hours.[60] Middlebrook demonstrates that, of the 32 infantry battalions which suffered casualties of 500 or more on 1 July, 20 (or 62.5 per cent) were New Army units – the highest losses being incurred at Fricourt by the 10th West Yorkshires (17th Division), who lost 22 officers and 688 other ranks, including the battalion commander, the second-in-command and the adjutant.[61] The 34th Division history states that the divisional 'wastage' for the whole of 1916, including those taken sick, totalled 733 officers and 15,253 other ranks. By my calculations, this means that the equivalent of about 81.5 per cent of the war establishment of the division (on the April 1915 scale) had to be replaced during the year, or immediately after the Somme offensive.[62] The 9th (Scottish) Division lost a total of 10,340 all ranks in its actions at Longueval-Delville Wood in July and near the Butte de Warlencourt in October.[63] At Guillemont and Ginchy, from 1 to 10 September, the 16th (Irish) Division suffered 4,330 casualties (or just under 40 per cent of the 10,845 who entered the battle), while the 12th (Eastern) Division incurred losses totalling 7,612 in a 6-week spell in July and August.[64]

The consequence was that brigades and battalions were often obliged to go into action with well under their nominal rifle strengths. In mid-October, relatively few battalions in Fourth Army could muster more than 400 men for an attack and many of these, according to the official historian, were only half-trained.[65] In short, the infantry battalions and brigades of the New Army divisions on the Somme – like their Regular, Territorial and Dominion counterparts – had to undergo a constant process of replacement, reorganisation and regeneration. However, their powers of recovery appear to have been remarkable, and their resilience beyond doubt, for, as I showed earlier, the collective success rate in attack of the New Army divisions did not drop below 60 per cent in the later stages of the battle during the months of September, October and November 1916.

During the battle, not many formations were afforded the luxury of refitting at a leisurely pace. Bringing a battalion or brigade up to strength, in terms of numbers, was one thing but rebuilding *esprit de corps* or training specialists such as bombers and Lewis gunners, could not be achieved in a few days. Furthermore, the cumulative effects of conscription earlier in the year, of frequent large-scale losses, and of changes in the reserve or drafting system, meant that it could no longer be guaranteed that casualty replacements would come, as they normally had before, from the parent regiment at home. Helen McCartney presents persuasive evidence that efforts *were* still made to draw such replacements from at least the same county or region, but this was not always possible and, inevitably, the highly localised character of many New Army units in mid-1916 was becoming diluted by the end of the offensive. The practical effects of this are summarised neatly by the historian of the 34th Division. The 15th Royal Scots, he writes, received 299 men from their 6th Battalion: 'these men had served in Egypt but none of them had handled a Mills bomb. The Suffolks drafts were from various battalions and regiments. The Lincolns was [*sic*] completed by parties of men from [the] Nothamptons, North Staffords, South Staffords, Middlesex, Oxford, Worcester and Leicester Regiments "and a few Lincolns". Many of these had only three months' service'. The divisional historian also comments that 'it was asking much of the few remaining officers and non-commissioned officers to expect them to weld such material into a first-class fighting instrument in a few days. Yet this is what was demanded not once but many times during this long-drawn-out war of every battalion staff …'.[66] Consistent success in battle depended, at least in part, on a division's ability to rebuild itself periodically and efficiently around a nucleus of seasoned officers and combat veterans, and to maintain its divisional ethos – a way of doing things well which could be passed on to others, however frequent the changes in personnel.

Morale and Discipline

Here too it would be foolish to claim that the New Army divisions suffered from no problems of morale. Robert Cude, an inveterate 'grouser' and barometer of ordinary soldiers' opinions in the 18th Division, wrote in January 1917 that peace was 'the heartfelt wish of all the troops operating on [the] Somme. Let the politicians fight the war now I have had enough'.[67] Clearly there were occasional crises of morale in front-line battalions. Brigadier-General L.A.E. Price-Davies VC, the GOC of the 113th Brigade in the 38th (Welsh) Division, was alarmed to see some of the troops 'running back in panic' following an attack at Mametz Wood on 10 July. He subsequently reported that, by the time the first objective had been reached,

> the sting had gone from the attack and a considerable degree of demoralisation set in … The demoralisation increased towards evening on the 10th and culminated in a disgraceful panic during which many left the wood whilst others seemed quite incapable of understanding, or unwilling to carry out, the simplest order. A few stout-hearted Germans would have stampeded the whole of the troops in the wood.[68]

In their book on the 15th Sherwood Foresters, part of the 35th (Bantam) Division, Maurice Bacon and David Langley recount an incident in the Guillemont sector on 20 July when Corporal Jesse Wilton ordered the evacuation of a dangerous and exposed position which had been under heavy shell fire – a decision which later led to Wilton's execution for quitting his post. Bacon and Langley state that officers 'drew revolvers to control some dreadful moments when a panicky retreat began to spread … It is scarcely doubted that Colonel Gordon feared for the steadiness of his battalion'.[69]

By the same token, so far as I can trace, this type of incident was by no means universal throughout the New Armies on the Somme, and events which might have been expected to cause a decline in morale in particular units sometimes had the opposite effect or a negligible impact. Tim Bowman, in his study of discipline and morale in Irish regiments, notes that the number of men tried by courts-martial in Irish units was generally higher than that in their counterparts from the British mainland, but he and other scholars contend that the Easter Rising in Dublin did *not* have a major adverse effect on morale in such units. Indeed, Bowman's assessment is that no acts of indiscipline occurred in the Irish regiments as a result of the Rising.[70]

In their book *Shot at Dawn*, Julian Putkowski and Julian Sykes assert that, on the Somme, Kitchener's Army 'provided the majority of victims for the firing squads'. They go on to say that, of the seventy-nine men executed for military offences during and after the main actions of the Somme in 1916 (and in the aftermath up to 31 January 1917), 'five-sixths were serving in New Army divisions'.[71] The inference here concerning the citizen-soldier as 'victim' is obvious. However, having analysed each of the case histories that Putkowski and Sykes present, I have come to some different conclusions. Applying *their* criteria regarding military offences, *and* the time-frame in which they were committed, very strictly, I would argue that twenty-two 'New Army' cases out of the overall total of seventy-nine can be interpreted as being the *direct* result of the Somme experience, while a further nine may have been – the evidence offered by Putkowski and Sykes being less detailed in the latter cases. In other words, even if one includes the nine cases which are less clear-cut, the total of New Army victims is still only thirty-one – a much lower figure than the 'five-sixths' (i.e. approximately sixty-five cases) suggested by Putkowski and Sykes. My figure is, in fact, well under half of the total number of Somme-period executions, thus putting a slightly different complexion on the matter. One might also point out, in passing, that one of these cases was an officer and another seven (or just under one-quarter of the thirty-one) were previous offenders. If one includes the 40th Division, which played no major part in operations on the Somme, twelve New Army divisions had no recorded executions for military offences in the period under review; a further seven each had only one definite recorded case; and six divisions had two or more definite cases. Again, if one lumps together the definite and less clear-cut cases, five divisions each had three or more executions which were, or might have been, a direct result of the Somme experience. These were the 25th, 30th, 31st, and 33rd Divisions – all with three – and the 35th (Bantam) Division with six. Note here that, with the exception of the 25th, all these formations were from the Fourth New Army, the group of divisions with the lowest collective success rate in the battle.

According to the evidence presented by Gerard Oram, 462 death sentences in all are known to have been imposed upon British and Dominion soldiers on the Western Front between 1 July 1916 and 31 January 1917, the vast majority of these being commuted to varying terms of penal servitude and/or hard labour. Of the overall total, 191 death sentences were meted out to NCOs and men serving in New Army front-line infantry battalions, including 15 in units transferred to Regular divisions in the 'stiffening' process of late 1915. Subtracting the latter 15 cases from the above total of 191, this signifies that death sentences were awarded to 176 NCOs and men who were serving in *New Army* divisions during the period under review, representing 38.09 per cent of the overall total of 462. Again, this proportion is much lower than the 'five-sixths' implied by Putkowski and Sykes. A total of 91 (or nearly 52 per cent) of the 176 death sentences in question were imposed on men in divisions of the first three New Armies (K.1 to K.3) and 85 (or just over 48 per cent) to men in divisions of the Fourth and Fifth New Armies (K.4 and K.5). Those divisions with the highest number of known cases in this period include the 35th (Bantam) Division with 35 death sentences awarded; the 15th (Scottish) Division with 14; and the 17th (Northern) and 30th Divisions with 10 each. The overall figures are, however, somewhat skewed by the fact that a large number of death sentences were handed out to NCOs and men of the 35th Division for incidents which occurred in the course of a single night in November 1916.[72]

The 35th Division – originally composed largely of diminutive men who were under 5ft 3in in height – was badly shaken by its experiences on the Somme and unquestionably suffered from a crisis of morale in the late autumn of 1916. This came to a head east and north-east of Arras on the night of 25–26 November when a number of posts held by the 19th Durham Light Infantry were penetrated by the Germans. Later that night, a raid mounted by the same battalion failed when some forty-five men became demoralised by their own barrage, which fell short in no-man's-land, and were thus reluctant to follow other small groups into the German trenches. As a consequence of these incidents, no less than twenty-six members of the 19th DLI were tried and sentenced to death for various offences, including cowardice, quitting posts and casting away arms, and three NCOs – Lance-Sergeant J.W. Stones, Lance-Corporal P. Goggins and Lance-Corporal J. McDonald – were ultimately executed. Major-General Landon, the divisional commander, attributed many of the formation's problems to the 'mental and physical degeneracy' and poor standards of recent replacements, although the division's troubles at least partly stemmed from the inherent weakness of the initial 'Bantam' concept, which could not be sustained in the long term. Landon was also determined to make an example of the NCOs involved 'as having especially failed in their soldierly duties and responsibilities'.[73] The 26 November episode hastened a radical overhaul of the 35th Division, effectively ending the Bantam experiment. With the active support of Landon, and of Aylmer Haldane, the commander of VI Corps, the division's Assistant Director of Medical Services (ADMS) carried out inspections which led, by 21 December, to the weeding out of 2,784 men who were judged to be physically or mentally unsuitable. Henceforth, the Bantam standard was to be 'disregarded for good and all'.[74]

Although there seems to be a strong correlation between morale and combat performance in the case of the 35th Division, one should perhaps be cautious about applying this deduction across the board. The great battles of attrition of 1916–1917 placed the citizen-soldiers of the BEF under enormous strain but, as Gary Sheffield has reminded us, the 'ultimate test of morale is willingness to engage in combat, and the BEF's divisions continued to fight throughout the campaigns'. Sheffield also cites a report of November 1916 which was based on the censorship of soldiers' letters and which stated: 'the spirit of the men, their conception of duty, their Moral [sic], has never been higher than at the present moment'.[75] Christopher Duffy's study *Through German Eyes: The British and the Somme 1916*, based on German intelligence reports – and in particular upon German interrogation of British prisoners of war – reinforces rather than undermines these conclusions. As one such German intelligence summary said of the British at the end of 1916: 'Most of the front-line soldiers … are extremely proud of what they have achieved so far. Again and again we hear from prisoners the self-satisfied question: "Don't you think we have done very well?"'[76]

It is, of course, impossible to quantify courage and gallantry with any precision in relation to battlefield performance, though clearly it is inextricably linked to the maintenance of morale and to questions of leadership and initiative in combat. For these reasons it is interesting to look at New Army Victoria Cross winners on the Somme. Of the 51 VCs won on the Somme in 1916, 25 (or nearly half) were awarded to officers and men in New Army formations; 6 out of the 9 VCs won on 1 July, and 14 out of the 26 won in July 1916 as a whole, went to officers and men in New Army divisions. The latter were also in the majority in September (7 out of 13) and November (2 out of 3), the only months in which they did not predominate being August (1 out of 5) and October (1 out of 4).[77]

Reflections

What, then, can one draw from this examination of the New Army divisions on the Somme? My own analysis of their combat performance in attack suggests that, in general, they were more effective in battle than the popular 'Blackadder'-type perception would lead us to believe. Even on 1 July 1916, some New Army divisions performed at least as well as, and in some cases better than, their Regular counterparts. Over the whole battle, the divisions of the First, Second, Third and Fifth New Armies achieved collective success rates in their attacks of 54 per cent or more, with only the Pals-based divisions of the Fourth New Army dipping to a figure as low as 40 per cent. This might indicate that the strong social cohesion and community links of the Pals formations by no means guaranteed success in battle. Indeed, although the original highly localised character of many of the battalions was inevitably, and increasingly, diluted by losses and replacements as the battle went on, the collective *monthly* success rates of the New Army divisions did not show a corresponding decline – quite the contrary, in fact, as the figures for September and October rose to 64.96 per cent and 71.87 per cent. Again, those New Army divisions which had been 'stiffened' with Regular battalions or brigades do not seem to have performed as well, in terms of successful attacks, as those which retained their original units. Frequency of employment during the battle did not always equate with a drop in standards. From the figures I have presented one can see that relatively 'fresh' divisions did not invariably perform well and, moreover, there was no corresponding reduction in the fighting capabilities of 'well-used' assault divisions the more they were employed. While not all New Army divisions maintained the same level of high morale – the 35th Division being an obvious example of a formation with problems – this did not, in the final analysis, seriously affect their collective willingness to fight. The courage, endurance, resilience and self-sacrifice displayed by those who fought – and continued to fight – on the Western Front never ceases to amaze and inspire.

Chapter Four

A Key Point in the Learning Process?: The 18th (Eastern) Division and the Capture of Thiepval, September 1916

For the majority of British and Commonwealth visitors who journey to the Somme each year to mark the anniversary of the battle, the annual service at Thiepval, beneath the great Lutyens Memorial to the Missing, almost invariably provides the main focal point for their commemorative activities. In recent years this experience has undoubtedly been enhanced by the new Visitor Centre, which was opened at Thiepval on 27 September 2004 and which is situated beside the road leading from the village to the Memorial to the Missing. I was personally involved in the planning and preparation of the Visitor Centre, having played a role – along with Nigel Cave, Michael Stedman and Jack Sheldon – in deciding upon its historical content and presentation, in undertaking relevant research, in drafting exhibition texts and in helping to select the photographs and film footage used in the displays. It was a privilege to be part of the Visitor Centre 'team' as I have been to Thiepval many times on battlefield tours since I first went there with my Imperial War Museum colleague Rose Coombs in the 1960s, and with the completion of the new Centre, I felt that at last I had been able to give something back to a place which has afforded me a great deal of rewarding study and inspiration over some forty years. Moreover, for much of that time, and particularly since the late 1970s, I have had a special interest in the 18th (Eastern) Division, the formation which captured the village on 26–27 September 1916. The 18th Division's memorial at Thiepval stands only some 200 yards west of the Visitor Centre and about 150 yards south-west of the site of the pre-1914 Thiepval Chateau.[1] However, my own observations over the years suggest that *most* visitors to the Lutyens Memorial or to the Ulster Tower, especially on 1 July, barely give the 18th Division's memorial a second glance.

This seems to me a pity because, like that of the 12th (Eastern) Division (see Chapter 8), the story of the 18th Division offers us a particularly rewarding case study. In the manner of its raising, in its composition, in its early painful experiences and shortages of uniforms and equipment, and in its battle honours, it was a typical British New Army division and, although not all British divisions could ultimately match its distinguished battlefield performance, it can nevertheless be seen as a symbol of the overall improvement of the BEF between 1915 and 1918. Its history reveals just what could be, and was, achieved, following an unpromising and chaotic start, by an 'ordinary' Kitchener division of citizen-soldiers which

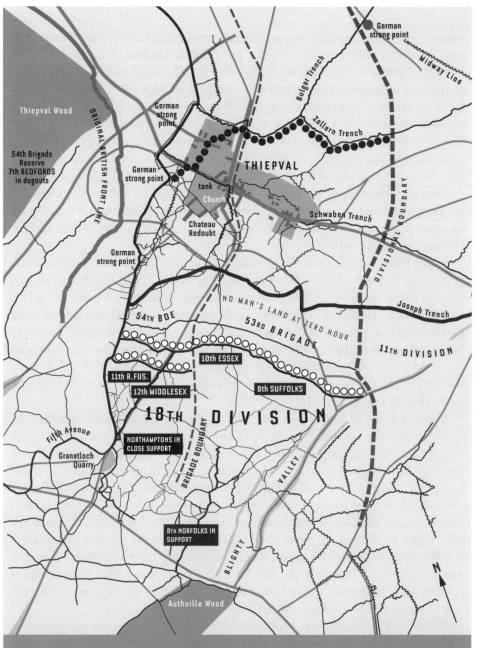

Thiepval Wood

54th Brigade
Reserve
7th BEDFORDS
in dugouts

German
strong
point

German
strong point

ORIGINAL BRITISH FRONT LINE

German
strong point

tank
Church

Chateau
Redoubt

Bulgar Trench

Zollern Trench

THIEPVAL

Schwaben Trench

German strong point

Midway Line

DIVISIONAL BOUNDARY

Joseph Trench

NO MAN'S LAND AT ZERO HOUR

54TH BDE

53RD BRIGADE

11TH DIVISION

10th ESSEX

11th R.FUS.

12th MIDDLESEX

8th SUFFOLKS

18TH DIVISION

Fifth Avenue

NORTHAMPTONS IN
CLOSE SUPPORT

Granatloch
Quarry

BRIGADE BOUNDARY

VALLEY

8TH NORFOLKS IN
SUPPORT

BLIGHTY

Authuille Wood

N

THE 18TH (EASTERN) DIVISION'S
ASSAULT ON THIEPVAL
26 SEPTEMBER 1916

British forming up trenches at Zero
Hour 12:35 on 26th September 1916
Position of leading British troops on
the evening of 26th/27th September
Brigade boundaries
Divisional boundaries
German lines

initially possessed neither the social and geographical cohesion of most Pals and Territorial units nor the sectarian and political binding of the 36th (Ulster) Division.[2] While the 18th Division made several successful assaults in the course of the Somme offensive, its capture of Thiepval in September 1916 was one of its most significant operations before 1918 and therefore, perhaps, deserves more detailed examination as a possible benchmark of the performance of New Army divisions on the Somme and of the tactical improvements wrought in the BEF as a whole during, and immediately after, the battle. In other words, was the capture of Thiepval a key point in what is now widely described as the BEF's 'learning curve' or 'learning process', given that the German defences in that sector, including the formidable Schwaben Redoubt, had successfully withstood previous British assaults by the 32nd and 36th Divisions on 1 July and by the 49th (West Riding) Division on 3 September?

At this point it might be useful to look at the actual course of the 18th Division's operations between 26 September and 5 October 1916. First, it has to be said that, in many respects, these operations did *not* represent the peak of tactical sophistication, becoming, in essence, a fierce and prolonged struggle at close quarters against a skilful and determined enemy – a 'soldier's battle' in short.[3] Nevertheless, an outline of the fighting will, in turn, indicate how far a division and its brigades really controlled their own battle in September 1916 and will also further test the the accuracy of Martin Samuels' claims about 'restrictive control' in the BEF at that stage in the war.[4]

The attack on 26 September was part of a major co-ordinated operation by II Corps and the Canadian Corps of Gough's Reserve Army, the aim of which was to take the ridge running from Thiepval to Courcelette. By seizing the crest line, the British and Canadians would deny the Germans observation over the battlefield southwards towards Albert while simultaneously giving the BEF good observation over the Ancre valley.[5] The 18th Division, under Major-General Ivor Maxse, on the left flank of this attack, was to assault northwards up the Authuille spur which runs from the tip of the Leipzig Salient to the present Memorial to the Missing. The cart-track which today runs roughly up the middle of this spur marks the boundary between the division's 53rd Brigade and 54th Brigade, which respectively advanced to the right and left of this line on 26 September with the task of securing Thiepval and the Schwaben Redoubt.[6]

The overall operation was supported by some 230 heavy guns and howitzers and 570 field guns and howitzers. Including batteries north of the Ancre, these provided an average of one field gun or howitzer to every 10.5 yards of front attacked and one heavy gun or howitzer to every 20 yards – a density comparable to that available to the Fourth Army at Flers-Courcelette just over a week earlier. The 18th Division's own artillery was, in fact, attached to the Canadian Corps at the time, so the field artillery components of the 25th and 49th Divisions were assigned to it instead. II Corps also placed a battery of 6in howitzers at Maxse's disposal and, of the six tanks allocated to II Corps, four were to support the 18th Division's assault. The preliminary bombardment, which began on 23 September, included 500 lachrymatory shells fired into Thiepval by No. 2 Special Company, Royal Engineers, on 24 September, helping to silence the German mortars there. During this phase some 60,000 field artillery rounds and 30,000 howitzer shells were fired in all, with the Corps artillery paying special attention to the isolation of German strongpoints such as Zollern Redoubt, Stuff Redoubt, Thiepval and the Schwaben Redoubt. The field guns of the 25th and 49th Divisions would support the 53rd and 54th Brigades from the left flank as they advanced, laying down a creeping barrage that would initially move at the rate of 100 yards in 3 minutes, speeding up to 100 yards in 2 minutes when the shelled area was passed. As Ivor Maxse told his troops: 'We want you to keep within 80 yards of your barrage. There you will be safe and can fight'. Overhead machine-gun barrages were arranged to fall between the artillery barrage lanes. The 53rd Machine Gun Company, for example, fired on Thiepval at a range of 2,150 yards, subsequently lifting to 2,800 yards in conformity with the artillery barrage.[7]

Zero hour for the assault was fixed at 12.35 p.m. on 26 September. The choice was undoubtedly influenced by Maxse, who firmly believed that, in dawn attacks, troops who reached objectives early would invariably have to hold on against counter-attacks and under hostile artillery fire for most of the day. A zero hour around noon, however, gave troops time to complete the capture of objectives an hour or so before sunset, when they were still relatively fresh, and they would then have the whole of the following night to consolidate under cover of darkness and free from *observed* artillery fire.[8]

On 26 September, the 53rd Brigade, under Brigadier-General Harold Higginson, attacked with the 8th Suffolks and 10th Essex leading and elements of the 8th Norfolks acting as 'moppers-up'. The creeping barrage was described by the official historian as 'excellent'. On the right of the brigade, the Suffolks – some of whom got within 30 yards of their own barrage – occupied the first objective, Schwaben Trench, within 12 minutes. On their left, the 10th Essex kept pace, encountering a number of Germans – who were apparently willing to surrender – in the sunken road running through Thiepval. One of the tanks supported the advance at this point and, though it soon became ditched in Schwaben Trench, the Essex gained *their* first objective, just beyond the village, on schedule. After a pause on the first objective, both battalions pushed on to the line of Zollern Trench and occupied it by 1.15 p.m. However, the advance to the final objective proved a much more difficult task. After covering another 250 yards, the Suffolks were checked by machine-gun and rifle fire and the Essex fared no better, coming under intense fire from two communication trenches which ran back to the Midway Line and Schwaben Redoubt. The two battalions therefore consolidated the Zollern line.[9]

54th Brigade's task was unquestionably the toughest of the day and the brigade quickly became involved in fighting which, in Maxse's words, was 'severe and bloody'. The brigade, under Brigadier-General Thomas Shoubridge, was expected to capture the western half of Thiepval and the original German front system of 1 July, its final objective being the Schwaben Redoubt. In the sector allotted to 54th Brigade lay not only the labyrinth of trenches of the former German front-line system covering Thiepval against attacks from the west but also at least 144 dugouts – not including a further cluster of dugouts around the Chateau and strongpoints near the Schwaben Redoubt. As Maxse himself recorded: 'It was plain that unless the left flank were effectively cleared the attack of the 18th Division must fail'. The frontage of 54th Brigade's attack was narrow (only 300 yards) and the final objective was 1,800 yards – just over a mile – distant. The job of clearing the village itself was entrusted to the 12th Middlesex, whose commanding officer, Lieutenant-Colonel Frank Maxwell VC, had personally led the 54th Brigade's successful assault at Trones Wood on 14 July. The 11th Royal Fusiliers were ordered to clear the network of trenches and dugouts to the left (or west) of the village. Because of the narrowness of the brigade front, the 11th Royal Fusiliers attacked on a frontage of only one platoon. The 6th Northants were in close support, ready to be used, if needed, to take the final objective, while the 7th Bedfords were in reserve.[10]

In this sector the assault started well but the Royal Fusiliers were soon engaged in a grim struggle amid the trenches and dugouts of the old German front system. Stubborn German resistance slowed their progress and the protection of the barrage was lost. The Middlesex, in contrast, were not checked until they reached the edge of the village, where machine-gun fire from the Chateau held up their advance. At this critical juncture, a tank (C.5, *Crème de Menthe*) appeared and helped to subdue the machine guns at the Chateau, enabling the 12th Middlesex to pass round the flanks of that stronghold. By 1 p.m. the men on the right of the Middlesex were pressing on to the next objective north of the village. An hour and a half later, Maxwell, who had established his headquarters at the Chateau, reported that, although his right was on the second objective, the left was held up. Another message, received at 3.20 p.m., stated that the two battalions were 'practically expended' and indicated the need for reinforcements. The 6th Northants, having suffered heavily from artillery fire on their way, and having already lost their CO, Lieutenant-Colonel G.E. Ripley – who was mortally wounded – now began to reach the vicinity of the Chateau. As their companies arrived they were sent to help the assault battalions, but their advance from the Chateau similarly came under machine-gun and sniper fire. When darkness descended, Maxwell – the only surviving battalion commander – took charge of the men from all three battalions and formed a defensive system of two lines, 50 yards apart, around the Chateau. This defensive position, on the right, was just clear of the village, but the north-west corner of Thiepval and the German front trenches facing west beyond their first objective were still in German hands.[11]

During the night, the 7th Bedfords relieved the men round the Chateau and, next morning (27 September), successfully assaulted the Germans still holding out in the north-west corner. The Bedfords had originally been expected to attack the final objective, but Maxse had by now informed Shoubridge that the assault on the Schwaben Redoubt should not be attempted before the afternoon of 27 September and would probably be postponed until 28 September. Both Gough and Claud Jacob, the GOC II Corps, visited Maxse during the day and agreed to the postponement. Nevertheless, by 11 a.m. on 27 September, the whole of Thiepval village and plateau had been secured by the division, at a cost of 1,456 casualties, including 64 officers.[12]

The task of taking the Schwaben Redoubt remained. It had originally been hoped, somewhat optimistically, to capture it on the first day, but the German resistance had been too strong and skilful. Maxse had concluded that an attack on it on the afternoon of 27 September would be a gamble, 'whereas on the 28th we could make almost a certainty of success and arrange for an overwhelming quantity of artillery to prepare the attack'. The hour of assault was eventually fixed for 1 p.m. on 28 September. Possibly because he had begun to have doubts about the GOC of the 55th Brigade, Sir Thomas Jackson, Maxse took two battalions from that brigade and attached them to Higginson and Shoubridge, who would continue the fight as initially planned. The 7th Queen's were assigned to Higginson and the 7th Royal West Kents to 54th Brigade. The 7th Buffs and 8th East Surreys were kept in reserve under Jackson. In the 54th Brigade, two fresh companies of the 7th Bedfords were to attack between the Redoubt and the old German front system.[13]

As on 26 September, all started well and both brigades covered the first 600–800 yards towards their objectives in good time. By 2.30 p.m. the Suffolks were nearing the eastern end of the Redoubt and, with the 7th Queen's, gained a footing in the eastern corner. To the left, the Bedfords, following the barrage closely, came up level with the northern edge of the communal cemetery, though they suffered badly on *their* right from fire from the Redoubt. A fierce struggle was also being waged for strongpoints in the old German front line and, with progress slowing, Shoubridge urged that efforts should be concentrated on the Redoubt, which commanded his brigade's sector on the slopes to the west. Meanwhile, in Higginson's sector, the Queen's won a foothold in the southern face of the Redoubt and secured the south-western corner. At 3 p.m. Shoubridge and Higginson conferred and agreed that their best course would be to push forward up the western face of the Redoubt. The fighting was extremely difficult to control in the maze of trenches and shell holes yet, by 5 p.m., the Queen's were in possession of the whole of the southern face and the Suffolks were in the Midway Line, while the 54th Brigade held Points 39, 19, 86 and 45. Though Higginson ordered his battalions to consolidate, fighting continued on the left, where the Bedfords helped to clear the western face by 8 p.m.[14]

The following day the 6th Royal Berkshires relieved the Suffolks. Higginson recognised that the 7th Queen's were now in no condition to mount further attacks, so the day was devoted to consolidation, with the 8th East Surreys relieving the Queen's at night. Early in the morning of this day (29 September), however, the Germans recaptured Points 39 and 19 in a strong counter-attack. A see-saw struggle continued on the Redoubt's western face all day until after 10 p.m. Late in the evening, Sir Thomas Jackson took over command of the whole divisional sector – now held by the Berkshires, East Surreys and Royal West Kents – from Higginson and Shoubridge.[15] At dawn on 30 September, a German counter-attack caught the East Surreys before they had settled down, driving them from the southern face, but the position was quickly retaken with the bayonet. The West Kents were likewise forced back from the western face, which stayed in German possession for the time being. At 4 p.m., under a heavy barrage, the East Surreys successfully attacked, and occupied, the whole of the northern face of the Redoubt but, to the left, the 7th Buffs, though supported by the West Kents, could not make any progress up the western face. The day's fighting was by no means over, for at 9 p.m. another German counter-attack, made from the west, struck the tired East Surreys in the northern face, compelling them to give some ground. When dawn broke on 1 October, the East Surreys still occupied Point 27, although powerful German bombing attacks seized Point 37. Two local attacks by the 18th Division from Point 27 failed to capture Point 99 but, in the afternoon, the Buffs reoccupied and held Point 37.[16]

At 5.15 a.m. on 2 October there was another strong German counter-attack, this time along all the trenches between the eastern end of the Redoubt and the old German front line. After bombing had continued all day, the Germans were left with a small gain of ground. Over the next three days, what Maxse called 'a series of spasmodic bombing attacks by various disjointed units of the 55th Brigade' took place. The Germans made a further counter-attack on 3 October, taking 200 yards of trench on the north-eastern face of the Redoubt, but bombers of the 7th Buffs, supported by Stokes mortars amd Lewis guns, regained all the lost ground and captured 100 yards more. 4 October saw a similar pattern of fighting. By the time the division was finally relieved on 5 October, virtually the whole of the Redoubt had been secured except for a small strip along the north-west corner – including Points 19, 39, 49 and 69 – which stayed in German hands. It was not until 14 October that the 39th Division drove the Germans from their last hold on the Schwaben Redoubt.[17] The fighting from 28 September cost the 18th Division another 1,990 casualties, including 80 officers. The division's total losses between 26 September and 5 October were returned as 3,344. Maxse's subsequent report on the operations, though full of understandable pride in the achievements of his division, contained perhaps a tinge of frustration in his remark that: 'We were disappointed at being obliged to relinquish our efforts to capture the last bit of the Redoubt but the troops required a rest even though it turned out to be only a short one …'.[18]

What, then, were the factors that had enabled the 18th Division to succeed in such a difficult and prolonged action and how far do its achievements at Thiepval and the Schwaben Redoubt reflect the learning process then taking place in the BEF? In this connection, we might first look again at command and control, the subject matter of the recent, and very important, volume of essays edited by Gary Sheffield and Dan Todman.[19] One of the recurring themes of that volume is the way in which the BEF sought, throughout the war and with varying degrees of success, to defer to the judgement of the 'man on the spot' – a principle enshrined in *Field Service Regulations* (*FSR*), which had been drawn up under Haig's aegis in 1909. A central problem was that, in the new conditions of warfare in 1916, and following the expansion and 'de-skilling' of the BEF, no one, including Haig himself, was quite sure when, or how far, to apply the principles of *FSR*. As we have noted elsewhere, this inevitably led to inconsistencies in command, planning and performance as well as contributing to the sort of tactical ambiguities and false assumptions that bedevilled British operations on the Somme. However, the Sheffield/Todman volume does examine and explain how operational planning and command *actually* worked in the BEF at different stages of the war. As Andy Simpson, among others, has shown, once the framework of the overall strategic plan and objectives had been agreed by GHQ and the army level of command (e.g. the Reserve Army), the corps would then be assigned the resources which it was hoped would be adequate for the task in question. While the general timetable for a big attack would probably come from the army headquarters, corps could make their own arrangements within it. Indeed, the role of corps in operations had grown by 1916 in parallel with the increasing importance of artillery and of the need to co-ordinate its activities in battle. Next, according to Andy Simpson, divisions would be informed of their objectives and were expected to produce detailed schemes of attack for their individual sectors. Thus divisions operated within the parameters set by corps but did not simply have plans forced upon them. During this process, there was usually discussion and and consultation at all levels, even down to brigade and battalion, though the extent to which the views of subordinates were listened to, or adopted, frequently depended on the command style and character of the corps or army commander.[20] However much historians such as Tim Travers may claim that the BEF, especially in 1916, was subject to over-centralisation, restrictive control and a one-way, top-down system of command, operating in a climate of fear of GHQ, I would argue that, even by the Somme, there was at least a degree of decentralisation and devolution of command in the BEF – which gradually, though not universally, increased during the battle – and that the identity and command style of the corps, division or brigade in which one served could, and often did, influence battlefield performance. It is my further conclusion that, in II Corps and the 18th Division at least, devolved command was being practised with some success by September 1916. As the earlier outline of the fighting at Thiepval has indicated, Gough and Jacob appear to have interfered comparatively little in decision-making 'at the sharp end', once the planned set-piece phases of the battle had begun, and to have left the conduct of the unfolding struggle for Thiepval and the Schwaben Redoubt very much to Maxse and his brigade commanders. They, in turn, were clearly prepared, when necessary, to delegate important tasks to battalion commanders such as Frank Maxwell.

Having said that, one should not underrate the role of the corps commander, Claud Jacob, in the operations at Thiepval. We have already seen (Chapter 3) that, when serving in II Corps on the Somme in 1916, New Army divisions had an overall success rate of 68.25 per cent in sixty-three attacks. Jacob has been described by John Bourne as a 'charming, thoughtful man' and 'an exceptional soldier'. When war was declared he was GOC of the Dehra Dun Brigade and took this formation to France with the Indian Corps, later assuming command of the Meerut Division. According to John Bourne, the Indian army was even more devoted to the concept of seniority than was the British and Claud Jacob was considered too young by the Indian government to command a division, even though he was 51. The Meerut Division was taken away from him in November 1915 but his career was rescued by Haig, who first gave him command of the 21st Division and then, in May 1916, promoted him to II Corps. Jacob was the only senior Indian army officer of the Indian Corps on the Western Front to remain in France and to be promoted there. He gained a reputation for being methodical and for being careful with the lives of his men. Personally unambitious, he also seems to have possessed the moral courage to question orders which he believed to be reckless and was one of the few officers willing to stand up to Hubert Gough, the commander of the Reserve (Fifth) Army.[21] The latter, to be fair, later paid a gracious tribute to the contribution made by II Corps in operations on the Somme. 'This', wrote Gough, 'called for an immense amount of mental and bodily energy, facing great anxieties, and overcoming an infinity of difficulties and worries, and all the time carrying heavy responsibilities. That Sir Claud Jacob and his Staff had met all this with such marked success proved their aptitude for war'.[22]

Maxse too praised the thoroughness of the preparations and the way in which his division was treated as soon as it came under the command of II Corps on 9 September 1916. Arrangements were made to acquaint all brigade, battalion and company commanders with the ground over which the attack was likely to take place. Motor cars and buses were placed at their disposal and parties of officers were then familiarised with the ground and the approaches to it. Above all, Maxse recalled:

an admirable lecture was given at my request to brigade and battalion commanders by Brigadier-General P. Howell [the BGGS] ... at Corps Headquarters, on the *local* situation and on recent fighting experiences on this particular front. To a division coming fresh from Flanders such a lecture was of inestimable value and several battalion commanders told me afterwards that it made them put life and intelligence into their work of preparation. They felt they were being trusted and liked being placed in direct touch with the Corps Commander's Chief Staff Officer on reaching new ground. At any rate the result was excellent, for when orders did come out every battalion and each company realised the importance of Thiepval and of the high ground about Schwaben and was determined to take both. Moreover, Brigadier-General Howell possessed in a special degree the art of imparting his thought and his subsequent loss was deeply felt in the Division.[23]

The division's growing reputation, by September 1916, as a reliable assault formation owed much to the calibre of its own commander, Ivor Maxse, who was GOC from October 1914 to January 1917. One of the BEF's foremost trainers and tactical thinkers, Maxse has been portrayed by historians, or those who served under him, as a 'hard swearing', 'bumptious and outspoken' or 'intolerant' officer who had little time for fools.[24] According to his biographer, John Baynes, Maxse became known throughout the 18th Division as 'the black man', and Basil Liddell Hart – who worked with him after the war – remarked that his long drooping moustache gave him the look of a Tartar chief, 'all the more because the descriptive term "a Tartar" so aptly fitted his manner in dealing with lazy or inefficient seniors and subordinates'. Liddell Hart took care to add, however, that Maxse's 'fierce' and 'electrifying manner' concealed a warm heart and 'he particularly liked people who showed that they were not afraid of him'.[25] What is beyond question is that his qualities as a trainer of troops were recognised and greatly appreciated by senior and subordinate officers alike. Harold Hemming, an officer in the 84th Brigade RFA in 1915, commented that Maxse's fortnightly conferences resembled 'a university course on how to make a fine fighting division out of 20,000 semi-trained albeit enthusiastic soldiers'.[26] At the other end of the command scale, Hubert Gough was also keen to acknowledge Maxse's abilities. As he subsequently wrote:

> Maxse had an immense capacity for grasping the important points in training … quick and energetic … he never failed to encourage initiative among his subordinates; he drove them hard but one and all, long before they had finished their experiences of fighting the Germans under his command, realised the soundness and value of his training and thanked him for it.[27]

Maxse was clearly convinced that 'Previous Preparation' was the key to success in trench-to-trench assaults. He wrote:

> Without it the bravest troops fail and their heroism is wasted. With sufficient time to prepare an assault on a definite and limited objective, I believe a well trained division can capture any 'impregnable' stronghold, and this doctrine has been taught to the 18th Division. Indefinite and frequently altered objectives involve wasted energies and diminish the confidence of the troops. Hurried attacks launched on the spur of the moment possess certain attractions for dashing platoon commanders, but they usually fail because they lack organised cohesion.

His policy was to tell subordinates as much as he could about impending operations – if possible long before they occurred – so that the Divisional Operation Order for an attack was merely the final embodiment of principles and decisions already covered by conferences etc. 'By this method', Maxse declared, 'an attack is built up bit by bit by the Divisional Commander acting in collaboration with his Corps Commander and with his subordinates in the Division. The result should engender the "team" spirit and [referring to Thiepval] in this instance did'. Maxse thought that it was better to risk information leaking out through captured prisoners 'than to run the greater risk of ordering infantry over the parapet unacquainted with what they are expected to do or where they are to go'. As if to underline these principles, conferences were held in every battalion on the eve of the attack at

Thiepval.[28] There is indeed precious little evidence here of the kind of 'restrictive control' that Martin Samuels and others see as being prevalent in the BEF on the Somme. The extent to which devolution and consultation were practised by the division by September 1916 is also reflected in the part played by the 53rd Brigade's staff in the preparations for the initial assault at Thiepval, including the organisation of last-minute training. Captain R.A. Chell of the 10th Essex recalled how, on 23 September, the Brigade Major, Captain C.H. Hoare, could be seen in the fields between Forceville and Lealvillers 'marking out a representation of the trenches we were to attack'. The battalion described itself as 'confident and completely satisfied' following three conferences held between brigade headquarters and battalion COs on 25 September.[29]

In the matter of assault formations, the division's policy was to 'Teach, drill and practice a definite form of attack so that every officer and man shall know it thoroughly. On this basis of theory and knowledge common to all any brigade, battalion or company commander varies his attack formation to suit any condition which may be peculiar to his front and his objective'. Though the formation, in Maxse's view, could indeed be varied according to circumstances and at short notice, experience had also shown that subordinate commanders did not *always* have the time or the opportunity to learn a new attack formation shortly before an assault. 'They can however invent and explain a variation of their normal procedure in a few moments', Maxse added, 'and this is just what they did in the case of the [11th Royal] Fusiliers at Thiepval'. The three-week course of battle training along these lines which the division underwent in the Third Army area west of Arras before 8 September obviously paid dividends in the subsequent operations at Thiepval. Maxse himself seems to have been in no real doubt that his troops would succeed. In a letter written after the capture of Trones Wood in July he had described his units from the southern and eastern counties as 'the boys to go fighting with', remarking that, although slow to become angry, 'suddenly in the battle they wake up and go for it like demons. They are simply splendid'. Maxse's confidence in his men underpinned the bold prediction he made in his pre-battle briefing on 25 September: 'The ... Wurttenburgers [*sic*] have withstood attacks on Thiepval for two years, but the 18th Division will take it tomorrow'.[30]

At Thiepval the division was fortunate to possess several subordinate commanders at brigade and battalion level who could meet Maxse's exacting standards. The 53rd Brigade, for example, was commanded by Brigadier-General H.W. Higginson, who later went on to command the 12th (Eastern) Division with distinction in 1918. On 26 September 1916, instead of automatically filling up the front and assembly trenches with his support waves once the assault waves had gone forward at zero hour, Higginson ensured that these trenches were left empty, so avoiding the worst effects of the inevitable German counter-barrage. Maxse was convinced that Higginson's 'forethought and instructions saved many casualties in his brigade'.[31] T.H. Shoubridge, the commander of the 54th Brigade, was nicknamed 'Harry Tate' because of his resemblance to the famous music-hall artist. According to Jonathan Walker, he was 'normally the last word in courtesy and elegance' but he sometimes lost his patience with argumentative or independent-minded subordinates. The following year, when elevated to the command of the 7th Division, Shoubridge removed the able H.R. Cumming from the command of the 91st Brigade when, at Bullecourt, the latter questioned his orders once too often.[32] There were also moments at Thiepval when Frank Maxwell came close to overstepping the mark in Shoubridge's eyes. Nevertheless, it would be quite wrong to dismiss Shoubridge as a prickly martinet, for his conduct of operations at Trones Wood *and* Thiepval suggests that he possessed both the inner steel to tackle tough assignments and enough flexibility to entrust battlefield command to talented mavericks such as Maxwell. Shoubridge's handling, with Lieutenant-Colonel G.D. Price, of the difficult night relief by the 7th Bedfords on 26–27 September earned Maxse's unqualified admiration. Maxse felt that this revealed a system of training in the 54th Brigade which reflected the greatest credit upon Shoubridge and his battalion commanders. 'They had the pluck', Maxse wrote, 'to attempt an operation which might have led to a disaster and they had sufficient confidence in the capacity of their subordinates to warrant them in the risk they took'. In contrast, Maxse was singularly unimpressed by the conduct of the 55th Brigade's attempts to take the Schwaben Redoubt. He quickly 'degummed' Sir Thomas Jackson, reporting that his brigade 'was not handled with firmness and the attacks were too partial. The situation should have been grasped more firmly by the brigade commander and he was so informed'.[33] The dismissal caused some bitterness in the ranks of the brigade, but it is also worth pointing out that Jackson's successor was Lieutenant-Colonel Price of the Bedfords – a promotion from within that avoided imposing a total outsider on the formation.

It has already been argued that the battlefield leadership of battalion commanders such as Maxwell and Price was of crucial importance at Thiepval. Maxwell had won his VC in South Africa and was a former ADC to Kitchener, who had nicknamed him 'The Brat'. The divisional historian describes his 'extraordinary personality' as combining 'a burning forcefulness' with 'an ice-cool exterior'. At Trones Wood on 14 July, Maxwell had, with Shoubridge's support, revived a flagging attack and had personally led men of the 54th Brigade through the wood like a line of beaters, even joining in an assault on a German strongpoint on the way to the final objective. Maxse did not always approve of battalion commanders going over the top with the *leading* infantrymen and had therefore, as he put it, kept them 'tight in hand' to reduce casualties among them on 1 July, but one feels that his description of Maxwell as 'my best platoon commander' after Trones Wood is not completely condemnatory. Maxwell's own letters to his wife suggest that his command style embodied a curious mixture of enlightened modern attitudes and old-fashioned 'gung-ho' aggression and intolerance. In June 1916, when addressing the 12th Middlesex, he instructed his men to gather close round him and to sit down, have a smoke and listen, assuring them that 'when we can be a family, we'll be one and talk to each other as one'. On the other hand, he saw shell-shock as 'a complaint which, to my mind, is too prevalent everywhere'. He added that 'I have told my people that my name for it is fright, or something worse, and I am not going to have it'. Following a church parade just over a month before Thiepval, Maxwell told his men that they should never retire from a position 'unless they saw a written order from me, which I guessed, and they guessed they would probably not get'. They should 'kill Germans and eat them, and not give them cigarettes, as if they were best friends'. After Thiepval, Maxwell was quick to comment that the Germans had fought stubbornly and bravely, 'and probably not more than 300 to 500 put their hands up. They took it out of us badly, but we did ditto; and I have no shame in saying so, as every German should, in my opinion, be exterminated. I don't know that we took one. I have not seen an officer or man yet who did, anyway'.

Even the firebrand Maxwell was not entirely enamoured with the task he had been given at Thiepval. He had been, in his own words, 'a sick man' for the three days prior to the assault, and:

> I hated the job from the first ... one knew it could only be a tough thing to take on, and I hadn't personally any hopes of accomplishing it, more especially as the distance to be covered – nearly one mile – was enormous for these attacks under any circumstances, and under the special one, of country absolutely torn with shell for three months, it was, I considered, an impossibility.

In the event, however, Maxwell threw himself in to the fight with all his customary determination. Maxse was particularly impressed by the manner in which Maxwell organised the defence of the captured Chateau and thus 'secured safety for the night ...'. When the 7th Bedfords came up during the night to continue the advance next morning, Maxwell – despite being ordered to 'clear out on relief' – stayed on to help Price, apparently much to the latter's delight. 'I was in no mind', Maxwell remarked, 'to lose what we had so hardly won by going before he had done his job'. Maxwell was subsequently given a serious dressing-down by Shoubridge, whose irritation was increased because, as Maxwell admitted, he knew 'I would do it again if even the King had given me the order'. It was popularly believed in the division that Maxwell had retorted to Shoubridge: 'What are you grousing about? I've got you another medal'.[34] Maxwell himself was awarded a Bar to his DSO and less than a month later was promoted to command the 27th Brigade in the 9th (Scottish) Division.

Junior leadership in the division was also often of a high order at Thiepval. It had to be, for as Maxwell observed, the ground 'was made for skulking, and every yard of it afforded opportunity for men to drop down unseen and stay there without being seen ...'.[35] Recalling the assault at Thiepval, Private C. Cooksey of the 10th Essex wrote:

> here I and the chaps in my section witnessed one of the bravest incidents of the day ... in my mind, I met the bravest man I had seen in my life. Lieut. Goddard of our company walking up and down the line ... with his map and his compass in his left hand and his revolver in his right one, stopping now and then to glance at his map or to shout an order as to direction to our

section leaders, cool as a cucumber taking no notice of their machine-gun bullets.

Sergeant Barrett, of the same company, remarked that Goddard was 'strolling along as if in the Strand' and called his officer's conduct 'thrilling'.[36]

Early on 27 September, Second-Lieutenant Tom Adlam of the 7th Bedfords displayed conspicuous bravery and great leadership when his platoon was held up by heavy rifle and machine-gun fire from several strongpoints. Adlam dashed across the open under this fire, collecting his men from shell holes for a combined rush, and also gathering up a quantity of German hand grenades with which he started a 'whirlwind' attack on the enemy. Though slightly wounded in the leg, he continued throwing from a kneeling position, out-throwing the Germans, and then seized the opportunity to lead his platoon to capture and kill all those who opposed him in the immediate vicinity. Commenting on the subsequent award of the Victoria Cross to Adlam, Maxse wrote that, by his bravery and example, and also by his skilful handling of his unit, Adlam was 'chiefly responsible for the success of the two companies of the Bedfordshire Regiment, who cleared and made good the last bit of the Thiepval objective ... It was, in fact, a successful minor operation without which the main attack on Schwaben Redoubt could not take place'. Adlam, a former private and sergeant in a Hampshire Territorial battalion before the war, took special care to keep the men happy, partly by being open-minded and aware of his own limitations. When interviewed in 1973, he declared: 'Some officers would think that they had to do better than their own men. But if I found a man who could do something better than me I'd say "Well, you do that". And I think they liked it ... A man likes to be recognised as being a responsible person'. [37] Another officer whose actions and example had an important local influence was Captain H.R. Longbourne of the 7th Queen's. In the assault on the Schwaben Redoubt on 28 September, his company was checked in its advance at about 2 p.m. by fire from Point 65 in the southern face of the Redoubt. Longbourne took a bag of Mills bombs and ran from shell hole to shell hole until he was 25 yards away from the strongpoint, then succeeded in knocking out a machine-gun. Re-supplied with grenades, he carried on an effective bombing duel for 45 minutes before charging and capturing the strongpoint with just a sergeant and a private by his side – a feat for which he was awarded the DSO.[38] Again, it is difficult to reconcile all these incidents with the patronising assertion of the American historian, Bruce Gudmundsson, that British small-unit leadership was largely in the hands of 'tactically incompetent schoolboys'.[39]

The capacity to show initiative and courage was, of course, not merely confined to officers. Privates Frederick Edwards and Robert Ryder – from 'B' Company of the 12th Middlesex – revealed these qualities in abundance at the height of the fighting for Thiepval itself, when most, if not all, of their officers had become casualties. Edwards knocked out a German machine-gun post with bombs while Ryder cleared a German trench by skilful use of his Lewis gun. Both won the VC. Edwards, then aged 21, was from County Cork. A soldier's son, he had enlisted in the Royal Garrison Artillery in 1908, when still only 14, and had served in

Hong Kong before transferring to the Middlesex Regiment. The 20-year-old Ryder, in contrast, was a former labourer from Harefield, Middlesex, and was a 1914 volunteer.[40] One could argue that, despite their different backgrounds and geographical origins, Edwards and Ryder typified the high standards of battle drill and training with which all ranks of the 18th Division were imbued by September 1916. The thoroughness of this training and of pre-battle briefings ensured that, when the set-piece phase of the attack was over and the outcome depended on an intense, close-quarters 'soldier's battle', the deeds of men like Edwards and Ryder were far from being isolated acts. As the official historian notes, the 'prowess of the individual soldier' largely determined the issue at Thiepval: 'For the most part, the enemy fought to the death; he was only to be overcome by desperate courage, skill-at-arms, and the enterprise of small groups of men, often led by privates after officers and NCOs had been killed or wounded'.[41]

I am personally inclined to believe that it was the divisional *ethos* (influenced, above all, by Maxse) and the quality of its training, rather than social cohesion or local unit identity, that provided the foundation for the 18th Division's consistently successful perfomance on the Somme. This success also depended – as in all divisions – on the formation's ability to rebuild itself periodically and efficiently, after heavy losses, around a nucleus of combat veterans and to uphold a way of doing things well which could be instilled in others, however frequent the changes in personnel. It is possible to trace figures in the 18th Division who *were* in a position to ensure the maintenance of standards. One was A.P.B. Irwin, who, as a captain in September 1914, was at that time the only Regular officer posted to the newly raised 8th East Surreys. Irwin was in command of the battalion by the Somme and still held the post two years later before becoming acting commander of the 55th Brigade shortly before the Armistice. Another such officer was T.M. Banks, who crossed to France with the 10th Essex in 1915 as a second-lieutenant and subsequently rose to command the battalion before becoming CO of the 8th Royal Berkshires, also in 53rd Brigade, towards the end of the war. The retention of the strong original local identity of units was, however, a different matter. Helen McCartney has shown that attempts *were* made by the authorities, from the autumn of 1916 onwards, to draw casualty replacements for units from at least the same county or region as before, and that the Liverpool Rifles and Liverpool Scottish, in particular, retained a marked *county* identity until the Armistice.[42] This may have been so in the case of the Liverpool Territorials but the story was by no means the same in the 18th Division, where the localised character of *some* units had already been diluted as early as September 1916.

In the absence of detailed and updated nominal rolls of the battalions of the 18th Division, it is, of course, impossible to be absolutely precise about the changes in their social and geographical composition but – adopting the same approach as Helen McCartney – I have examined the relevant lists of casualties in *Soldiers Died in the Great War*, as these do offer at least some evidence about places of birth, residence and enlistment. From a sample of nine of the division's battalions, I found, at one end of the scale, that the 8th Norfolks, for example, still had a very strong *county* identity in late September–early October 1916. Of the NCOs and men of the battalion who died during or as a direct result of the fighting at Thiepval, 88.09 per cent had been born in Norfolk and 92.85 per cent had enlisted in the county. The 8th Suffolks too still had a reasonably strong local character, with 53.33 per cent of its fatal casualties having been born in the county and another 28.88 per cent being natives of neighbouring Cambridgeshire. However, the composition of other battalions appears to have been much more varied. Only 17.70 per cent of the NCOs and men of the 7th Bedfords who fell at Thiepval were born in Bedfordshire itself, while 27.98 per cent enlisted there. Similar numbers of NCOs and men were born, or enlisted, in neighbouring Hertfordshire, though this still meant that almost 60 per cent were born outside these two counties and over 55 per cent enlisted elsewhere. In the 12th Middlesex, Frank Maxwell's battalion – which lost 142 other ranks killed or died of wounds at Thiepval – just over half (53.52 per cent) are known to have been born in and around London, and a very high proportion (72.53 per cent) can be identified as having enlisted there, though only 35.21 per cent are known to have been living in or around the city at the time of enlistment. The birthplace of the non-Londoners extended from Aberdeenshire to Cornwall and Jersey within the British Isles and Channel Islands, while a handful hailed from such far-flung locations as New York, Auckland, Cairo and India. A total of twenty-three (or 16.19 per cent) had formerly served in the Royal Fusiliers and nineteen of these (or 82.6 per cent of the 23) were non-Londoners. In the 8th East Surreys, 16.16 per cent of the Thiepval dead had formerly served in the Middlesex Regiment and another 13.88 per cent had been in the Royal Sussex Regiment, helping to explain why the battalion contained men from Brighton and Midhurst. At the other end of the scale from the Norfolks one finds the 7th Queen's. By 13 July 1916, when it went into action at Longueval Alley, near Trones Wood, the battalion had received no drafts since the start of the Somme offensive and was only 280 strong. Though reinforced by a company of the 7th Buffs, it lost another 200 in this attack – quite apart from the losses to the Buffs' company – and, for a brief period, in the words of the official historian, it 'ceased to exist as a battalion'. Judging from the known details of those who fell while serving with the battalion at Thiepval, by then only 24.29 per cent were Surrey-born NCOs and men; 29.9 per cent had been living in Surrey at the time of enlistment; and 27.1 per cent had actually enlisted in the county. 75.7 per cent had been born outside the county and 72.89 per cent had enlisted elsewhere. 17.75 per cent had been transferred from the Royal Sussex Regiment and 12.14 per cent from the Middlesex Regiment. Some of the NCOs and men came from as far afield as Bootle, Sunderland, Leamington Spa and Devon.[43]

The evidence indicates, therefore, that while the 18th Division, on 26 September 1916, retained traces of a very broad regional (i.e. Home Counties) identity, few, if any, of its battalions were from specific communities as *was* the case in the 31st, 32nd, 34th and 36th Divisions. Given the figures presented elsewhere (see Chapter 3) about the performance of divisions of the Fourth New Army on the Somme, and bearing in mind the 18th Division's own high levels of performance, one might thus reasonably conclude that tight-knit social cohesion and strong local identity did not *necessarily* lead to consistent success in battle. By the same token, dilution of social or geographical identity did not always lead to a decline in a formation's fighting capabilities.[44]

Despite the protestations of historians such as Denis Winter, Bruce Gudmundsson and Martin Samuels, there can scarcely be little doubt that various aspects of the BEF's command, organisation and tactics *did* show a marked improvement during, or as a direct result of, the Somme. Whether one calls it a 'learning curve', 'learning process' or 're-skilling', it is possible to trace a steady process of improvement in the BEF from 1916 – albeit one that was never uniform and which contained periodic mistakes, setbacks, steps backward and false dawns. While, from the evidence I have seen, the 18th Division at Thiepval appears to have been one of the earliest British divisions to employ an overhead machine-gun barrage in a major set-piece attack, I would not seek to claim that, in 1916, it was particularly innovative in a tactical sense.[45] One can contend, however, that, at Thiepval, its battle drill, training and devolved command *did* contribute significantly to its achievements and that these factors *were* recognised by the BEF as being among the likely keys to future success. It was in this way that the 18th Division helped to shape the template for the highly effective limited-objective assaults carried out by Second Army and the Canadian Corps the following year, and to encourage the kind of devolved command which was to prove so vital in the Hundred Days offensive of 1918. After Thiepval, Ivor Maxse received a letter from Herbert Plumer, the commander of Second Army, asking him to send 'a few lines describing your attack and how you carried it out – as you say trouble in training and careful organisation of the smaller units pays over and over again'.[46] If that request doesn't reflect a willingness to learn at all levels of the BEF in late 1916, it is difficult to know what does. Certainly, both the enemy and the allies of the BEF also acknowledged the 18th Division's achievement at Thiepval. Oberstleutnant Alfred Bischler, of the German 180th Infantry Regiment, described the event as 'absolutely crushing ... every German soldier from the highest general to the most lowly private had the feeling that now Germany had lost the first great battle'. The French official historian, General Palat, saw the 18th Division's success as an indication that the BEF had finally ended its apprenticeship and could now genuinely face and defeat the professional German army.[47]

It might be appropriate to conclude this chapter with an extract from the passage on Thiepval in the published history of the 10th Essex. The battalion historians seem slightly apologetic about the fact that they had only captured two of their three objectives: 'Subsequently we heard that General Maxse had said something like this: "If you take and hold your first objective you do well; if you take and hold your second objective you do just about as much as is humanly possible; and higher command sets a third objective in case of a possible breakdown of the enemy's morale"'.[48] As one hopes that this chapter and others demonstrate, New Army divisions such as the 18th – on many occasions on the Somme – *did* secure their first and second objectives and sometimes all of them. One surely cannot ask, or expect, more of citizen-soldiers than that.

Chapter Five

Somme Footnote: The Battle of the Ancre and the Struggle for Frankfort Trench, November 1916[1]

If the capture of Thiepval in September 1916 bore distinct evidence of a learning process and of improvements in command, training and tactical methods in the BEF, the final throes of the Somme offensive – the struggle for Munich and Frankfort Trenches in November that year – also showed that developments and improvements were, at that time, still imperfectly understood and certainly not yet universally applied by all formations serving under Sir Douglas Haig on the Western Front.

On 18 November 1916, in the very last phase of the Allied offensive on the Somme, the British 32nd Division attacked the Munich and Frankfort Trenches, which were situated on Redan Ridge, about a mile north-east of Beaumont Hamel, while other units attacked towards Grandcourt, south of the River Ancre.[2] Although the 19th Division reached the western edge of Grandcourt, the latter village was to remain in German hands until the following February. Similarly, as so often happened when the British launched attacks on a limited scale in 1916, the 32nd Division's assault on Munich and Frankfort Trenches was, in the main, a costly failure, despite the considerable gallantry and powers of endurance displayed by all ranks in dreadful conditions. By nightfall on 18 November most of the survivors of the attack had fallen back to positions in or near their own front line. Remarkably, however, more than 100 other ranks and a handful of officers from the 11th Battalion, Border Regiment, and the 16th Battalion, Highland Light Infantry (HLI), not only penetrated as far as Frankfort Trench but held out there, largely unaided, for eight days. This courageous stand in Frankfort Trench merits only a footnote in the British official history yet, like the 32nd Division's attack as a whole, the episode illustrates many of the best and worst features of the battlefield performance of the BEF in 1916.[3]

Following the disastrous British assault on 1 July, and the more successful attack on the German second main position between Bazentin le Grand and Longueval a fortnight later, the offensive had developed into a grim battle of attrition. Haig himself came to accept that the prospects of an early breakthrough had receded, now seeing the BEF's operations on the Somme more in terms of a 'wearing-out' fight in preparation for the next large-scale set-piece assault, which was planned for mid-September and which Haig hoped would prove to be the decisive stroke.[4] During the period from 15 July to 14 September, the British Fourth Army, under General Sir Henry Rawlinson – apart from its repeated attempts to win Delville Wood and High Wood – was also embroiled in a bitter contest for Guillemont

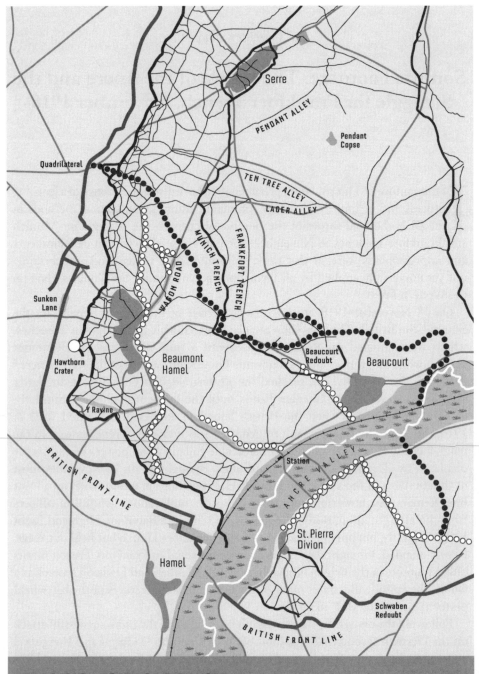

Serre

PENDANT ALLEY

Pendant
Copse

Quadrilateral

TEN TREE ALLEY

LAGER ALLEY

MUNICH TRENCH

FRANKFORT TRENCH

WAGON ROAD

Sunken
Lane

Beaucourt
Redoubt

Beaucourt

Hawthorn
Crater

Ravine

Beaumont
Hamel

BRITISH FRONT LINE

Station

ANCRE VALLEY

St. Pierre
Divion

Hamel

BRITISH FRONT LINE

Schwaben
Redoubt

**THE SECTOR NORTH OF THE ANCRE
AND THE STRUGGLE FOR FRANKFORT
TRENCH 13-24 November 1916**

British front line 13 November ————

Line reached 14 November ○○○○○○○○○

Line consolidated 19 November ●●●●●●●●●

and Ginchy, both of which were captured in the first half of September. In the meantime, General Sir Hubert Gough's Reserve Army, which had gradually assumed responsibility for operations north of the Albert–Bapaume road, was beginning to figure more prominently in the offensive. After a fierce struggle, starting on 23 July, Australian troops of I Anzac Corps had, by 5 August, captured Pozières on the Albert–Bapaume road, as well as the ruined mill on the ridge line beyond the village. The gains at Pozières had undoubtedly provided the BEF with better observation over the central portion of the battlefield, although the Australians suffered some 23,000 casualties in 5 weeks. Moreover, Pozières was only a prelude to the long and painful slogging-match which the Reserve Army had still to face in order to take the successive German trench lines north-west of the Albert–Bapaume road, and on the slopes and spurs of the Morval–Grandcourt ridge, so that it could unlock the German defences at Mouquet Farm and Thiepval from the rear.

A large proportion of the British attacks from mid-July to early September were comparatively small-scale affairs, the aims of which were to push forward the British line at various points, to win local tactical advantages and to improve the starting positions for the major attack in mid-September. In a war dominated by artillery, it was often vital to straighten the start line before a big assault to ensure that the preliminary bombardment and supporting barrage would be as accurate as possible, but the price of such 'line-straightening' operations was a serious erosion of the BEF's combat strength. In their analysis of Rawlinson's performance on the Somme, Robin Prior and Trevor Wilson have observed that, in 62 days, the Fourth Army lost 82,000 men while advancing a mere 1,000 yards on a 5-mile front. Only on some five occasions out of ninety operations were twenty or more battalions involved and only four attacks were delivered across the whole of the Fourth Army front between 15 July and 14 September.[5] Gough too showed a predilection for frequent attacks with moderate numbers to keep the enemy off balance. 'Once we allow him to get his breath back', he told Lieutenant-General Sir William Birdwood, the commander of I Anzac Corps, 'we shall have to make another of these gigantic assaults ... I think our way keeps down casualties and brings the best results'.[6] What his statement appeared to overlook was the fact that limited attacks on narrow fronts permitted the Germans, in most cases, to concentrate much of their available firepower on the threatened sector. Even Haig, who was usually willing to leave the *detailed* planning and conduct of operations to subordinate commanders, reminded them on 2 August that they must practise 'economy of men'.[7] Later the same month, as we have seen, Haig left Rawlinson in little doubt that he was dissatisfied with attacks on narrow fronts by insufficient forces and with inadequate supervision from senior commanders. For the mid-September attack, he stressed, 'a sufficient force must be employed in proper proportion to the extent of front ...'.[8]

The major British assault which took place on 15 September against the German third main position was notable for the first-ever use in battle of a new weapon, the tank. The objectives of the Fourth Army on that day included the German third position in front of Flers and the capture of Gueudecourt, Lesboeufs and Morval. The Canadian Corps, part of the Reserve Army, was to seize Courcelette. In the event, the British XV Corps, helped by four of the tanks assigned to the 41st Division, took Flers and High Wood. Martinpuich and Courcelette were also secured. Advancing about 2,500 yards on a front of 4,500 yards, the British gained, in square miles, roughly twice the amount of ground that they had won on 1 July, although it required a renewal of the offensive in the last week of September to seize all the objectives. After a particularly effective preliminary bombardment and creeping barrage on the right, where the divisions of XIV Corps were attacking, Leboeufs and Morval fell on 25 September and Gueudecourt and Combles followed suit the next day. On Gough's front on 26 September, the Reserve Army undertook its biggest operation to date, attacking from Courcelette to the Schwaben Redoubt. The 18th Division cleared Thiepval itself of Germans by noon on 27 September but again the early impetus was lost. The stubborn defenders of the Schwaben Redoubt were not completely forced out until 14 October, while the fight for, and around, Regina Trench on the Canadian Corps sector dragged on into November.

The question has often been asked as to why Haig, having once more failed to achieve the hoped-for breakthrough, persisted with the offensive after the end of September. Many commentators suggest that, fed by optimistic reports from Brigadier-General Charteris, his Chief of Intelligence at GHQ, Haig firmly, if wrongly, believed that the Germans on the Somme were close to collapse.[9] Gary Sheffield, in his excellent recent biography of Haig, agrees that the latter was convinced that the battle of attrition was working in favour of the Allies but adds that Haig also judged that the battlefield skills of his forces were improving and saw the grinding down of the German as being in itself a valid military objective. Other factors included the military situation on other fronts and Haig's over-estimation of what was physically possible for his troops in the mud and rain of autumn on the Somme. However, Sheffield argues that perhaps the most significant factor was the pressure that the French high command brought to bear upon Haig.[10] Certainly, when Haig wrote to Sir William Robertson, the Chief of the Imperial General Staff, on 7 October, he contended that the offensive 'must be continued without intermission as long as possible'. Haig admitted that he could not say how near to breaking-point the enemy actually was, but thought that:

he has undoubtedly gone a long way towards it. Many of his troops have reached, and even passed, it at times during the last few weeks, and though the great difficulties of our advance, and the severity of the German discipline, have enabled the enemy's leaders to reorganise resistance afresh after every defeat, this cannot go on indefinitely if constant pressure is maintained.[11]

The reality was that, after their crisis of late September, the Germans rapidly recovered their operational equilibrium. It is also true that, in several respects, the BEF was demonstrating considerable improvements in tactical thinking by the last quarter of 1916. The creeping barrage, providing a moving curtain of artillery fire behind which the infantry advanced to their objectives, was becoming standard in the BEF. On the other hand, the Germans had swiftly revised their own defensive tactics by withdrawing their machine-gunners just beyond the normal range of a creeping barrage. The key role of artillery in the preparation of an assault had been amply revealed by the British successes on 14 July and 25 September, when the preliminary bombardments had been sufficiently intense and concentrated, in terms of weight of shell per yard of trench attacked, to ensure success.[12] Nevertheless, the fact that the formula was not consistently applied in 1916 indicates that Haig, Rawlinson and Gough had not yet fully grasped its implications or importance.

It was against this strategic and tactical background that the focus of operations shifted partly back to the sector immediately north and south of the Ancre which, except for an abortive attack by the 39th and 49th Divisions towards St Pierre Divion on 3 September, had stayed comparatively dormant since 1 July. Once the Thiepval ridge was in British possession, Haig wanted Gough to strike hard in this sector. The instructions which GHQ issued on 29 September for the new phase of the offensive called for the Fourth Army to advance towards Warlencourt, Le Transloy and Beaulencourt, while the Reserve Army was to launch a two-pronged attack converging on Miraumont, with one blow being delivered northward from the Thiepval ridge and the other coming eastward from the Beaumont Hamel–Hébuterne front.[13] The provisional date selected for the joint attack was 12 October but, as the month wore on, rain turned the battlefield into a morass. The thick mud and mist added greatly to the problems of infantry and gunners alike. In the words of the British official historian, the infantry, 'sometimes wet to the skin and almost exhausted before zero hour, were often condemned to struggle painfully forward through the mud and heavy fire against objectives vaguely defined and difficult of recognition'.[14]

In the circumstances, GHQ was forced to modify its plans and delay Gough's operations on the Ancre. On 17 October, after Haig had consulted Gough and Rawlinson, it was decided that, instead of making a converging advance from both sides of the Ancre valley, the Reserve Army would now attack astride the Ancre, possibly on 23 October, in conjunction with the Fourth Army's efforts to secure Le Transloy. However, the weather remained mostly wet and stormy until, on 3 November, Haig authorised Gough to postpone the Ancre operations indefinitely, so long as arrangements were made to commence the assault without further delay as soon as the weather showed signs of becoming more settled.[15] Five days later, following a visit from Lieutenant-General Sir Launcelot Kiggell, Haig's chief of staff, Gough conferred with his corps commanders and ruled that, provided no more rain fell, the Fifth Army – as the Reserve Army had now been renamed – would launch its attack on 13 November.[16]

It seems reasonably clear from the evidence that, in the end, it was Gough who was largely responsible for deciding that the Ancre operations should proceed. On the morning of 12 November, when the preliminary bombardment was already in progress, Kiggell visited Gough's headquarters at Toutencourt to ascertain how satisfied the Fifth Army commander was about his chances of success and to underline the fact that Haig did not, in any way, wish to bring on a battle in unfavourable conditions.[17] Gough rated the prospects as 'quite good' and replied that he must either attack on 13 November or withdraw and rest the divisions which were currently in position. In the afternoon, Haig himself rode to Toutencourt where Gough, having been to see all the divisions concerned during the day, recommended that the assault should 'go in'. Haig confirmed that a success on the Ancre was highly desirable, not only because it might have a beneficial influence on the Allied situation on the Russian and Romanian fronts – partly by dissuading the Germans from switching any divisions from France – but also because it would create a favourable impression at the inter-Allied military conference at Chantilly, which Haig was due to attend on 15–16 November. As Haig noted in his diary: 'The British position will doubtless be much stronger (as memories are short) if I could appear there on top of the capture of Beaumont Hamel for instance, and some 3,000 German prisoners ... But the necessity for a success must not blind eyes to the difficulties of ground and weather. Nothing is so costly as a failure ...'.[18]

Nonetheless, Haig was reassured by Gough and agreed that the Fifth Army should attack the following day. Writing to the official historian after the war, Kiggell observed that 'as things turned out the later stages of the fight were hardly justified, but Gough was so keen and confident the C-in-C decided to permit them'.[19] General Sir George Jeffreys – who as commander of the 57th Brigade in the 19th Division in November 1916, was deeply involved in the Ancre battle – was less circumspect in his criticisms of Gough's misplaced optimism. 'The Army commander and his staff', he recalled, 'had simply no conception of the conditions in the forward area, which were, in fact, about the worst I can remember at any time in the war'.[20]

Considering the obduracy with which the Germans were about to defend the sector, it is perhaps surprising to find that, on the eve of Gough's attack, several senior German officers had grave misgivings regarding their positions on the Ancre. Crown Prince Rupprecht of Bavaria, whose Army Group faced the British on the Somme, favoured evacuating the salient between St Pierre Divion and Beaumont Hamel. Ludendorff, the First Quartermaster-General, shared this view and Colonel von Lossberg – the chief of staff of the German First Army and one of the most gifted of all German tacticians – also judged the Serre–Ancre angle to be particularly vulnerable to concentrated artillery fire. However, General Fritz von Below, commanding the German First Army, was reluctant to yield high ground which offered his troops valuable observation, so, in practice, the line north of the Ancre was strengthened by the arrival of the German 12th Division which, from 22 October, took over the Beaumont Hamel sector between the 52nd Division at Serre and the 38th Division at Beaucourt.[21]

In the British Fifth Army's attack on 13 November, II Corps (Jacob), south of the Ancre, was ordered to eject the Germans from the remains of their front system between the Schwaben Redoubt and St Pierre Divion and establish a line facing north-east, abreast of Beaucourt. The principal blow was to be delivered north of the Ancre by V Corps (Lieutenant-General E.A. Fanshawe). Here, from right to left, the 63rd (Royal Naval), 51st (Highland), 2nd and 3rd Divisions were to assault the original German defences between Beaucourt and Serre which had resisted capture on, and since, 1 July. The first objective of V Corps, in what was intended to be a three-stage operation, extended from Beaucourt station on the Ancre, up the Beaumont Hamel valley and around the eastern edge of the village, and then across Redan Ridge and the slope in front of Serre. An average advance of 800 yards would be necessary to complete this stage. A further 600 to 1,000 yards on lay the second objective, which ran from the western edge of Beaucourt and along the eastern slope of Redan Ridge before bending around the eastern edge of Serre, where a defensive flank was to be formed. The third corps objective was Beaucourt, on the right near the Ancre. On the part of the front which concerns us most – that of the 51st (Highland) and 2nd Divisions – the objectives included Munich Trench which, in July, had formed an intermediate line between the German front defences and their second position from Grandcourt to Puisieux. Frankfort Trench, the second and final objective of the 51st and 2nd Divisions on 13 November, was 200–400 yards beyond Munich Trench, on the reverse slope of Redan Ridge.

There were 1,401 artillery pieces available to prepare and support the British assault. In the case of V Corps, they comprised 472 field guns and howitzers and 173 heavy guns and howitzers. This meant that, to support V Corps, there was one field gun to every 13.5 yards and one heavy gun to every 31 yards of front. In comparison, there had been one field gun to every 21 yards and one heavy gun to every 57 yards on 1 July, and one field gun per 10 yards and one heavy gun per 21 yards on 15 September.[22]

The attack, launched in a dank fog at 5.45 a.m. on 13 November, had mixed fortunes. On the II Corps front, the 39th Division, and two battalions of the 19th Division, took most of their initial objectives, including St Pierre Divion, at a cost of under 1,000 casualties. On the other side of the Ancre, the 63rd (Royal Naval) Division, in its first battle on the Western Front, had a tough fight for Beaucourt but, with the help of units from the 37th Division, finally secured the village the following morning. The 51st Division cleared the ruins of Beaumont Hamel by the late afternoon of 13 November to give Haig the prize he particularly wanted in time for the Chantilly conference. Unable, for the moment, to push on to the next objective, 250 yards of Frankfort Trench overlooking the Beaucourt–Ancre valley, the Highlanders paused to consolidate their gains.

Further north the assault was generally less successful. On the left flank, opposite Serre, the troops of the 76th Brigade (3rd Division) were hampered by clinging mud, which was waist deep in places. Finding few gaps in the German wire, they were only able to enter the enemy trenches in small groups. Some of the men of the 8th Brigade, also part of the 3rd Division, crossed the German support and reserve trenches to reach the first objective, Serre Trench, but, again, they were only in isolated parties and were inevitably overpowered. The British

2nd Division, between the 3rd and 51st Divisions, attacked the German positions along Redan Ridge. Its 5th Brigade arrived, on schedule, at its own first objective, Beaumont Trench, which stretched northward from Beaumont Hamel, though the leading troops suffered heavily from rifle and machine-gun fire. The 6th Brigade, on the left, soon ran into difficulties, especially around the Quadrilateral. Mud, intact German wire and enfilade fire from German machine guns all impeded progress. While parties of the 13th Essex Regiment and 1st King's (Liverpool) Regiment pressed on to the first objective near the junction of Beaumont Trench and Lager Alley, most survivors of the leading wave of battalions were held up in the German front trench.

By 7.30 a.m., when the battalions of the second wave were expected to attack Frankfort Trench, only those of the 5th Brigade were in any position to adhere to the programme and even they could barely muster 120 men from the 17th Royal Fusiliers and the 2nd Oxfordshire and Buckinghamshire Light Infantry. Joined by a handful of men from the 13th Essex and 1st King's of the 6th Brigade, they reached various sections of Frankfort Trench but nowhere in sufficient numbers to hold it. The scattered groups were eventually compelled to fall back, at first to Munich Trench, 200 yards to the rear, and then to Wagon Road and Beaumont Trench. At 9.30 a.m. orders were received from V Corps for a fresh attack in co-operation with the 3rd Division. These orders were cancelled when the 3rd Division's true situation became known and the renewed assault was postponed until the following morning. With Gough still confident that V Corps could capture its original objectives, a formal operation order was issued by that corps to its divisions two hours before midnight. The 51st and 2nd Divisions would once more attempt to carry Frankfort Trench. The Germans, however, used the hours of darkness to reinforce their troops on the Ancre, parts of the 26th Reserve and 223rd Divisions moving up to support the 12th Division north of the river. Of these formations, the 12th and 26th Reserve Divisions had already fought, and suffered severe casualties, on the Somme during the summer. The 223rd Division was a new formation but it comprised regiments which had previously seen service at Verdun and in Lorraine. All three were regarded by the Allies as good divisions.[23]

It was frequently the case in 1916 that, once the set-piece phase of a British assault was over, and the early momentum was lost, subsequent attacks became piecemeal, hastily organised affairs which lacked both weight and co-ordination. The efforts of V Corps to seize Munich and Frankfort Trenches on the morning of 14 November followed this depressingly familiar pattern. The 51st Division's 152nd Brigade was meant to attack Munich Trench at 6.20 a.m., at the same time as the 2nd Division, but the attached 1/7th Argyll and Sutherland Highlanders received their orders late and could do little other than to send forward strong patrols against stubborn opposition. A two-company advance at 7.30 a.m. secured the southern portion of Munich Trench after about an hour, the troops observing that Frankfort Trench appeared to be bristling with Germans. Before any further advance could be attempted, Munich Trench was shelled in error by a British heavy battery and the Highlanders were forced to withdraw some distance.

The 2nd Division at least started its attack on time at 6.20 a.m., using the battalions of the 99th Brigade from divisional reserve. An erratic supporting barrage caused many casualties and, being new to the ground, some troops lost direction. The 1st King's Royal Rifle Corps got as far as Munich Trench but in insufficient numbers to effect a permanent lodgement, likewise dropping back to Wagon Road during the morning. The one bright spot of the morning for the British was the fact that the barrage covering the left of the assault broke up a German counter-attack from Serre while the 22nd Royal Fusiliers came up to strengthen the 2nd Division's position on this flank.[24]

Undeterred by the events of the early morning, V Corps ordered a resumption of the attack on Frankfort Trench by the 2nd and 51st Divisions at 2.45 p.m. As before, the orders reached the Highlanders too late, leaving the battalions of the 112th Brigade (37th Division) – lent to the 2nd Division for the purpose – to attack alone. It was a measure of the poor communications on the battlefield that the divisional headquarters did not know that the previous attack on Munich Trench had failed. Consequently, when the 11th Royal Warwickshires and 6th Bedfordshires advanced, after an exhausting approach march, they ran into unexpected machine-gun fire from that quarter and could do no more than add to the congestion of units along the sunken Wagon Road. Most of the available German troops in the Munich–Frankfort position had been needed to halt the attack and British artillery fire had prevented them from being re-supplied with bombs and small arms ammunition, although part of the German 208th Division, following a two-month spell on the Eastern Front, began to relieve the hard-pressed 12th Division. That night, on the British side of no-man's-land, Pioneers and Royal Engineers of the 51st Division hurriedly dug a new line, called 'New Munich Trench', about 200 yards west of Munich Trench itself.[25]

Fanshawe, the V Corps commander, had been visited by Gough at noon on 14 November. With Gough's consent, orders were issued for a general resumption of the attack the next day. Apparently ignorant of the fact that Munich Trench was still occupied by the Germans, V Corps ordered the 2nd and 51st Divisions to mount a fresh assault towards Frankfort Trench at 9 a.m. on 15 November. During the evening of 14 November Haig, who was now in Paris, learned of Gough's plans for the morrow and immediately telephoned GHQ to indicate that he did not want the Fifth Army to embark upon any more large-scale operations before he returned from Chantilly.[26] Kiggell went to see Gough at 9 a.m. on 15 November to make sure that Haig's views about the resumption of the offensive were not lost on the Fifth Army's commander.[27] Even as the two officers met, however, the joint attack by the 2nd and 51st Divisions was being delivered.

Many of the ingredients common to hastily prepared minor operations and follow-up attacks were evident in the assault of 15 November and, predictably, they again combined to produce a recipe for failure. The 1/7th Argyll and Sutherland Highlanders advanced from New Munich Trench, about 500 yards further forward than the jumping-off positions of the 2nd Division in Beaumont Trench, and partly as a result of this difference in alignment, ran into their own barrage. Some

Highlanders reached Frankfort Trench and lobbed bombs into dugouts but, being outnumbered, withdrew to their starting point, covered by Lewis guns. The 2nd Division employed two more battalions – the 8th East Lancashires and 10th Loyal North Lancashires – from the attached 112th Brigade (37th Division) – and these units did not arrive at their assembly trenches until 40 minutes before zero hour. Major-General W.G. Walker, commander of the 2nd Division, had tried in vain to persuade V Corps to postpone the attack until 1 p.m. to allow these troops time for reconnaissance. Not surprisingly, when their assault was made, the Lancashire battalions soon lost direction and, having sustained heavy casualties in officers, withdrew to Wagon Road like several units before them in the past 50 hours or so.

After Kiggell's visit on the morning of 15 November, Gough met his corps commanders, Jacob and Fanshawe, and subsequently telephoned GHQ to tell Kiggell that all were agreed that a resumption of the Ancre attack had good prospects of success. Pointing out that further gains would improve the Fifth Army's line, he proposed two more days of offensive operations, beginning on 17 November, if Haig was willing to let them proceed. Gough was certainly overstating the case in claiming that 'all ranks were keen to attack again', for, as George Jeffreys later asserted, 'he had no notion of the physical strain on the troops of even a few hours in the line under such conditions'. Nevertheless, when Kiggell discussed the situation with Haig in Paris that evening, Gough's proposals were approved. To be fair to Gough, even his seemingly unshakeable optimism was dented by the failures of 15 November. Meeting Jacob and Fanshawe again on 16 November, he admitted that, although Munich and Frankfort Trenches had yet to be captured, the Fifth Army had already used up more men than anticipated; it was doubtful if enough troops could be assembled to launch a further attack on Serre; and Grandcourt too might be out of reach. While V Corps still had the task of seizing Frankfort Trench, the main role in the next attack was now allotted to II Corps, south of the Ancre, where it was to advance 500 yards towards Grandcourt Trench, secure a line south of Grandcourt and push forward to the western edge of the village.[28]

At this juncture, the British 32nd Division, under Major-General W.H. Rycroft, was transferred from the II Corps reserve to V Corps, and came up to relieve troops of the 2nd and 51st Divisions, these formations having incurred some 3,000 and 2,200 casualties respectively since 13 November. Seven of the 32nd Division's twelve infantry battalions were locally raised Pals battalions. They included three battalions raised in Glasgow: the 15th Highland Light Infantry (HLI), originally recruited from the city's Tramway Department; the 16th HLI, recruited largely from current and former members of the local Boys' Brigade; and the 17th HLI, raised by the Glasgow Chamber of Commerce from students and ex-pupils of the Glasgow Academy, Royal Glasgow Technical College and various high schools as well as from the city's business houses and offices.[29] The 16th Northumberland Fusiliers (Newcastle Commercials) contained many volunteers from businesses on the Newcastle Quayside, whilst the 15th and 16th Lancashire Fusiliers had been raised in and around Salford by a committee headed by Montague Barlow MP.[30]

The 11th Battalion of the Border Regiment – known as the 'Lonsdales' – had been recruited by the Earl of Lonsdale and an executive committee in Cumberland and Westmorland.[31] The remaining infantry formations in the division were mostly Regular units, except for an amalgamated Territorial battalion, the 5/6th Royal Scots, formed from two units which had served on Gallipoli. This battalion had joined the division on 29 July 1916.[32]

The 32nd Division had fought bravely at Thiepval from 1 to 3 July, suffering 4,676 casualties. Its 97th Brigade, deployed in no-man's-land before zero hour on 1 July, took and held the Leipzig Redoubt at the tip of the Leipzig Salient but, apart from this brilliant feat, the division had largely failed to secure its objectives in the opening days of the offensive. It had later participated in attempts to complete the capture of Ovillers between 13 and 15 July before moving north for three months of routine trench warfare in the Cambrin, Hulluch and Cuinchy sectors near Béthune. Despite their losses in July, and the subsequent changes in the reserve and drafting system which meant that reinforcements and casualty replacements no longer necessarily came from a unit's parent regiment or recruiting area, most of the division's Pals battalions still contained a small nucleus of their original members.[33]

There is evidence to suggest that all was not well in the command and staff echelons of the division. Austin Girdwood, who was a GSO2 on the staff of the division in July and commanded the Lonsdales in November 1916, accused Rycroft, a cavalryman, of being ignorant about, and unsympathetic towards, the infantry.[34] Girdwood complained, in particular, that before 1 July Rycroft had exhausted the infantry by keeping them in the line too long and using too many of them on working parties. 'Naturally I got myself disliked', wrote Girdwood, 'and the proof is in the fact that … I was given command of a Battalion to get me out of the Staff Office'.[35] Lieutenant-Colonel E.G. Wace, the division's GSO1 from 2 May to 28 November, remarked that Gough had been 'furious' with the 32nd Division after its failure at Thiepval and that Rycroft was terrified of the Fifth Army commander:

> Rycroft knew he'd 'got it in for us', and when at Béthune we got orders to go back to the Somme in October he turned to me and said wryly that this would be his undoing unless we went to Rawly's Army! So he just hadn't the kick in him to stand up to Gough, when all initiative was taken out of his hands.[36]

It should be added that at least one battalion commander, Lieutenant-Colonel H.J.N. Davis of the 15th HLI, maintained that Rycroft always gave him 'a feeling of confidence and fair play'.[37]

Rycroft seems to have summoned up enough resolve on 16 November to argue that it would be practically impossible for his division to attack the next day since the line had not been properly reconnoitred and forming-up positions had not been marked out.[38] The attack was put back until 6.10 a.m. on 18 November but this was by no means the sole problem facing the 32nd Division. Both Wace and

Davis asserted that the GSO1 and some battalion officers of the 2nd Division, when being relieved, could not give them correct positional 'fixes' for the front line or their own headquarters. Davis found that the 15th HLI were consequently 300 yards or more south of the sub-sector they were supposed to have taken over, a factor which had serious implications for the accuracy of the creeping barrage on the day of the assault.[39] To make matters worse, the 32nd Division's own artillery was elsewhere in the line, having been assisting the 51st Division, so much of the assault on 18 November would be covered by gunners of the 2nd Division. 'In this way', wrote one of the 32nd Division's artillery brigade commanders, 'the mutual confidence and knowledge of each other was wasted'.[40]

The ground itself, pitted as it was with shell holes from the recent fighting, also militated against rapid movement or re-supply in the front line area. An officer who served on the staff of the 14th Brigade in November 1916 went so far as to say that 'the climatic conditions alone made it clear from the start to the very stupidest brain that no success could possibly result'.[41] The 2nd Manchesters, part of that brigade, 'were so overdone with working parties and fatigues that they were not too fit for the attack when it came …'.[42] But, even with the extra day, the division's principal problem was the lack of time allowed for preparation. The Fifth Army operation order for the attack was issued at 8 p.m. on 16 November and the 32nd Division's own operation order at 3.45 p.m. the following day, although the latter appears to have reached the 14th Brigade's headquarters, for example, too late to enable the brigade staff to issue their own orders until 11.30 p.m. on 17 November, less than 7 hours before the attack. Because of the difficulties of communication in the forward area, some of these orders did not reach assaulting battalions until 4.30 a.m. on the morning of the assault. Units on their way to the line became lost and only 10 minutes remained before zero hour when the last of the 16th HLI's attacking troops arrived, half-frozen and exhausted, in their jumping-off positions, having had no hot food for 15 hours.[43]

The assault at 6.10 a.m. was launched in sleet and snow, which later turned to rain. The conditions underfoot became extremely slippery while the problems facing the gunners – who were already hampered by poor visibility – were compounded by the intense cold, which affected the shell fuses and made an accurate barrage even more difficult to achieve.[44] On the left, the 14th Brigade attacked with two battalions, the 2nd Manchesters and the 15th HLI, to carry the defensive flank forward some 500 yards to the line of Ten Tree Alley. The 97th Brigade was ordered by V Corps to use all its four infantry battalions in the attack on Munich and Frankfort Trenches, a decision which appears to have been influenced by Gough himself. The order greatly reduced Rycroft's options if things went wrong, although it had the virtue of giving added weight to the assault.[45]

As their commanding officer had feared, the 15th HLI, the left-hand battalion of the 14th Brigade, received negligible help from the covering barrage, which fell up to 600 yards too far ahead. The troops endeavoured to bomb their way forward and made slight gains on the left, near the Quadrilateral, but further progress was blocked by close-range machine-gun fire.[46] The 2nd Manchesters, unable, in the time available, to dig forming-up trenches, pushed eastward along Lager Alley before zero hour and, when the overall attack was delivered, advanced down into the valley in the direction of Serre. A few small groups even reached that village where, with ammunition supplies running out, they were overwhelmed, during the afternoon, by a counter-attack involving elements of the German 52nd and 223rd Divisions. Nothing was subsequently heard from the three leading companies of the 2nd Manchesters.[47]

The British barrage was similarly erratic on the 97th Brigade's front. When it opened, it was particularly short on the right, killing and wounding many men of the 17th HLI, who were lying out in front of New Munich Trench prior to the assault. The Germans, manning Munich Trench in some force, were relatively untouched by the ragged barrage and stopped the 17th HLI's attack with rifle and machine-gun fire, driving the survivors back on New Munich Trench.[48] The right-hand company of the 16th HLI – 'A' Company – which was next in line, shared the same fate. However, on the 16th HLI's left, the barrage was much better and three platoons of 'D' Company not only stormed across Munich Trench but also took and held a portion of Frankfort Trench, the final objective. The 11th Border Regiment was another battalion which suffered the consequences of supporting artillery fire that fell short. 'To say that the British barrage was ineffective is too mild altogether', wrote the commanding officer of the Lonsdales. In spite of this bad start, parties of the Lonsdales succeeded in joining the 16th HLI in Frankfort Trench. The 2nd King's Own Yorkshire Light Infantry (KOYLI), on the 97th Brigade's left flank, could not render any real assistance in the crucial sector, its own right-hand companies being held up by a strongpoint in Munich Trench. German retention of Munich Trench condemned the 97th Brigade's attack to failure. The remainder of the 16th HLI and the Lonsdales withdrew to Wagon Road following a German counter-attack, leaving their comrades cut off, behind German lines, in Frankfort Trench.[49]

Some German units in the Redan Ridge area, such as the 62nd Infantry Regiment (12th Division) were now down to a fraction of their former strength. Rycroft wished to bring up battalions of his divisional reserve, the 96th Brigade, at dusk for a further attack against Munich Trench. The corps commander agreed but the plan was vetoed by Gough's headquarters.[50] In fact, given the conditions and its own losses, it is doubtful whether the 32nd Division was capable of another major assault so soon. The 16th HLI alone, for example, had lost 13 officers and 390 NCOs and men killed, wounded and missing on 18 November and, as a staff officer of the 14th Brigade remembered, this was 'the only occasion on which I saw men dead from exhaustion from their efforts to get out of the mud'.[51] The division's post-battle analysis argued, however, that, if Brigadier-General J.B. Jardine's 97th Brigade had not been obliged to attack with all four battalions at zero hour on 18 November and had been permitted to keep troops in hand to give the assault more depth and exploit any early success, then the Germans might have been driven out of their positions.[52]

Estimates vary as to the size of the party which remained isolated in Frankfort Trench, although the most detailed contemporary reports put it at 7 officers and just over 120 other ranks, including 3 officers and 60 other ranks from the 16th HLI, the same number of officers and men from the 11th Border Regiment, and 1 officer and 3 other ranks from the 2nd KOYLI. Of these, between 30 and 50 men were wounded, some severely.[53] The tiny garrison occupied two dugouts in the captured portion of trench, one being allocated to the wounded and the other to those still fit to fight. They had four Lewis guns and a limited quantity of ammunition, which they supplemented by taking what they could from the dead lying in the open. Most men handed over their small arms ammunition to the Lewis gunners and armed themselves with German rifles and cartridges. Bombs were scarce and there was very little food and water. Many of the men had already consumed their water and iron rations. Again, the dead were searched at night for additional rations, while water was collected from shell holes and boiled over improvised lamps, using rifle oil as fuel and fragments of cleaning flannel as wicks.[54]

On 19 November, as the 97th Brigade was relieved by the 96th Brigade along Wagon Road and New Munich Trench, the British troops in Frankfort Trench consolidated their defences, placed their machine-guns at vital points and organised a system of sentry duties – the Germans, at this stage, apparently being unaware of their presence. This state of affairs did not last much longer for, on 20 November, the third day of the isolated garrison's ordeal, a strong German raiding party moved across the open and bombed the captured portion of Frankfort Trench on the right. Beaten off with rifles, machine guns and bombs, the Germans retired, leaving behind many casualties. Heartening as this was to the dogged defenders, they too had incurred more losses, compelling them to evacuate the smaller of the two dugouts and to shorten their line to economise on manpower.[55] Half an hour before midnight, two members of the beleaguered garrison – Company Sergeant-Major Johnstone and Private Dixon of the 11th Borders – crawled out of Frankfort Trench and, guided by a bright star and the occasional illumination afforded by Very lights, evaded the German sentries and working parties and reached the 96th Brigade's lines in the early hours of 21 November.[56]

As the fourth day of the siege of Frankfort Trench dawned, the garrison's plight was becoming desperate. The men were now weakened by hunger and an almost unbearable thirst. Many of the wounds were turning gangrenous, but there was no water available to wash bandages, nor drugs to ease the pain. Hopes rose, however, when a signaller managed to attract the attention of a British pilot by using pieces of a torn shirt. Several more aircraft arrived after an interval to flash the message that relief was on the way. Two soldiers of the 16th HLI, in particular, displayed outstanding leadership during this phase of the siege. One was Company Sergeant-Major George Lee, a roads foreman with the Glasgow Corporation in civilian life, who was subsequently described as 'the heart and soul of the defence'. The other was Lance-Corporal John Veitch, the son of a sergeant in the Scots Greys, who played a key role in the deployment and handling of the Lewis guns in the captured trench. Neither survived the battle but both earned a posthumous mention in depatches.[57]

When the first definite news of the situation of the isolated party had reached the 32nd Division's headquarters, it had been decided to send out, on the night of 21–22 November, a party of two officers and sixty men – drawn equally from the Lonsdales and 16th HLI – in an attempt to rescue their stranded comrades. The party was to be guided by Company Sergeant-Major Johnstone, who had escaped from Frankfort Trench the previous night. The relief party left Wagon Road at 9.30 p.m. and arrived at the German wire in front of Munich Trench about 75 minutes later. Johnstone then worked his way along the wire to the south and the north, but the night was very dark, so he was unable to find a suitable gap through which the patrol might pass in order to cross Munich Trench. The officer in command therefore withdrew the party to Wagon Road, which was reached at 2.25 a.m. By this time Haig had told Gough that Rycroft was unfit to command a division and that his brigadiers 'had not been taught anything by him'. Brigadier-General R.W.R. Barnes of the 111th Brigade, 37th Division, was chosen by Haig as Rycroft's successor, one of his earliest acts on 22 November being to report to V Corps on the previous night's attempt to relieve Frankfort Trench. His conclusion was that Company Sergeant-Major Johnstone had exaggerated the extent to which the German wire represented an obstacle, though Barnes did admit, somewhat condescendingly, that Johnstone 'had gone through a very trying 24 hours and was probably feeling the strain of it'.[58]

According to the published battalion history of the 16th HLI, the Germans launched a powerful attack from both the front and flanks against the dwindling British band in Frankfort Trench on the afternoon of the sixth day, 23 November. The weary defenders somehow mustered the strength and the courage to beat back the Germans, even taking eight prisoners in a fierce fight at close quarters.[59]

At 11 p.m. on 21 November – while Johnstone was still trying to find a way through the German wire, and two more men – a lance-corporal and a private – were escaping from Frankfort Trench, Fanshawe, the V Corps commander, had held a conference at which it was decided to make another effort to relieve the marooned party. The operation was to be undertaken by three companies of the 16th Lancashire Fusiliers and one company of the 2nd Royal Inniskilling Fusiliers, all from the 96th Brigade, attacking in four waves. The second wave was given the vital task of passing over the initial objective – Munich Trench – and pressing on to rescue the Frankfort Trench garrison. Reports from officers who reconnoitred the German wire on the night of 22–23 November revealed that Johnstone had, in fact, been right and that the wire in front of Munich Trench was relatively intact. The gunners were therefore directed to begin wire cutting as soon as possible on 23 November. Shortly before noon, divisional headquarters fixed zero hour for 3.30 p.m.

The 96th Brigade's attack on 23 November started well. Keeping close to the covering barrage, the troops reached Munich Trench with little opposition but, because of the nature of the ground and the remains of the German wire, they did not reach the objective simultaneously at all points. This early loss of cohesion notwithstanding, the men of the first wave jumped into Munich Trench as they arrived to deal with the German garrison there. The second wave crossed Munich Trench as ordered and pushed on until they ran into their own barrage. Pausing to reorganise, they resumed their advance although all the officers and NCOs were killed or wounded as they encountered heavy machine-gun fire from a trench on the right which had not been subdued by the British artillery. The survivors of the second wave were forced back to Munich Trench where, because some portions of the objective had not been immediately secured, the Germans had been able to emerge from dugouts to engage the attackers in bombing duels. The fight continued until about 4.20 p.m. when the British were at last compelled to retire, suffering further casualties as they did so from machine guns on both flanks. In total, the 96th Brigade lost 7 officers and 224 other ranks – over 60 per cent of those taking part in the operation.[60]

The failure of 96th Brigade's attack removed any lingering hopes that the Frankfort Trench garrison might be saved. During the night of 23–24 November, the 7th Division began to relieve the 32nd Division, which left the sector having suffered 2,524 casualties in six days, a large proportion of these having been posted as missing.[61] On the seventh day of the siege of Frankfort Trench, the Germans, under cover of a white flag, sent a message calling upon the garrison to surrender. When, after due consideration, the request was ignored, the Germans shelled the trench heavily, killing Company Sergeant-Major Lee among others. On 25 November the Germans delivered an attack in force from all points of the compass. There could only be one outcome. The tiny garrison was finally overrun and the survivors taken prisoner. Only fifteen of the original number were left unwounded and even they were so weak that they could barely stand.[62]

The Somme offensive was now over. It had cost the BEF 419,654 casualties for a strip of territory approximately 6 miles deep by 20 miles wide. Although Beaumont Hamel and Beaucourt had fallen, the Germans had stopped Gough's attempts to secure the Munich–Frankfort position on the Redan Ridge in the last phase of the battle. The capture of Munich Trench by the 7th Division on 11 January 1917 made it possible to clear the crest of the Beaumont Hamel spur in the second half of that month, but Serre was held by the Germans until they abandoned the sector on 24 February, during the preliminary stages of their withdrawal to the Hindenburg Line.

The gallantry of the 32nd Division was eventually acknowledged by the award, after the Armistice, of a large number of decorations to the survivors of Frankfort Trench – an unusual step in that it was comparatively rare to confer decorations upon prisoners of war. To be fair, Gough warmly endorsed the recommendations, stating that the attack on 18 November had demanded considerable 'grit and courage' and that the feat of the Frankfort Trench garrison deserved recognition as a 'magnificent example of soldierly qualities'.[63] Indeed, the achievement of the front-line troops of the division in storming and holding Frankfort Trench, given all the disadvantages arising from poor planning and appalling conditions, demonstrated how good the raw material of the New Armies actually was in 1916. Responsibility for the sacrifice of the best part of two divisions for a limited objective lies elsewhere. Gough must bear the brunt of the overall blame for persisting with hurriedly planned and badly co-ordinated small-scale operations after the capture of Beaumont Hamel on 13 November. His performance at Bullecourt in April–May 1917 and at Langemarck during the Third Battle of Ypres in August that year suggests that he had learned little from the experience of the Ancre, either in terms of curbing his natural impetuosity or in the art of planning and conducting operations in bad conditions. Gough, a friend of Haig, survived the setbacks of 1916 and 1917 whereas, in addition to Rycroft, the GSO1 of the 32nd Division (Lieutenant-Colonel Wace) and two brigade commanders – Compton of 14th Brigade and Yatman of 96th Brigade – were removed in the week following the Ancre battle. If this clear-out of senior officers was, perhaps, a trifle unfair and drastic, there is no doubt that bad staff work contributed to the division's failure. As Austin Girdwood later wrote:

> I know what the same units could do when the Division was commanded by a man like 'Tiger' Shute who worked us hard but sensibly and who damned us all to heaps but whom we all adored all the same because he understood infantry ... He had Macnamara [*sic*] and Lumsden to back him up and that is why the Division did so brilliantly afterwards.[64]

The most senior commanders involved in the Munich and Frankfort Trench operations from mid-Novmber onwards should not escape their share of censure for the mistakes and failures which beset their successive assaults. As Andy Simpson has underlined, the desire to continue attacks after 13 November was not restricted to Haig and Gough.[65] Fanshawe, of V Corps, for instance, appears to have glimpsed the prospect of 'a serious break' on his front and therefore wished to attack.[66] He had submitted the scheme for his corps to seize Munich and Frankfort Trenches to Gough, who agreed to it. As Simpson relates, the failure of the 2nd and 51st Divisions on 15 November had been the subject of 'a detailed post-mortem' with the divisions concerned being asked to provide details of how they had carried out the plan.[67] G.M. Harper, the GOC 51st Division, attributed that failure partly to the men being caught in their own barrage, arguing that this was due to their own impetuosity and the fact that they were accustomed to a faster-paced creeping barrage than that employed on the day. There was also implied criticism of Fanshawe in his comment that 'the chances of success would have been greatly increased if the attack had been carried out by a formation under one command'.[68] Major-General W.G. Walker, of the 2nd Division, if more circumspect, stated that he had told Fanshawe that the only available troops were unfamiliar with the ground and that the previous attack by the attached 112th Brigade from the 37th Division 'had been very hurried and had failed and I was afraid if this was carried out in a hurry it would fail too'.[69] Having been informed by Fanshawe that there was 'no alternative', Walker had requested that the operations should be delayed to permit the brigade assigned to the task at least to see the ground in daylight. This proposal was turned down and, in a report to Fifth Army, Fanshawe made it clear that he did not accept all these points since the positions had been attacked before and should thus have been familiar.[70] Simpson suggests that, in the ongoing review of operations on or after 15 November, Harper and Walker 'were more prepared to stand up for themselves to Fanshawe than he was to Gough. Indeed, rather than blame his brigade commanders, Harper was prepared to blame corps'. The reverse was true of Fanshawe, who even tried to deflect Gough's wrath downwards. Rycroft, of the 32nd Division, seems to have been resigned to his likely fate at an early stage but Walker too was relieved of his command of the 2nd Division on 27 December 1916. It is easy to agree with Simpson's verdict that the whole episode 'reflected far less well on both Gough and Fanshawe than the other protagonists; the former for his poor reasoning and indifference to the views of the men on the spot, and the latter for his dishonest transfer of blame'.[71]

Gough undoubtedly exercised a more prescriptive and restrictive command style in the struggle for Frankfort Trench than he had at Thiepval in September. This may have had something to do with the fact that Jacob was a more reliable corps commander than Fanshawe and could more easily be left to get on with the task in hand. But Gough cannot avoid responsibility for urging the continuation of operations from 14 November onwards. Thus, although decentralisation of command to the 'man on the spot' had worked elsewhere in the Reserve (Fifth) Army – as at Thiepval – it was noticeably less effective, or even allowed, in November. The fight for Frankfort Trench reveals that, in late 1916, the BEF still had a fair way to go before such devolution of command was more evenly and more widely practised.

Chapter Six

'The Absolute Limit': British Divisions at Villers-Bretonneux, 1918

On 4 April 1918, Sir John Monash, then a major-general commanding the 3rd Australian Division, wrote:

> A new British Division came into the line on my right flank, South of the Somme last night, and was this morning biffed out, making a bad break in the line, and exposing my right flank ... Some of these Tommy Divisions are the absolute limit, and not worth the money it costs to put them into uniform. However, – I mustn't let myself go. You can doubtless read between the lines of all I have written in the recent past – bad troops, bad staffs, bad commanders.[1]

These words were written at the time of the first German attack at Villers-Bretonneux. On 26 April, shortly after the *second* German attack on the town, he commented:

> It was the same old story. My 9th Brigade had held securely, and kept the Bosch out of the town of Villers-Bretonneux for three weeks. They were then withdrawn for a rest on April 23rd, and the 8th British Division (regulars) took over the sector from them.
>   Naturally, on April 24th, the Bosch attacked ... and biffed the Tommies out of the town. Late at night we had to organise a counter-attack. This was undertaken by 13th and 15th Brigades in the early hours of Anzac Day. They advanced 3,000 yards, in the dark, without Artillery support, completely restored the position, and captured over 1,000 prisoners ... It was a fine performance.[2]

Both of these extracts, written during, or in the immediate aftermath of, the two battles of Villers-Bretonneux, are certainly less than complimentary to British troops and formations and they give no credit whatsoever to British units for their part in the defensive operations or counter-attacks which finally ensured the security of the town and, with it, the safety of Amiens. Even in his book *The Australian Victories in France*, published after the war, Monash is equally ungenerous and makes scarcely any references to the British units involved in the fighting for, and around, Villers-Bretonneux. The impression given by Monash is that the successful defence of the town was almost entirely due to Australian troops.

The evidence available in surviving letters, diaries and unpublished accounts indicates that a large proportion of the officers and men of the AIF shared Monash's view of the poor quality and performance of many British troops in the face of the German spring offensives in 1918. Major-General Sir J. Talbot Hobbs – himself British-born – commanded the 5th Australian Division, whose 15th Brigade played such a key part in the decisive counter-attack at Villers-Bretonneux on the night of 24–25 April 1918. Towards the end of that month he recorded: 'the conduct of some of the [British] troops through the ignorance neglect or I am almost tempted to say – but I won't, I'll say nervousness of their officers has had a very depressing effect on me and disgusted many of my officers and men'.[3]

Such sentiments were not confined to senior officers. Lieutenant Sydney Traill, of the 1st Battalion AIF, noted in his diary on 9 April: 'Every day come fresh rumours about the Tommies. It seems that whole divisions retreated for miles without putting up any show of fight. The cold-footed hounds, it is enough to make one weep'. Traill wrote in a similar vein on 25 April, after the German capture of Mount Kemmel, observing: 'The name of the Tommy stinks in a good many quarters now …' .[4] Lieutenant J.W. Axtens, of the 8th Australian Machine Gun Company – writing home to his parents in New South Wales on 2 May 1918 – pointed out that there was 'a lot of strong feeling among our chaps against the Tommies … There are some very scathing jokes against them; this is one. A Tommy brigadier is reported to have overtaken a hare on the road towards Amiens and said savagely "Get out of the road you brute and give a man a chance who can run" …'.[5] The prevalence of this type of comment was sufficient to persuade Sir William Birdwood, then still commanding the Australian Corps, to urge his senior officers on 30 April to do everything in their power to put a stop to 'disparaging comparisons' between British and Dominion troops. 'The Dominion soldier', he emphasised, 'has so established his merits that depreciation of his kith and kin is not necessary for the acknowledgement of the great work Dominion troops are doing. We are of the same blood, and the creation of friction by criticism is only playing the German's game'.[6]

A few pertinent points of my own need to be made at this juncture, I feel, for it is very far from being the intention of this chapter to underplay the role of the Australians in the defence of Amiens and the operations at Villers-Bretonneux and elsewhere in March and April 1918. Indeed, Australian officers and other ranks had every reason to be proud of *their* performance in April 1918 and there were at least *some* grounds for their criticisms of that of the British units alongside them. It also has to be said that, on the whole, the Australian official historian, C.E.W. Bean, is very fair in his description and assessments of the First and Second Battles of Villers-Bretooneux, apportioning credit to British units, and individual officers and men, where it is due and levelling criticisms against them where they are justified.[7] In turn, the Australian deeds at Villers-Bretonneux – particularly those of the 35th and 36th Battalions of the AIF on 4 April, and of the 13th and 15th Australian Brigades in the counter-attack of 24–25 April – are given reasonable prominence in the relevant accounts in the *British* official history.[8] However, Sir James Edmonds rarely, if ever, attempts to cover the exploits of individual junior officers, NCOs and men in the same way as Bean does, and much of the spirit and character of the defence and counter-attacks is thereby lost or obscured in Edmonds' drier and less vivid narrative. Moreover, whereas Bean devotes some 212 pages to the fighting in and around Villers-Bretonneux, Edmonds deals with it in only 34 pages. But neither Bean nor Edmonds would be classed as light reading, and, of the more recent popular accounts of 1918, only one or two – such as Gregory Blaxland's *Amiens 1918* and Peter Pedersen's *Villers-Bretonneux* – pay any real attention to the efforts of British units in these operations.[9] In these circumstances, it is hardly surprising that the story of Villers-Bretonneux does not loom large in the *British* national folk-memory. Outside of specialist miltary historians and members of the Western Front Association, one ventures to suggest that few British people would even have a clear idea as to where Villers-Bretonneux is located, let alone know what happened there.

My own observations and experiences would also suggest that this assessment would be much less true in the case of the *Australian* public. Today, visitors to Villers-Bretonneux, which lies some 10 miles east of Amiens, can see several potent symbols of Australia's connections with the town, not least the Australian National Memorial – unveiled by King George VI in 1938 – which stands on the crest of Hill 104 just to the north of the town and very close to the ground crossed by the 15th Australian Brigade during its night counter-attack on 24–25 April 1918. Villers-Bretonneux was adopted by Melbourne after the First World War and the local school, situated in a street called the *Rue Victoria*, was rebuilt in the 1920s with money collected by children from the schools of that state. Since the 1970s, the building has housed a museum with displays on the AIF and its operations, especially those in Picardy and the Somme region in 1918. The town is twinned with Robinvale, Victoria, and inside the *Mairie* is a room containing further material marking the links with Australia. In contrast, apart from graves in the area's war cemeteries and a memorial on the Cachy road to the first-ever tank versus tank action, it is very difficult to find any comparable physical reminders of the presence of British troops in and around the town in 1918.

How significant, then, was the contribution of British units to the defence of Villers-Bretonneux, and to what extent were Australian criticisms of the quality and performance of the British troops there actually justified?

The German March Offensive

It is still difficult to understand why the Germans did not make the key rail centre of Amiens a *primary* objective of their March offensive from the very outset. Approximately half of the BEF's supplies came in through its three main southern ports (Rouen, Le Havre and Dieppe) and had to pass through or skirt the rail hub at some stage, as did 80 per cent of the north–south traffic, including trains from the Lens coalfields for French munitions factories.[10] The loss of Amiens would therefore have seriously, perhaps fatally, impaired the Allied war effort and the BEF's logistics and operational capacity. In the plans for Operation *Michael*, the German March offensive, Amiens does not appear to have featured as a main objective, though General von Hutier predicted in his operation orders for the German Eighteenth Army on 14 March that the French would use its vital rail centre to bring up reserves. On 21 March, the opening day of the German offensive, von Below's Seventeenth Army and von der Marwitz's Second Army, of Crown Prince Rupprecht's Army Group, were to attack south of Arras, pinching off the Flesquières salient and advancing towards Bapaume and Péronne and across the old Somme battlefield before swinging north-west in a great left hook, enveloping Arras in the process. The object of the wheel to the north was to roll up the BEF and press it back against the sea. Von Hutier's Eighteenth Army, of Crown Prince Wilhelm's Army Group, was to advance beyond the Somme and the Crozat Canal to protect the left flank of the offensive, defeating any French reserves which might come up from the south to help the right flank of the British Fifth Army. Von Hutier might thus also sever the connection between the French and British armies.[11]

By 23 March, parts of the British Fifth Army had been driven back over 12 miles and the German Eighteenth Army was pushing on westwards to seize crossings over the Somme and Crozat Canal. At this point, Erich Ludendorff – who as First Quartermaster-General at German General Headquarters (OHL) was the de facto director of Germany's war effort – allowed the tactical opportunity presented by von Hutier's impressive progress to deflect him from the declared strategy, a tendency which bedevilled the German high command throughout the war. Ludendorff now issued new orders, directing the Seventeenth Army towards St Pol and Abbeville and the Second Army westwards to Amiens. The Eighteenth Army, originally given the flank protection role, was now to drive north-west, pushing back the French as well in a much more clearly defined attempt to separate the French and British armies. Instead of being concentrated for the gigantic left hook, the German armies would henceforth be advancing in divergent directions – to the north-west, the west and south-south-west – like a hand with the fingers spread wide.[12]

On 25 March, with the centre and left wing of the German Second Army, on either side of the Somme, beginning to lag behind, Ludendorff agreed with a suggestion from Crown Prince Wilhelm that, while the Second Army remained directed on Amiens, the weight of the Eighteenth Army should be transferred to its right wing so that, together with the Second Army, it might gain the old French line from the Avre valley to Caix (6 miles south-east of Villers-Bretonneux). The following day, with the French line being dangerously thrust back and the right of the German Eighteenth Army having advanced over 9 miles, Ludendorff continued to probe for the weakest spots. That evening, he ordered Second Army to make its principal effort south of the Somme and to press forward to the Avre with its left on Moreuil, a few miles south-east of Amiens, while its centre captured Amiens itself. The Eighteenth Army was also to maintain its drive from the line Noyon-Chaulnes south-west to the Avre, where it would secure crossings with a view to a further advance.[13] As a 9-mile gap opened between the French First and Third Armies, Montdidier was abandoned by the French on 27 March, forcing the French First Army, under General Debeney, to move its assembly area back to St Just, on the only remaining direct railway line from Paris to Amiens. The focus of attention temporarily switched back to the north with the launching of Operation *Mars*, an attack against Arras, on 28 March, but the failure of this operation with heavy losses effectively sealed the fate of the *Michael* offensive as a whole. The only direction which offered any prospect of success was where the front was still fluid – namely opposite the left wing of the German Second Army and opposite the Eighteenth Army. It was no longer a question of what was desirable but what was possible.[14]

The grandiose objectives of Operation *Michael* had plainly proved to be beyond the strength and capacity of the forces employed and the colossal sweep of the original plan had been reduced in a few days to the scope of a local operation to seize a railway centre. Yet, as Bean notes, Ludendorff, despite the advice of his subordinate commanders, was now simply too close to the prize of Amiens to resist an attempt to grasp it, even if it meant only that the railway centre was brought under artillery fire. To this end, the inner wings of the Second and Eighteenth Armies were to push on towards Amiens by the shortest routes. This involved an advance on both sides of the Avre in a north-westerly direction beyond Moreuil to throw the enemy back over the Noye, some 5 miles west of the Avre.[15] Even these more modest objectives were beyond the immediate powers of the exhausted Second and Eighteenth Armies and, although both armies carried out a series of small local attacks after 30 March, Ludendorff postponed further serious operations until 4 April, to allow time for rest and reorganisation. Above all he needed to bring up fresh supplies of ammunition along his over-stretched lines of communication over the old Somme battlefield, so that the next big attack would have adequate artillery preparation.

It should be borne in mind that the increasing resistance which the divisions of the British Third Army, stiffened by the 4th Australian Division and the New Zealand Division, were able to mount between Arras and the Somme – particularly after 26 March – was a not insignificant factor in causing the Germans to shift the weight and direction of the *Michael* offensive further to the left, or south-west. For example, Bean fully acknowledges the part played by the British 19th, 42nd and 62nd Divisions, with the New Zealanders, in blocking the German advance near Hébuterne in the Third Army area on 26 March. The British stragglers whom the Australians encountered in scenes of near-panic and confusion near Hébuterne that day – and who were roundly condemned by Australians in their letters home – appear mostly to have belonged to transport echelons, labour battalions and a divisional ammunition column. 'The panic nowhere extended to the front-line troops', Bean asserts.[16] Even on the extreme British right flank, astride the Oise, where the British III Corps had been temporarily placed under French command, the hard-pressed formations of the British Fifth Army remained capable of springing some unpleasant surprises on the Germans, a case in point being the counter-attack delivered by the 18th Division at Baboeuf on 25 March, when its 54th Brigade retook the village and captured ten machine-guns.[17]

Between the Oise and the Avre, however, the front of the French First and Third Armies on the British Fifth Army's right, was, for the moment, comparatively soft, encouraging the Germans to focus their attention on the Noyon–Montdidier–Moreuil sector. By 27 March, twelve French infantry divisions and three cavalry divisions had arrived, or were arriving, on the front held by Fayolle's Reserve Army Group, and another thirteen infantry divisions and a dismounted cavalry division were either on their way or had been warned to prepare to move to the threatened sector. Nevertheless, these units invariably arrived with limited supplies of small arms ammunition, little or no artillery and without their cookers and other transport, and they were often committed piecemeal to the battle. When the British were driven back, pivoting on Arras, the French – for a crucial few days – formed a line facing not east but *north*, between the original right of the British Fifth Army at La Fère and its subsequent positions as far back as Moreuil. Thus, as Edmonds puts it, 'instead of the British holding the base of a triangle, La Fère-Arras, they held one side, Moreuil-Arras, while the French occupied the other side, La Fère-Moreuil, with the Germans in the angle'.[18]

The brief, but alarming crisis of 24–25 March, when it seemed that the French and British armies might retire in different directions, led, on 26 March, to an inter-Allied conference at Doullens, at which General Foch was made responsible for the co-ordination of Allied operations on the Western Front.[19] At a time when the German offensive was beginning to lose momentum through fatigue, heavy casualties and supply problems, Foch unquestionably helped to boost Allied morale and inspire confidence, and he acted promptly to ensure the maintenance of the link between the French and British armies, giving priority to the protection of Amiens. Even so, there was little he could do, in practical terms, to influence the immediate tactical situation. The twenty-nine British divisions which had been in the line on 21 March were now, six days later, greatly weakened by battle losses, sickness and straggling and were very tired, having had precious little rest or sleep. On 27 March, nine divisions, including the 4th Australian and New Zealand Divisions, had arrived from GHQ Reserve or other armies to reinforce them, and the 3rd and 5th Australian Divisions were also on their way south from the Second Army area and about to reach the Somme–Ancre region. But there was not much else left in the British locker.[20] In fact, Foch was anxious to build up a strong reserve in the Amiens area for a future counterstroke and, with the French then under pressure in the Montdidier area, he could not yet fulfil his promise to relieve the British Fifth Army up to the Somme. All this meant, in essence, that the British Fifth Army would not only have to struggle on, existing at least partly on its own dwindling resources and reorganising itself where it stood, but would also, for some days to come, actually have to take over more of the front, from the Luce southwards to the line Mezières–Moreuil. Such developments clearly had a powerful bearing on the condition and performance of the British units at Villers-Bretonneux the following month.

To adhere to Foch's directive that there was to be no further withdrawal was easier said than done. All the same, on 27 March, when the French gave way at Montdidier, the troops of the British Fifth Army managed to cling to a line not far short of that which Foch, the previous day, had ordered them to hold. On 27 March the 8th Division, under Major-General W.C.G. Heneker, stood its ground in the morning at Rosières, about 9 miles south-east of Villers-Bretonneux. In the early afternoon, two of its battalions, which had been sent hurriedly northwards to restore the situation around Proyart – just north of the Roman road from St Quentin to Amiens – made a gallant counter-attack that drove the advancing Germans back 1,000 yards and temporarily halted the enemy's progress along the main Amiens road. And, as if these achievements were not enough for one day, three more of the 8th Division's infantry battalions, together with engineers and the personnel of three brigade headquarters, helped to re-establish the 50th (Northumbrian) Division's line and briefly recapture Vauvillers in another counter-attack.[21] Unfortunately, German successes to the north and south rendered the position of the British XIX Corps in this key sector virtually untenable.

A misinterpretation of orders by VII Corps in the sector south of Albert had resulted in much of the right wing of the British Third Army falling back towards the Somme at Sailly-le-Sec, about 6 miles further west than the left flank of the Fifth Army. Exploiting this situation, the Germans crossed the Somme at Cérisy and Chipilly and thrust south-westwards, occupying Lamotte and the adjoining village of Warfusée Abancourt on the main Roman road in the evening, placing them only some 3 miles east of Villers-Bretonneux and barely a dozen miles from Amiens itself. A counter-attack on Lamotte and Warfusée on 28 March by the 61st (2nd South Midland) Division, supported by the 1st Cavalry Division, made some initial progress but was stopped 200 yards short of the Germans. The 61st Division subsequently withdrew south-westwards beyond Marcelcave. On the left of the XIX Corps line, infantry of the 16th Division, with the assistance of the 1st Cavalry Division – and men of the improvised formation of British, Canadian and American engineers and railway troops known collectively as Carey's Force – repulsed a strong German attack on Hamel, to the north-east of Villers-Bretonneux. By the end of 28 March, having absorbed the rump of XVIII Corps, the British XIX Corps – under Lieutenant-General Sir Herbert Watts – was, to all intents and purposes, the sole surviving remnant of the Fifth Army still operational. Its frontline troops now only comprised the 39th, 61st and 66th Divisions, with the 20th Division in close support of the French on the right, and the 16th Division and 1st Cavalry Division to the left of Carey's Force on the other flank.[22]

One could argue, with some justice, that these actions by the divisions of the Fifth Army in the last days of March ought to be borne in mind in any discussion of the defence of Amiens, and – with the subsequent operations between the Avre and the Luce from 30 March to 2 April – they could be said to constitute the first of the four phases of that defence. Given the exhaustion of the infantry, their inadequate level of training in open warfare, and the heavy casualties they had suffered, the troops of Fifth Army had displayed remarkable powers of resistance in this period. As Edmonds comments, not only 'did they hold the enemy's advance with little loss of ground, but they also often counter-attacked with success'. Bean too praises the tenacity of the Fifth Army at the end of March: 'its unrelieved remnant was stubbornly holding an almost equally exhausted enemy … in maintaining the one condition vital to its side – a generally unbroken front – it was entirely successful; and … with reinforcements denied, its surviving wing still managed to keep the British right in touch with the arriving French'.[23]

For all that, Fifth Army was desperately weak by 28 March, when General Sir Hubert Gough was removed from command and replaced by General Sir Henry Rawlinson. Five days later, on 2 April, the Fifth Army was officially renamed the Fourth Army. On taking over from Gough on 28 March, Rawlinson telephoned Watts at his headquarters for a briefing on the situation facing XIX Corps. Watts replied breezily that 'they may well get us by lunch-time and you by tea-time'.[24] The prospects certainly did not appear to be rosy. Returns left by Gough put the total infantry strength of Fifth Army on 27 March at an estimated 21,650, of whom around 8,000 were still with the absent III Corps, and one should remember that this calculation had been made before the actions of 28 March diminished the strength still further. Of the individual divisions, the 8th, 30th and 50th were reckoned to have a fighting strength of perhaps 2,000 men each, while the 66th had only some 500. The divisions from Lieutenant-General Sir Ivor Maxse's XVIII Corps, which was then being absorbed by the XIX Corps, were all graded as 'unreliable', 'quite unreliable' or 'rather unreliable' and the 61st Division, with a strength of perhaps 1,500, was classed as 'all but tired out'. By 30 March some of these figures had been adjusted upwards, with the 50th Division now estimated to have a fighting strength of 3,000, the 8th Division 2,600, the 24th Division 1,800, the 66th Division 880 and the 39th Division 800 men. The position with regard to artillery was not quite so serious. Roughly half the 500 guns lost since 21 March had already been replaced and Gough bequeathed 783 to Rawlinson, including 225 medium and heavy pieces. In the words of Gregory Blaxland, these 'could provide a much greater density of fire on the reduced frontage than was available on March 21st'.[25] Even so, the overall situation was sufficiently gloomy for Rawlinson to write urgently to Foch on the evening of 28 March. Unless fresh troops were sent to him in the next two days, Rawlinson said that he doubted 'whether the remnants of the British XIX Corps which now hold the line to the east of Villers-Bretonneux can maintain their positions'. Expressing his anxiety for the security of Amiens and seeking to impress upon Foch the seriousness of the threat to it if the Germans renewed their attacks from the east before the desired reinforcements arrived, he also predicted that XIX Corps was no longer capable of executing a counter-offensive.[26]

In the event, Rawlinson's worst fears proved unfounded. Over the next three or four days more units *did* arrive to bolster the defences around Villers-Bretonneux, some of these formations having been requested by Gough before his departure. These included the 2nd and 3rd Cavalry Divisions, which had previously been operating with the French, much of the time in a mounted infantry role. Less emasculated than the standard infantry formations by the huge battles of attrition of earlier years, they contained a greater proportion of surviving Regulars who were expert with small arms and their Hotchkiss machine guns. The three divisions of Lieutenant-General Sir Richard Butler's III Corps had also been relieved by the French, with whom they had been operating on the Oise, and had been moved around to the Amiens sector. All three had been in the front line on 21 March – when the 14th (Light) Division had been faced by no less than *four* German divisions with another two in the enemy's second line and one in the third (a total of seven German divisons in all). Butler's divisions had each incurred heavy casualties in the week following the start of the German offensive, the 58th (London) Division having lost 832 killed, wounded and missing, the 18th Division 2,445 and the 14th Division 3,197.[27]

These divisions had had a few days' respite from battle – if not much actual *rest* – and had been partly filled up with new drafts, but they were still under-strength and particularly weak in officers and experienced NCOs. There had been no real opportunity to absorb or train the new arrivals properly, and the historian of the 18th Division recorded that its fresh recruits, 'most of them raw youths', had not yet had time to become imbued with 'the corporate spirit of the division'.[28] However, the 18th Division possessed some able senior officers, including its commander Richard Lee, a sapper of 'quick grip and decision' according to the divisional historian.[29] They also included H.W. Higginson, the commander of the 53rd Brigade, a gifted tactician who was soon to take over the 12th (Eastern) Division; and the doughty Brigadier-General E.A. Wood, an extraordinary officer and one of those individuals for whom the First World War was their crowning moment. Wood, who stalked the battlefields in 1918 with a cigar clenched between his teeth and using a lance as an alpenstock, captured over twenty Germans later in the year by pelting them with lumps of chalk and old boots. Bean describes him as an officer 'of stout build and of most stalwart disposition'.[30] During the Great War, Wood won four DSOs, was Mentioned in Despatches nine times, was wounded five times, gassed twice and buried once. Small wonder, then, that Robert Cude, a runner with Wood's 55th Brigade in 1918, wrote that he 'would not mind going through Hell itself' so long as Wood was in command.[31]

The 14th Division, however – which had been hard-hit on 21 March – had some problems in this regard. Its commander at the start of the German offensive, Major-General Sir Victor Couper, had been relieved on 22 March by Butler, who judged him to be 'not in a fit state to handle the situation for the time being'.[32] Couper was succeeded by Major-General W.H. 'Bob' Greenly from the 2nd Cavalry Division, but he too broke down under the pressure and was thought 'not fit to continue operations' by 28 March. Haig's diary says, more bluntly, that

Greenly 'went off his head with the strain'.[33] By early on 25 March Butler believed that the 14th Division should be pulled out of the fight. The division's performance in March was damned with faint praise by Butler in his subsequent report, and Couper's eventual successor, P.C.B. Skinner – previously the commander of its 41st Brigade – did not take over until 31 March. The 58th Division, the last to be released by the French, was on its way to XIX Corps, but only two of its battalions, the 6th and 7th Londons, would be close at hand on 4 April. Last, but by no means least, there was the 9th Australian Brigade, which had been detached from Monash's 3rd Australian Division and hurried to Villers-Bretonneux on the night of 29 March. Its commander, Charles Rosenthal, brought to the brigade, in Bean's words, 'a robustness and audacity intensely welcome to its members'.[34] The Australians had not been in a major action since Third Ypres and they were therefore fresher than the troops of III Corps. In addition, while the manpower crisis of early 1918 had forced the British to reduce the number of battalions in a brigade from four to three, the Australians still retained the old four-battalion organisation, and, although their divisions were also under-strength and the reservoir of trained reinforcements was running low, the rate at which their drafts arrived was nevertheless above that for British divisions.

During the period 30 March–2 April a series of actions took place to the south and south-east of Villers-Bretonneux, especially between the Avre and the Luce, as the Germans strove to seize features of local tactical advantage and to straighten the line preparatory to the next big assault. On 30 March, the Canadian Cavalry Brigade, of the 3rd Cavalry Division, fighting both mounted and on foot, distinguished itself by driving the Germans out of Moreuil Wood and recapturing it for a time.[35] The same day, on the other side of the Luce, the 33rd Battalion of the AIF, under Lieutenant-Colonel Leslie Morshead – preceded by the 12th Lancers from the 2nd Cavalry Division – counter-attacked from the east of Cachy in an attempt to retake Aubercourt. The Lancers, galloping forward in lines of squadrons, succeeded in forcing the Germans out of a feature henceforth known as Lancer Wood, but the 33rd Battalion AIF, supported by companies of the 34th Battalion, came under heavy machine-gun fire 200 yards beyond the wood and failed to reach the objectives, the Australians losing 200 killed and wounded in the process.[36] On the credit side, the very presence of the Australians and cavalry gave a lift to the spirits of the men of XIX Corps at a critical moment, and Morshead was quick to record his admiration for the 12th Lancers, writing that it was a privilege for him to work with such a fine regiment. 'All ranks', he noted, 'were eager to give every possible help to us ... One was able, too, to judge of the splendid work they are doing for the army at the present time, and they cannot be too highly praised'.[37] To the north, between the Roman road and the Somme, engineers and pioneers of the 16th Division, and the 5th Dragoon Guards from the 1st Cavalry Division, combined to eject the Germans from trenches they had entered in front of Hamel, beating off a second attack later that afternoon. Next day, the Germans made some headway between the Avre and the Luce, gaining possession of Moreuil Wood and Rifle Wood, though a counter-attack of the 8th Division's 25th Brigade – only some 200-strong – retook the copse at the north-west corner of Moreuil Wood at 4 p.m. On 1 April, around 1,000 men of the 4th, 5th and Canadian Cavalry Brigades, after an intense artillery bombardment and covered by a machine-gun barrage – advanced on foot in 3 waves to recapture Rifle Wood, along with over 100 prisoners and 13 machine-guns.[38] Finally, on the evening of 2 April, companies of the 11th Royal Fusiliers and 7th Bedfords of the 54th Brigade, 18th Division – backed up by the 7th Royal West Kents from the 53rd Brigade – made an attempt to take a German trench on the high ground north-west of Aubercourt. They were spotted by German observers as they were forming up and were subjected to severe artillery and machine-gun fire, the leading companies losing over 100 officers and men before the attack was called off.[39]

It is worth re-emphasising, then, that the operations between Moreuil and Hamel at the end of March and the beginning of April, and the performance of the British divisions – particularly the cavalry formations – in these actions, were of no little significance to the defence of Amiens and Villers-Bretonneux. The determined stands and counter-attacks made during this period all played a part in keeping the Germans at arm's length and in preventing an enemy breakthrough along the Roman road or from the south-east. They delayed the Germans sufficiently to allow time for further French reinforcements to arrive and take over, by 3 April, the sector from Moreuil to Hangard (inclusive); and they provided a bit of extra breathing space for Rawlinson and Watts to build up the defences at Villers-Bretonneux.

By the eve of First Villers-Bretonneux, the front line east of the town was held by the 18th Division on the right and the 14th Division on the left. Between them, from the Chaulnes–Amiens railway to the Roman road, was the 35th Battalion of the 9th Australian Brigade, now attached to the 18th Division. In support and reserve were the 6th Cavalry Brigade and the 33rd Battalion AIF. Behind them, in the so-called Gentelles Line, were the 24th Division, the 11th King's (Liverpool Regiment) – who were the Pioneers of the 14th Division – the two remaining battalions of the 9th Australian Brigade and the 7th and Canadian Cavalry Brigades. Further back still, near Amiens itself, was the 2nd Cavalry Division. Thus, if not in overwhelming strength, XIX Corps – as Edmonds comments – was at least 'disposed in considerable depth'.[40] The front was also covered by the field artillery of five divisions as well as five heavy artillery brigades. But the unfortunate 14th (Light) Division represented a potential weak spot in the defence. It had first re-entered the line to the south, near Hangard, on the night of 1–2 April. The next night it was relieved by the French and was then transferred northwards to the left flank where, on the night of 3–4 April, it relieved the 1st Cavalry Division between the Roman road and the Somme.[41] When considering its performance in the coming battle, it is therefore wise to remember that the 14th Division had been involved in reliefs on three successive nights and had not even seen, in daylight, the ground it was now expected to defend.

The First Battle of Villers-Bretonneux

The first major German assault on Villers-Bretonneux began at 6.30 a.m. on 4 April, after a heavy 75-minute artillery bombardment on the British–Australian front line, artillery positions and rear areas. If successful, the Germans intended to follow it up next day with a drive against Amiens itself. Twelve German divisions attacked on a 9-mile front against the French and five more on a 6-mile front against the British and Australians. On the front held by the Australian 35th Battalion and the 55th Brigade of the 18th Division – where the 7th Buffs and the left of the 7th Royal West Kents were in the line – the Germans made little or no progress for most of the morning. At least three German attacks, in which the enemy infantry came forward in dense masses, were stopped by intense artillery, machine-gun and rifle fire. Eventually an attack against the line of posts occupied by the 7th Buffs, on the immediate right of the Australians, caused the Buffs to waver and leave their trenches, but they returned to the line when provided with covering fire by the Lewis guns of the 35th Battalion. According to Bean, the Buffs retired again shortly afterwards, although the 7th Royal West Kents stood firm.[42]

It was on the left flank, to the north, that the main crisis occurred. The 41st Brigade of the weak 14th Division, immediately north of the Roman road, fell back hurriedly in some disorder and, after rallying for a while on a support position 500 yards behind the front line, then retired another 3,000 yards to a ridge west of Vaire Wood, reaching this point about 10 a.m. The neighbouring 42nd Brigade, under Brigadier-General G.N.B. Forster, stood its ground but – with its flank exposed by the retirement of the 41st Brigade – it too withdrew in some haste, abandoning Hamel. Forster himself remained in Hamel to the last, was captured about midday and was killed by a stray bullet shortly afterwards.[43]

As the 14th Division gave way, the Australian 35th Battalion found the Germans behind their left flank and carried out a fighting withdrawal to a support position roughly a mile east of Villers-Bretonneux, where it linked up again with the men of the 7th Buffs who had retired earlier. Meanwhile, Lieutenant-Colonel Henry Goddard of the 35th Battalion – who had been placed by Rosenthal in local command of the Australian reserves in Villers-Bretonneux – ordered up three companies of the 33rd Battalion to protect his own left north of the railway and the Roman road. XIX Corps sent forward the two remaining battalions of the 9th Australian Brigade (the 34th and 36th) which, at Rosenthal's urging, were kept concentrated for a possible counter-attack and placed in positions north-west and south of Villers-Bretonneux. General Lee, of the British 18th Division, commanding all the troops south of the Roman road, had summoned up the 6th Londons, from the 58th Division, giving them to Brigadier-General Wood of the 55th Brigade as a reserve. Wood, who was always at his best in the heat of battle, moved part of his own reserve battalion, the 7th Queen's, and a company of the 6th Londons to his left flank to support the Buffs and hold the line of the railway south of the town, warning the other two companies of the 7th Queen's to be ready to counter-attack in the event of further withdrawal.[44] In the critical sector north of the Roman road, the day was saved by the British artillery, sometimes firing over open sights and with the Germans only 1,500 yards away; by the efforts of the 58th Battalion of the 5th Australian Division, holding the Somme crossings at Vaux; and by the three regiments of the 6th Cavalry Brigade, which came up to plug gaps in the line and whose Hotchkiss guns helped to beat off the attacking Germans. By the early afternoon, therefore, a new line (of sorts) had been formed and the situation temporarily stabilised.

This, however, was not the end of the day's fighting. At around 4 o'clock in the afternoon, following an hour's hurricane bombardment, two German divisions made a new attack from the south-east towards Cachy and Villers-Bretonneux, striking the 18th Division's front hard. On the right, where the French were simultaneously driven out of Hangard cemetery, the 6th Northamptonshires, of the 54th Brigade, were forced back to the Cachy–Hangard road and the 8th East Surreys, of the 55th Brigade – now down to under 100 officers and men – likewise yielded ground. The 55th Brigade, hampered by the rain and mud which clogged many rifles and made them unserviceable, was pushed out of its positions and the Germans entered the northern part of Lancer Wood, threatening to outflank the 7th Royal West Kents, who were holding a line in front of its south-eastern corner. The West Kents therefore withdrew to the eastern edge of Hangard Wood to escape being surrounded. A swift counter-attack by the 8th Royal Berkshires of Higginson's 53rd Brigade brought the Germans to a temporary halt but the battalion commander, Lieutenant-Colonel R.E. Dewing, was killed and the Berkshires were reduced to less than sixty men as a result of this action. Thereafter, the 53rd and 54th Brigades were able to hang on to their new positions and resist further attacks. The 55th Brigade, however, was still in some confusion and as the Buffs and East Surreys continued to retire, they took the Australian 35th Battalion, and the right of the 33rd Battalion, with them. The Germans had now nearly reached the Demuin road, leading directly to Villers-Bretonneux from the south, and, but for a few Canadian motor machine-gun batteries and six armoured cars, the way into the town appeared to be open.[45]

At precisely this moment – the second truly critical point in the battle – Lieutenant-Colonel Goddard ordered the Australian 36th Battalion, under Lieutenant-Colonel John Milne (once a private in the British army), to counter-attack south of the railway. Launched at around 5.45 p.m., it was supported by the reserve company of the 35th Battalion on the left and 180 men of the 7th Queen's – rallied and led forward by Brigadier-General Wood himself – on the right, with the 6th Londons acting as a 'second wave'. Advancing with great dash in the face of intense small arms and machine-gun fire, the Australians and 7th Queen's, despite taking heavy casualties, caught the Germans off-balance and swept them back nearly a mile on the left and half a mile on the right. Within an hour or so, a line east of Villers-Bretonneux was once more securely held.[46] Even so, units of the 18th Division were called into action again on the evening of 5 April. At 7.20 p.m. that day, the 54th Brigade delivered a counter-attack in conjunction with the French, who had been thrown out of Hangard cemetery and wood in the late afternoon. The 6th Northants had to cross 1,500 yards of ground and were silhouetted against the light of a burning haystack, yet they got to within 50 yards of their objective – the sunken road running from Hangard to Hangard Wood – where they dug in. The French, on the right, pushed the Germans out of Hangard cemetery and regained the village.[47]

What then were the results of the first German attempt to seize Villers-Bretonneux and how well had the British units performed? The town had indeed been held, although Rawlinson's Fourth Army had been driven back along its whole front and up to 2 miles at some points. The French XXXVI Corps on the right had similarly been pushed back 2 miles beyond the Avre, to the west of Moreuil, and the Germans were in part of the Bois de Sénécat, from the edge of which the outskirts of Amiens could be seen. On the other hand, more French reinforcements were arriving in the sector and the German penetration at this part of the line was thin, if deep. Bean reasonably gives most credit to the 3rd Cavalry Division and the 9th Australian Brigade for averting the danger to Villers-Bretonneux along the most direct line of approach north and south of the Roman road. The 14th Division, even when all the mitigating circumstances have been taken into consideration, cannot be said to have performed well. Parties of the Australian 58th Battalion near Vaire, south of the Somme, had tried in vain to stop officers and men of the 14th Division from withdrawing and many had already dumped their rifles and equipment. 'Pompey' Elliott, of the 15th Australian Brigade, issued an order to the 58th Battalion 'to stop all stragglers and compel them to fight'. The Australians on this flank noted the difference in the spirit of the cavalry and Captain H.D.G. Ferres of the 58th Battalion later remarked that no men 'could have done more than these cavalry men did'. Even in the centre, where the 35th Battalion and elements of the British 55th Brigade had retired, one unnamed Australian officer – who is quoted at length by Bean – was struck by the contrast between the British and Australians. Every single Australian still carried a rifle, recorded the officer in his diary, and they were easier to rally. The British, by way of comparison, 'though only walking as if from a football match', were, in his opinion, 'quite spiritless'.[48]

This may all be justified comment, but it cannot be fairly applied to the British gunners, some of whom had kept their guns in action until the Germans were less than half a mile away. Neither would the 18th Division fully deserve such criticism. The division had suffered only slightly less than the 14th in the March Retreat, yet, with the possible exception of the 7th Buffs – who were unsteady and difficult to handle throughout much of the day – most of its battalions had fought hard. The 7th Queen's had played a useful part in the decisive counter-attack in the late afternoon and early evening, while the 8th Royal Berkshires and 6th Northants also had enough spirit and determination left to mount telling counter-attacks of their own during the later stages of the fighting. On the command side, Watts and Lee, at corps and divisional level, had, in the main, contributed effectively by feeding in reinforcements and moving reserve units at appropriate moments. But, in the final analysis, it was the brigade, the battalion and, often, the company commanders who conducted the battle. Officers such as Rosenthal, Goddard and

Milne among the Australians and, for the British, Wood, Higginson, Dewing and Lieutenant-Colonel C.B. Benson of the 6th Londons, all provided control or front-line leadership when and where it mattered most and certainly helped to compensate for the lack of experienced junior officers and NCOs, especially in the British units. It is interesting to note, in passing, that Goddard of the 35th Battalion AIF was born in England while Benson of the 6th Londons was born in Queensland.

An Unquiet Sector

The most important result of all from the defence of Villers-Bretonneux on 4 April was that it played a major part in persuading Ludendorff to call off Operation *Michael* and to transfer the main German effort to the *Georgette* offensive on the Lys, preparations for which were already in train. However, this did not mean that the front north and south of the Roman road at Villers-Bretonneux was altogether quiet. Rawlinson was now better off with regard to reserves but the tactical position still left much to be desired, since there were two big dents in the Allied line and the German artillery was now a mile closer to Amiens. South of the Luce, the alignment of the French formations ran back well behind that of the British Fourth Army, this being a constant source of anxiety to Haig and Rawlinson over the next two or three weeks, as it provided the Germans with a tempting route of attack from the south-east towards Cachy to outflank both the Fourth Army and Villers-Bretonneux. Immediately after First Villers-Bretonneux, tactical control of the Fourth Army's front at Villers-Bretonneux passed from XIX Corps to Butler's III Corps, though the front line itself was taken over entirely by Australian units – with the Australian Corps as a whole being transferred from the Third Army to the Fourth Army on 7 April. The 15th Australian Brigade, from the 5th Australian Division, occupied the new line between the Somme and Villers-Bretonneux; the 5th Australian Brigade, from the 2nd Australian Division, came in between Villers-Bretonneux and the French; and the 8th Australian Brigade – also from the 5th Australian Division – relieved the tired 24th Division as the reserve behind the southern sector of the Fourth Army's line.[49]

Rawlinson was somewhat reassured by the presence of the Australians and confided to his diary on 5 April that he thought that the Fourth Army would now 'be able to keep the Bosche out of Amiens'. But, whatever his inner thoughts, he continued to impress upon Haig and Foch his worries about the right flank. As he wrote to Haig on 15 April: 'I have discussed this question with the III Corps commander and his Divisional Commanders and they are all agreed that unless something is done by the French to restore the situation on the right it may become serious and the safety of Amiens compromised'. Haig duly wrote to Foch in much the same vein two days later.[50]

To be fair to Foch, he was clearly aware of the need for some action on the Avre–Luce sector, although what could be achieved in practice was quite another matter. Even before First Villers-Bretonneux, Foch, on 3 April, had issued a general directive for continued Franco-British operations 'with a view to freeing Amiens' by driving the Germans 'farther away' from the important rail centre. The forces available would only permit this to be attempted in two stages. Another directive from Foch, issued on 6 April, laid down that, in preliminary operations, the French would seek to drive the Germans from part of the west side of the Avre, while the Fourth Army cleared up the rather messy tactical situation around the ravine and woods to the north and north-east of Hangard, near its junction with the French First Army. Then, once these initial steps had been taken, a joint attack would be launched to reach a line stretching from Moreuil, through Demuin and Aubercourt, to Warfusée – i.e. approximately the position held on 28 March.[51] The combined attack was scheduled for 9 April but the French were not ready and it was postponed until 13 April. 'The French do not seem out to do v[ery] much fighting', Rawlinson noted on 8 April. He was also unhappy about Foch's decision to place reserve divisions immediately west of Amiens in the Fourth Army area: 'It is an infernal nuisance as it blocks all the roads and I feel sure they will be too far off there to be of much real value'. Nevertheless, Rawlinson grudgingly acknowledged that Foch was now 'Generalissimo' and had 'issued the order in writing so it has to be obeyed'.[52]

As part of the preliminary operations called for by Foch, the 19th and 20th Battalions of the 5th Australian Brigade provided a company each on 7 April to attack and capture Hangard Wood. The attack was made with considerable dash and bravery – Lieutenant P.V. Storkey of the 19th Battalion winning the VC for his gallantry during the action – but it did not succeed and cost the battalions concerned 151 officers and men. Butler attributed the failure to enfilade machine-gun fire from south of the Luce but Bean disputes this and certainly the relative weakness of the attacking force, the thin and ragged supporting artillery barrage, and the poor selection of the objective for the 19th Battalion – which, in the event, proved untenable – were the main reasons for the lack of success, and all were at least partly Butler's responsibility.[53]

The Germans too were not content to remain passive during this period. On the evening of 9 April they attacked Hangard, got into the village, and temporarily captured the cemetery to the east of it, until a French counter-attack, the same night, drove them out. At dawn on 12 April, a weighty bombardment heralded a fresh German attack, delivered in greater force than its predecessor. The 5th Australian Brigade's sector of the front, next to the French, was at this time held by the 34th and 36th Battalions (lent by the 9th Australian Brigade), with two of the 18th Division's battalions – the 7th Royal West Kents and 10th Essex – standing by in close support for a possible counter-attack. The German assault quickly penetrated into Hangard and the French managed to retain only the chateau. At 10.15 a.m. the Royal West Kents counter-attacked alongside the French. The latter failed to retake Hangard and some of the West Kents apparently wavered as they came under fire en route to the Australian front line, but the remainder went on and, with the French, reached and held on to the western edge of the copse above the village. At 6.30 in the evening, the Germans at last captured the chateau, only to be subjected, at 7.20 p.m., to yet another Franco-British counter-attack, in which the 10th Essex played a distinguished part. Advancing steadily in artillery formation through a German barrage, the 10th Essex lost about half their strength, but 'went straight through the German position, as did the French on their right'. Although the cemetery and the copse 200 yards to its north-east stayed in German hands, the much-disputed village of Hangard was recaptured with over 120 prisoners. 'It was desperate, it was costly, it was successful', observed the historians of the 10th Essex.[54] The bitter fighting around Hangard on 12 April caused the cancellation of the joint attack which III Corps and the French were to have launched the following day, but the struggle in this sector flared up again briefly on 15 April, when the 18th Battalion AIF, from the 5th Australian Brigade, attacked with the French in a minor operation to recapture the cemetery and its neighbouring copse. The Australians failed to secure the copse, losing 84 out of 180 officers and men who participated in the attack, though the French seized and held on to the cemetery.[55]

The fighting for, and around, Hangard – which may be said to have constituted the *third* of the four phases of the defence of Amiens and Villers-Bretonneux – unquestionably contributed to Rawlinson's unease about the security and alignment of his right flank and, as we have seen, impelled him to keep up the pressure on Foch, through Haig, to take appropriate action. At last, on 18 April, the French First Army, under General Marie-Eugène Debeney, launched an attack without British assistance, seeking to force the Germans back across the Avre. Edmonds does not waste the opportunity to comment tartly that this 'was the first offensive action taken by the French to relieve the British since the fighting began on the 21st March'. Debeney's operations were only partly successful, gaining just 500 yards on average, and no progress was made east of the Avre, yet, by clearing the enemy out of the Bois de Sénécat and the ridge north of it, the French deprived the Germans of their observation over the rear areas of the British III Corps. In this respect, therefore, the French attack was not totally without value to Rawlinson.[56]

While all this was happening on the southern flank, 'Pompey' Elliott's 15th Australian Brigade – though not, in the end, required to take part in the proposed Franco-British attack – had, under Elliott's dynamic and energetic leadership, made good use of its time in the sector between Villers-Bretonneux and the Somme. As Bean remarks, the brigade was then 'at the zenith of its form; a magnificent instrument, fit, like Cromwell's Ironsides, for the hardest military tasks', even if Elliott's frequently voiced contempt for the quality of British troops and his 'hot-headed tendency to use his brigade as if it were independent of the rest of the BEF' often caused trouble.[57] From 7 April, by means of aggressive patrolling and methodical reconnaissance, the Australians were able to advance at night in successive bounds of 500 yards or so, bringing the front line closer to Hamel. When the 15th Australian Brigade went into reserve and was replaced at the front by its sister brigade, the 14th, Elliott – with the approval of Hobbs – kept one battalion in the Bois l'Abbé, in part of the Aubigny line a mile behind the town, ordering it to be in constant readiness to counter-attack should Villers-Bretonneux fall. Elliott ensured that his staff and battalion commanders knew the ground, of which he ordered contour models to be made, and he also drew up contingency plans for the counter-attack operation. After inspecting the Australian Corps on 14 April, Rawlinson remarked on the contrast between them and Butler's troops. 'They are a splendid body of men', he noted, 'and Hobbs and Monash are both very good commanders. They are ready for any emergency, which is comforting; for Butler's III Corps, which has recently been reinforced, has little or no chance of training its drafts and is short of officers'.[58]

With Haig insistent that both sides of the Somme, to the north, should be held by one formation, the Australian Corps, the Villers-Bretonneux front was reorganised in mid-April. The Australian front now lay astride the Somme and, on its right, extended to the summit of Hill 104, the inter-corps boundary being about 1,300 yards north of the Roman road. The defence of the Villers-Bretonneux plateau and the town itself became the responsibility of Butler's III Corps and, in particular, the 8th Division, which had been transferred to III Corps to replace the shattered 14th (Light) Division and which took over this key sector between 19 and 21 April. As the evidence increased that another German thrust against Villers-Bretonneux was imminent, Rawlinson had some cause for concern about the current condition of III Corps. The 8th Division, for example, had lost some 250 officers and 4,693 other ranks – roughly half its infantry – during its splendid fighting withdrawal in March. The two battalions which had suffered the most were the 2nd Middlesex and the 2nd West Yorkshires, the latter having recently received drafts of no fewer than 11 officers and 700 other ranks and the 2nd Middlesex almost as many.[59] In addition, the division's own artillery was currently refitting and training elsewhere, which meant that, in the immediate future, the formation would have to work with the less familiar gunners of the 20th (Light) Division. There was, however, no shortage of quality among its senior officers. Brigadier-General Clifford Coffin, of the 25th Brigade, had won the VC at Third Ypres while Brigadier-General George Grogan, of the 23rd Brigade, was destined to win the same decoration on the Aisne in May 1918. W.C.G. Heneker, the long-serving divisional commander, was described by one of his former battalion commanders, James Jack, as 'a fine but exacting chief'. John Bourne says that his command style was that of an auditor, with nothing escaping his 'penetrating and unrelenting attention'. Hubert Essame recalled, many years later, that Heneker expected to be saluted by everyone within eye range: 'His eagle eye could detect an unshaven chin, the need for a hair cut, a grease stain or an unpolished button at a considerable distance. His comments were unequivocally clear, vividly expressed and long remembered'. Heneker's GSO1 from November 1916 to December 1917, Lieutenant-Colonel E.H.L. 'Moses' Beddington, admitted that his commander was 'a bit of a bully' but thought him to be a good tactician and 'a good man to serve so long as one stood up to him'.[60] The performance of the 8th Division in the final week of March 1918 should leave no room for doubt about Heneker's genuine capabilities as a divisional commander in battle.

The 18th Division faced similar problems in having to incorporate and train new drafts as quickly as it could. The 7th Royal West Kents at least received strong drafts of third-line Yeomanry and Kent Cyclists, who had undergone a fair amount of training in England and who brought the battalion's ration strength up to 700; the 8th Royal Berkshires contained 350 youngsters under the age of 19; and 60 per cent of the 7th Queen's were also boys under 19 who, until the week before, had never fired a round. On 23 April eight new officers joined the 10th Essex. Within three days all but one would be dead or wounded. Rawlinson was right to be worried by the need to rely upon those he subsequently described as 'children'.[61] It is true that the overall strategic situation, with the Germans preparing further operations in Flanders, left Haig and Rawlinson with a limited range of options. However, it is reasonable to ask whether they might have been wiser to leave the defence of Villers-Bretonneux in the hands of well-integrated and combat-hardened Australian formations rather than entrust it to the divisions of III Corps, which were weakened and embodied recent drafts of uncertain quality. Moreover, Richard Butler, who had previously spent three years on Haig's staff, latterly as Deputy Chief of Staff at GHQ, lacked experience as an operational corps commander. Not surprisingly, 'Pompey' Elliott, invariably a vociferous critic of British troops and generals, questioned Rawlinson's judgement in this regard and expressed his concerns forcefully to Hobbs.[62]

The reorganisation of the front was carried out in stages between 13 and 21 April. The 58th (London) Division – also barely rested and refitted after the March crisis – took over the southern sector from Monument Wood down through Hangard Wood to the junction with the French, holding the front line with all three battalions of the 173rd Brigade, and with the 2/10th Londons from the 174th Brigade attached for counter-attack purposes. In the course of the reorganisation, on 17 April and the following days, the Germans drenched Villers-Bretonneux, the Bois d'Aquenne to the south-west of the town, and the village of Cachy to the south, with mustard gas, phosgene and irritant gases, causing some 1,074 casualties, chiefly in the 58th Division and in Australian units. By the eve of the next German attack, the 8th Division completed its deployment, if only just. The 23rd Brigade, under Grogan, was on the right next to the 58th Division, and had the 2nd West Yorkshires and 2nd Middlesex in the front line, to cover Villers-Bretonneux, with the 2nd Devons, as counter-attack battalion, behind them and immediately to the south of the town. Coffin's 25th Brigade, had the 2nd Rifle Brigade in the front line to the left of the Middlesex and on the other side of the Roman road; the 2nd East Lancashires were placed in trenches around the town for close defence; and the 2nd Royal Berkshires, the counter-attack battalion, were located to the north of Villers-Bretonneux. The 24th Brigade was in divisional reserve, but two companies of the 1st Worcestershires were in the Cachy Switch, protecting the village of Cachy with a scratch formation known as Shepherd's Force – which included two companies of the 6th Northants and the 83rd Brigade, Royal Field Artillery, from the 18th Division.

A vaulable addition to the strength of Butler's forces was made with the arrival of a dozen or so Mark IV tanks, some of which were placed in front of the Bois l'Abbé to prevent the Germans from gaining a foothold in the Bois d'Aquenne, while the remainder were held in reserve to check, by immediate counter-attack, any German advance near Gentelles and Cachy. Seven light Whippet tanks were also available in a wood a mile south of Blangy. The German gas bombardment, however, seriously affected the crews of the three tanks near the Bois d'Aquenne, causing the forward tanks to be moved south of the Bois l'Abbé to reduce the danger of this happening again. A total of 7 field artillery brigades and 89 guns of the III Corps heavy artillery supported the 8th and 58th Divisions.[63]

Thanks to a lot of hard work since 5 April, there were now four rear defence lines in front of Amiens between the Avre and the Somme. The Gentelles-Bois l'Abbé–Aubigny line, or reserve line, behind Villers-Bretonneux had one switch running to the front line from Gentelles past Cachy to the Bois d'Aquenne and the south-east face of Villers-Bretonneux, and another switch, as right flank protection in their area, dug by the Australians. Approximately 1,500 yards behind the reserve line was the Bois line, in front of the Bois de Blangy and Bois de Gentelles. Then, 2,500 yards behind this was the Blangy-Tronville line and, finally, a further mile to the rear, the Glisy line. Edmonds points out that the III Corps defences had some depth even though the trenches were shallow and lacked dugouts and adequate wire protection. He emphasises too that, for want of troops, there was no large body of men available for *immediate* counter-attack.[64] Elliott and Hobbs, indeed, were disturbed to find that, on 20 April, when the 8th Division took over the southern part of Elliott's area, only one platoon of the incoming 22nd Durham Light Infantry (DLI), a Pioneer battalion, was assigned to relieve the battalion which he had kept for counter-attack. When protests were made to III Corps, the response was that Butler had sanctioned different arrangements for the weaker brigades of the 8th Division. More anxious than ever, Elliott maintained one of his battalions, the 59th, at the southern end of the Aubigny line in the Bois l'Abbé, ready to counter-attack should the Germans break through.[65]

The Second Battle of Villers-Bretonneux

The second big assault by the Germans on the Fourth Army's front at Villers-Bretonneux began in thick fog at 6 a.m. on 24 April, preceded by a bombardment – which included gas shells – lasting 2 hours and 15 minutes and covering the Allied front positions and rear areas between the Bois de Sénécat and the Somme. The attack had two principal objects: one was to straighten out and blunt the German salient facing Amiens and south of the Luce by capturing Villers-Bretonneux and the plateau on which it stood; the other was to divert Allied attention from German operations in Flanders, where a final attempt was to be made to seize Kemmel. It was hoped that, at least, the attack at Villers-Bretonneux would bring the German artillery within even closer range of Amiens, and if Villers-Bretonneux, the main objective, was taken, the success was to be exploited. Four divisions – the 228th, 4th Guard, 77th Reserve and 208th, and the left flank of a fifth, the 243rd Division – were to attack the front held by the British 8th and 58th Divisions while the Guard Ersatz Division struck Hangard and demonstrated on the front of the

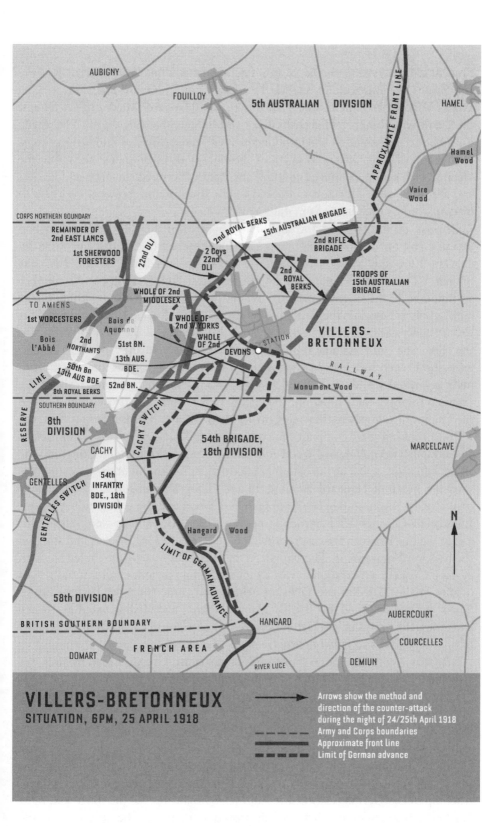

AUBIGNY

FOUILLOY

5th AUSTRALIAN DIVISION

HAMEL

Hamel Wood

Vaire Wood

APPROXIMATE FRONT LINE

CORPS NORTHERN BOUNDARY

REMAINDER OF 2nd EAST LANCS

1st SHERWOOD FORESTERS

22nd DLI

2nd ROYAL BERKS

15th AUSTRALIAN BRIGADE

2nd RIFLE BRIGADE

2 Coys 22nd DLI

2nd ROYAL BERKS

TROOPS OF 15th AUSTRALIAN BRIGADE

WHOLE OF 2nd MIDDLESEX

TO AMIENS

1st WORCESTERS

Bois de Aquenne

WHOLE OF 2nd W. YORKS

VILLERS-BRETONNEUX

Bois L'Abbé

2nd NORTHANTS

51st BN.

WHOLE OF 2nd DEVONS

STATION

13th AUS. BDE.

RAILWAY

50th Bn 13th AUS BDE

52nd BN.

Monument Wood

8th ROYAL BERKS

SOUTHERN BOUNDARY

8th DIVISION

CACHY SWITCH

54th BRIGADE, 18th DIVISION

MARCELCAVE

RESERVE LINE

CACHY

GENTELLES

GENTELLES SWITCH

54th INFANTRY BDE., 18th DIVISION

Hangard Wood

N

58th DIVISION

LIMIT OF GERMAN ADVANCE

BRITISH SOUTHERN BOUNDARY

HANGARD

AUBERCOURT

COURCELLES

FRENCH AREA

DOMART

RIVER LUCE

DEMIUN

VILLERS-BRETONNEUX
SITUATION, 6PM, 25 APRIL 1918

Arrows show the method and direction of the counter-attack during the night of 24/25th April 1918

Army and Corps boundaries

Approximate front line

Limit of German advance

French 131st Division to the south. The German 19th, 9th Bavarian Reserve and *Jäger* Divisions were in reserve. The 228th and 4th Guard Divisions were to assault Villers-Bretonneux, the 77th was to take Hangard Wood and Cachy and the 208th would secure Hangard village and its neighbouring copse. The attack would be accompanied by thirteen German A7V tanks, divided into three groups. One group of three advanced north of the railway directly against the town; the second, with six tanks, moved south of the railway between the town and Cachy; and the third, with four tanks, attacked Cachy itself. Flamethrowers were also to be employed by the Germans in the assault.[66]

Because of the fog and the din of the bombardment, the leading German infantry and tanks crossed no-man's-land and reached the British line virtually unseen. Edmonds states that wherever tanks appeared the British line was broken.[67] The young soldiers had no effective anti-tank weapons, and a number surrendered to the German infantry. When the Germans attacked without direct tank support, however, the British generally succeeded in beating them off. This was certainly the case in the sector of the 173rd Brigade of the 58th Division. On the right, the 3rd Londons repulsed all attacks and held their position all day, until the French lost Hangard yet again in the evening, forcing the battalion to make a limited withdrawal. The left battalion, the 2/4th Londons, resisted the German infantry for a time, but the enemy tanks eventually drove them back to the Cachy Switch, where they reorganised about 10 a.m. The centre battalion, the 2/2nd Londons, were compelled to conform to this movement and to fall back to a position between Hangard Wood and Cachy. The 2/10th Londons, the counter-attack battalion, tried, at the battalion commander's own initiative, to restore the situation north of Hangard Wood at 10 a.m. They were checked, short of their objective, by machine-gun fire from Hangard Wood and the commanding officer, Lieutenant-Colonel W.F.J. Symonds, became a casualty, but they were able to fill a gap in the line between the centre and left battalions of 173rd Brigade and stopped the backward movement. The Fourth Army War Diary partly attributed the lack of deep German penetration in this sector to the inexperience and generally poor quality of the 77th Reserve Division, which had come from the Eastern Front. Their progress slowed by British machine-guns, and disheartened by heavy casualties, the troops of the 77th Reserve Division came to a halt 2,000 yards short of their objective and failed to take Cachy as planned.[68]

The story was different on the 8th Division's front. Grogan's 23rd Brigade was attacked by two groups of tanks, with infantry and flame projectors, and the front line was rapidly overrun. The three forward companies of the 2nd West Yorkshires, raked in enfilade by the machine guns of the tanks as they crossed the British trenches, were completely overwhelmed. The battalion, down to 140 men and with only its support company left in action, was driven back, first to the railway west of Villers-Bretonneux and ultimately to the reserve line in the Bois l'Abbé. The two southernmost companies of the 2nd Middlesex were also swiftly overcome, whereupon the Germans worked round the right and rear of the third, and most northerly, front-line company and destroyed it in turn. The survivors of the

1. A platoon of the 7th Bedfords (18th Division) marching through a French villlage shortly before the start of the Somme offensive, 1916.

2. Troops of the Tyneside Irish Brigade (34th Division) advance from the Tara–Usna line to attack La Boisselle, 1 July 1916.

3. A British 18-pounder field gun in action in the Carnoy valley, near Montauban, 30 July 1916.

4. Men of the Border Regiment in 'funk holes' near Thiepval, August 1916.

5. British support troops moving up under fire to attack Ginchy, 9 September 1916.

6. View from close to the Albert–Bapaume road near La Boisselle, looking along a captured German trench towards Ovillers, September 1916.

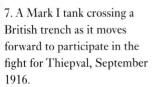

7. A Mark I tank crossing a British trench as it moves forward to participate in the fight for Thiepval, September 1916.

8. Portrait drawing by Francis Dodd of Lieutenant-General Sir Ivor Maxse in 1917.

9. Lieutenant-Colonel (later Brigadier-General) Frank Maxwell VC.

10. The axis of the 18th Division's advance towards Thiepval on 26 September 1916. The track in the centre marks the boundary between the 53rd and 54th Brigades.

11. A congested road at Fricourt in October 1916.

12. A working party in the rain near St Pierre Divion, November 1916.

13. Brigadier-General T.W. Glasgow (left), GOC 13th Australian Brigade, with his staff at Blangy-Tronville, 25 April 1918.

14. Villers-Bretonneux, as seen from the German lines in 1918.

15. Brigadier-General H.E. 'Pompey' Elliott, GOC 15th Australian Brigade, in 1918.

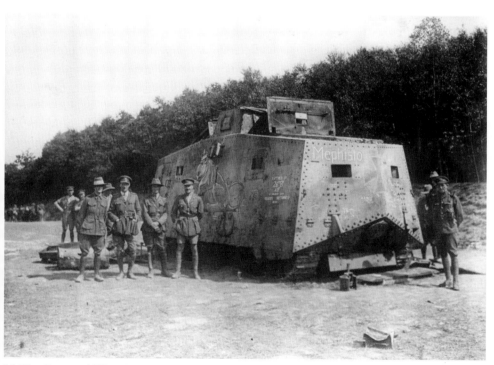

16. The German A7V tank 'Mephisto' after its capture in Monument Wood, near Villers-Bretonneux, by the 26th Battalion AIF in July 1918.

17. Brigadier-General A.J. McCulloch, the commander of the 64th Brigade (21st Division) in August 1918.

18. Major-General H.W. Higginson, GOC 12th (Eastern) Division from April 1918 to March 1919.

19. Lieutenant-Colonel W.R.A. 'Bob' Dawson, who commanded the 6th Royal West Kents in the Hundred Days.

20. Mark V tanks moving up near Bellicourt on 29 September 1918 for the assault on the Hindenburg Line.

2nd Middlesex similarly withdrew along the railway in stages until they reached the reserve line. Grogan's counter-attack battalion, the 2nd Devons, waiting south of Villers-Bretonneux, had its two left companies driven in by tanks and powerful German infantry support, which opened the way for the 4th Guard Division to enter the Bois d'Aquenne. The two right companies, with two more from the 1st Worcesters, did succeed, on the other hand, in clinging to their positions in the Cachy Switch, even though the Germans in the Bois d'Aquenne were behind their left flank.[69]

In Coffin's 25th Brigade, the 2nd Rifle Brigade, who were *not* attacked in front by tanks, stood their ground for a time, but the tanks which had overrun the 2nd Middlesex turned north and struck the Rifle Brigade's two right-hand companies from the rear. The left company maintained its position with accurate fire for much of the day and helped to form a defensive flank with the 2nd Royal Berkshires – the counter-attack battalion – who swung back to face south-east in order to oppose any German attempt to advance northwards from the town. The 2nd East Lancashires, defending the town itself, had been prevented by gas from keeping men actually in Villers-Bretonneux and occupied only its eastern outskirts. They too were outflanked from the south and retired to the north-west of the town where, with the assistance of some Australian troops, they were able to stop the enemy from debouching from Villers-Bretonneux in that direction. In this they received the invaluable support of artillery of the 20th Division, firing at the Germans over open sights. To the south, as the 8th Division's infantry retired, similar deeds were performed by 'B' Battery of the 83rd Brigade RFA, part of the 18th Division. One 18-pounder, under Second-Lieutenant A.I. Butler, sited first behind the railway embankment near the Bois l'Abbé and later moved up onto the embankment, engaged and hit a German tank. Butler's gun fired continuously for 7 hours and expended 1,100 rounds before it was pulled back to safety.[70]

Heneker knew by 7.20 a.m. that the Germans were using tanks and Lieutenant-General Butler, at III Corps headquarters, had been informed by 8 a.m. Acordingly, Butler placed the available seven Whippet tanks at the disposal of Major-General A.B.E. Cator's 58th Division to operate in front of the Cachy Switch. Cator was also told to employ his reserve brigade, the 174th, to restore the situation, their place in the reserve line being taken by the 54th Brigade of the 18th Division. The 8th Division had ordered forward three Mark IV tanks of the 1st Battalion, Tank Corps, from the Bois l'Abbé–Bois d'Aquenne area and assigned them to Grogan of 23rd Brigade. He, in turn, ordered them to help in the defence of the Cachy Switch, where they arrived about 9.30 a.m.[71]

As a result of these moves by Butler, Heneker and Grogan, the first two British counter-attacks of any real significance were, in fact, delivered by tanks. Shortly after 9.30 a.m., in front of the Cachy Switch, the three Mark IVs of Captain J.C. Brown's No.1 Section of 'A' Company, 1st Battalion, Tank Corps, engaged three German tanks in the first ever tank-versus-tank action. Two of the British tanks were 'Females', armed only with machine-guns, and were soon disabled, but the third – a 'Male' tank armed with 6-pounder guns and commanded by Lieutenant

F. Mitchell, hit the leading German tank three times in succession, causing its crew to abandon it and driving the accompanying infantry back. Mitchell's own tank was hit by artillery fire but not before he had also forced the other two German tanks to withdraw. Next, about noon, the Whippets of the 3rd Battalion, Tank Corps, under Captain T.R. Price – who, by another curious coincidence, had once served with the 6th Northamptonshires in the 18th Division – swept into action past the north of Cachy and on across the plateau to the spur leading southwards in the direction of Hangard Wood. Driving through a a line of Germans in shell holes, they surprised two or three German battalions on the reverse slope, scattering them in all directions and running over and crushing many who were trying to escape. One of Price's Whippets received a direct hit, killing its crew, and 3 other Whippets were disabled on the return journey but the detachment lost only 5 officers and men and had inflicted an estimated 400 casualties on the luckless 77th Reserve Division, whose second-phase attack towards Cachy was thereby halted.[72]

Two more tanks – a 'Male' and a 'Female' – had been handed over to Heneker at his request at 8.40 a.m. and, during the latter part of the morning, these were used to support the 1st Sherwood Foresters, the reserve battalion of the 24th Brigade, in an attempt to clear the Bois d'Aquenne of Germans and, if possible, capture the line of road running north-south through the town. The battalion, advancing in artillery formation, reached the southern edge of the wood at about 12.30 p.m. and turned northwards, driving the Germans towards its eastern edge. The battalion commander, Lieutenant-Colonel R.F. Moore, was, however, badly wounded at this critical juncture and, deprived of his leadership, the troops were unable to press home their attack, digging in on the road running north-east between the Bois l'Abbé and the Bois d'Aquenne. Here they were shelled and suffered heavy losses, but they blocked any further German progress – this road, some 8 miles from Amiens, being the closest point to the city reached by the Germans in 1918. Although the 'Male' tank was hit by a German field gun, the 'Female' pressed on to the north-western outskirts of the town where, at about 4 p.m., it helped to clear a number of enemy machine guns and encouraged remaining elements of the 2nd East Lancashires, the 2nd Royal Berkshires and patrols of the Australian 59th Battalion to join in a spontaneous attack which advanced approximately 150 yards to a small outlying copse. Bean observes that this minor action was the only counter-attack carried out with success by the 8th Division during the daylight hours of 24 April.[73] The truth is that the 8th Division, by late morning, could no longer seriously be classed as a cohesive fighting force and, as a consequence of the break in the centre of the line, the Germans had occupied a pocket 4 miles wide and 1 mile deep and had taken the town.

It must also be stressed that, even when all their difficulties are taken into account, Butler and Heneker failed, during the morning, to exercise any immediate grip on the situation, and the few minor counter-attacks that had taken place were piecemeal and largely unco-ordinated, thereby merely adding to the frustration of Australian commanders such as Elliott and Hobbs. Butler's subsequent claims that the situation was not sufficiently clear, until well on in the day, to warrant the launching of a counter-stroke, and that Heneker was 'very rightly of [the] opinion that partial attacks would not meet with success' are undermined by the fact that both he and Heneker permitted just such partial attacks during the morning. Indeed, in this respect, Butler's report, submitted in August 1918, contains more than a hint of retrospective self-justification.[74]

The story of how the plan for a major counter-attack *did* evolve as the day progressed is both illuminating and complex, throwing some interesting light upon the command and control problems faced by the Fourth Army and its subordinate formations during the crisis of 24 April. It is instructive to see how, and by whom, these various command problems were tackled and, in most cases, solved. Alerted by the German bombardment and some time *before* the actual German tank-infantry assault, 'Pompey' Elliott, as early as 4.10 a.m., had ordered the battalions of the 15th Australian Brigade to stand to arms. Within the hour, at 4.50 a.m., Elliott was issuing provisional orders for a counter-attack by battalions of his brigade. The 59th Battalion was to assault up the high ground on which Villers-Bretonneux was located and the 60th Battalion was to advance along the western spur of Hill 104 adjacent to it. On reaching the Hamelet road, these units were to turn south-eastwards. The 60th Battalion would then push on to the Hamel road while the 59th Battalion, once at the Roman road, would swing south-west to face the town. The 57th Battalion was to be prepared to move along the railway on the *south* side of Villers-Bretonneux in an attempt to cut off the Germans. Like Elliott, Brigadier-General T.W. Glasgow, of the 13th Australian Brigade, then in Fourth Army reserve, had also anticipated the turn of events and had similarly warned his own battalions to be ready to move.[75]

Shortly after 8.30 a.m., on receiving reports that Villers-Bretonneux had fallen and that the Germans were attacking north from it, Elliott asked Hobbs, his divisional commander, whether he could now launch a counter-attack at his own discretion. He was told by Hobbs that he was only to act within his allotted area unless he received an 'urgent request' to assist the British on his right. If such a request was received, he could then use his discretion, keeping Hobbs informed of his actions. A little before 9 o'clock, Hobbs, who was also increasingly concerned about the 8th Division's plight, contacted Heneker to enquire if he was going to counter-attack and to offer the services of Elliott's 15th Brigade. Heneker's reply, according to some sources, was off-hand and non-commital.

As the battalions of the 15th Brigade moved off to their start line, their headstrong commander, disgusted and alarmed by reports of unnecessary withdrawals by British soldiers, ordered that 'All British troops [were] to be rallied and reformed, as our troops march through them, by selected officers and on any hesitation to be shot' (Hobbs later curtly instructed Elliott to delete the offending sentence). By this time Hobbs was as annoyed as Elliott by the lack of communication from Heneker. He complained to Lieutenant-General Birdwood, the Australian Corps commander, that he could not obtain any information from 8th Division and did not know if that formation intended to counter-attack. Heneker had, in fact, referred the question, and the offer of the 15th Australian Brigade, to Butler and, by 10 a.m., Hobbs and, in turn, Elliott were duly told that the British were 'endeavouring to restore the line themselves'. The battalions of the 15th Australian Brigade were to stand fast 'pending further orders' but to be 'ready for instant action'.[76]

Knowing the ground and convinced that their troops would ultimately be required to participate in a counter-attack, Hobbs and Elliott, who were now straining at the leash, fumed at the delays and apparent inactivity of III Corps and the 8th Division. However, on learning, at 9.30 a.m., of the fall of Villers-Bretonneux, Rawlinson, from the first, insisted that the town should be retaken as quickly as possible, before the Germans were given time to consolidate, regarding this as 'imperative for the security of Amiens'. One of his earliest steps to this end was to order Glasgow's 13th Australian Brigade to march south to the battle area to assist in the recapture of Villers-Bretonneux. Glasgow's brigade, part of the 4th Australian Division, was to be placed at the disposal of III Corps for the purpose. Heneker was told by Butler at 10.50 a.m. that, on arrival, the 13th Australian Brigade would come under the orders of the 8th Division. The brigade began its 8-mile approach march at 11.15 a.m. It was intended that three of Glasgow's battalions would take part in a projected attack to retake the town while the fourth (the 49th Battalion) was to be used to strengthen the reserve line.[77]

At 10.50 a.m., now under pressure from Rawlinson, Butler ordered Heneker to involve the 15th Australian Brigade in the 8th Division's counter-attacks and, soon afterwards, directed Hobbs to keep in touch with Heneker and 'to act as far as possible in close co-operation' with him, though Butler then confused matters by reporting that Heneker 'considered he would be able to clear up the situation with his own troops'. While these exchanges were taking place, Heneker, at 11 a.m., had ordered his own 25th Brigade to prepare for an attack from the north in which the 2nd Royal Berkshires and two companies of the 2nd Rifle Brigade were to recapture the northern part of the town. Having consulted his battalion commanders, Brigadier-General Coffin responded that the 25th Brigade currently had neither the strength nor the organisation for such an operation and that, with the Germans occupying the northern edge of the town and enjoying a perfect field of fire from the plateau, any advance in daylight without proper artillery preparation would be suicidal and likely to result in heavy losses for little or no gain. The proposed attack was therefore cancelled but Coffin's advice appears to have had an influence, either directly or indirectly, on subsequent plans. At 11.30 a.m. – some time before the attack by the 1st Sherwood Foresters was delivered – Rawlinson proposed that Villers-Bretonneux should be retaken by means of a double counter-stroke, north and south of the town. Through Butler, Heneker, who would command the operation, was instructed to contact Hobbs and to arrange for the 5th Australian Division to join in a combined attack, starting at 2 p.m. Hobbs once again offered the 15th Australian Brigade, then still in reserve at Aubigny, or two reserve battalions of the 14th Brigade, which were even nearer.[78]

The evidence presented by Bean indicates that it may have been Heneker's GSO1, Lieutenant-Colonel C.C. Armitage, who proposed that the counter-attack should be made by two brigades, ignoring the town itself but passing to the north and south and meeting to the east of it. However, as Bean points out, probably the same idea – 'a common and fairly obvious one for attacks on villages and small towns' – had suggested itself to most of the commanders and staffs concerned, and 'Pompey' Elliott, for some time, had not only been advocating a not dissimilar plan but also aching to carry it out. A further refinement was added by Heneker, who, following the advice he had received earlier from Coffin, considered that a daylight attack across the open plateau would be doomed to failure. As the moon would be full, Heneker felt that the attempt might be made more successfully that night and urged Butler to postpone the operation for a few hours. The overall idea for a two-brigade advance on either side of the town at night – having been submitted to III Corps – was approved by both Butler and Rawlinson. The latter, indeed, spent some time on the telephone to Butler, explaining how he wished the plan to be executed and sent Lieutenant-Colonel Beddington, now a member of his staff, to Heneker's headquarters to ensure that his instructions were not misinterpreted.[79]

The French did not offer a great deal of help at this point. General Debeney was informed of the plan and promised to co-operate if the attack were postponed until 25 April. This, of course, did not suit Rawlinson, who continued to demand that the operation should take place before the Germans had settled down. Debeney's only immediate measure, however, was to order the Moroccan Division forward to a position behind the British right, where it occupied part of their reserve line near Gentelles and so freed some of the 58th Division's own reserves. Even so, Debeney told Butler during the morning that the Moroccan Division must not, under any circumstances, be used piecemeal to counter-attack or to reinforce the front, and would only be employed, in a counter-attack, as a complete formation. When Haig visited Rawlinson's headquarters at 12.30 p.m., on his way to lunch with Butler at Dury, he was briefed on the situation with regard to the French and directed that a telephone message be sent to Lieutenant-General Sir John Du Cane, his senior representative on Foch's staff, asking for the Moroccan Division to join in the counter-attack rather than remaining in reserve. It was thus with some irritation that, in mid-afternoon, Haig received a written message from Foch – delivered by Du Cane – which stated patronisingly that the importance of recapturing Villers-Bretonneux would not have escaped Rawlinson and pressed the British to launch a powerful counter-attack like the one Debeney had mounted that morning. Haig lost no time in making it clear to Foch that Debeney had not attacked at all and, at 6.30 in the evening, he asked Foch to direct the Moroccan Division, or another French division, 'to co-operate energetically and without delay' with III Corps to retake Villers-Bretonneux. But, by this time, most of the key decisions concerning the counter-attack had been made and it was too late for the French to play a meaningful role in it, though Foch *did* order Debeney to co-operate more actively on 25 April and to see what could subsequently be done to relieve the units of III Corps. Rawlinson was highly critical of Debeney's conduct during the crisis. 'I have found Debeney v[ery] difficult', Rawlinson complained in his diary on

24 April, accusing the French First Army commander of having 'misrepresented his ability to use the Moroccan Div. to Foch saying he was ready to attack with it'.[80]

While all this was going on, Hobbs and Elliott were becoming more and more puzzled and disturbed by the ongoing delays in launching the counter-attack. However, at around 3 o'clock on the afternoon of 24 April, Hobbs was at last informed that the 5th Australian Division had been placed under III Corps for the forthcoming operation, meaning that Butler could now call upon both the 13th and 15th Australian Brigades for the counter-attack. In a telephone call 10 minutes later, Hobbs suggested to Butler that Elliott's brigade should strike with three battalions past the northern side of Villers-Bretonneux and in a south–easterly direction. He then rang Heneker at 3.30 p.m., when he was told that the 8th Division's part in the attack would, in fact, be carried out by the 13th Australian Brigade, which was to make its thrust to the south of the town so that the two main attacking formations would meet on the farther side. On learning of these developments from Hobbs, Elliott expressed his pleasure that the 13th Brigade would be on his right and stated that he was willing to attack by moonlight, preferably without previous artillery preparation.[81]

Glasgow had initially reported in person to Heneker's headquarters at Glisy at 1 p.m. The commander of the 13th Australian Brigade has been portrayed as tough and tactiturn. Bean, who obviously admired him, describes Glasgow as an 'Australian counterpart of the best type of English country gentleman … but rugged as the Queensland hills' and writes glowingly of his 'good sense, force of will, and honesty of purpose', Glasgow was evidently as forceful and resolute as Elliott, if less volatile. When he met Heneker early in the afternoon, the latter was unable to give him all the information he needed, simply explaining that the picture was 'changing from moment to moment'. As he had not seen the ground over which his troops were to counter-attack, Glasgow therefore wisely insisted that he should go forward to assess the situation for himself before the plans were finalised, a proposal which Heneker accepted. There can be little doubt that the delays which so vexed Elliott and Hobbs were partly caused in the afternoon by Glasgow's request to conduct a personal reconnaissance and, in any case, once the decision had been made to attack in the evening, Heneker was more justified than he had been that morning in deferring further action until satisfactory arrangements had been made. Though under pressure from Rawlinson and Butler and all too aware of the tricky task ahead, Heneker must have been reassured by the availability of the Australian brigades. In this respect, Ross McMullin's depiction of an increasingly jittery Heneker during the afternoon of 24 April does not quite ring true and 'rattled' and 'quailing' are not terms which are usually associated with the 8th Division's commander.[82]

Upon his return to Heneker's headquarters at 2.30 p.m., Glasgow made two or three important contributions to the counter-attack plan. One of these was to persuade Heneker to drop Butler's scheme to launch the southern arm of the attack from Cachy and to accept instead that it should start from a north–south line between the Bois d'Aquenne and Cachy. By doing this the 13th Brigade would avoid attacking across the enemy's front and would thereby have more protection on its right. 'Tell us what you want us to do, Sir', said Glasgow to Heneker, 'but you must let us do it our own way'. Glasgow similarly dissuaded Heneker from beginning the counter-attack at the time Butler wished, namely 8 p.m., which was only a few minutes past sunset. 'If it was God Almighty who gave us the order, we couldn't do it in daylight', Glasgow protested. In the end, after discussion, 10 p.m. was chosen as zero hour, only 30 minutes earlier than the time Glasgow himself had advocated. He also let it be known that, partly because the front was still semi-fluid – with the location of the German guns unknown and some British guns still settling into new positions after the withdrawal – and partly to achieve surprise, he wished to dispense with a preliminary bombardment and creeping barrage.[83]

All of these key proposals were incorporated in the operation orders issued by III Corps at 5.30 p.m. and confirmed later by the 8th Division. In the absence of a creeping barrage, all the available artillery was to fire standing barrages, with well-defined targets, including the town, the railway south of it, and the eastern part of Hangard Wood, from 10 p.m. to 11 p.m. Then the heavy batteries were to switch to a protective barrage 500 yards beyond the objective, while the field guns fired a similar barrage 300 yards beyond it. The artillery's contribution would be co-ordinated by III Corps. Two battalions of the 8th Division – the 2nd Northamptonshires and the Pioneer battalion, the 22nd DLI – were to be attached to the 13th and 15th Australian Brigades respectively to attack and mop up Villers-Bretonneux itself from the south and the north. On Glasgow's right, the 18th Division's 54th Brigade, lent to the 58th Division for the purpose, was also to advance eastwards. On this occasion the 54th Brigade would consist of its own 7th Bedfordshires, the 7th Royal West Kents from the 53rd Brigade and the 9th Londons from the 175th Brigade of the 58th Division. It could therefore hardly be described as a cohesive force with battalions who were accustomed to fighting regularly alongside each other. Furthermore, as Edmonds comments, the whole operation was to be carried out by three brigades from three different divisions rather than by a single, well-integrated formation.[84]

In the late afternoon and early evening, first Glasgow and then Elliott conferred with their respective battalion commanders. At 8 p.m. Glasgow reached Blangy-Tronville, where he would share Elliott's headquarters. This was the first real opportunity the two brigade commanders had to co-ordinate their inter-brigade arrangements. Perceiving that the line of advance of the 15th Brigade's 57th Battalion, to the south of the town, might cross that of the two British 'mopping-up' battalions and cause confusion, Glasgow persuaded Elliott to make a last-minute alteration to the plan and shift the 57th Battalion to the northern side of Villers-Bretonneux.[85]

The night counter-attack at Villers-Bretonneux – made in the dark, across partly unfamiliar ground and without previous artillery preparation – was fraught with difficulties but was nevertheless one of the truly outstanding Australian operations of the First World War. The 13th Australian Brigade, which started more or less on time at 10.10 p.m., was held up for a while by the wire in front of the Cachy Switch, running diagonally across the front of the leading battalions. The 52nd Battalion on the right eventually surmounted this obstacle and then overcame the German troops beyond it after a charge and what Edmonds calls 'some sharp fighting with the bayonet', so reaching the objective. It was, however, subsequently brought back a little, with the right extending across the Hangard Wood road towards the Domart road, in order to maintain contact with the 7th Bedfords. The 51st Battalion, on the left, was enfiladed by machine guns on the southern face of the Bois d'Aquenne and had to deal with these by using bomb and bayonet. Lieutenant C.W.K. Sadlier won a Victoria Cross during this fighting. The battalion continued to take heavy losses but the advance went on and, by the early hours of 25 April, the 13th Australian Brigade, if not on its objective, *was* in a position to help pinch out the town should Elliott's brigade also achieve success.[86]

The battalion commanders of the 15th Australian Brigade had not returned from their crucial final conferences until 8 p.m. and, as a result of the darkness and detours to avoid lingering gas, the brigade was approximately 2 hours behind schedule in beginning the advance. The battalions reached the first objective, over a mile away, with relative ease but opposition then stiffened. At this point, Captain E.M. Young, of the 59th Battalion, gave the order to charge and the whole line went forward with a ferocious yell, carrying all before it. The German line was broken and the Hamel road reached with the loss of no more than 150 men. While the old front line had not been retaken, the Australian counter-attack had almost encircled Villers-Bretonneux and the Bois d'Aquenne and had regained most of the ground on the northern part of the battlefield which had been lost earlier.[87]

The British units participating in the counter-attack had mixed fortunes. On the extreme right, elements of the 9th Londons (Queen Victoria's Rifles) got as far as Hangard Wood, but were unable to hold on and were forced to fall back to their start line. The 7th Royal West Kents, meeting heavy machine-gun fire from German posts in shell holes which had escaped the barrage, lost 230 men in an hour and dug in about half-way to their objective. The 7th Bedfords met little opposition over the first thousand yards of their advance and had crossed the Hangard Wood–Villers-Bretonneux road when they came under artillery fire from the right. The survivors withdrew to a position 500 yards behind the road where they found themselves virtually surrounded by Germans in nearby shell holes. Their only remaining officer, Second-Lieutenant W. Tysoe, resisted German calls to surrender. The Bedfords too held on and maintained touch with the 13th Australian Brigade until relieved in the early hours of 26 April. Indeed, as darkness was falling on 25 April, Tysoe and his force – who averaged 19 years of age – even mounted a counter-attack with the bayonet to drive off a German attempt to overwhelm their position.[88]

The two battalions from the 8th Division which had been detailed to mop up the town encountered problems, and the continued firing from the town during the night gave the Australian commanders the impression that the attack of the 2nd Northants and 22nd DLI had not been conducted with the required vigour. Elliott even informed Heneker at 4.15 a.m. that he suspected that the Durhams had not moved at all, while Glasgow similarly reported that nothing had been seen of the Northamptonshires. The truth, as Bean concedes, was that the task assigned to these two battalions was far harder than Elliott or Glasgow assumed, for while 'the thrust of the two Australian brigades was directed where the Germans did not expect it, the 22nd DLI and 2nd Northampton had to strike where the blow was expected, and the Germans were in strength with great numbers of machine-guns and fully prepared'. The 2nd Northants, on the south of the town, quickly came under artillery fire – their commanding officer, Lieutenant-Colonel S.G. Latham, being killed and the adjutant wounded – and then, some 500 yards from the railway embankment, were subjected to fierce machine-gun fire and were unable to progress further. Their casualties, by the end of the fight, totalled 295 officers and men. The Durhams likewise found the town to be strongly defended and, after efforts by two companies to approach it had been driven off by intense fire, the battalion did not try again that night. Elliott's message to Heneker concerning the lack of progress of the Durhams had, however, prompted Heneker to send forward the 2nd Royal Berkshires of the 25th Brigade, to attack and enter the town from the north. This they did in some style at 6.30 a.m. and, with the assistance of the Australian 57th Battalion, cleared a considerable area of the town. As the light improved, the 22nd DLI managed to enter Villers-Bretonneux from the north-west. Gradually, during the day on 25 April – the third anniversary of the Anzac landings on Gallipoli – the pockets of German resistance in the town were eliminated, while parties of the 2nd Middlesex, 2nd West Yorkshires and 1st Sherwood Foresters cleared the Bois d'Aquenne.[89]As Edmonds writes, because of 'General Rawlinson's grasp of the situation and resolution to act without French assistance, the enemy had been deprived of a considerable proportion of his gains of the morning of the 24th. He had been cleared out of Villers-Bretonneux, although the original front had not quite been recovered, and he had been foiled in his object of diverting attention before the attack on Kemmel took place and of getting nearer to Amiens'.[90]

Apart from some local counter-attacks to adjust the line on 25 April – one of which involved the use of three Whippets west of Hangard Wood – the last major scene in the drama was enacted in the early morning of 26 April when the French, in the shape of the splendid Moroccan Division, belatedly made their advance. The Moroccan Division, in the words of its own war diary, was 'in superb condition and the troops impatient to attack'.[91] To restore and straighten the line in the Cachy area and to the south, the division was ordered to recapture the ground between Monument Wood and Hangard Wood. At the same time, two tired battalions of the 18th Division, the 7th Queen's and the 10th Essex, were placed temporarily under French command and were to attack Hangard Wood. The French 131st Division would endeavour to retake Hangard village. The French unwisely rejected Butler's advice that they should not attempt to launch the whole Moroccan Division in daylight across ground registered by the German gunners. It has to be admitted, on the other hand, that the vagueness of the British line in this sector, and the imperfect knowledge of the British troops themselves as to their exact positions, contributed to the French decision – since they, unlike the

Australians and the British, were not prepared to attack from an ill-established line across open ground at night and wished to employ a barrage. When the Moroccan Division advanced at 5.15 a.m. on 26 April, under a creeping barrage but without a preliminary bombardment, resistance was met several hundred yards further west than anticipated, The barrage was lost and, having taken heavy casualties, the Moroccans were driven back by a counter-attack. The 131st Division failed to recapture Hangard village and the only success was achieved by the 10th Essex and the 7th Queen's who, despite incurring heavy losses from machine-gun and rifle fire, retook the western part of Hangard Wood and held on there until relieved next day.[92]

The British divisions, by then, had little more left to give. Since 5 April, the 8th Division had lost 3,553 officers and men; the 18th Division some 2,446; and the 58th Division 3,530. The casualties of the 2 Australian brigades in the second battle were 455 for the 15th Brigade and 1,009 for the 13th Brigade. However, Edmonds estimates that, with gas casualties before 24 April included, the 15th Brigade lost as many as 50 officers and 1,284 other ranks. Bean estimates the overall German casualties as being around 10,400.[93]

The performance of the British divisions at Second Villers-Bretonneux – as on 4 April – had been variable. The battalions from the 18th and 58th Divisions, on the right, had certainly prevented any fatal German penetration in this sector and had attacked and counter-attacked, with some success, when required. The fact that this right flank, if not totally secure, did not significantly collapse in either battle undoubtedly gave the Australian counter-attacks a better chance of succeeding. The 18th Division, in particular, could be reasonably proud of its record at Villers-Bretonneux. One should take into account that the division had already been in action several days at the start of the German March offensive before fighting in *both* battles at Villers-Bretonneux. Besides their contribution to the defensive operations on 4 and 24 April, the infantry battalions of the division had, between them, also taken part in at least eight attacks or local counter-attacks in the period from 2 to 26 April, a higher total, I believe, than any other Allied division at Villers-Bretonneux could claim.

The 8th Division did not have its finest hour at Second Villers-Bretonneux and, as in the case of the 14th (Light) Division on 4 April, its early reverses in the face of the German attack had created a critical situation. Like the 14th Division, the 8th Division had been seriously weakened by the March fighting, though the 8th had unquestionably performed with greater distinction than the hard-hit 14th in the first week or so of the German offensive. Moreover, *unlike* the 14th, it had faced tanks when attacked by the Germans at Villers-Bretonneux – *not* an everyday experience for British soldiers in the Great War and an extremely alarming one for a good, but weakened, division which had not yet fully recovered from its previous trials nor properly absorbed its large proportion of raw young recruits. One might therefore contend that there were *some* excuses for its partial collapse on 24 April, while it could also be pointed out that a number of its battalions had regained sufficient cohesion, spirit and strength to participate in the mopping-up operations on 25 April. The divisional history asserts that, while it was the splendid fighting qualities of the Australians which had turned the enemy out of the positions he had gained, 'it was the 8th Division, on which the full weight of the blow fell, who stopped the advance before its purpose had been accomplished'.[94] The 8th Division, however, was unfortunate enough to be caught up in the German offensive on the Aisne in May and it was consequently not surprising that its performance in the Hundred Days, between August and November 1918, was moderate at best. The 14th Division was another formation which had a relatively unimpressive performance level during the final British offensive. The 58th and 18th Divisions, in contrast, had success rates of 63 per cent and 78 per cent respectively in opposed attacks between 8 August and 11 November.

Australian criticisms of the British divisions at Villers-Bretonneux were thus, I would suggest, only partly justified and were sometimes based on over-hasty judgements without full knowledge of the circumstances. It is also suggested by Bean that the 'forcefulness' of Elliott and Glasgow was 'not wholly relished' by Heneker, under whose command they had fought at Second Villers-Bretonneux. From what others – such as Hubert Essame, who also served under him as adjutant of the 2nd Northamptonshires – have written about Heneker, this assumption itself appears to be at least questionable, for the commander of the 8th Division was not the type of man who could be easily bullied. Bean is possibly on safer ground when he remarks that 'amid all the telegrams of congratulation that afterwards reached the two [Australian] brigades, there came no message from the divisonal commander to whom they had been lent'. Though Bean notes that 'two senior members' of Heneker's staff rode over and thanked Glasgow for the 13th Australian Brigade's efforts, this failure by Heneker himself to acknowledge the part played by Elliott and Glasgow and their troops was, if deliberate, a petty and mean-spirited act which does him no credit.[95] Happily, others were more than ready to give the Australians the praise that they had so richly earned. Rawlinson noted in his diary that the 13th and 15th Australian Brigades 'did brilliantly' while the Fourth Army War Diary similarly describes the performance of the 13th Brigade – given the lack of time for preparation and reconnaissance – as 'exceptionally brilliant'.[96] Grogan, of the 23rd Brigade, later called the night operation of 24–25 April 'perhaps the greatest individual feat of the war – the successful counter-attack by night across unknown and difficult ground, at a few hours' notice, by the Australian soldier'.[97] Butler too wrote in his official report on the operations: 'My thanks are especially due to the Australian brigades placed under my orders for the counter-attack on Villers-Bretonneux, who carried out the night attack with magnificent dash ...'.[98] It is worth noting that the Australians were also willing to reverse earlier judgements and give credit where it was due. The 2nd Royal Berkshires were reported by Australian officers and NCOs who visited them on 24 April to be 'badly shaken and probably liable to panic', yet, after the battalion's work with the Australian 57th Battalion in helping to mop up Villers-Bretonneux on the morning of 25 April, a message was sent by the 5th Australian Division to say 'Well done Royal Berks'.[99]

Most of the commanders involved in the operations of 24–25 April had made an important contribution either to the handling of the desperate defence of the morning of 24 April or to the planning of the successful counter-attack – or, indeed, to both. It should be recognised that Haig himself was personally in touch with the situation, having spent time at the headquarters of Fourth Army and III Corps on the afternoon of 24 April. He does not appear to have interfered in the detailed conduct of the battle, but he did what *was* expected of a Commander-in-Chief and put pressure on the French to co-operate, not only by attacking with the British as soon as possible but also by relieving the divisions of III Corps. Rawlinson, for his part, had quickly appreciated the need for a swift counter-attack and had tried to ensure that it was carried out before the Germans had been allowed time to consolidate and move all their guns into new positions. Butler, the commander of III Corps, had to be persuaded to drop some of his own ideas concerning the direction and timing of the counter-attack, but at least he remained open to reasonable argument, while Haig – who lunched at III Corps headquarters – was impressed by the 'quiet methodical way' in which he issued orders and made his arrangements with Hobbs and Heneker over the telephone.[100] Heneker and his staff, as well as Elliott, can claim to have helped shape the plan to pinch out Villers-Bretonneux in the counter-attack, but, while Elliott and Hobbs imparted a considerable sense of urgency to the command deliberations and discussions on 24 April, Heneker's refusal to panic, plus his readiness to listen to good ideas and act accordingly were vital ingredients in the formula for success. As Bean admits, it was Heneker, above all, who, 'following the advice of Brigadier-General Coffin and the battalion commanders of the 25th Brigade, prevented the wasting of the 15th Brigade at midday, and induced General Butler, despite Rawlinson's pressure, to acquiesce in postponement until evening'.[101] Finally, Glasgow's vital input, particularly with regard to the timing of the counter-attack and the start line for his brigade, should be re-emphasised.

In reporting on the performance of his divisions between 21 March and First Villers-Bretonneux, Butler had remarked on the lack of training or initiative of junior officers in 'open warfare operations on a large scale'.[102] Edmonds was also critical of the standards of British junior leadership in both the March–April fighting and, later, the Hundred Days. Yet, as I have argued elsewhere, I believe that, if standards of junior leadership in the British divisions was really so low, the achievements of the young conscripts in stopping the German thrusts of March and April, and subsequently in advancing to victory between August and November, would simply not have been possible. In this respect, the experience of March and April helped young officers and NCOs to shake off the habits of trench warfare and almost certainly gave those who survived a greater degree of confidence and self-reliance that stood them in good stead later in the year. The determination shown by Second-Lieutenant Tysoe, who, as the only remaining officer of the 7th Bedfords, won a DSO for maintaining his position to the right of the 13th Australian Brigade throughout 25 April, illustrates what could be achieved by relatively inexperienced officers when the challenge came. According to the historian of the 18th Division, the 'fine example of gallantry and leadership by this young officer was entirely instrumental in holding the ground gained, with many young soldiers who were in action for the first time'.[103]

The often complex chain of command at First and Second Villers-Bretonneux could have been a recipe for disaster. Australians were placed temporarily under the command of XIX Corps and III Corps and under the 8th and 18th Divisions in one or other of these actions, while elements of the 58th Division were attached to the 18th Division and vice versa between 2 and 26 April. But, despite differences of command style and personality clashes, the command system at Villers-Bretonneux could be judged to have worked remarkably well in difficult and dangerous circumstances. This was partly due to the willingness of Butler and Heneker to accept sensible advice from below, while the fact that Haig and Rawlinson were prepared to leave the tactical conduct of a critical battle largely to their subordinates made it easier for those at corps, divisional and brigade level to respond effectively and flexibly to the changing demands of the situation. Villers-Bretonneux can therefore be seen as indicative of the extent of the devolution of battlefield command and decision-making in the BEF by 1918. A number of historians, including myself, have recently argued that, so far as the day to day conduct of operations was concerned, Haig, GHQ and the army commanders were far less relevant by mid-1918 than they had been two years, or even a year, before. One could also contend that the experience of the March Retreat and of Villers-Bretonneux may have accelerated this process, for the nature of tactical command in the BEF during the Hundred Days was, in many ways, quite different to that which had existed at Arras or Third Ypres in 1917. Mistakes and failures would continue to occur in 1918, but there is now wider agreement among historians and students of the First World War that those in the BEF who were ready to learn from difficult experiences, to embrace new tactics and techniques, and to encourage greater individual self-reliance and initiative, were exerting a more marked influence on the course of operations by the time the Hindenburg Line was breached. It is surely more than a coincidence that that the British infantry divisions which performed best at Villers-Bretonneux – namely the 18th and 58th – also had a good or above average success rate in attacks during the final and victorious Allied offensive.

Chapter Seven

'Somewhat Ambitious': V Corps and the Recapture of Thiepval and the Ancre Heights, August 1918

The story of the recapture of the Thiepval plateau and the Ancre Heights by V Corps in August 1918 offers a graphic illustration of the principal differences between the BEF's operational and tactical methods as practised in 1916 and those which it employed in 1918. The episode also reveals the changes in the BEF's collective mindset during that period, including the greater willingness of its senior commanders in 1918 to take risks which, earlier in the war, would have been unthinkable.

The Challenge

The preliminary phases of the attempt by V Corps to retake the Thiepval plateau – which had been lost to the enemy in the German March offensive – encompassed an attack on a village and efforts by strong fighting patrols from the three divisions chiefly concerned to negotiate the floods and marshes of the Ancre valley while establishing footholds and posts on the further side of the river and repairing, under fire, its damaged bridges and causeways. These efforts continued on the second day of operations while elements of one division had to beat off German counter-attacks. At the same time, the 18th Division of III Corps, the left-wing formation of the Fourth Army, had to clear Albert in order to give the right wing of V Corps room to deploy south of the flooded area prior to an attack, east of the town, on La Boisselle. On the third day, attempts were made to drive the Germans further from Albert and to seize the Tara and Usna Hills while units in the centre and on the left of the V Corps front strove to secure better jumping-off positions for the main assault on the Thiepval heights and ridge, which was to take place on the night of 23–24 August. To avoid both the flooded area and the need to deliver a direct assault on the Thiepval stronghold itself, converging attacks were to be launched from the north and south, thus outflanking two major obstacles.

It will immediately be apparent that, quite apart from the considerable problems caused by the ground in the Thiepval sector, the divisions of V Corps, along with the 18th Division of III Corps, faced a number of challenging tasks, including a river crossing; the construction or repair of bridges and causeways; the clearance of a ruined town; co-operation between neighbouring formations across inter-corps and inter-army boundaries; convergent attacks; and a planned advance of several hundred yards *at night* over part of the old 1916 battlefield. As if these operations were not complex enough, they were to be carried out by divisions which – as the official historian suggests – contained a large proportion of 'boy' soldiers, many of whom would be in action for the first time.[1] The nature of the crossings over the Ancre and its marshes meant that, initially, only pack transport could be used to move supplies of small arms ammunition and water up to the forward troops, and some time would elapse before field guns could be brought up over the river to afford close support to the infantry. Except on the right, near the Albert–Bapaume road, tanks were of little or no help in the difficult terrain of the Ancre valley and heights and, because the major attack by V Corps was launched under cover of darkness, aircraft too could provide no real support in its early stages. Hence at least two possible components of a true 1918-style combined-arms operation were largely absent during the crucial phase of the operation. Moreover, the night advance by some units was made with a partial and deliberate disregard for open flanks. The potential for setbacks and even disaster in this complicated scheme was therefore only too obvious. In the event, when parts of the plan *did* begin to unravel, it would be good old-fashioned leadership by the 'man on the spot' at brigade, battalion and company level that enabled V Corps to achieve its aims. If some of the remaining limitations and weaknesses in the BEF's operational capabililties were also exposed by the actions of 21–24 August 1918, the value of the continuing devolution of command and control *downwards* was, at the very least, re-emphasised in a striking fashion.

Background

The Germans had retaken their former stronghold of Thiepval and the Ancre Heights, and had occupied the town of Albert, on 25–26 March 1918, during Operation *Michael*, but the British Third Army – and, in particular, V Corps, then still under the command of Liieutenant-General Sir Edward Fanshawe – had managed to organise a relatively stable defensive line along the high ground and western approaches to the River Ancre, effectively halting further German progress in the sector from just north of Albert to the village of Hamel. From the latter point, where the river itself begins to swing north-east towards St Pierre Divion, Beaucourt, Grandcourt and Miraumont, the Third Army's front ran roughly due north in the direction of Auchonvillers, Hébuterne and Bucquoy. The Albert–Arras railway, which became the main German line of resistance facing the British Third Army, followed the course of the Ancre on its left (or west) bank as far as Miraumont, whence it ran north-east and then north beyond Achiet le Grand.

In the final days of March and the first week of April 1918, the Germans succeeded in establishing themselves on the west bank of the Ancre between Albert and Hamel, gaining possession of much of Aveluy Wood, which was a little over a mile in length and nearly a mile across. This feature was, in effect, the principal German 'citadel' on the west bank, covering the river crossings. The site of the once-pretty village of Hamel was now – in the words of the British official historian – 'a shell trap situated on a forward slope', and was wisely abandoned by V Corps.[2] To the north of Aveluy Wood and around Hamel, the Germans rarely occupied the same position two nights running, and were hard to locate, sometimes holding one series of posts, sometimes another. More than one British officer described the Ancre valley as a happy hunting ground for night patrols. The struggle for domination of Aveluy Wood and the Ancre valley continued throughout the summer months into July, with various divisions taking their turn in the line, and raids, patrols and skirmishes were frequent.[3] However, the pressure of events elsewhere on the Western Front, including the decisive Franco-American counter-stroke between Reims and Soissons from 18 July onwards, induced the Germans to evacuate the salient they held between Hamel and Bucquoy and withdraw from their bridgeheads on the west bank of the Ancre. In the V Corps sector there were early indications of a German retirement on 1 August and, the following day, the British 17th (Northern) Division had secured a north–south line across the middle of Aveluy Wood with outposts on the railway close to the west bank of the Ancre. Three days later the whole of the wood was clear of the enemy and by mid-August the German retirement to the east bank was largely complete. These developments, and the abandonment by the Germans of the salient immediately to the north, permitted Third Army to re-enter Serre and Beaumont Hamel and enabled V Corps to take possession of Hamel village and the ground to its east as well as close up to the western outskirts of Beaucourt.[4]

Plans and Priorities

Serious consideration of future offensive plans involving General Sir Julian Byng's Third Army on the front between Albert and Arras, had begun to gather pace on 16 July 1918, when Haig instructed Byng to prepare a scheme for recapturing the Moyenneville–Ablainzevelle ridge, south of Arras and, if things progressed satisfactorily, to seize the Serre ridge, 7 miles north of Albert. At that stage, Haig envisaged that the principal purpose of the orders he had given to Third Army was merely to divert German attention away from the forthcoming operations of Fourth Army at Amiens and, as things turned out, the German withdrawal from their salient near Beaumont Hamel partly negated the need for an attack to secure Serre ridge.[5] However, further orders were given to Third Army on 10 August when the Anglo-French offensive at Amiens, though still only in its third day, was already encountering stiffer German resistance and losing momentum. That morning, Foch – now a Marshal of France and General-in-Chief (Generalissimo) of the Allied armies on the Western Front – arrived at Haig's advanced headquarters at Wiry, bringing with him a general directive regarding the development of operations. The directive was consistent with Foch's concept of the *bataille générale*, whereby, instead of seeking a deep penetration or breakthrough along a narrow axis, the Allied armies would mount a series of shallow attacks on different fronts to keep the enemy off-balance, sap his strength and prevent him from concentrating his reserves. While Foch wanted the British Fourth and French First Armies to press on east of Amiens, he also intended that the French Third Army should exploit the situation by clearing the Noyon–Montdidier area of Germans and that the British Third Army, to the north of Albert, should also take advantage of any additional success that the Fourth Army achieved in the direction of Ham, on the River Somme, by advancing towards Bapaume and Péronne. The French Tenth Army was to remain prepared to extend the battle to the right and follow the progress of the French Third Army, south of the River Oise. After some discussion concerning the increasing German opposition to the British Fourth Army and French First Army, it was nevertheless agreed that the offensive east of Amiens should continue but, following the meeting, Haig issued fresh instructions to Byng. His Third Army was to 'carry out raids and minor operations in order to ascertain the enemy's intention on the Albert–Arras front' and to 'take immediate advantage of any favourable situation which the main operations may create and push advanced guards in the general direction of Bapaume'.[6]

By the late evening of 11 August it had been decided that, in view of the growing German resistance, the Amiens offensive should be suspended for the time being, although it was planned to resume operations on that front around 15 August. Foch retained hopes that the British might still reach the Somme but consented to the objective being limited to the Ham–Brie sector, 4 miles south of Péronne. He also expressed the wish that the Third Army might take the offensive as soon as possible. Next morning (12 August) he sent Haig a new directive aimed at exploiting to the utmost the gains made by the British Fourth Army and French First Army between 8 and 10 August. Foch wished to do this by making powerful concentrated attacks on selected points 'whose possession would increase the enemy's disorganisation' and disrupt his communications. Foch similarly believed that, independently of such actions, the two wings of the present battle could profitably be extended by (a) an attack of the French Tenth Army east of the Oise, towards Chauny (between Soissons and St Quentin) and (b) an advance by the British Third Army towards Bapaume and Péronne, in order to outflank the enemy's defensive line on the Somme and force him to make another, deeper, retirement.[7]

On 13 August, Haig issued a formal order to Byng regarding the Third Army's role in the forthcoming operations. Promising Byng reinforcements of four infantry divisions and two cavalry divisions, as well as tanks and additional artillery, Haig decreed that the Third Army was to break into the German positions on a 4-mile front south of Arras and then to exploit the success gained in the direction of Bapaume and to drive south and south-east towards Péronne to outflank the forces facing Rawlinson's Fourth Army. The breach might also be widened to the north to include the recapture of the key observation point of Monchy le Preux, east of Arras. The date of the Third Army's attack was provisionally fixed as 20 August. Byng was told to submit an outline of his plan of operations as soon as he could.[8]

Over the next two or three days, the importance and potential scope of Byng's projected operations were enhanced. Shortly before noon on 14 August, Third Army reported that the German Seventeenth Army was falling back on a front of over 6 miles between Bucquoy and the Ancre, even if this affected only their outpost zone and not the main German line of resistance.[9] Meanwhile, a serious difference of opinion had arisen between Foch and Haig as to the respective degrees of priority to be given to the operations of the British Fourth and French First Armies on the one hand and those of the British Third Army on the other. Foch wanted the attack of the former to be 'hastened as much as possible' and *followed* 'as rapidly as possible' by that of the British Third Army. Haig, however – accepting the advice of Rawlinson and Lieutenant-General Sir Arthur Currie, the commander of the Canadian Corps – ordered the date of the Fourth Army's attack to be postponed.[10] On the morning of 15 August, Haig conferred with Byng, General Sir Henry Horne (commander of the First Army) and Lieutenant-General Sir Charles Kavanagh (of the Cavalry Corps). The Commander-in-Chief directed that the Third Army should press on with its offensive, even before the promised reinforcements arrived; that the First Army should take advantage of the Third Army's advance by capturing Orange Hill and Monchy le Preux near Arras; and that the Fourth Army should continue its preparations south of the Somme and exploit any opportunities which arose to gain ground. North of the Somme, Rawlinson's left wing was to co-operate with the right wing of Third Army in exerting pressure on the enemy and following him up. An operation order confirming these instructions and amending those given to Byng two days earlier was subsequently issued.[11]

The same afternoon, Haig and his chief of staff, Lieutenant-General Sir Herbert Lawrence, visited Foch's own advanced headquarters at Sarcus to explain their plans. Foch urged Haig to assault the Roye-Chaulnes position, south-east of Amiens, the next day, but Haig declined, in view of the heavy casualties likely to be incurred if the attack was delivered without adequate artillery preparation. He also reminded Foch that he (Haig) was responsible to the British government and his fellow citizens for the handling of the BEF. At this point Foch accepted the wisdom of temporarily shifting the main weight of the British offensive effort to the Third Army front rather than persisting with costly major operations against prepared German positions east of Amiens. It is worth noting that improved British logistics had at last made it possible, by 1918, for the BEF to raise its operational tempo, rapidly switch its main point of attack and mount concurrent, or successive, operations in more than one sector. Once he had returned to Wiry, Haig, in accordance with Foch's apparent wishes, despatched a letter to the Generalissimo to reassure him that, south of the Somme, Rawlinson's Fourth Army would not relax its pressure and that, north of the Somme, it would co-operate with the Third Army and make every effort to advance. He added that the Third Army was likewise already attempting to push the Germans back and would increase its efforts as reinforcements reached it. Horne's First Army too would launch an attack, though the precise date of this would be determined by the progress achieved by Byng.[12]

Third Army's orders for its attack were issued and circulated on 18 August. As a preliminary operation, on a date to be notified later, the left wing of Lieutenant-

General Sir Montague Harper's IV Corps and the right wing of Lieutenant-General Sir Aylmer Haldane's VI Corps were to capture the remainder of Bucquoy and Ablainzevelle together with the Moyenneville–Ablainzevelle spur, in a limited advance of only a mile or two. Should these actions prove successful, IV Corps and VI Corps were to exploit the gains by pushing infantry and tanks through the line Gomiecourt–Bihucourt–Irles in the south and to the Albert–Arras railway further north. Harper's IV Corps was also to seize the remainder of the Serre–Miraumont ridge, including the Beauregard Dovecot. All this would require IV Corps to advance more than 4 miles in some parts of its sector. V Corps, now commanded by Lieutenant-General C.D. Shute, had only a subsidiary role in the attack, being told to prepare to cross the Ancre in a south-easterly direction towards the Pozières ridge and to extend the right of IV Corps. Byng – who some historians portray as being seemingly 'war-weary' by August 1918 – was certainly erring on the side of caution in his planning for the offensive. Corps commanders were advised not to persist with attacks in the face of very stubborn resistance or severe casualties, while only one of the two cavalry divisions allocated to Byng was given a part to play. The ground was considered to be 'not very favourable for mounted action' and, as opportunities 'would probably be fleeting', the commander of the 1st Cavalry Division, Major-General R.L. Mullens, was allowed 'a free hand in carrying out his general task of exploitation …'. He *was* expected, however, to grasp any chance which presented itself to pass through exploiting troops and press on towards Bapaume. Because of the need for secrecy, the hour and date of the attack (4.55 a.m. on 21 August) was not revealed until 19 August.[13]

It was on 19 August that Haig and Lawrence visited the Third Army headquarters so that Byng could explain his plan. Haig, struck by its overriding caution, bluntly commented that he thought the plan was 'too limited in its scope'. He told Byng that his objective was to break the enemy's front, prevent the Germans from destroying roads and bridges and '*gain Bapaume as soon as possible*' (Haig's italics), reassuring him that his right and left flanks would be well protected by the developing operations of the Fourth and First Armies. Haig also criticised Byng's lack of audacity with regard to the employment of the cavalry, saying that it must be used to the fullest possible extent. 'Now is the time to act with boldness and in full confidence that, if we only hit the enemy hard enough and combine the action of all arms in pressing him, his troops will give way on a very wide front and acknowledge that he is beaten'. Having moved on to see Harper at IV Corps headquarters, Haig subsequently sent John Dill, his BGGS (Operations) at GHQ, to direct Byng to assign a cavalry regiment to each of his attacking corps and to instruct him that it was necessary to deploy advanced guards of all arms first to reconnoitre and then to push on when the enemy's line of resistance had been pierced.[14] Despite these instructions, which Haig confirmed in writing on his return to his headquarters train at Wiry, Byng appears to have taken little action to alter his basic plan of operations.[15] Haig also let Foch know that, owing to delays in the arrival of tanks and 'other troops', the Third Army offensive would not now begin until the morning of 21 August. First Army was to remain ready to attack Orange Hill and Monchy le Preux and to reinforce or exploit Third Army's advance. The operations of Fourth Army north of the Somme were scheduled to begin on 22 August and its attack south of the Somme was fixed for 23 April.[16]

As Foch had always intended, the Allied offensive was extended on its right wing on 20 August, when General Mangin's French Tenth Army attacked northwards with twelve divisions on a 12-mile front between Soissons and the Oise, gaining an average of 3,000 yards. Ludendorff, the German First Quartermaster-General, called this 'another black day' for the German army. Mindful of the need to strike an equal blow on the left wing, Foch wrote to Haig that evening to report on the Tenth Army's progress and to emphasise his desire that Byng's attack should proceed on 21 August '*with violence*, carrying forward with it the neighbouring divisions of the First Army and the whole of the Fourth Army. After your brilliant successes of the 8th, 9th and 10th, any timidity on their part would hardly be justified in view of the enemy's situation and the moral ascendancy you have gained over him'.[17] The scene was now set for the British Third Army and V Corps to join the *bataille générale*.

V Corps

Shute's V Corps had three divisions in or near the front line at the start of Third Army's August operations. These were the 17th (Northern) Division (Major-General P.R. Robertson), the 21st Division (Major-General D.G.M. Campbell) and the 38th (Welsh) Division (Major-General T.A. Cubitt). All three had done tours of duty in the Ancre sector at various times during the spring and summer months. The 17th Division had seen action in the opening days of the German March offensive but, unlike some formations, had escaped reorganisation or reconstitution in the summer. Expecting a period of rest and training in mid-August, the division was instead attached to the Australian Corps east of Amiens and was only returned to V Corps on the eve of the Third Army's attack. Indeed, its move back to the V Corps area was not completed until 2 a.m. on 21 August, giving it precious little time to settle in and re-acclimatise before seeing action again.[18] The morale of all ranks was reported to be high and unit strengths as 'practically up to establishment', except in the 51st Brigade, which had suffered 700 gas casualties, including 2 battalion commanders, when the division was in the Australian Corps area. The 17th Division's state of training was described in its war diary as 'fair', though not up to the standard required for successful open warfare offensive operations: 'The main deficiencies were lack of tactical knowledge, which resulted in formations not being adapted to suit ground, and lack of power to apply the principle of fire covering movement, also lack of intelligent patrolling'.[19] Some, though not all, of the war diarist's comments would be borne out in the first phase of the offensive.

The 21st Division had so far experienced a tough year in 1918. After an epic defence of Epéhy on the first day of the German March offensive, the division had conducted a spirited fighting retreat in the following week or so until, at the end of March, when it was relieved, its battalions had an average combat strength of just over 200 men. It was then heavily engaged once more in the German *Georgette* offensive on the Lys in April and, having been sent to a supposedly quiet sector on the Aisne to recuperate, it was unfortunate enough to become embroiled in a *third* German attack, the *Blücher* offensive along the Chemin des Dames, in late May. In June the 8th Leicesters in the 110th Brigade had been replaced by the 1st Wiltshires but otherwise, perhaps surprisingly, the division, like the 17th, had avoided major reorganisation. It too had been allowed only a few days of rest and training in the first half of July before receiving orders to move to the Ancre–Thiepval sector. Captain D.V. Kelly, who served with the 6th Leicesters and as Intelligence Officer of the 110th Brigade, recalled that it 'seemed odd and a little discouraging to be back again in the old trenches where the Ulstermen had fought in 1916, as though so much blood and effort had been wasted'. Since the move the division had carried out ceaseless patrolling. In the words of Brigadier-General Hanway Cumming, the commander of the 110th Brigade, these fighting patrols had been 'boldly and skilfully handled' but had cost 'a certain number of casualties at a time when the Brigade was by no means fresh …'.[20] The 38th (Welsh) Division, in contrast, had been lucky enough to have a relatively undemanding year. Although its artillery had seen considerable action on the Lys in April, its infantry formations had spent much of the spring and summer on the Ancre front, mostly near Aveluy Wood and Hamel. The division had borne its share of raids and patrols but, overall, was undoubtedly suffering from less battle fatigue than the 21st Division. Despite this, an outbreak of influenza early in July prompted Captain J.C. Dunn, the Medical Officer of the 2nd Royal Welsh Fusiliers, to record on 4 July that the 'general tone and health of the troops was not good'. The morale of this particular battalion was, however, reinvogorated by the arrival of a new commanding officer, Lieutenant-Colonel J.B. 'Cocky' Cockburn. By 10 July, as Dunn observed, a 'new spirit and keenness and a new thoroughness were evident'.[21]

In his study of British corps command on the Western Front, Andy Simpson convincingly argues that, during the Hundred Days offensive, Third Army and its component formations excercised as decentralised a style of command as was consistent with operational common sense, and that they did this by adhering to the principles laid down in *FSRI* and the 1918 version of *SS 135*. As some operations took the form of set-piece attacks, 'corps at these times exerted closer control over divisions than during phases of pursuit. However, this approach was entirely flexible and corps varied its style of command as the situation demanded'. In the case of the opening phase of the 21 August operation, which was basically a set-piece attack, Third Army was prescriptive in some aspects of its orders to corps but, on the eve of the assault, Third Army exhorted corps to stress to division and brigade commanders 'the importance of being actually on the ground with their formations during the operations. The delay caused by the Commander not being on the spot to handle the reserves may possibly annul initial success and prevent surprise being exploited to the utmost'. In other words, as Andy Simpson puts it, 'if authority and control were passed down to the man on the spot, it was essential that he actually be on that spot'.[22]

Largely following this template, V Corps allowed a fair amount of latitude to divisional commanders regarding operational decisions on the ground. For example, by way of contrast to common practice in 1917, matters arising from the need to act in conjunction with divisions from neighbouring corps were now left to the divisions themselves, rather than being discussed at corps level. For the set-piece attack of 21 August, the GOCRA at corps level still co-ordinated the corps artillery plan, allocating the field artillery to cover the divisions in question and apportioning the majority of the heavy artillery pieces to counter-battery tasks, although divisions were to inform corps of any special targets which they required the 'heavies' to suppress. The organisation of the crossings of the Ancre was also placed in divisional hands. Yet, lest it be concluded that divisions were more or less free to do as they pleased, it should be pointed out that on 20 August, the day before the attack, V Corps produced a detailed critique of the 21st Division's plans.[23]

In view of the degree of decentralisation and flexibility being conceded to corps, divisions and brigades, once Third Army had issued relatively short summaries of objectives and of the different stages of the operation, much depended on the calibre of the 'men on the spot'. Opinions about the V Corps commander, Cameron Shute, are mixed. Unfortunately for his long-term reputation, he is perhaps most widely remembered as 'that shit Shute' – the object of A.P. Herbert's scorn in a song written in response to Shute's unsympathetic and critical attitude to the idiosyncrasies of the 63rd (Royal Naval) Division, which he commanded, before and after the Battle of the Ancre, between October 1916 and February 1917. Major-General Reginald Pinney, whose 33rd Division formed part of V Corps in the 'Hundred Days', resented Shute's fussiness and interference, having been told by the latter that 'the drive must come from you – ring up the brigadiers every 15 minutes'.[24] David Campbell, the commander of the 21st Division, called Shute 'a very hard man to satisfy', while Pinney noted that the fortnight's 'Bosh [sic] hunting' to which Campbell had 'looked forward all his service had been absolutely miserable owing to Shute's fussing'.[25] In Shute's defence, however, one should note that, while in command of the 32nd Division from February 1917 onwards, he had done much to restore its fighting reputation and had become known in that formation as 'Tiger' Shute. He was rewarded with promotion to the command of V Corps at the end of April 1918 and led it capably and with no little flexibility in the final British offensive.[26]

The 17th (Northern) Division was commanded by Major-General Philip 'Blobs' Robertson, an officer of the Cameronians (Scottish Rifles). He had served as GOC of the 19th Brigade for just over a year before being promoted to divisional command on 13 July 1916, when he was 50 years old. He remained with the 17th Division for the remainder of the war and, by the Armistice, he was the sixth longest-serving divisional commander in the BEF. Treating his new command as if it were a large battalion, he insisted on pre-war Regular Army standards of discipline, duty and efficiency. Robertson was not a man to court easy popularity and, like Shute, would forcibly point out cases of slackness during his frequent tours of the trenches but, if not loved by his men, he *was* always trusted by them and turned his division into a solid 'workhorse', rather than an élite, formation. J.C. Dunn, of the 2nd Royal Welsh Fusiliers, who was often unimpressed by senior officers, called him a 'dud'.[27] On the other hand, W.N. Nicholson, who was Robertson's AA and QMG for the best part of two years, stated that he was 'in every respect a most excellent divisional Commander'.[28] Whatever his strengths and weaknesses may have been, he certainly did not lack moral courage, as he showed in April 1917, when he was one of three divisional commanders to take the uncommon and risky step of registering a formal protest against General Sir Edmund Allenby's tactics at the Battle of Arras.[29]

T.A. Cubitt, a gunner aged 47, had only been in command of the 38th (Welsh) Division since 23 May 1918. Before taking over the division he had served in Somaliland in the first half of the war and had commanded the 57th Brigade in the 19th (Western) Division from 6 April 1917 to 22 May 1918. Perhaps not surprisingly, Dunn portrays him as a brusque, critical and often discouraging fire-eater 'with a marvellous flow of language' but, as in other cases, not all shared Dunn's opinion. One officer wrote that Tom Cubitt was 'a perpetual joy to the soldier world' because of his picturesque language, that his 'magnetic personality' suited the 38th Division and that he had 'a shrewd head, a kind heart and great wit … a charming and lovable personality'. Another remembered him as a 'fighting soldier' who was 'daring and unafraid' and who possessed 'a heart of gold' beneath his outspoken manner and forceful language.[30]

The 21st Division, as already indicated, was under the command of Major-General David 'Soarer' Campbell, whose nickname was derived from the name of the horse he had ridden to victory in the 1896 Grand National. Campbell had been CO of the 9th Lancers at the outbreak of war and was promoted to the post of GOC of the 6th Cavalry Brigade in November 1914. He had been promoted again, this time to the command of the 21st Division, on 22 May 1916, when he was 47.[31] He played a key role in nursing the formation back to fighting efficiency after its disastrous baptism of fire at Loos the previous September and by the end of the war was the BEF's fifth longest-serving divisional commander. Like Philip Robertson, he applied to the division the standards he had followed as a pre-war regimental officer, seeing it as his duty to pay regular visits to the front line. John Bourne writes that Campbell 'did not suffer fools gladly, and he was quite prepared to protest to his seniors when he thought that their orders were unreasonable, which was quite often'.[32] This did not endear him to Shute, who was to tell Haig, on 25 August, that Campbell 'had not shown up very well; he was always raising objections and difficulties'. As will be seen, 21st Division actually fought with some skill and determination under difficult circumstances on 23–24 August, so Shute's remarks may well have been prompted more by Campbell's argumentativeness than by any perceived shortcomings in the division's commnd and performance. A month later Shute acknowledged that the division had 'done splendidly'.[33] Probably the most glowing tribute to Campbell was paid by his subordinate, Hanway Cumming, who portrayed him as very 'quick and alert, with an inexhaustible supply of energy, a great sense of humour and a fund of common sense' making him, in Cumming's eyes, 'the perfection of a Divisional Commander'. Cumming further commented that Campbell was very popular with all ranks because of his concern for their comfort and welfare: 'Added to which he was a fine soldier, with sound and original ideas on training, and possessed a strong will of his own without being in any way obstinate'.[34]

Campbell's division in August 1918 was fortunate in being able to call upon a trio of truly outstanding brigade commanders. The GOC of 62nd Brigade was George Gater who, apart from service in the Officers' Training Corps at Winchester, had had no previous military experience before the war and, having obtained a history degree and a Diploma in Education at Oxford, was Assistant Director of Education for Nottinghamshire in 1914. Commissioned in the 9th Sherwood Foresters soon after the outbreak of hostilities, he served with the unit on Gallipoli and was in temporary command of the battalion at the time of its evacuation from the peninsula in December 1915. He subsequently served with the 9th Sherwood Foresters in France until August 1916, when he was given command of the 6th Lincolnshires. On 1 November 1917 he was promoted to the command of 62nd Brigade at the age of 30. His remarkable rise from civilian to brigadier-general had taken just over three years.[35] Hanway Cumming described Gater as 'a first-class Brigade Commander, very able and quick ... A delightful companion and a good comrade, he was universally liked throughout the Division'. David Campbell also portrayed Gater in glowing terms in a report forwarded to GHQ in October 1918, judging him to be a brigadier 'of the very highest class' and 'a very good disciplinarian' who had 'proved himself to be an excellent organiser, trainer and fighter' and had won 'the absolute confidence of all serving under him'. Campbell considered him 'thoroughly qualified to command a division'.[36]

Andrew McCulloch, the commander of 64th Brigade, had only been in the post since 28 July. He was 42 years old. The son of a Scottish judge, he too was an Oxford graduate and had qualified as a barrister before the South African War apparently changed the direction of his life and career. Having joined the ranks of the City Imperial Volunteers, he was awarded the Distinguished Conduct Medal and commissioned in the field into the Highland Light Infantry. McCulloch graduated from the Staff College, Camberley, in 1910 and by the beginning of the First World War was a captain in the 7th Dragoon Guards, serving on the staff, later transferring to the 14th Hussars. However, in the autumn of 1917, he reverted to an infantry role when he was given command of the 9th King's Own Yorkshire Light Infantry in the 21st Division. His elevation to the 64th Brigade the following summer was therefore a promotion from within the division. McCulloch was destined to play a leading part in the events of 23–24 August.[37] The 110th Brigade was commanded by Hanway Cumming, who was 50. Cumming had gained a Regular commission in the Durham Light Infantry (DLI) in 1889, had attended the Staff College in 1901–1902 and had held a variety of staff and regimental appointments before taking command of the 2nd DLI on the Somme in August 1916. His attention to detail and insistence on rigorous training quickly led to him being considered for further promotion and he was given command of the 91st Brigade in the 7th Division on 26 November that year. For all his undoubted positive qualities, Cumming tended to question orders that he deemed unwise and, after pushing his luck once too often at Bullecourt in May 1917, was compelled to relinquish his command by Major-General Thomas Shoubridge, by then GOC of the 7th Division. Haig, indeed, wrote to the Military Secretary at the War Office on 18 May 1917 that he thought Cumming was 'unfit at present' for a brigade or battalion command in the field, although the position should be reviewed after 'not less than six months'. As Commandant of the Machine Gun Training School at Grantham between August 1917 and February 1918, he had played a pivotal role in the reorganisation of machine-gun companies into battalions with sixty-four guns, a reform which gave the BEF the potential to achieve greater concentrations and tighter tactical control of automatic firepower. Clearly too talented an officer to leave at home, Cumming was rewarded with the command of 110th Brigade, joining his new formation in France only three days before the Germans launched their March offensive. Campbell found his advice to be of 'inestimable value' and described Cumming as 'not only a magnificent leader of men, but also a soldier of the very highest class' who was 'beloved by every one in the Brigade'.[38] Gater, McCulloch and Cumming had all commanded hastily improvised composite formations with distinction in 'puttying-up' the line during the desperate defensive battles in the spring of 1918 and were therefore well-equipped to meet the demands of decentralised command in the semi-open warfare of the 'Hundred Days'.[39]

21 August 1918

As already indicated, the terrain in the V Corps sector posed its own series of problems for an attacking force. The Ancre had been canalised at a higher level than the swampy approaches to the river and, because shelling had damaged the banks, much of the valley was flooded to a width of 300 yards. The main stream was now indistinguishable and the Ancre valley had become a stretch of marsh and water which was covered, in places, by a tangle of fallen trees and branches, reeds, barbed wire and mangled railway track. 'Nowhere is there any solid ground' wrote one soldier of the 6th Leicesters in the 21st Division. Bridges and causeways had been largely destroyed by artillery fire while German artillery and machine guns were ranged on the existing crossing-places. Indeed, the Ancre valley resembled a moat defending the Thiepval heights which loomed above the men of V Corps 'like a great, black hump', scarred with old trench lines.[40]

Shute's orders to his divisions for 21 August outlined three main tasks, the first two of which were assigned to Campbell's 21st Division. This formation was (a) to prolong the right of the neighbouring IV Corps, by approximately 1,000 yards, to the Ancre near Beaucourt and (b) to exploit any initial success by pushing strong battle patrols over the Ancre, between Hamel and Miraumont, in a south-easterly direction. The 38th Division, similarly deploying strong fighting patrols, was to probe the German defences and press on if the enemy displayed any signs of weakening. However, if either division met serious opposition, they were not to commit themselves to a costly attack. Having just returned to the sector, the 17th Division remained in corps reserve, although its artillery would augment that of the 21st Division for the operations scheduled to begin at 5.45 a.m. In all, six field artillery brigades and four brigades of corps heavy artillery supported the two divisions in action that day.[41]

In the 21st Division, the advance on the left was entrusted to George Gater's 62nd Brigade, with the 2nd Lincolnshires in the lead. The latter unit had not been granted a quiet night, having first been called upon to beat off a heavy German raid and then, barely 2 hours before its attack, subjected to a mustard gas bombardment which put around one-hundred men out of action. Nevertheless, in the misty early morning of 21 August, assisted by the fire of 12 Stokes mortars and an 8-minute hurricane bombardment of the village by 18-pounder field guns, the battalion captured Beaucourt by 6.15 a.m., and took 93 prisoners at a cost of only 30 casualties. An advance to the railway was subsequently effected and the 1st Lincolnshires, passing through the lead battalion, pressed on along the sunken road, west and north-west of Baillescourt Farm, in the direction of Miraumont, gaining contact with the 42nd Division from IV Corps in the process.[42] To the south of Beaucourt, the artillery was unable to suppress the fire of German machine guns and it was mid-afternoon before two companies of the 12th/13th Northumberland Fusiliers succeeded in crossing the Ancre and establishing a precarious bridgehead 500 yards beyond the river.[43]

Four companies of the 6th and 7th Leicesters, from Cumming's 110th Brigade, had managed to slip across the Ancre in the early morning mist but, when this lifted, they were exposed to heavy machine-gun fire and could not hold on to their gains. For many of the Leicesters it was their first taste of action. One of them was R.H. Kiernan, who wrote that the air 'was singing with bullets, and fellows were dropping and lying still, all spread out ... The firing stopped. But when we moved it started again. We crawled back as best we could'. The war diary of the 6th Leicesters notes that the companies which returned to the west bank of the Ancre had been badly shaken by the experience. That night, however, the crossings were improved by the 98th Field Company, Royal Engineers, who built two footbridges, enabling the 6th Leicesters to push patrols over to the east bank once more.[44]

The 38th Division, on the right of V Corps, had much the same experience as the 21st Division. Patrols of the 114th Brigade (Brigadier-General T. Rose Price) attempted to cross the Ancre at four different spots during the day but made no headway. Battle patrols of Brigadier-General W.B. Hulke's 115th Brigade did manage to negotiate the water on their part of the front but found the opposite bank too strongly held to make any meaningful progress. Even so, under cover of darkness on the night of 21–22 August, six sections from one company of the 14th Welsh Regiment, part of the 114th Brigade, crossed the river near Hamel and secured a foothold in an unoccupied trench on the southern edge of Thiepval Wood, where they held on against all attacks until reinforced two nights later.

Second-Lieutenant L.O. Griffiths undertook the task of keeping the post supplied with rations, which necessitated him having to swim the Ancre several times. As Cumming indicates, these small unit actions, though not substantial in themselves, represented 'the first step towards gaining complete possession of the high ground which was so important for further operations Eastwards'.[45]

Overall, the Third Army registered a reasonable degree of success on the first day of its offensive. VI Corps took the Moyenneville–Ablainzevelle spur, its first objective, early in the morning (zero hour in this sector was 4.55 a.m.) and reached the Albert–Arras railway along its whole attack frontage, except for half a mile on the right, by about 11.30 a.m. Harper's IV Corps had gained its first objective by around 6 a.m., but, over most of its sector, the railway lay outside the range of the field artillery from its initial positions. With insufficient support from the gunners, IV Corps was unable to overcome resistance from Achiet le Grand and the 42nd (East Lancashire) Division captured, but failed to hold on to, the Beauregard Dovecot that day. Despite advancing some 3 miles, IV Corps did not hold the line of the railway at any point. Thus, although a number of important villages had been secured by Third Army – including Moyenneville, Courcelles, Achiet le Petit, Bucquoy and Puisieux – the results might have been better.[46] The day had turned hot and sultry after a foggy start and Byng – anxious not to overtax inexperienced troops and wishing to move his guns forward – ordered a temporary halt for Third Army on 22 August to allow the men to rest and regroup. In view of the continuing opposition to a crossing in force of the Ancre, he also told V Corps to instruct the 38th Division to remain where it was until III Corps of the Fourth Army had resumed its offensive on 22 August and had taken the town of Albert as already planned. When Albert was in British hands, the German left flank on the Ancre would be turned, clearing the way for the 38th Division to deploy east of the town. Even Byng's initial plans for 23 August were more than a trifle over-cautious, being limited to a VI Corps advance north of Moyenneville to establish a good jumping-off position for a 'further possible advance', against a spur extending north-east from Hamelincourt, on an unspecified date. Byng's apparent lack of drive contrasted sharply with the approach of the French Tenth Army, which had thrust forward 5 miles in two days on 20–21 August. It is therefore scarcely surprising that, at 10.30 p.m., when Herbert Lawrence informed Haig that Byng had decided to suspend major operations the following day, the Commander-in-Chief was quick to voice his frustration and disappointment. 'I expressed *the wish* that the attack should be resumed at the earliest possible moment', he recorded in his diary.[47]

22 August 1918

All too aware of Haig's obvious impatience and displeasure, Byng and his staff – working closely with Haldane, the commander of VI Corps – were goaded into a flurry of activity on the morning of 22 August, substantially revising their plans for the following day and preparing a wider and more vigorous attack. The new plans were subsequently approved by Haig's chief of staff, Herbert Lawrence. Instead of a limited advance by VI Corps alone against the spur running north-east from Hamelincourt, all three corps in the Third Army would be in action, with support from aircraft and tanks. After capturing Gomiecourt on the night of 22–23 August, VI Corps was to push on east towards Ervillers and Sapignies. Once Gomiecourt had fallen, Harper's IV Corps was to advance and attack Irles and Achiet le Grand. In the V Corps sector, the 38th Division was to co-operate with III Corps of Fourth Army in operations designed to drive the Germans away from Albert and thereby turn the southern flank of the Thiepval position. As Paul Harris puts it, the aim of Third Army on 23 August would now be 'to break the front of the German Seventeenth Army that day and to inflict a major defeat'.[48] Shortly before noon on 22 August, GHQ issued another 'hurry-up' order, urging that the Third Army's offensive should be resumed with maximum energy: 'The enemy is being pressed from the Scarpe to Soissons and it is essential ... that he should be attacked continuously and with the utmost determination'.[49] Since Third Army's plans had largely been revised by then, this latest directive from Haig was virtually redundant.

Byng's apparent caution and limited ambition on the previous day did have one fortunate spin-off, in that, on 22 August, General Otto von Below, of the German Seventeenth Army, was encouraged to order a general counter-stroke against the divisions of Third Army. Organised in haste and ill-co-ordinated, the localised counter-attacks which resulted made little impression, failed to achieve a serious penetration at any point and merely weakened the German Seventeenth Army even further.[50] The 62nd Brigade of the 21st Division was, however, subjected to a number of such attacks by part of the German 40th Division during the early morning and evening of 22 August. One of these drove its extreme left flank back slightly while another got within 30 yards of the line. All the enemy assaults were repulsed with significant losses, although the 62nd Brigade's own casualties were reported to be 'fairly heavy'. In the meantime, on the right, units of Cumming's 110th Brigade had been busy establishing themselves over the Ancre. Two companies of the 6th Leicesters crossed the river north of St Pierre Divion and gained contact with the forward companies of the 12th/13th Northumberland Fusiliers, from the 62nd Brigade, which were already on the opposite bank. Bombing parties and fighting patrols of the 110th Brigade, despite machine-gun fire from the Thiepval ridge, also secured important footholds in several trenches on the east bank, including Logging Trench, Logging Support, Luff Avenue and Candy Avenue. Having gradually consolidated a vital bridgehead across the Ancre, 110th Brigade was relieved that night by the 50th Brigade of the 17th (Northern) Division.[51]

Until Albert was recaptured, it would remain extremely difficult for V Corps and, in particular, the 38th Division, to negotiate all the swamps and marshes of the Ancre and keep pace with the rest of Third Army. The job of clearing Albert, on 22 August, was entrusted to the 18th (Eastern) Division, the left-wing formation of Fourth Army. The division had been commanded, since January 1917, by Maxse's successor, Major-General Richard Lee, a sapper of 'quick grip and decision'.[52] The redoubtable E.A. Wood (see Chapter 6) was still in command of 55th Brigade, which was handed the task of securing the ruined town and pushing along the narrow-gauge railway to its east. This was no easy assignment, as the town was full of land mines and booby traps (136 were removed by the Royal Engineers that day) and the 8th East Surreys, detailed to carry out the operation, were shelled with high-explosive and gas shells while assembling for the attack. Even so, advancing under a barrage at 5.45 a.m., the East Surreys took many German posts by surprise in the morning mist and by 10 a.m. the town was practically free of the enemy. When the 7th Buffs, under Lieutenant-Colonel A.L. Ransome, tried to advance from the East Surrey line, they encountered such severe machine-gun fire from the western slopes of Tara Hill that they suffered many casualties, persuading Ransome that it would be wiser to abandon the assault for the time being.[53]

It was clear that, to make satisfactory progress on this flank, the Tara and Usna Hills, astride the Albert–Bapaume road, must be seized. Major-Generals Lee, of the 18th Division, and Cubitt, of the 38th Division, duly conferred and decided that, early on 23 August, a combined attack should be made, with the 53rd Brigade of the 18th Division moving against Tara Hill and the 113th Brigade of the 38th Division, passing through Albert, assaulting Usna Hill. But, so that both brigades would have adequate room in which to deploy east of Albert, it would first be necessary for the 55th Brigade to gain the final objective on the Albert–Bapaume road, which it had been unable to reach in daylight. This preliminary operation was at least partly organised by Lieutenant-Colonel Ransome and Brigadier-General Wood in what Mark Connelly terms a 'vignette' of devolved command to the 'men on the spot' by 1918. Following a 4-hour preparation by all available artillery, machine-guns and mortars between 7 p.m. and 11 p.m., the 7th Buffs, covered by patrols, advanced again 'with great dash' in a classic fire and movement attack, gaining their original final objective by 2.30 a.m. on 23 August.[54] At the same time, during the night of 22–23 August, the 114th Brigade of the 38th Division sent two companies of the 15th Welsh Regiment, under Captain G.W. Lancaster and Lieutenant Glyn Williams, across the Ancre near Hamel, though these parties were compelled to wade through chest-high water under fire. The companies then established positions near St Pierre Divion and held them throughout the next day and night against repeated attacks. Like those achieved by the 21st Division, these small bridgeheads would be of considerable value as the V Corps operations developed and were the product of good junior leadership by the officers and NCOs involved.[55]

To inject even more 'ginger' into his troops on the eve of the resumed offensive, Haig despatched a telegram to the commanders of all the British Armies on the Western Front at 11.30 p.m. on 22 August. In this message Haig requested the army commanders to point out to 'all subordinate leaders' the changed conditions under which operations were now being conducted and to instil in them the need for all ranks 'to act with the utmost boldness and resolution' so that full advantage could be taken of the enemy's apparent exhaustion and disorganisation. The methods which had applied hitherto in battles with limited objectives were, Haig claimed, 'no longer suited' to present circumstances. He added:

> It is no longer necessary to advance in regular lines and step by step. On the contrary, each division should be given a distant objective which must be reached independently of its neighbour, and even if one's flank is thereby exposed for the time being ... Reinforcements must be directed on the points where our troops are gaining ground, not where they are checked.[56]

Haig's latest exhortation came too late to influence events the following day but, as will be seen, it does appear to have had an effect on command decisions and the conduct of operations at corps and divisional level on 24 August.

23 August 1918

As Paul Harris has noted, the operations of the BEF and Third Army on 23 August have a rather 'ragged appearance'. Under pressure from Haig, Byng had been forced to mount an attack on a wider scale than he had originally envisaged, so 'the planning at corps level was inevitably somewhat hurried and unco-ordinated', with formations going into action at different times. Nevertheless, Third Army had a very successful day and won a major victory. Haldane's VI Corps duly seized Gomiecourt before taking Hamelincourt, Boiry Becquerelle, Ervillers and the St Léger ridge. In a preliminary operation launched by IV Corps, units of the 42nd (East Lancashire) Division and the New Zealand Division finally secured the Beauregard Dovecot and the ridge to its north-east which commanded the valley traversed by the Albert–Arras railway. Harper's troops subsequently gained possession of Irles, Bihucourt and Achiet le Grand. In all, Third Army advanced between 2,000 and 3,000 yards and had taken over 5,000 prisoners.[57]

V Corps was less heavily involved in Third Army's operations on 23 August, since its own main effort was to be made the following night. The principal action was that carried out by the 113th Brigade of the 38th Division in co-operation with the 18th Division of III Corps, its aim being to drive the Germans further away from Albert and secure a line over the Tara and Usna Hills, along Rubber Trench and down to the Ancre marshes south-east of Aveluy. When this had been achieved, an attempt was to be made on the left by 115th Brigade to press on out of the Ancre valley to Crucifix Corner, the site of a strongpoint. On the night of 22–23 August, the 113th Brigade (Brigadier-General H.E. ap Rhys Pryce) had passed through Albert across reconstructed bridges which were under continual shell fire. The men had then formed up, within 100 yards of the enemy, in the angle between the Ancre and the Albert–Bapaume road, a manoeuvre which required the two attacking battalions, the 13th and 14th Royal Welsh Fusiliers, to leave Albert by the Bapaume road and then perform a flank movement to their left. The 18th Division's part in the operation would be executed by Brigadier-General M.G.H. Barker's 53rd Brigade, attacking with three battalions abreast: the

10th Essex, the 7th Royal West Kents and the 7th Queen's (attached from 55th Brigade). Michael Barker was a worthy successor to Harold Higginson (see Chapters 4 and 6). A tall young officer, still in his early thirties, he was highly praised by the divisional historian: 'His tirelessness, his pride in his brigade, his dash, his very youth proved to be great assets, particularly in the swift moving warfare of the Hundred Days'.[58]

The joint attack began at 4.45 a.m. The 53rd Brigade, supported by six tanks and a divisional artillery barrage, met strong opposition at first but, despite the fatigue of its young recruits, overcame the enemy, thanks to outstanding local leadership by company and platoon officers. For example, with the assistance of one NCO, Captain C.F. Bland – a Territorial officer attached to the 10th Essex – successively eliminated three German machine-gun posts. By 6 a.m. Tara Hill and 350 prisoners were in the Brigade's hands. The Welsh Division's attack was aided by two tanks and covered by divisional artillery and machine-gun barrages. It proved equally successful. Usna Hill was taken, the enemy line was outflanked and another 194 Germans surrendered, but the cost was not light. The 13th Royal Welsh Fusiliers alone lost 1 officer and 20 other ranks killed and 5 officers and 117 other ranks wounded.[59]

To the left of this attack, the crossing of Brigadier-General W.B. Hulke's 115th Brigade was made easier by the initiative of two small parties on 23 August. The site of the bridge at Aveluy was under fire from German posts on a spur to the south. A party led by Lieutenant Connell of the 13th Royal Welsh Fusiliers captured one of these posts with seven machine guns. Another strongpoint was captured by 'A' Company of the 2nd Royal Welsh Fusiliers, under Second-Lieutenant J.O. Smith. This officer made several attempts to ford the river and floods below Aveluy before finding a suitable crossing-point. He then got his company across in small groups, rushed the post and killed or captured thirty Germans as well as seizing eight machine guns. The 115th Brigade was now able to cross the Ancre, clear Crucifix Corner – the site of yet another German strongpoint – and come up on the left of 113th Brigade.[60] Brigadier-General T. Rose Price's 114th Brigade, on the left of the divisional front, also had to engage in some hard fighting on 23 August and, here too, the men had to swim or wade the Ancre, though the brigade pushed more posts into Thiepval Wood.[61] The strength of the German position at Thiepval was being progressively undermined.

Early in the morning of 23 August, the 50th Brigade of the 17th Division had relieved the 110th Brigade east of the Ancre. Even this proved difficult, as all the crossings – particularly the long narrow track over damaged causeways near St Pierre Divion – were frequently swept with enemy artillery and machine-gun fire, and the valley was full of gas. The leading battalion, the 6th Dorsets, dribbled over the river and floods in single file and in small groups, all becoming soaked to the skin in the process, but, by 5 a.m., had taken over the line of Logging Trench. As daylight was now coming, the other two battalions, the 10th West Yorkshires and the 7th East Yorkshires, remained on the west bank. In the course of the morning the Dorsets pushed on up the hillside for another 400 yards, consolidating a line, already won from the enemy, along Logging Support and its southern extension known as Common Lane. During the rest of the day, by means of almost continuous skirmishing, patrols of the 6th Dorsets strove to occupy Cannon and Cash Trenches near the crest and thereby secure a better starting-point for the planned night attack on the ridge. Partly because the 38th Division as yet had too few troops across the Ancre in this area to offer effective support, the Dorsets could not quite reach Cannon and Cash Trenches and eventually established themselves in an advanced line just 300 yards short of the desired jumping-off position.[62]

The Night Advance, 23–24 August 1918

To maintain the momentum of the offensive, as Haig wished, it had been decided that the next phase of the advance would begin at 1 a.m. on the night of 23–24 August, thus taking advantage of bright moonlight. It was hoped that launching the attack at this hour would not only surprise the Germans but would also leave a full day on 24 August for exploitation. The official history states that Byng's orders for the continuation of Third Army's advance eastward were issued at 5.35 p.m. on 23 August but it is clear from the evidence that detailed planning of the night attack was already well under way at corps and divisional level by that time. Shute, for example, had held a conference at the headquarters of the 38th Division at 10.30 a.m. on 23 August and 21st Division's initial operation order had been issued at 3.15 p.m. that afternoon.[63]

As noted earlier in the chapter, the obstacles presented by the floods and marshes of the Ancre from Aveluy to nearly half a mile north of Authuille persuaded Shute to plan converging attacks from north and south of the swampy area. These attacks would subsequently link up on a line running from Grandcourt to Ovillers and La Boisselle. Shute's scheme would also enable V Corps to avoid having to make a direct assault on the Thiepval position itself, which was located just to the north of the sector protected by the floods. The northern attack, to be made in a south-easterly direction, would be carried out by the 21st Division, the 50th Brigade of the 17th Division and the centre and left of the 38th Division. It was intended that these formations would take Thiepval from the flank, secure the high ground beyond it as well as Grandcourt, and then join up with the southern attack approximately half a mile north-north-east of Ovillers. The southern attack, which was to be directed north-eastwards, was assigned to the right wing of the 38th Division, acting together with the left of the 18th Division. If successful, V Corps would push on to a line stretching from Contalmaison and Pozières to a point roughly 1,000 yards south-east of Miraumont. Morval would be the objective of a further advance, should that prove possible. A creeping barrage would be fired at zero hour by 144 field guns and 60 heavy guns. The official historian remarks that this was a small number of artillery pieces to cover a front of more than 8,000 yards but was nevertheless 'sufficient to satisfy the infantry at this stage of the war'. The remainder of the heavy guns were to keep firing on the ground between the southern and northern wings of the advance until Cubitt's 38th Division was in a position to finish mopping-up. The principal feature of the ground facing

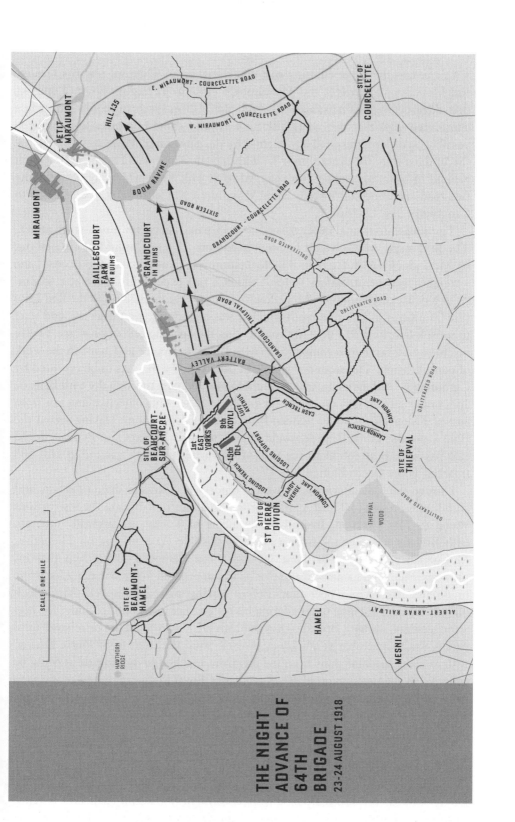

THE NIGHT
ADVANCE OF
64TH
BRIGADE
23-24 AUGUST 1918

SCALE : ONE MILE

HAWTHORN
RIDGE

SITE OF
BEAUMONT-
HAMEL

HAMEL

MESNIL

ALBERT-ARRAS RAILWAY

SITE OF
ST PIERRE DIVION

LOGGING TRENCH

COMMON LANE
AVENUE

CANDY
AVENUE

THIEPVAL
WOOD

SITE OF
THIEPVAL

SITE OF BEAUCOURT-SUR-ANCRE

1st EAST YORKS

15th DLI

9th KOYLI

LUKE AVENUE

LOGGING SUPPORT

CASH TRENCH

CANNON TRENCH

CANNON LANE

BATTERY VALLEY

GRANDCOURT-THIEPVAL ROAD

OBLITERATED ROAD

OBLITERATED ROAD

OBLITERATED ROAD

GRANDCOURT IN RUINS

SIXTEEN ROAD

GRANDCOURT - COURCELETTE ROAD

BOOM RAVINE

BAILLESCOURT
FARM
IN RUINS

MIRAUMONT

PETIT
MIRAUMONT

HILL 135

W. MIRAUMONT - COURCELETTE ROAD

E. MIRAUMONT - COURCELETTE ROAD

SITE OF
COURCELETTE

V Corps was the ridge running east-south-east from Thiepval towards Ginchy and Morval with Pozières and Martinpuich close to its highest point. A spur of that ridge overlooked Miraumont, which was still in German hands, and it was considered vital that this particular high ground should be taken as rapidly as possible, in order to forestall any attempt by the garrison of Miraumont to destroy the bridges over the Ancre prior to withdrawal. The task of securing the high ground in question (sometimes referred to as Hill 135), which lay between the two roads running southwards from Miraumont to Courcelette, was allotted to Campbell's 21st Division.[64]

The initial divisional order, issued at 3.15 p.m., called for a two-stage attack. The first stage, which would begin at zero hour (1 a.m.), would be carried out by McCulloch's 64th Brigade. The formation was to advance to the Brown Line – roughly the line of Battery Valley – which it was expected to reach at 1.40 a.m. After a pause of 10 minutes, McCulloch's troops were to press on to the Red Line (the Grandcourt–Thiepval road) which it was hoped they would secure, and start to consolidate, by 2.30 a.m. After augmenting the opening artillery barrage, twelve machine guns were to accompany the 64th Brigade advance and assist in the work of consolidation. The second stage of the attack, at 5 a.m., was to be executed by Cumming's 110th Brigade, which would follow and pass through the 64th Brigade and, under a fresh barrage, make for the Blue Line. This objective line ran from east of Thiepval and along Sixteen Road to Petit Miraumont. Having seized the Blue Line, the 110th Brigade would exploit towards Le Sars and Pys but would also pay special attention to the task of capturing the high ground at Hill 135 (marked as the Green Dotted Line).[65]

During the late afternoon, however, reports of German demoralisation and withdrawal prompted Third Army to order last-minute changes to the instructions issued to 21st Division. Instead of advancing at 1 a.m., as originally ordered, 64th Brigade was now to attack as soon as possible. At 5.30 p.m. on 23 August, McCulloch received a telephone message from Campbell telling him that his previous orders were amended and that he was to proceed to divisional headquarters to discuss the revised operation. Before leaving to see Campbell, McCulloch himself issued a warning order altering his own earlier instructions. Under the new arrangements, the 64th Brigade – less the 15th DLI, who could not be relieved until dark – was to assemble as quickly as possible amid the ruins of St Pierre Divion, with as many machine guns from the company attached to the brigade as could be collected in the time now available. A section of Royal Engineers would continue to work on the Ancre crossings and would mark out jumping-off places with pickets, while the 64th Light Trench Mortar Battery was to stand ready to bombard enemy positions on the railway passing north of Grandcourt.[66]

When McCulloch arrived at divisional headquarters, he received confirmation that his new first objective would be the ridge line immediately east of the Grandcourt–Courcelette road. On reaching this, the 64th Brigade would no longer wait for the 110th Brigade to pass through but would itself now advance to seize the high ground at Hill 135 on the Green Dotted Line. 110th Brigade was to advance echeloned in rear of McCulloch's brigade with the object of linking up with the right of 64th Brigade and the left of the 17th Division on the Green Dotted Line. A creeping barrage would be provided by the 21st Division's artillery and sixteen heavy guns of the XVII Brigade, Royal Garrison Artillery. Not surprisingly, McCulloch tried to explain to Campbell that he would prefer to carry out the original plan 'rather than a hurried and impromptu performance' which, because of the scattered positions of his units, could not commence before 10.30 p.m. at the earliest. Although he admitted that 'others knew the situation in rear of the German outposts better than I did', McCulloch later wrote that, at the time, he 'did not care much for the idea' of advancing at night, without troops on his right or left, to an objective some 3 miles away. 'At the first blush', he commented, the scheme 'appeared somewhat ambitious'. McCulloch's protests were in vain and a new zero hour was fixed for 11.30 p.m. that evening.[67]

Back at his brigade headquarters, McCulloch encountered further problems. One company of the 1st East Yorkshires had somehow got lost; orders for the one available company of the 15th DLI had 'miscarried'; and it became obvious that there was every chance that the Vickers guns would not all be ready in time to accompany the brigade forward. Taking steps to put these matters right, McCulloch called his battalion commanders together to brief them in person. 'It was dark and raining at the time and other conditions did not admit of elaborate written orders', he recalled. Urging his battalion COs 'to push on boldly regardless of the presence or otherwise of our troops on the flank of the brigade', he instructed them to halt and reorganise on the first objective, at which point he would give them orders for the advance to the Green Dotted Line. To maintain cohesion in the dark, McCulloch adopted an interesting and unusual attack formation. Preceded by a brigade guide in the centre, the 9th KOYLI on the right and the 1st East Yorkshires on the left – each less one company – would lead the advance. Behind them would be the brigade reserve, consisting of the two detached companies of the 9th KOYLI and the East Yorkshires, the one available company of the 15th DLI, and eight Vickers guns. Each of the lead battalions was to have two companies in the front line with a third in support, and each company would move in a square formation, with a platoon at each angle of the square. The platoons would be 20 yards apart in either direction and a similar distance would separate the companies. The brigade reserve was to march about a hundred yards behind the centre, while brigade headquarters would be immediately in rear of the reserve. Any Germans who offered resistance from close in front were to be charged at once, and the battalions were also to post a party on their exposed flank ready to rush out and capture any Germans or machine guns endangering that flank, but the troops were to ignore enemy fire which came from some distance away.[68]

The 64th Brigade duly passed through the line held by the 62nd Brigade and entered Battery Valley around midnight. The barrage was on time and generally successful in subduing enemy fire but some heavy guns failed to lift their fire at the prescribed time of 11.45 p.m., with the result that the 64th Brigade received three bursts of 'friendly' fire and suffered some thirty casualties. Soon after this incident, the leading troops rushed the German outpost line in Battery Valley, getting to within fifteen yards of the outposts before the enemy opened fire. Here several Germans were killed and thirty prisoners were taken, although McCulloch had to intervene personally when one platoon, whose own leaders had been killed or wounded, showed signs of wavering and came back towards the rear. McCulloch reported:

> I do not think these men were panic-stricken. They simply had faced a blow – had their directing hand removed and were in a sort of invertebrate state with no will to guide them … [It] is in this that the danger of night fighting lies. Directly these men met me and found someone who meant business they responded willingly and went on with their task.

From this point on the men advanced 'full of confidence', charging more German positions and taking additional prisoners. The brigade's first objective was reached at 1 a.m. on 24 August.

By now the Germans were beginning to attack 64th Brigade from the south, so McCulloch used the brigade reserve and the available Vickers guns to deal with this threat to his right flank. This measure too was successful, although McCulloch admitted that the enemy soldiers involved in the action were of poor quality. 'They evinced no desire to close with us and find out what was doing. The prisoners we caught were frightened'. At the first objective, McCulloch ordered a pause for reorganisation until 3.15 a.m., when the advance would be resumed. As there were still numbers of German troops in the vicinity, he hoped that the pause would be long enough to allow 110th Brigade the opportunity to arrive, meaning that he would no longer have to continue his attack unsupported. On the other hand, he could not wait too long, as he wanted to have at least 90 minutes on the final objective before daylight so that adequate defences could be arranged and dug. To McCulloch's relief, the rest of the 15th DLI, at least, reached him at 2.15 a.m. and were deployed on the right of the 9th KOYLI. On the left the support and reserve companies of the 1st East Yorkshires mopped up the village of Grandcourt, seizing more than 100 prisoners together with 4 field guns and 20 machine guns.[69]

When the advance began again, some opposition was met in Boom Ravine – a difficult enough obstacle in itself with its precipitous sides and limited eastern exits. The Germans in front, once some of their comrades had been killed or captured, fled in all directions, throwing away their rifles and equipment. The 9th KOYLI arrived on the final objective at Hill 135 around 4.30 a.m., with about 15 minutes remaining before daylight in which to occupy a line of shell holes. The Durhams, who had been attacked on the right while crossing Boom Ravine, came up 45 minutes later and established a short defensive flank to the right of the 9th KOYLI. The 1st East Yorkshires were similarly held up and did not manage to reach the line gained by the 9th KOYLI, so took up positions – about 1,000 yards to the rear – where they hoped to be able to protect the brigade's left flank. Having reached his main objective, however, McCulloch was granted little time in which to organise its consolidation and defence for, on proceeding south for a few hundred yards in an effort to locate the 15th DLI, he was hit in the thigh by a machine-gun bullet and obliged to hand over command to Lieutenant-Colonel C.E.R. Holroyd-Smyth of the Durhams. Despite its outstanding success, the 64th Brigade's position was still far from secure. No other troops had yet arrived on its flanks, which were both in the air. Rifle and machine-gun fire assailed the troops from all quarters and casualties steadily mounted, while Germans were filtering back into Boom Ravine and Battery Valley, threatening the brigade's communications to the rear. At risk of being cut off, the three battalions were counter-attacked by the Germans and called upon to surrender but all such moves by the enemy were repulsed or rejected and the officers and men of the 64th Brigade stood their ground. Towards midday, the situation began to ease. British troops could be observed to the north, advancing on Miraumont and, elsewhere, the general advance of the Third and Fourth Armies was now well under way. The Germans facing the 64th Brigade – apparently from the 30th and 68th Reserve Infantry Regiments of the 16th Reserve Division – at last started to retire and leave the brigade 'in comparative peace'.[70]

The 110th Brigade, meanwhile, had been ordered to concentrate in Battery Valley at midnight and form up for its advance with the 6th Leicesters on the right, the 7th Leicesters in the centre and the 1st Wiltshires on the left. Although the night assembly involved a march over difficult ground and a river crossing over narrow footbridges, it was carried out without any major hitch. However, as the leading battalion, the 6th Leicesters, had approached Battery Valley, they discovered that the southern end, and a trench line south of it, was still in German possession. The commanding officer of the 6th Leicesters, Lieutenant-Colonel M.C. Martyn, at once launched an assault on these positions, driving the Germans out and effectively clearing the valley – at least for the time being. The action, nevertheless, necessitated a change in the attack formation. Now the 7th Leicesters and the 1st Wiltshires would lead, with the 6th Leicesters, who had to reorganise after the skirmish, following in support. R.H. Kiernan, of the 6th Leicesters, remembered chasing 'a lot of Jerries along a trench, just as it was getting light, we on the top and they on the inside ... [They] were all very young and small ... and they sang and danced when they had to form fours and march back as prisoners'.[71]

At 5 a.m. Cumming's brigade started to advance eastwards out of Battery Valley towards their objective. By 7.40 a.m. divisional headquarters was aware of the 64th Brigade's fragile hold on Hill 135 and Campbell directed Cumming to proceed by the quickest possible route to protect the 64th Brigade's right flank. The 110th Brigade moved steadily forward even though there was as yet no sign of the 17th Division on its own right. Thus, with its flank in the air, the 110th Brigade was subjected to continual machine-gun fire from the right during the whole of its advance. In spite of this, the brigade pressed on and at about 9 a.m. Cumming decided to shift his headquarters forward to a sunken road, around 1,000 yards west of Boom Ravine, where the advance temporarily stalled. On arrival at this spot, Cumming ordered the left battalion, the 1st Wiltshires, to drive on, while he sent word back to the supporting guns to lengthen their range – the barrage having been overrun. The 7th Leicesters were told to follow slightly in echelon on the right and to push out a company to protect that flank. At 1.15 p.m. Cumming was able to report that, although small parties of Germans were still present in Boom Ravine, his troops had gained touch with those of the 64th Brigade and were extending their line to the right. However, the whereabouts of the 17th Division remained unknown.[72]

For a time there was some anxiety about the fate of the two leading companies of the 7th Leicesters, under Captain H.R. Horne and Captain J.C. Vanner. These companies had been diverted from their true line of advance by enfilade fire from the right and had ended up on the outskirts of Courcelette, which was in the 17th Division's sector. Ignoring the potential perils of their situation, the two companies proceeded to enter the village, where they overcame four machine guns and strongpoints and rounded up a large number of prisoners, including a battalion commander. Despite the worries they had caused him, Cumming described the action as 'quite a brilliant little affair' which reflected much credit on the leadership of the two officers concerned.[73]

The late changes to the 21st Division's orders undoubtedly caused some dislocation to the 17th Division's plan at the beginning of its own advance, as the bringing forward of the 64th Brigade's start-time meant that, for some hours, there would inevitably be a considerable space between the right of the 21st Division and the left of the 17th Division's 50th Brigade. The changes also involved an extension to the 17th Division's frontage on that flank of around 500 yards. 'A' Company of the 7th East Yorkshires was therefore deployed on the left of the 6th Dorsets to prolong the front and protect the exposed flank. 50th Brigade's assault at 1 a.m. was led by the 10th West Yorkshires on the right and the 6th Dorsets on the left, under a barrage fired by the divisional artillery and sixteen guns of the LXII Brigade, Royal Garrison Artillery. One company of the West Yorkshires actually passed through the supporting barrage and contributed to the success of the battalion's right by attacking the Germans there in flank and rear. The Dorsets, however, met tougher resistance and it was not until the remainder of the East Yorkshires were brought up on the left that the 50th Brigade, now with all three of its battalions engaged, was able to make more significant progress. The labyrinth of old trenches around the Stuff and Schwaben Redoubts – which had given the BEF such trouble in 1916 – were outflanked and secured and the brigade pushed across the desolate zone of ruins, tree stumps and shell holes that had once been the site of Thiepval village, chateau and park. By 8 a.m. the 50th Brigade was reported to be on the Red Line, the first objective on the crest of the ridge east of Thiepval, having taken 214 prisoners, including 6 officers.

On receipt of this news, V Corps ordered the advance to be continued 'with the utmost vigour', so Robertson quickly issued new instructions, by telephone, for the 50th Brigade to press on towards Courcelette, with the 52nd Brigade (under Brigadier-General W. Allason) coming up in support on its right as early as possible. Unfortunately, at this point, the 50th Brigade – operating on ground largely devoid of notable landmarks – failed to execute a half-swing to the left towards Courcelette and instead veered south-east in the direction of Pozières. The error could be seen by the brigade staff from the western slopes of the Ancre. Attempts were made to contact the 50th Brigade, first by flag signals and then by sending forward a mounted staff officer, but the latter was too late to rectify the mistake. The 52nd Brigade, following in support, was seriously delayed by the difficulties of crossing the Ancre, yet did manage to maintain the right direction, reaching a position within 1,000 yards of Courcelette by the late afternoon. Here it discovered that the 50th Brigade was not in front as it should have been and that, despite the gallant action of the 7th Leicesters, the village was still in German hands. A line of outposts was therefore formed and contact was eventually made with the 50th Brigade. Even so, a wide gap remained around Courcelette between the 21st and 17th Divisions, enabling the Germans who had been holding up the advance in Battery Valley and Boom Ravine to slip away to the east.

The 50th Brigade occupied the ruins of Pozières at about 4 p.m., being boosted by the arrival of the first of a few 18-pounders which had been moved forward across the Ancre, albeit with restricted ammunition supplies. The mistake in direction by the 50th Brigade also had a fortunate by-product in that its seizure of Pozières trapped a large body of Germans who were retiring before the 38th Division's advance up the Albert–Bapaume road. The Germans, however, were reluctant to relinquish such a tactically important site, launching two determined counter-attacks, supported by artillery, against the 50th Brigade's positions at Pozières. Both were repulsed with heavy losses to the German infantry. When the fighting in this area died down, the 50th Brigade had been in action for more than 17 hours, had advanced approximately 3 miles and had taken nearly 350 prisoners.[74]

In the 38th Division's sector, on the right of the attack frontage of V Corps, the 14th and 15th Battalions of the Welsh Regiment, part of 114th Brigade, still had to cross the Ancre near Hamel to reach the start-line at Thiepval Wood. The 15th Welsh found a bridge ready, but the men of the 14th Welsh were not so lucky and the majority of the latter battalion had to wade through chest-high water in the dark. While forming up on the far bank, they were counter-attacked and, although the Germans here were driven off, only one company reached Thiepval Wood by zero hour. To add to the mounting problems, the Vickers and Lewis guns available for the assault arrived some 90 minutes late. Nevertheless, at 1 a.m. – supported by a barrage fired by four field batteries and twelve heavier guns of the XXXV Brigade, Royal Garrison Artillery – the companies which *were* present attacked in a south-easterly direction. Meeting only relatively light opposition, they stormed the heights, assisted in the capture of Thiepval and formed up on the right of the first objective of the 50th Brigade.[75]

It was intended that, as the 114th Brigade pushed south-east, the 113th Brigade and the right of the 115th Brigade would attack in a north-easterly direction, converging with the 114th at a point well to the east of Aveluy Wood. In the centre of the divisional front, the 2nd Royal Welsh Fusiliers, of the 115th Brigade,

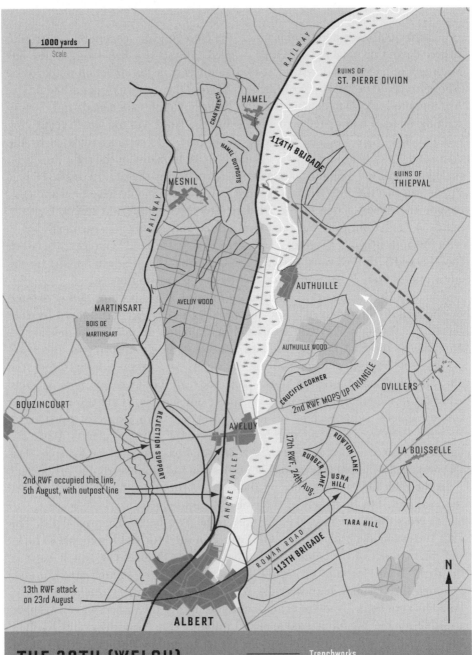

1000 yards
Scale

RAILWAY

RUINS OF
ST. PIERRE DIVION

CRAB TRENCH

HAMEL

114TH BRIGADE

HAMEL OUTPOSTS

RUINS OF
THIEPVAL

MESNIL

RAILWAY

AUTHUILLE

MARTINSART

AVELUY WOOD

AUTHUILLE WOOD

BOIS DE
MARTINSART

CRUCIFIX CORNER

2nd RWF MOPS UP TRIANGLE

OVILLERS

BOUZINCOURT

REJECTION SUPPORT

AVELUY

ROWTON LANE

LA BOISSELLE

RUBBER LANE

17th RWF, 24th Aug.

USNA
HILL

ANCRE VALLEY

2nd RWF occupied this line,
5th August, with outpost line

TARA HILL

ROMAN ROAD

113TH BRIGADE

13th RWF attack
on 23rd August

ALBERT

N

THE 38TH (WELSH)
DIVISION'S SECTOR
23-24 AUGUST 1918

Trenchworks

Railways

Roads

 Ancre Valley Marshes
and River

Brigade boundaries

were assigned the task of mopping-up the triangle of territory around Crucifix Corner, Authuille Wood and Authuille village, between the converging arms of the division's attack. The main assault on the right was led by the 16th and 14th Royal Welsh Fusiliers of 113th Brigade and the 17th Royal Welsh Fusiliers of 115th Brigade. According to the official history, the village of La Boisselle was taken 'without much difficulty' by the 16th Royal Welsh Fusiliers, but the same could not be said of the old 1916 mine crater (now known as Lochnagar Crater) which, together with a few nearby strongpoints, resisted capture until late in the day. It was not until after 8 p.m. that the position was finally taken, under a Stokes mortar bombardment, with a great deal of help from the 8th Royal Berkshires of the 18th Division. Further to the left, the advance of the 17th Royal Welsh Fusiliers was halted by Germans in a trench in front of Ovillers. The 10th South Wales Borderers, of the 115th Brigade, who had previously been assisting with the work of mopping-up, were sent up on the left of the 17th Royal Welsh Fusiliers, only to be stopped by fire from a northern continuation of the same trench. The 2nd Royal Welsh Fusiliers, however, had a happier experience, successfully clearing the triangle around Authuille Wood and taking over 200 prisoners and 17 machine guns in the process.[76]

The continued German resistance at Ovillers persuaded V Corps to direct Major-General Cubitt to 'pinch out' the village, so the latter ordered a fresh advance, beginning at 4 p.m. Aiming to envelop Ovillers, Cubitt instructed the 113th Brigade on the right to drive on towards Contalmaison. The 115th Brigade, in the centre, would avoid a direct assault on the village and, instead, push past it on the higher ground to its north, and the 114th Brigade, coming south-eastwards from Thiepval, was to proceed towards Pozières. The new attack did not, in fact, get under way until 5.30 p.m. and then made very slow progress in the face of heavy machine-gun fire. The 113th Brigade was stopped in front of Contalmaison and the 114th Brigade, finding that Pozières had already been occupied by the 17th Division, halted on the Ovillers–Courcelette road, yet the enveloping movement ultimately had the desired effect. Realising that they were in danger of being outflanked to the north by 115th Brigade, the Germans eventually abandoned Ovillers and the ruins of the village were clear of the enemy by 10 p.m. that evening. As a result of the day's fighting, the 38th (Welsh) Division had taken 643 prisoners and 143 machine guns.[77]

Thus ended a highly successful night and day for V Corps. Thiepval, La Boisselle, Ovillers and Pozières – which, collectively, had resisted capture for weeks in the summer of 1916 – had all fallen into British hands once more, but this time within the space of 24 hours. In addition, thanks partly to the seizure of the high ground to its south-east by McCulloch's 64th Brigade, Miraumont too was cleared by the 42nd Division, of the neighbouring IV Corps, by the late afternoon of 24 August. Although a small gap still existed between the 17th and 21st Divisions around Courcelette, the Germans were in no state to take advantage of the situation and the village was finally secured by the 51st Brigade of the 17th Division the following day as V Corps pressed on towards Flers, Mametz Wood, High Wood and Gueudecourt. As the official historian himself records, the audacity of some of the operations of V Corps on 24 August had been duly rewarded.[78]

The recapture of Thiepval and the Ancre Heights on 24 August had certainly *not* been the product of a massively supported, limited-objective, 'bite and hold' attack, as seen at Vimy Ridge, Messines Ridge and the Menin Road Ridge in 1917. Nor had it been a carefully orchestrated, classic combined-arms assault of the type delivered at Hamel and Amiens in the summer of 1918. Orders for the attack of 23–24 August were by no means elaborate, were generally issued at relatively short notice and were subject to changes at the eleventh hour. As we have observed, much had to be hastily improvised. In the words of the historian of the 17th Division, painfully acquired skills in set-piece attacks did not necessarily count for a great deal on 24 August, as keeping direction 'from trench line to trench line up communication trenches in an assault rehearsal on model trench lines, explained in detail and marked out on large scale trench plans, was not an experience that helped towards guiding an advance over a desolate wilderness of ground like the battlefield of that day'.[79] Furthermore, key elements of the BEF's 1918 combined-arms tactical weapons system – such as tanks and ground-attack aircraft – had either been absent or of comparatively little assistance in the V Corps sector on 23–24 August and, once the local divisional barrages had been fired, the river crossings and the nature of the terrain dictated that field guns could, at first, only be dribbled forward individually or in sections to provide close support for the advance. For all the difficulties faced, losses were not necessarily excessive in this battle. The 9th KOYLI, in McCulloch's brigade, for example, suffered only twenty-three fatal casualties, including one officer, on 23–24 August.[80]

The advance had not, of course, been conducted without its share of mistakes. The war diarist of the 17th Division confessed that map reading in his formation was 'deplorably bad' and this no doubt accounted for the division's mistake in direction on 24 August. He also complained that, in previous months, the division had been in the line for long periods and that training, while fair, was not up to the standards 'required for successful open warfare offensive operations'.[81] Such a statement may indeed point to a continuing lack of uniformity – for a variety of reasons – in the BEF's tactical training in the summer of 1918, but it may also betray command weaknesses within the division itself, as other formations in the BEF, like the 12th Division (see Chapter 8), *had* succeeded in identifying and rectifying shortcomings in training before the start of the 'Hundred Days'. What, surely, cannot be in doubt is the outstanding quality of leadership displayed at brigade, battalion and company level – especially by officers such as McCulloch, Gater and Cumming – in V Corps between 21 and 24 August. In his own after-battle report on the night attack of 23–24 August, McCulloch emphasised that in 'an operaton of this nature, the presence of the Bde. Commander is essential ... if the troops know that the Bde. Commander is near their morale is increased'.[82] These, indeed, are the words of a true front-line general – the 'man on the spot'.

The story of the action on 23–24 August tends to support the view of Jonathan Boff that, on this as on other occasions, the Third Army revealed 'an impressive level of flexibility at the small-unit tactical level'. Doctrine from above played a part, writes Boff, but units, even within the same division, also modified their tactical methods according to the nature of the challenge faced or simply their own commander's personal preferences. This, he adds, undercuts the argument 'that combined arms was both a standard method, and a consistent solution, to the problems of the 1918 battlefield'.[83] Harris and Barr appear to agree with this assessment, declaring that the first few days of the Battle of Albert in August 1918 proved that the BEF as a whole, and not just its Dominion formations, could still inflict serious defeats on the Germans 'with a lesser degree of surprise, with a much less pronounced superiority in artillery, and with much less armour than it had used on 8 August'.[84] Boff is surely right in asserting that decentralisation of command was not consistently achieved in the Hundred Days and that a variety of factors – including a range of 'cultures of command' partly driven by the personalities, temperament or preferences of individual senior officers – underlie the complexity of the picture.[85] Yet, equally, it cannot be denied that, in the operations of 23–24 August, as on other occasions, delegation of command did actually work. The fact also remains that – for all its complexity, diversity, faults and inconsistencies – it was the BEF's peculiar and evolving mix of 'command cultures', rather than the practices of the German army, that ultimately won success in 1918. In this respect at least the underlying principles of *Field Service Regulations* and *SS 143* had been vindicated and, as I have written elsewhere, the fighting of late August 1918, on the old Somme battlefield, showed that the BEF had come a long way tactically, if not geographically, since 1 July 1916.[86]

Chapter Eight

'Up the Sharp End': The Experience of the 12th (Eastern) Division in the Hundred Days, August–November 1918

It has already been noted, in an earlier chapter, that in attacks against meaningful opposition during the 1916 Somme offensive, the 12th (Eastern) Division achieved a creditable success rate of 63.63 per cent.[1] Two years later, in the 'Hundred Days' offensive of August to November 1918, it performed even better, achieving an overall success rate of 69.5 per cent in opposed attacks.[2] This illustrates the high tactical standards that could be, and were, maintained by ordinary – i.e. non-élite – infantry units in the last months of the Great War. But what factors, or combination of factors, enabled the 12th Division to make such an effective contribution to the BEF's final weeks of operations?

Organisation and Composition

Like almost all *British* formations on the Western Front, the 12th Division had experienced changes in organisation and composition in the first half of 1918, particularly in February when manpower problems and the cumulative effects of casualties had caused the reduction of the majority of the BEF's infantry divisions from twelve battalions to nine. At the same time, infantry brigades were reduced from four battalions to three. This reorganisation saw the disbandment of three of the 12th Division's original 1914 battalions – namely the 8th Royal Fusiliers and the 11th Middlesex (from 36th Brigade) and the 7th East Surreys (from 37th Brigade). During this period too, the 5th Royal Berkshires, originally part of the 35th Brigade, were transferred to the 36th Brigade. The changes did not stop there. In the wake of the German March offensive in Picardy – when, according to its historians, the 12th Division was 'greatly reduced in numbers' and lost, by their calculations, 368 killed or died of wounds, 1,853 wounded and 704 missing (a total of 2,925 casualties, or the equivalent of just under one-third of its nominal infantry strength) – the 7th Suffolks, one of the original battalions of the 35th Brigade, was reduced to cadre. As a result, 11 officers and 408 other ranks were absorbed by the 1/1st Cambridgeshires – a Territorial battalion which took the place of the Suffolks in 35th Brigade on 10 May 1918, having previously served with the 39th Division from February 1916. Fortunately, the 12th Division mostly avoided the next round of major organisational changes in the late spring and early summer of 1918 when nine divisions – nearly one-fifth of the British divisions in the BEF – were reduced to cadre and then reconstituted, generally with a completely different set of battalions. At least the 12th Division kept *eight* of its original twelve infantry battalions, plus its original Pioneer battalion (the 5th Northamptonshires), giving it a greater degree of continuity in its organisation and composition than many other British formations were able to call upon in the final stages of the war.[3]

The battalions which constituted the division's infantry strength in the Hundred Days were, therefore: the 7th Norfolks, 9th Essex and 1/1st Cambridgeshires in the 35th Brigade; the 9th Royal Fusiliers, 7th Royal Sussex and 5th Royal Berkshires in the 36th Brigade; and the 6th Queen's (Royal West Surrey Regiment), 6th Buffs (East Kent Regiment) and 6th Queen's Own (Royal West Kent Regiment) in the 37th Brigade. It should also be noted that from 1 March 1918, as part of the overall reorganisation of the Machine Gun Corps, the three machine-gun companies were removed from the control of the infantry brigades and grouped together with the addition of a fourth (from Divisional troops) to form the 12th Machine Gun Battalion, with a total of 64 Vickers guns.[4] This greater concentration of automatic firepower under *divisional* control compensated, to some extent, for the reduction in the division's infantry strength.

Whatever the reasons for the success of the 12th Division in the Hundred Days, it cannot really be claimed that a strong sense of local identity in each of the infantry battalions was necessarily a major factor. If one takes a detailed sample of the relevant information about the places of birth and enlistment of the other ranks of each battalion who fell in the summer and autumn of 1918 – as listed in *Soldiers Died in the Great War* – one finds that in only two battalions, the 9th Royal Fusiliers and 7th Royal Sussex, had more than 25 per cent of the dead actually been born in the home county or principal recruiting area of the parent regiment. In the case of the 9th Royal Fusiliers, 41.26 per cent of the men in question are known to have been born in Greater London, while 28.18 per cent of the 7th Royal Sussex dead in the Hundred Days appear to have hailed from the battalion's home county. Similarly, the percentages of the fallen who are known to have *enlisted* in the battalion's home county or main recruiting area generally vary between 15.38 per cent in the case of the 5th Royal Berkshires and 25.97 per cent in the case of the 6th Royal West Kents. Again, the 9th Royal Fusiliers, with a figure of 50.55 per cent, and the 7th Royal Sussex, with a proportion of 39.54 per cent, are the exceptions at the higher end of the scale.[5]

In fact, the cumulative effects of heavy casualties, conscription and changes in the reserve and drafting system from 1916 onwards meant that it was simply no longer possible to guarantee that replacements would come from the parent regiment and the *localised* character of units at the front inevitably became increasingly diluted in many cases as the war went on. Again, it is therefore necessary, in my judgement, to search for factors other than strong geographical cohesion when one is attempting to explain the successful battlefield performance of the 12th Division between August and November 1918.

Summary of Operations

The 12th Division had five prolonged spells in the line or in actual battle during the Hundred Days. The first was during the Battle of Amiens, from 8 to 13 August, when it fought alongside its sister formation, the 18th (Eastern) Division, as part of III Corps in Rawlinson's Fourth Army. At Amiens, the 12th did not initially operate as an integrated formation. Prior to the battle, on 6 August, the 18th Division had been attacked by the 27th Württemberg Division and its 54th Brigade had suffered so many casualties that the 36th Brigade from the 12th Division had to replace it in the planned assault towards Gressaire Wood at the start of the main battle two days later. The task of the 35th and 37th Brigades on and after 8 August was to secure Morlancourt and the high ground between the Somme and the Ancre on the left flank of III Corps. The ground in the 12th Division's sector was difficult, consisting of a long, narrow plateau which not only had steep slopes running down to the Somme but was also intersected by a series of ravines. The nature of this terrain, and the disruption to the original plan, helps to explain why the division's progress, though steady, was not as spectacular as the advances achieved by the Australian and Canadian formations on the more level ground to the right (or south).

The division's second period of action was from 22 to 30 August, when, after taking Méaulte and the high ground east of the Bray–Méaulte road, it advanced – this time on the *right* of 18th Division – across the southern part of the old 1916 Somme battlefield from Bécordel-Bécourt to the Carnoy–Montauban area and then, past Bernafay Wood, to the Hardecourt–Maltz Horn Farm ridge. After an all-too-brief rest, the division was in action again, from 4 to 8 September, at Nurlu, north-east of Péronne. Next, from 18 to 30 September, the division was engaged in a tough battle for the outlying defences of the Hindenburg Line at Epéhy, Malassise Farm and Little Priel Farm before pressing on to Vendhuile, near the St Quentin Canal, on the left flank of Fourth Army's assault on the main Hindenburg Position. At times, the bitter see-saw fighting during this twelve-day period was reminiscent of operations on the Somme in the high summer of 1916. After this ordeal the division was transferred to VIII Corps in Horne's First Army and, in its fifth period of operations, from 6 to 29 October, it advanced from the Lens–Arras area in Artois, across the Haute Deule Canal to Buridon, Bruille and Chateau l'Abbaye on the banks of the Schelde – a distance of 32 miles.[6] Despite casualties totalling 6,940 – including 86 officers and 879 other ranks killed – and the fact that it was almost continuously in action after 8 August, with only short periods of rest, the 12th Division, in the Hundred Days, still achieved a success rate of 69.5 per cent in opposed attacks, only half a percentage point lower than the élite Guards Division.

What did this mean, in terms of 'battle days', for the infantry of the 12th Division? I have analysed all the significant operations mentioned in the official and divisional histories, and in such battalion histories as were available to me, and have found that six (or two-thirds) of the division's nine infantry battalions had seventeen or more battle days during the final offensive, the highest total being experienced by the 7th Royal Sussex in 36th Brigade, with twenty-one such battle days. The 9th Royal Fusiliers and the 5th Royal Berkshires, in the same brigade, each had nineteen, as did the 6th Queen's in 37th Brigade. The 7th Norfolks in 35th Brigade and 6th Royal West Kents in 37th Brigade appear to have had the fewest days of serious action, with eleven and thirteen battle days respectively.

It should also be pointed out that all the infantry battalions often found themselves in action on *consecutive* days. The 6th Queen's, for instance, were in action on consecutive days on five occasions – twice in August, once in September and twice in October. On *four* of those five occasions the 6th Queen's were fighting, or leading the advance, on *three* consecutive days. The 7th Royal Sussex had a similar experience, being in action on consecutive days twice in August and three times in October. During the latter month, the battalion appears to have been in action for a three-day spell from 15 to 17 October, and on no less than *five* consecutive days from 23 to 17 October.[7]

These bald statistics conceal a number of outstanding operations by the division. For example, on 28 August, the 35th and 36th Brigades stormed the Hardecourt–Maltz Horn Farm ridge. The action of the 9th Royal Fusiliers in clearing Favière Wood, occupying Hardecourt and capturing 16 machine guns was remarkable in that the battalion contained some 350 recruits, aged 18½ to 19½, who had been in France barely a week. At Epéhy in September, five battalions of the division succeeded in driving twelve *Jäger* battalions of the famed Alpine Corps from a position which the latter had been ordered to hold at all costs.[8] Just over a month later, on 23–24 October, the 6th Buffs, from 37th Brigade, crossed the Scarpe, moved along the banks of a small tributary, the Traitoire, to reach Cubray and Haute Rive prior to seizing Buridon under covering fire from skilfully sited Lewis guns. On 25 October the same battalion delivered a swift attack on Bruille, a large village on the banks of the Schelde Canal. Making the assault without artillery preparation, the Buffs caught the Germans unawares, captured the village with little loss to themselves and thus turned the German position between two waterways, causing the enemy units on the left to be withdrawn.[9]

I do not subscribe to the view that all the victories of the Hundred Days were won, almost by default, against declining or low-grade opposition. At Amiens the men of the 12th Division faced, among others, troops of the formidable and experienced 27th Württtemberg Division. The brilliant attack by the young conscripts at Hardecourt on 28 August overcame Fusilier battalions of a Guard Grenadier regiment from the German 2nd Guard Division, while, as seen above, the 12th Division, at Epéhy, was up against the Alpine Corps.[10] As Captain E.S. Ellis, of the 7th Royal Sussex, wrote of the captured warrant officers he saw at Epéhy: 'They were old regular soldiers, fine big bearded men whose moral[e] was untouched. Their influence among the young German private soldiers was most marked, and they showed none of the glad-to-be-out-of-it-at-any-price attitude which we had noted with other prisoners recently'.[11] Clearly then a number of factors, other than low-grade opposition or a strong local identity and geographical cohesion, contributed to the division's relatively high success rate.

Command and Control

The 12th Division was fortunate to have a high-quality team of senior officers whose ability and leadership contributed in no small measure to the formation's good battlefield performance in the Hundred Days. The divisional commander was Major-General Harold Higginson, arguably one of the more gifted and underrated tacticians in the BEF.[12] His successes in command of the 18th Division's 53rd Brigade in 1916 were described in Chapter 4 and, despite some setbacks, he had continued in much the same vein the following year. On 17 February 1917, in the assault on Boom Ravine, near Grandcourt, the 53rd Brigade, in tricky conditions, took Grandcourt Trench and Coffee Trench, though the important height of Hill 130 stayed in German hands.[13] The brigade's part in the capture of Irles, north-east of Miraumont, on 10 March, was a model attack in both planning and execution, the village being secured after a converging rather than a frontal assault. An oblique, instead of an overhead, barrage was employed and, to ensure that his troops kept as close as possible to it, Higginson even issued diagrams illustrating the bursting patterns of shrapnel. The divisional historian called this a 'very pretty little victory'.[14] Again, having experienced difficulties in the Sanctuary Wood–Glencorse Wood sector on 31 July and 10 August 1917, during the Third Battle of Ypres, Higginson bounced back on 22 October to become one of the few divisional or brigade commanders to emerge with any credit from the messy operations at Poelcappelle. On this occasion, 53rd Brigade took Poelcappelle Brewery, Meunier House and Tracas Farm after Higginson had bluffed the Germans with a dummy attack south of the village and then outmanoeuvred them with a thrust to the north.[15]

Higginson kept a cool head under tremendous pressure in the defensive battles of March–April 1918, particularly at Villers-Bretonneux in the defence of Amiens, where, by my calculations, the 18th Division was in the line longer than any other single British or Australian division. On 4 April, for example, at the height of the first German assault on Villers-Bretonneux, 53rd Brigade delivered a telling counter-attack at Hangard Wood.[16] Higginson's achievements as a brigade commander were finally rewarded later that month by his appointmnt to the command of the 12th Division, with the rank of major-general, a big farewell dinner being held for him at 53rd Brigade headquarters on the evening of 23 April, only hours before the Germans launched their second major onslaught on Villers-Bretonneux.[17] Higginson identified a number of weaknesses in his new command after elements of the 12th Division had taken part in a costly and unsuccessful attempt to clear the prominent Bouzincourt spur, north of Albert, on 30 June 1918. In his subsequent report he highlighted the need for junior officers to retain close control over their inexperienced men in action. He also endeavoured to rectify the problems which had arisen by overseeing a programme of training in the latter half of July which involved attack procedures and formations, the forming of advanced guards, and the tactical employment of Lewis guns as well as lessons in map-reading for junior officers and conferences for company commanders. The training programme culminated in a practice attack on a village.[18] Higginson clearly adjusted quickly to divisional command and a Bar to his DSO was gazetted on 16 September 1918. The 12th Division's success rate in the Hundred Days showed that he had not lost his sure tactical touch. This was underlined by the manner in which he rotated his brigades in action during the late August movement across the old Somme battlefield, enabling the division to maintain the momentum of the advance. During this period he employed a variety of means, including creeping and box barrages, advanced guards and concentrated overhead machine-gun fire, to solve a succession of different tactical challenges.[19]

During the final offensive 35th Brigade had two commanders. Its permanent commander was Brigadier-General Berkeley Vincent, a 46-year-old gunner who had been attached to the Japanese army during the Russo-Japanese War before transferring to the cavalry in 1908. His career had appeared to stutter early in 1911 when Douglas Haig, then Chief of Staff in India, engineered his removal from the post of Instructor at the Staff College, Quetta, on the grounds that Vincent was a 'mediocrity' with an inadequate knowledge of cavalry tactics. However, his career did not suffer in the long term for, after acting as a GSO2 with the Indian Corps in France in 1914, and as GSO1 of the 37th Division from April 1915 to January 1917, he then succeeded Arthur Solly-Flood as GOC of the 35th Brigade and held the post – obviously with Haig's acquiescence or even approval – for the rest of the war.[20] Though Solly-Flood was a hard act to follow, Vincent swiftly demonstrated that, as a commander of infantry, he too was outstanding. On 9 April 1917, the first day of the Battle of Arras, he brought his brigade into action, ahead of schedule, at just the right moment to help break German resistance on Observation Ridge. Two of his battalions subsequently charged down the eastern slopes of the ridge to capture more than thirty German field guns deployed in Battery Valley. Next day, he again revealed his finely tuned tactical instincts when he turned the Wancourt–Feuchy Line in his sector by ordering one battalion to wheel right and move down *behind* it while the other three battalions advanced frontally.[21] On 24 November 1917, at Cambrai, a company of the 5th Royal Berkshires – then still in his brigade – seized Quarry Post, north-west of Banteux, under cover of a rifle grenade and trench mortar barrage, while the 7th Suffolks moved down Breslau and Breslau Support Trenches to threaten the garrison from a flank. The skill with which a variety of weapons was employed in this action suggests that the 35th Brigade was, by this point, thoroughly versed in the new infantry tactics which Vincent's predecessor, Solly-Flood, had done so much to promote.

That Vincent was not simply an 'attacking' general was demonstrated on 30 November 1917, when the Germans launched their damaging counter-stroke at Cambrai. He showed considerable powers of leadership in organising and conducting a masterly fighting withdrawal from Villers Guislain to Revelon Ridge with a scratch force which included headquarters personnel, machine-gunners,

Royal Engineers and divisional Pioneers. Boosted by the arrival of Canadian railway troops, Vincent's men held their position on Revelon Ridge until relieved on 3–4 December.[22] The Brigade was, in fact, deprived of the leadership of this remarkable officer when he became a gas casualty on the very eve of the Battle of Amiens in August 1918 and had to relinquish his command for a few weeks. Nevertheless, he had recovered sufficiently to resume command of the brigade by 20 September, in the midst of the bitter fighting for the Hindenburg Line outposts, and he led his formation throughout the First Army's final advance from Lens in October 1918.[23]

Recalling the transfer of the Cambridgeshires to 35th Brigade, M.C. Clayton, the second-in-command and later commanding officer of the battalion, commented: 'I saw at once that we were fortunate. Vincent had Cavalry and India stamped all over him. Coupled with many years of staff experience he had a profound admiration for, and a sound understanding of, the men in the ranks …'. He also wrote of Vincent's return to the brigade in September:

We were all glad to see him recovered from his injuries. His experience, skill, and the support he afforded his C.O.'s through thick and thin were worth an extra battalion to [the] Brigade at this juncture. He took in the situation at a glance; his little pat on the back for our efforts during the two days' fighting [at Epéhy] did a lot to dispel the feeling of weariness and strain from which we were all suffering.[24]

There was little doubt about the warrior or leadership credentials of Vincent's temporary replacement, Brigadier-General Arthur Beckwith, aged 43. Before deputising for Vincent, Beckwith had served with two of the most famous fighting divisions in the BEF – the 29th and 51st (Highland) – and had been wounded three times and gassed once. He had commanded the 2nd Hampshires during the Gallipoli campaign and was awarded the DSO for gallantry and devotion to duty. After distinguishing himself again at Monchy le Preux in April 1917, he was given command, in August that year, of the 153rd Brigade in the 51st Division. It was typical of Beckwith that, although gassed in March 1918, he had remained on duty until 11 April, when he had at last collapsed, plainly too ill to carry on. Following his eventful five weeks with the 35th Brigade in August–September 1918, he commanded the 13th Brigade in the Regular 5th Division until the end of the war.[25]

The youngest of the 12th Division's brigade commanders was Charles Owen, who was still only 39 at the start of the Hundred Days. C.S. Owen is probably best known from the pages of J.C. Dunn's *The War the Infantry Knew*, having been a captain in, and adjutant of, the 2nd Royal Welsh Fusiliers at the outbreak of war. Nicknamed 'Bingo', the Welsh-born Owen was renowned in the battalion for his salty language. Before taking over the 36th Brigade in November 1916, he had commanded the 6th Royal West Kents in the 37th Brigade since late 1915, so had, in effect, been promoted from within the 12th Division. Owen too had been awarded a DSO in 1915. At the time of the Hundred Days he was the division's longest-serving brigade commander. Alan Thomas, who served under him as a young officer in the 6th Royal West Kents in 1915–1916, recalls that Owen was known as 'The Fire-eater' with 'an eye as clear as a crystal, a tongue as sharp as a razor and a command of language that a sailor would have envied'. Whatever other faults he possessed, Thomas wrote, Owen 'was without vice of hesitation. No one could have called him a ditherer. He never left you guessing: in conversation as in action, he went directly to the point. Toughness was all: and when we were out of the line he saw to it that neither officers nor men lacked opportunities for strengthening their fibre'.[26]

Perhaps the least-known of the division's brigade commanders was the 42-year-old Adrian Incledon-Webber, who had commanded the 1st Royal Irish Fusiliers in the 4th Division for several months before taking over the 37th Brigade in October 1917. Prior to that he had held successive staff posts with the 1st Canadian Brigade between late 1915 and January 1917, having been awarded a DSO during that period. There is evidence to suggest that he shared Higginson's views concerning the importance of training and firm leadership. After the action at Bouzincourt, Incledon-Webber observed, in July 1918, that recent operations had shown that young and inexperienced troops did not always support and follow their leaders. Some of these leaders, he asserted, 'must bring up the rear and deal summarily if necessary with any recalcitrants'. Anticipating the more mobile and semi-open warfare of the forthcoming offensive, he also foresaw that battalion commanders had to exercise initiative, since they could not rely upon a regular flow of detailed orders in the changed conditions.[27]

What is absolutely clear about these senior officers is that they all had considerable front-line and/or staff experience and were not found wanting in courage or leadership qualities. All of them had seen active service before 1914: Higginson in the South African War, West Africa and the Sudan; Vincent in China and South Africa; Owen in the relief of Peking in 1900; and Incledon-Webber also in the South African War. All except Vincent had been awarded the DSO. Such officers unquestionably possessed more collective and individual experience of combat than their German counterparts had accrued prior to 1914. Indeed, they had been schooled to accept personal danger and discomfort and to display bravery, devotion to duty and a paternalistic concern for the welfare of their men.[28]

Battalion Commanders

In the semi-open warfare of the Hundred Days, when fresh tactical challenges presented themselves almost daily and each front-line infantry battalion contained a significant proportion of inexperienced junior officers and young conscripts, the battalion *commanders* themselves obviously played a key role in the operational performance of their respective units. Of the nine in post at the start of the Hundred Days, three had been in command for a year or more. These were Lieutenant-Colonel W.R.A. 'Bob' Dawson of the 6th Royal West Kents, who had taken over his battalion from C.S. Owen in November 1916, twenty-one months earlier; Lieutenant-Colonel Arthur Smeltzer, who had led the 6th Buffs for fourteen months; and Lieutenant-Colonel W.V.L. Van Someren of the 9th Royal Fusiliers, in command for thirteen months since July 1917. E.T. Saint had assumed command of the 1/1st Cambridgeshires ten monhs before, in October 1917. The other five had commanded their battalions for four months or less, Lieutenant-Colonel A.L. Thomson of the 7th Royal Sussex having taken over his unit as recently as July 1918. These latter five at least partly owed their promotion to the increased turnover of battalion commanders during and after the German spring offensives. Lieutenant-Colonels P. Whetham and G. Green had been given command of the 6th Queen's and 9th Essex respectively in April; Lieutenant-Colonel H.A. (Ashley) Scarlett had taken over the 7th Norfolks on 21 May; and Lieutenant-Colonel H.T. Goodland, formerly second-in-command of the 5th Royal Berkshires, had been elevated to command his battalion in June. Thomson, of the 7th Royal Sussex, had served with the 1st Battalion in India before joining the 7th Battalion as second-in-command in April 1917. Ashley Scarlett had been second-in-command of the 9th Royal Fusiliers before transferring, within the 12th Division, to the 7th Norfolks.[29]

Not all of the battalion commanders in question survived in post throughout the Hundred Days. Green, of the 9th Essex, was gassed during the operations near the Bray–Méaulte road on 22 August and was succeeded by Lieutenant-Colonel W. Russell Johnson, who was himself slightly wounded on 13 October and replaced, for a few days, by an officer from the Duke of Wellington's Regiment.[30] Edward Saint, of the Cambridgeshires, was mortally wounded by a shell during the attack on Hardecourt and the Maltz Horn Farm ridge on 28 August and died the next day, his place being taken by his second-in-command, M.C. Clayton.[31] Bob Dawson, of the 6th Royal West Kents, was hit by a shell after inspecting the battalion's bridgeheads across the flooded Scarpe, near St Amand, on 23 October – on what was practically the last day the battalion was in action before the Armistice. When struck by shell fragments in the back, chest, left leg and spine, Dawson was, according to Alan Thomas, picking some celery in the garden of an empty house on his way back to his headquarters. Dawson died of his wounds on 3 December 1918.[32] H.T. Goodland, of the 5th Royal Berkshires, handed over to the unit's former commander, Lieutenant-Colonel E.H.J. Nicolls, in October, though Goodland was certainly back in post a few weeks after the Armistice.[33]

Between them these battalion commanders could call upon a considerable amount of combat experience. All except Green were recipients of the DSO and *he* had won the MC. Edward Saint of the Cambridgeshires had enlisted in his battalion as early as 1900 and had been commissioned in 1906. When the battalion landed in France in February 1915, Saint was in command of 'B' Company and was one of the first officers to see action. Clayton, his successor, was another pre-war officer of the battalion who had also commanded a company in 1915.[34] The CO of the 9th Essex from August 1918 onwards – W. Russell Johnson – had served on Gallipoli with the 1/7th Essex before becoming second-in-command of the

9th Battalion. His predecessor, Green, had accompanied the 9th Essex to France in May 1915 and had taken command of 'C' Company the following month. Both Green and Johnson had even commanded their battalion before, albeit for a very brief period, in the course of 1917.[35] H.T. Goodland, of the Berkshires, won the DSO for his gallantry and leadership at Amiens on 8 August 1918, when he led elements of his battalion through a barrage to reinforce the firing line and then supervised the consolidation of a position under direct fire from machine guns and from field guns firing over open sights. E.H.J. Nicolls, who resumed command of the 5th Berkshires in October, had already led the unit from August 1917 to June 1918.[36]

Few, however, could match the combat record of Bob Dawson of the Royal West Kents. As a young Regular officer he had been posted to the 6th Battalion on its formation in 1914 and served continuously with it until mortally wounded shortly before the Armistice. He had been promoted Temporary Captain in March 1916 and Temporary Major in August 1916 before succeeding Owen in command of the battalion towards the end of that year. He won the DSO and *three* Bars and, when he was hit on 23 October 1918, he had already been wounded six times. Alan Thomas viewed Dawson as a 'natural' commanding officer who 'knew his job' and possessed an 'instinctive grasp of soldiering'. Richly endowed with both charisma and courage, Dawson understood the importance of being a role model and of being seen to cope, factors which underpinned his 'hands-on' style of leadership and helped to maintain the *esprit de corps* of the battalion. His habit of going out alone on patrol in no-man's-land prompted Thomas to comment that rarely 'can a C.O. have been so reckless and foolhardy – or have commanded such devotion from his men'. Thomas added that, from his officers, Dawson 'expected as much as he gave – which was everything'.[37]

Another notable battalion commander, also in the 37th Brigade, was Lieutenant-Colonel A.S. Smeltzer of the 6th Buffs. Smeltzer was aged 36 when he became CO of the battalion in June 1917, and he won a DSO and Bar as well as the MC, being mentioned in despatches four times. He had spent over fourteen years in the ranks and, according to Mark Connelly, was a company sergeant-major in the 1st Buffs in 1914. After being commissioned in the field as a second-lieutenant in October 1915, he served with the 6th Battalion and was wounded in an attack at Triangle Crater, near Loos, in March 1916. His swift rise to the battalion command in the next fifteen months completed what Connelly calls 'an impressive career trajectory in the Buffs'. Alan Thomas pithily described him as 'an old soldier, keen as mustard and as brave as they make them …'.[38] In the course of the Hundred Days, Smeltzer displayed a blend of initiative, common sense and a firm grasp of combined-arms tactics. Following the actions at Favière Wood and Maurepas in late August, he called a meeting of all officers to discuss the lessons to be gleaned from recent operations.[39] On 19 September, in the fighting at Braeton Post and Bird Trench, during the struggle for Epéhy and the Hindenburg Line outposts, the 6th Buffs encountered strong machine-gun fire and Smeltzer, anxious to husband his precious troops, halted his attack 100 yards short of the objective.[40] Then, in the assault on the Hindenburg

Line itself on 29 September, Smeltzer personally directed his battalion's attempt to overcome resistance emanating from a group of quarries at Vendhuile. Joined by both an artillery and a machine-gun officer in his observation post, Smeltzer effectively co-ordinated the fire of their respective arms, enabling his own men to advance and capture the quarries along with 150 prisoners and many machine guns.[41] But this resourceful officer was perhaps seen at his best in the battalion's final actions of the war, on 23–25 October 1918. Having seized Cubray on 23 October, Smeltzer quickly organised a night operation to burst through a thin German screen covering Haute Rive. In a subsequent attack on the morning of 24 October, he sent forward Lewis gun teams to establish positions in Buridon and help overcome that village in addition. Not content with these successes, Smeltzer ordered the 6th Buffs to push on to Bruille, which was taken in a surprise attack while most of the German garrison were still having breakfast.[42]

It is not difficult to find alternative examples of good personal leadership or effective tactical control by the division's battalion commanders during the Hundred Days. At a tricky stage of the struggle for Nurlu on 5 September, M.C. Clayton – described by his own former commanding officer as 'a Cambridgeshire to the tips of his fingers' – conducted a dangerous personal reconnaissance with a runner so that he could better understand the problems his forward companies were encountering. Similarly, at Epéhy on 18 September, Clayton went forward from battalion headquarters at least twice at critical moments in the attack. On the second occasion he got as far as the main street of the village before losing his way and being forced, in his own words, to 'beat an undignified retreat in a series of dives from shell-hole to shell-hole'. The following morning, Clayton, armed with a rifle and fixed bayonet which he picked up on the battlefield, joined a mixed group of some thirty officers and men from the Cambridgeshires and the 5th Northamptonshires in seizing a section of Ockenden Trench, literally coming face to face with the enemy in the process.[43] So too did Ashley Scarlett of the 7th Norfolks, who, with his orderly, personally captured four prisoners and a machine gun at Boujon, in the advance from Lens, on 18 October.

In the action at Courcelles on 12 October, when the 9th Essex took the village after a great deal of street and house-to-house fighting, Lieutenant-Colonel W. Russell Johnson called for volunteers to subdue a troublesome machine-gun firing from the gates of the chateau. He, another officer and four or five men then dashed forward about 200 yards to the shelter of a row of houses. As the regimental history records: 'It was an apparently mad thing to do, but audacity paid …'. As Russell Johnson neared the machine gun, and another on a slag heap to the left, the crews fled.[44] Dawson of the 6th Royal West Kents was a constant inspiration to his battalion. East of Epéhy on 21 September, his troops had become 'weary and depressed' after five unsuccessful attempts to secure Braeton Post. Dawson, portrayed by the divisional historians as 'one of the great leaders of every fight of the Division', came forward and, 'calling on Lieutenant Berger and four or five men, put such enthusiasm into this small body that the post was rushed, and the enemy driven out in confusion'.[45]

Sometimes, however, the bravery of these battalion commanders verged upon foolhardiness. Near Morlancourt on 9 August, Dawson – seeking to set an example of courage and calmness under fire – led his men into action on horseback.[46] An even more eccentric command decision was taken by Russell Johnson on 24 August. In the advance east of Mametz towards Carnoy, he ordered the company commanders of the 9th Essex to lead their men into action on their chargers. One of the officers involved later wrote: 'We did so for about fifty yards, when owing to the chargers' loathing for barbed wire and two particularly nasty shells, they were sent back again, only too thankfully, by the company commanders'. The strain of commanding battalions in successive actions, often day after day during the final offensive, was, of course, immense. After a day of fighting for Carnoy on 24 August, Russell Johnson, whose battalion headquarters were established under a waterproof sheet, was – according to a company commander – 'too tired to say much'.[47] M.C. Clayton felt that he badly needed a rest after the events of August and September, but his spell of leave behind the lines was cut short when his second-in-command was hit on 12 October. On reaching Sameon on 20 October, Clayton and his adjutant, Captain Walker, slept in real beds for the first time since July.[48]

These were by no means old men. When they died, E.T. Saint and Bob Dawson were, respectively, 33 and 27 years old, while Saint's successor, Clayton – though already with the battalion for eight years – had only just celebrated his 26th birthday. The resource, initiative, courage and, above all, experience of such front-line commanders were priceless assets to their battalions, and to the division as a whole, in the Hundred Days. Embodying as they did the ethos and fighting traditions of their units, their tactical knowledge and instincts were invaluable in helping to shepherd their less-experienced junior officers and other ranks through the successive ordeals of the final offensive. It seems highly likely that, had the war continued into 1919, and had they survived, officers such as Dawson, Smeltzer and Clayton would soon have been given brigade commands.

Junior Leadership

Like all major offensives during the Great War, the Hundred Days made huge demands upon junior officers in terms of leadership and, all too often, self-sacrifice. But what, precisely, did this mean to individual battalions in practice? Officer losses were high, particularly in August and September, though they appear to have diminished somewhat in the generally less-intensive fighting of October. For example, in two days' fighting at Amiens–Morlancourt in the second week of August, the 9th Essex lost two officers killed and six wounded. In the advance of 22 August, six officers were killed and the then commanding officer, Lieutenant-Colonel Green, was gassed and taken to hospital. Despite the arrival of some replacement officers, all the companies in the operations east of the Maricourt–Montauban road on 28 August were led by second-lieutenants. The following day, 'A' Company was reduced to one officer, one sergeant, one lance-corporal and about forty men. 'C' Company's sole remaining officer, Lieutenant Kay, had been wounded in the previous attack. Two newly joined officers took part in the advance of 29 August and one of these was wounded soon after the start of operations, again leaving only one officer in 'C' Company.[49] In the 1/1st Cambridgeshires, during three weeks in August, the battalion commander (E.T. Saint), the adjutant, the signals officer and twenty-four company officers became casualties. M.C. Clayton, who took over the battalion at this juncture, wrote that, at that stage of the war, 'we had to budget for the loss of anything up to a dozen officers in one attack, and the position worried me'.[50]

The Appendices to the published history of the 7th Battalion, Royal Sussex Regiment, contain detailed lists of officers who served with the unit, not only in the Hundred Days but also in the war as a whole. From this sample one is able to draw some useful and instructive statistics to illustrate the impact of the final offensive upon the battalion so far as officer losses were concerned. The lists in question show that 86 officers in all served with, or were attached to, the 7th Royal Sussex in the Hundred Days, of whom 19 (or 22.09 percent) died and 67 (or 77.9 per cent) survived. Of the 67 officers who survived, 26 (or 38.8 per cent) were wounded at some point in the offensive. The 19 officers who died included 1 captain, 4 lieutenants and 14 second-lieutenants. The overall total of battalion officers who died in the war was 57, which meant that *one-third* of all the battalion officers who were killed or died of wounds between May 1915 and the Armistice actually died during the Hundred Days – a significant proportion. Of the 19 dead officers, 8 were lost as a result of the fighting around Epéhy from 18 to 24 September. The final offensive was thus by no means a 'walkover' for those called upon to carry it out.

The *average* length of service with the battalion of those officers who died in the final offensive was just under 170 days, or 5.6 months. To some extent this figure further undermines the myth of the 'six-week subaltern', though not completely so. When he died of wounds suffered at Epéhy, Lieutenant A.C.W. Uloth MC had been with the battalion 2 years and 3 days, while Captain E.C. Gorringe MC had served with the battalion only 1 day less when he was killed at Nurlu on 5 September. Of the other fallen officers, 2 had been with the battalion for over a year, 1 of them for a year and 290 days. On the other hand, 7 of the dead were with the battalion for a month or less. The shortest length of service was that of Second-Lieutenant T.P. Ashby, who joined on 30 August and was killed at Nurlu, only 6 days later, on 5 September; 3 others lasted only 10 days while 4 more served between 13 and 19 days before they became casualties. Thus, in all, 8 of the 19 officers who died in, or as a result of, the final offensive, served for 3 weeks or less. At the other extreme, Major H.S. Bowlby MC, Major G.F Osborne MC, Captain G.L. Reckitt MC and Bar, and Captain J.E. Clarke OBE (the Quartermaster) were all original 1914 officers who had crossed to France with the battalion in 1915 and who survived the war.[51]

The 12th Division as a whole suffered 2,105 officer casualties during the war, including 435 killed, 1,415 wounded and 255 missing. Of these officer casualties,

336 were incurred during the Hundred Days. Therefore, of the division's total officer casualties from 1915 to the Armistice, 15.96 per cent occurred in the final offensive.[52]

The wastage of officers in the more fluid operations of the Hundred Days, when units were often in action or on the move for several days at a stretch, was a constant source of anxiety to battalion commanders. Commenting on the situation at the beginning of September, Clayton wrote: 'Hitherto it had always been possible for new officers to have a turn of trench duty to enable those above and those under them to assess their value. Now the newly-joined officer was expected within a few hours of joining to lead his men over the top'.[53] Lieutenant-Colonel Thomson, of the 7th Royal Sussex, wrote in a similar vein of the effects of the fighting later in September: 'Practically all the officers were new to the battalion', he observed, 'and just after Nurlu we had a whole batch of officers, most of who had been in the 11th, 12th and 13th Battalions; almost all of them became casualties by the end of the Epéhy period'.[54]

The losses just described did *not*, in my judgement, necessarily lead to a decline in the standards of leadership displayed by junior officers. Not all historians would share my opinion. In the two volumes of the official history which cover the Hundred Days, Sir James Edmonds, for example, is repeatedly critical of the standards of junior leadership in *British*, as opposed to *Dominion*, divisions. The late Paddy Griffith was surely right in laying the blame at Edmonds' door for encouraging the belief that British junior leaders were poor in 1918. In Griffith's view, the decentralisation of tactical command and control to the level of temporary officers and citizen-soldier NCOs was a profoundly unsettling innovation to many Regulars since, in effect, it eroded the powers and mystique of the old Regular Army and its long-serving officers. Thus Edmonds' critical comments may be explained partly in terms of a backlash against this erosion.[55] My own view is that the BEF's ability to overcome such a wide variety of tactical obstacles and challenges in the Hundred Days – ranging from formal set-piece assaults to street fighting and canal crossings on improvised bridges and rafts – would simply not have been possible without high standards of leadership and initiative on the part of its junior officers.

A few examples from the 12th Division's own operations will suffice to support this point. At Maurepas on 29 August, the 6th Buffs infiltrated to the rear of a German company without being seen, and partly due to the reconnaissance of the position by, and the leadership and initiative of, Lieutenant S.H.S. Marchant, they cut off and captured two officers and 60 men. In the attack on the Quarries, east of Epéhy, one month later, Lieutenant Fiske, of the same battalion, on finding his company held up by two German machine guns, worked round the flank, rushed the guns and bombed and killed the teams, enabling his men to advance.[56] At Auby on 14 October, Clayton of the Cambridgeshires observed Captain T.H. Harding-Newman of 'D' Company – 'immaculate as ever' – preparing for action 'as though he were going for a walk down Bond Street'. 'D' Company and Captain Charles Tebbutt's 'A' Company risked casualties from their own patchy artillery barrage and, with shells falling all around them, pushed forward so quickly that they caught the Germans still emerging from their cellars and reached their objective without a check. Harding-Newman again distinguished himself at Sameon on 20 October. His company and 'A' Company – this time led by Lieutenant J.A. Hardman – worked to the right and left of the village respectively and advanced in platoon rushes, with Harding-Newman's men providing covering fire with rifles and Lewis guns. The village was captured at minimal cost to the companies involved.[57] Such company and platoon actions were common in the changed tactical conditions of the Hundred Days.

Sometimes, at trying moments, the younger officers could prove a real inspiration to their seniors. Captain E.W. Barltrop of the 9th Essex, when recalling the fighting at Nurlu in early September, wrote:

> I was awarded the DSO but I have to thank the men for it. Tom Comber and Joe Mussett (subalterns) came to me on return from leave or training courses in the middle of the night of 5th–6th September, when I was in the depths of despair at the order to attack again, as it seemed inevitable annihilation to me. These two men were like the strongest wine. I knew them for tried and brave fellows and they cheered and encouraged me in a way I shall never forget.[58]

Nevertheless, even the most courageous officers were not immune to battle fatigue. Clayton relates how, at Epéhy, he found Captain A.E.M. Coles, who was 'brave as a lion' and 'had led "D" Company consistently well in a series of attacks', looking 'as miserable as Hell'. It was clear to Clayton that Coles had 'nearly reached the limit'. Indeed, during the ensuing operations, Coles suffered a bad wound, from which he eventually lost a leg.[59]

NCOs

As always when officers fell, much of the burden of junior leadership was borne by the warrant officers and NCOs. Again, there are plentiful examples of gallantry and initiative by NCOs which contributed substantially to the successful outcome of battalion actions. On 9 August, near Morlancourt, Sergeant Thomas Harris MM of the 6th Royal West Kents won a posthumous Victoria Cross. When his battalion's advance was held up by machine guns hidden in the standing crops and shell holes, Harris rushed one of the guns at the head of his section and captured it. Later, on two successive occasions, he attacked other machine-gun posts single-handed. On the first occasion he killed the entire crew and captured the gun. Though he was killed when trying to repe at the feat a second time, the battalion was able to resume its advance.[60] The same day, 'C' and 'D' Companies of the Cambridgeshires came under enfilade machine-gun fire from the southern end of the village when endeavouring to clear Morlancourt. Company Sergeant-Major Betts, of 'D' Company, worked his way forward alone until he was in the rear of the machine-gun nest in question. Then, with a blood-curdling yell, he rushed the machine-gun crew at bayonet point.

Those Germans who survived the onslaught surrendered and Betts captured, in all, four machine guns and thirty men. Betts, who was a company sergeant-major at the age of 21, was a fenman from Wisbech and had enlisted at March in Cambridgeshire. He already held the DCM and Bar and was awarded the Military Medal for the action at Morlancourt. Unfortunately, he was killed in the advance to the Bray–Méaulte road on 22 August, less than two weeks later.[61]

Another highly decorated NCO was Sergeant A. Trevor DCM, MM, of the 7th Royal Sussex, who, on 22 August, had captured thirty Germans from a large dugout in the sandpit beside the Bray–Albert road, and then won a Bar to his DCM in the fighting around Epéhy in September.[62] In the street fighting at Auby on 14 October, much depended upon the leadership of the NCOs. Company Sergeant-Major W.C. Parry, of the 7th Norfolks, took command of a platoon when the officer was wounded, and later of a *second* platoon when *its* officer fell, eventually leading half the company successfully through the village. Sergeant C.W. Clarke and Lance-Corporal Sammons likewise distinguished themselves in clearing a portion of the village.[63] As with the junior officers, such leadership often came at a heavy price. Four sergeants from 'A' Company of the 7th Royal Sussex – one of whom held the MM – were killed, for instance, in the advance from the Bray–Albert road to the Carnoy–Montauban area between 22 and 26 August.[64] It is noteworthy that, if one takes a sample from *Soldiers Died in the Great War* of *decorated* infantry NCOs who fell in the August to November advance, a significant proportion of those were born, or had enlisted in, the counties from which their regiments and battalions had originated. This suggests that they may well have been 1914–1915 volunteers who, by 1918, were approaching veteran status, and also that they represented the type of experienced NCOs who both embodied the fighting traditions of the battalion and were able to nurse the young conscripts through the successive attacks of the Hundred Days.

Other Ranks

In the final analysis, however, it was the courage, resilience and sheer persistence of the other ranks that ultimately carried infantry divisions such as the 12th through to victory. During the Hundred Days, 879 of the division's other ranks were killed, 4,987 were wounded and 738 were posted missing – a total of 6,604 casualties among the officers and men. This represented 14.34 per cent, or just under one-seventh, of the total casualties incurred by other ranks of the division from June 1915 onwards.[65] Though drafts of reinforcements appear to have arrived regularly, battalions repeatedly found themselves under-strength. For example, after the initial attack at Epéhy on 18 September, the 7th Royal Sussex could muster a total of only 3 officers and 197 other ranks in its 4 front-line companies, including 1 officer and 87 men in 'A' Company, 1 officer and 37 men in 'B' Company, no officers and just 23 men in 'C' Company and 1 officer and 50 men in 'D' Company. Two days later the battalion had to be temporarily reorganised into a two-company unit. As the battalion historian later wrote: 'We had now been through seven weeks of practically incessant fighting, and the original battalion that had gone into action on the 8th August had almost ceased to exist. More than 40 officers and 800 other ranks had become casualties – nearly twice its fighting strength. There was not a unit in the Division but had suffered equally'.[66] Captain J. Macey, who was then commanding 'A' Company of the 9th Essex, remarked that, as early as 24 August, his company had one officer (himself), one sergeant, three corporals 'and about fifty tired men'. Following the battalion's action on 28 August, the company was 'very much exhausted' and 'it was difficult to keep the men awake'.[67] M.C. Clayton of the Cambridgeshires also recalled that, by 28 August, his battalion badly required a rest: 'Not only were we all spent both bodily and mentally, but the whole Battalion had to be reorganised. "A" and "B" Companies needed completely rebuilding, and all sections of the Battalion had sorrowful gaps to be filled'.[68]

Clayton also commented on the quality of the 350 other ranks who arrived in drafts of reinforcements at this stage, noting how they were soon integrated into the battalion:

> About 50 of these were old hands, including several good N.C.O.'s, but the other 300 were boys called up in the Spring. Their average length of service was about fifteen weeks. They had fired a musketry course but knew nothing about Lewis guns. They had come straight from the base and had never been under fire ... On the other hand I had about three hundred men who had been through some or all of the attacks of the preceding month, and the framework of the Battalion – H.Q. and Company, Platoon and Section leaders – was sound and reliable.[69]

Clayton's interesting observations help to explain how, despite recurrent losses, battalions – given a nucleus of surviving veterans – were able to regenerate themselves, and maintain their fighting ethos, after each major battle or series of actions. Indeed, he recorded that at Nurlu on 5–6 September – an action that 'would have been trying at any time' – the veterans 'were playing their part magnificently' and Clayton felt that the battalion 'could not be in too bad a trim after all'. He also stated, revealingly:

> I could not, however, but admire the way in which these ... youngsters had carried out their job; it was a baptism of fire such as might have dismayed more experienced troops. As long as they had leaders they kept steadily on, but when, as in 'B' Company, the officers (all four) and the platoon sergeants became casualties they quickly lost cohesion and were scattered in depth, to become victims of their inexperience in how to make use of ground and cover ... We mourned the loss of these lives, but I felt confident that, given breathing-space and opportunity for training, we could weld this new material into a weapon which would add further to the reputation of the Cambridgeshires.[70]

Tanks and Artillery

Some recent interpretations of the Hundred Days – particularly those by Commonwealth historians such as Tim Travers and Robin Prior and Trevor Wilson – suggest that the success of the BEF's rolling limited-objective attacks in the final offensive depended, above all, on mechanical means – i.e. tanks and overwhelming artillery firepower – and upon the infantry advancing only within the range of their own field artillery support.[71] There is, of course, a large element of truth in this interpretation but it does not, in fact, *wholly* stand up to rigorous scrutiny. As one examines the operations of divisions such as the 12th, it quickly becomes clear that there were repeated occasions on which the support of tanks and artillery was either inadequate or non-existent (sometimes by choice) and it was left to the infantry to fight their way forward using their own resources.

Looking at tanks first, the nature of the terrain did not always favour their use, especially en masse. At the Battle of Amiens in August, the Morlancourt ridge, where the bulk of the 12th Division were in action, was bounded by steep slopes and intersected by a series of ravines, thus being unsuitable for the employment of tanks on the scale seen elsewhere on the battlefield. Nevertheless, on 8 August, one tank, which, in the mist and smoke, had strayed into the 12th Division's area from the neighbouring 18th Division sector, helped 35th Brigade to mop up a pocket of German resistance south-east of Morlancourt, over 300 prisoners being taken.[72] Next day, another single tank destroyed a German machine-gun post which had been holding up the 6th Queen's, allowing the battalion to push on, yet, of three tanks allotted to the 1/1st Cambridgeshires, one was knocked out by a field gun and the other two were late arriving, leaving the Cambridgeshires to advance unaided for 300 yards across a fire-swept zone to Morlancourt village.[73] Just over a week later, on 22 August, elements of the division again had contrasting experiences with tanks. Four tanks materially helped the 5th Royal Berkshires to overcome resistance in Méaulte – two of them silencing a German field battery and dispersing the crews of a second – but only one of three tanks assigned to the 35th Brigade got beyond the intermediate objective, and it then turned back, pursued by enemy artillery fire which caused casualties to the 9th Essex.[74] Of three Whippet tanks ordered to help the 6th Royal West Kents attack two strongpoints on 24 August, two were disabled while the guns of the third jammed.[75] On 18 September, at Epéhy, and on 30 September, near Vendhuile, the 7th Royal Sussex and 6th Buffs were respectively fired upon by friendly tanks.[76] It would seem self-evident, therefore, that, in practice, tanks by no means offered a solution to all tactical problems.

The same can be said of the artillery. On the first day of the Battle of Amiens, the British dispensed altogether with a preliminary bombardment, in order to achieve surprise. It has already been pointed out how the 6th Buffs at Bruille on 25 October decided, for the same reason, to attack without artillery preparation. The initial assault by the 35th Brigade on 8 August was made under a creeping barrage fired, in its sector, by just forty-eight field guns. This proved weighty enough to help the 7th Norfolks and 9th Essex reach their objectives but did not prevent the Cambridgeshires from suffering heavy casualties. A second attack by the Cambridgeshires at 12.25 p.m., after a 10-minute bombardment by four batteries of 18-pounders, was entirely successful.[77] Such artillery barrages may have proved effective, but, from a divisional standpoint, they were scarcely on the scale of the huge five-layered barrages fired by the Second Army in September 1917.

Like the tanks, the artillery also became involved in unfortunate incidents, such as on 13 August, when difficulties of registration led to a very uneven barrage and 'C' Company of the 7th Royal Sussex was overwhelmed by a rain of 'friendly fire'. Similarly, on 14 October, on the banks of the Haute Deule Canal, guns which were worn out by incessant work were unable to fire an accurate barrage, the latter resembling instead an 'area shoot' in which shells fell all round the leading companies of the Cambridgeshires.[78] M.C. Clayton described the dawn barrage at Nurlu on 5 September as 'very meagre' and a second barrage, at 7.45 a.m., as being 'miserably thin'.[79] Much of the fighting in October was carried out by all-arms brigade groups and advanced guards – operations in which big bombardments and barrages were too difficult and complex to organise quickly and which were, in any case, inappropriate or unnecessary. Moreover, by this late stage of the offensive, the division was often attacking, or advancing towards, villages which still contained civilian inhabitants, so heavy bombardments could not be risked.

In truth, it was often the proximity of a few field guns which could provide effective and timely support, rather than massive bombardments or barrages, which was of most assistance to the infantry. On 7 September, Major J.B. Kindersley, commanding 'A' Battery of the 63rd Brigade, Royal Field Artillery, (RFA) was in the front line and directed the fire of his battery with such success that the 6th Buffs were able to advance and occupy Guyencourt, to the north-east of Nurlu.[80] Likewise, in the struggle for Room and Ockenden Trenches, near Epéhy, on 19 September, a crucial intervention was made by Major T. Stamper of 'B' Battery, 62nd Brigade RFA, when the Cambridgeshires were checked 150 yards short of their objective. As M.C. Clayton recalled, Stamper's signaller:

> ran out a line, whilst he moved a section of his guns further left behind Epéhy to enable him to enfilade Ockenden Trench. One or two ranging shots, rather close to 'B' Company, and then he got the exact range. He was an artist at his job; he burst shrapnel only a few feet high over the trench; he traversed the length of it; he lifted the range a few yards to encourage the Boche to remount his machine-guns, only to switch back onto the trench.

The Cambridgeshires subsequently pressed forward and seized a portion of Ockenden Trench.[81] Sometimes this type of vital close support came from sources other than the artillery. At Méaulte on 22 August, 'D' Special Company of the Royal Engineers projected fifty drums of burning oil into the village at zero hour, and in the attack on the Hardecourt–Maltz Horn Farm ridge on 28 August, the overhead machine-gun fire from the 12th Machine Gun Battalion 'for a considerable time' greatly assisted the progress of the 35th and 36th Brigades.[82]

However, for all the BEF's superior logistics, improved technology and highly effective combined-arms tactics in the Hundred Days, the doggedness and resilience of the British front-line soldier remained as important – and perhaps even more important – than the methods he employed. It should be remembered that the German divisions, after dazzling early successes in March, April and May 1918, had largely run out of steam after one or two weeks of each of their offensives. The average British division, such as the 12th, had, in contrast – and allowing for periods of rest – the capacity to keep up the pressure on the enemy over much of the three-month period of the Hundred Days. This relentless pressure surely did as much as anything to ensure the battlefield defeat of the Imperial German Army.

Notes

Foreword

1. Peter Simkins, *Kitchener's Army: The Raising of the New Armies, 1914–16* (Manchester University Press, 1988).
2. Peter Simkins, 'Haig and The Army Commanders', in Brian Bond and Nigel Cave (eds), *Haig: A Reappraisal 70 Years On* (Leo Cooper/Pen and Sword, Barnsley, 1999), pp. 78–106.
3. Peter Simkins, 'For Better or Worse: Sir Henry Rawlinson and his Allies in 1916 and 1918', in Matthew Hughes and Matthew Seligmann (eds), *Leadership in Conflict, 1914–1918* (Leo Cooper/Pen and Sword, Barnsley, 2000), pp. 13–37.

Introduction

1. Professor Stephen Badsey, 'Haig since Terraine', paper given at the University of Birmingham, 22 June 2013.

Chapter 1

1. A shorter version of this essay was given as the President's Address at the Annual General Meeting of the Western Front Association at Oxford, April 2012, and is reproduced here by kind permission of the Editor of the *Bulletin* of the Western Front Association (WFA) and of the Trustees of the WFA. The shorter version was published in the *Bulletin* in July 2012, No. 93.
2. Brian Bond (ed.), *The First World War and British Military History*, Clarendon Press, Oxford, 1991, pp. 289–313.
3. Richard Holmes, *Tommy: The British Soldier on the Western Front, 1914–1918*, Harper Collins, London, 2004.
4. Holmes. *Tommy*, pp. xvii, xviii, xxiii.
5. *Ibid.*, pp. xxiii–xxiv.
6. Desmond Morton, *When Your Number's Up: The Canadian Soldier in the First World War*, Random House, Toronto, 1993.
7. Tim Cook, *At the Sharp End: Canadians Fighting the Great War, 1914–1916*, Viking, Toronto, 2007, and *Shock Troops: Canadians Fighting the Great War, 1917–1918*, Viking, Toronto, 2008.
8. Peter Pedersen, *The Anzacs: Gallipoli to the Western Front*, Viking, Camberwell, Victoria, 2007.
9. Glyn Harper, *Dark Journey: Three Key New Zealand Battles of the Western Front*, Harper Collins, Auckland, 2007.
10. Malcolm Brown, *The Imperial War Museum Book of the Somme*, Sidgwick and Jackson, London, 1996 and *The Imperial War Museum Book of 1918: Year of Victory*, Sidgwick and Jackson, London, 1998.
11. Ian Passingham, *Pillars of Fire: The Battle of Messines Ridge, June 1917*, Sutton, Stroud, 1998; Jonathan Walker, *The Blood Tub: General Gough and the Battle of Bullecourt, 1917*, Spellmount, Staplehurst, 1998; Paul Cobb, *Fromelles 1916*, Tempus, Stroud, 2007; Charles Messenger, *The Day We Won The War: Turning Point at Amiens, 8 August 1918*, Weidenfeld & Nicolson, London, 2008; Bryn Hammond, *Cambrai 1917: The Myth of the First Great Tank Battle*, Weidenfeld & Nicolson, London, 2008; Paul Kendall, *Bullecourt 1917: Breaching the Hindenburg Line*, Spellmount, Stroud, 2010; Dale Blair, *The Battle of Bellicourt Tunnel: Tommies, Diggers and Doughboys on the Hindenburg Line, 1918*, Frontline Books/Pen and Sword, London, 2011; Scott Bennett, *Pozières: The Anzac Story*, Scribe, Melbourne, 2011; Chris Baker, *The Battle for Flanders: German Defeat on the Lys, 1918*, Pen and Sword, Barnsley, 2011.
12. See, for example, *The German Army at Ypres 1914 and the Battle for Flanders* (2010); *The German Army on the Western Front 1915* (2012); *The German Army on the Somme* (2006); *The German Army on Vimy Ridge 1914–1917* (2008); *The German Army at Passchendaele* (2007); and *The German Army at Cambrai* (2009). All were published by Pen and Sword, Barnsley.

13. Peter Hart, *1918: A Very British Victory*, Weidenfeld & Nicolson, London, 2008, pp. 2–3, 5–6, 474, 517–18, 521.
14. K.W. Mitchinson and Ian McInnes, *Cotton Town Comrades: The Story of the Oldham Pals Battalion, 1914–1919*, Bayonet Publications, 1993; Matthew Richardson, *The Tigers: 6th, 7th, 8th and 9th (Service) Battalions of the Leicestershire Regiment*, Leo Cooper/Pen and Sword, Barnsley, 2000; Jack Alexander, *McRae's Battalion: The Story of the 16th Royal Scots*, Mainstream, Edinburgh, 2003; Derek Clayton, *From Pontefract to Picardy: The 9th King's Own Yorkshire Light Infantry in the First World War*, Tempus, Stroud, 2004; John Stephen Morse, *9th (Service) Battalion The Sherwood Foresters (Notts and Derby Regiment)*, Tommies Guides, Eastbourne, 2007; and Wayne Osborne, *The 10th Notts and Derbys in the Great War: Volume One, Dorset 1914 to Ypres 1915*, Salient Books, Nottingham, 2009.
15. K.W. Mitchinson, *Gentlemen and Officers: The Impact and Experience of War on a Territorial Regiment, 1914–1918*, Imperial War Museum, London, 1995; Jill Knight, *The Civil Service Rifles in the Great War: 'All Bloody Gentlemen'*, Pen and Sword, Barnsley, 2004; Alec Weir, *Come on Highlanders! Glasgow Territorials in the Great War*, Sutton, Stroud, 2005; Derek Bird, *The Spirit of the Troops is Excellent: The 6th (Morayshire) Battalion, Seaforth Highlanders in the Great War, 1914–1919*, Birdbrain Books, Moray, 2008; Leonard Sellers, *The Hood Battalion*, Leo Cooper/Pen and Sword, Barnsley, 1995.
16. Helen B. McCartney, *Citizen Soldiers: The Liverpool Territorials in the First World War*, Cambridge University Press, 2005, see, in particular, Chapters 3 to 6.
17. Dale Blair, *Dinkum Diggers: An Australian Battalion at War*, Melbourne University Press, 2001, see pp. 1–16, 37–68, 150–164, 188–194.
18. Peter Stanley, *Men of Mont St Quentin: Between Victory and Death*, Scribe, Melbourne, 2009.
19. Kenneth Radley, *We Lead, Others Follow: First Canadian Division, 1914–1918*, Vanwell, St Catherine's, 2006.
20. Mitchell A. Yockelson, *Borrowed Soldiers: Americans under British Command, 1918*, University of Oklahoma Press, 2008; Mark Ethan Grotelueschen, *The AEF Way of War: The American Army and Combat in World War I*, Cambridge University Press, 2007; Leonard V. Smith, *Between Mutiny and Obedience: The Case of the French Fifth Infantry Division during World War I*, Princeton University Press, New Jersey, 1994.
21. Smith, *Between Mutiny and Obedience*, see, for example, pp. 89–98, 107–114, 126–129, 155–174 and 176–214.
22. John Peaty, 'Capital Courts-Martial during the Great War', in Brian Bond et al., *Look to Your Front: Studies in the First World War by the British Commission for Military History*, Spellmount, Staplehurst, 1999, pp. 89–104.
23. Cathryn Corns and John Hughes-Wilson, *Blindfold and Alone: British Military Executions in the Great War*, Cassell, London, 2001.
24. Gary Sheffield, *Leadership in the Trenches: Officer-Man Relations, Morale and Discipline in the British Army in the Era of the First World War*, Macmillan, London, 2000, pp. 1–28, 61–78, 80–102, 107–164.
25. Timothy Bowman, *The Irish Regiments in the Great War: Discipline and Morale*, Manchester University Press, 2003, pp. 127–9, 194–6, 202–9.
26. John Lewis-Stempel, *Six Weeks: The Short and Gallant Life of the British Officer in the First World War*, Weidenfeld & Nicolson, London, 2010, pp. 7, 9.
27. Christopher Moore-Bick, *Playing the Game: The British Junior Infantry Officer on the Western Front, 1914–1918*, Helion, Solihull, 2011, particularly pp. 17–18, 21, 263.
28. Alexander Watson, *Enduring the Great War: Combat, Morale and Collapse in the German and British Armies, 1914–1918*, Cambridge University Press, 2008, especially Chapters 5 and 6, and pp. 7, 139 and 183.
29. John Bourne and Bob Bushaway (eds), *Joffrey's War: A Sherwood Forester in the Great War (Geoffrey Ratcliff Husbands)*, Salient Books, 2011, p. 524.

Chapter 2

1. Ian Malcolm Brown, *British Logistics on the Western Front, 1914–1919*, Praeger, Westport CT and London, 1998, pp. 1–13.
2. Gary Sheffield and Dan Todman (eds), *Command and Control on the Western Front: The British Army's Experience, 1914–1918*, Spellmount, Staplehurst, 2004, p. 2.

3. Lieutenant-Colonel J. Shakespear, *The Thirty-Fourth Division, 1915–1919: The Story of its Career from Ripon to the Rhine*, Witherby, London, 1921, pp. 72–3.

4. See C.H. Dudley Ward, *The 56th Division (1st London Territorial Division)*, John Murray, London, 1921, pp. 89–92.

5. Brigadier-General A.H. Hussey and Major D.S. Inman, *The Fifth Division in the Great War*, Nisbet, London, 1921, pp. 110–111, 118, 133–134.

6. Lieutenant-Colonel M. Kincaid-Smith, *The 25th Division in France and Flanders*, Harrison, London, 1919, p. 21.

7. Cyril Falls, *The History of the 36th (Ulster) Division*, M'Caw, Stevenson and Orr, Belfast and London, 1922, pp. 61–62.

8. Captain A.D. Ellis, *The Story of the Fifth Australian Division: Being an Authoritative Account of the Division's Doings in Egypt, France and Belgium*, Hodder and Stoughton, London, 1920, p. 143.

9. Brian Bond, *The Unquiet Western Front: Britain's Role in Literature and History*, Cambridge University Press, 2002.

10. *Ibid.*, p. 31.

11. *Ibid.*, p. 28; see also Martin Stephen, *The Price of Pity: Poetry, History and Myth in the Great War*, Leo Cooper, London, 1996, pp. 138–147.

12. Charles Edmonds (Charles Carrington), *A Subaltern's War*, Anthony Mott edn, London, 1984, pp. 11, 14, 91.

13. Peter Pedersen, 'Introduction' to the 1982 University of Queensland Press edition of C.E.W. Bean, *The Official History of Australia in the War of 1914–1918, Volume III, The AIF in France, 1916* (hereafter Bean, *AOH III*), pp. xxx–xxxi; see also pp. 862–863 of main text. Volume III was originally published by Angus and Robertson, Sydney, 1929.

14. Bean, *AOH III*, pp. 875–876.

15. Bean to Gellibrand, 14 September 1944, Gellibrand papers, Australian War Memorial (AWM), Box 190.

16. Pedersen, 'Introduction', p. xxviii; Bean, *AOH III*, pp. 873–876; see also Captain Wilfrid Miles, *Military Operations: France and Belgium, 1916, Volume II*, Macmillan, London, 1938 (hereafter *OH, 1916, II*), pp. 147–148.

17. Lieutenant-Colonel J.H. Boraston (ed.), *Sir Douglas Haig's Despatches (December 1915–April 1919)*, Dent, London, 1919 and 1979, pp. 19–59, 319–321.

18. Bean, *AOH III*, pp. 943, 945, 947.

19. *Ibid.*, p. 948.

20. There is a brief summary of the improvements in tactical methods in the BEF on pp. 946–947 of Bean, *AOH III*, while the important changes in artillery organisation and the structure of the infantry platoon which were made as a result of the fighting in 1916 are dealt with in less than two pages in Bean, *Volume IV, The AIF in France, 1917*, see pp. 17–18.

21. David French, 'Sir James Edmonds and the Official History: France and Belgium', in Brian Bond (ed.), *The First World War and British Military History*, pp. 69–86, particularly pp. 71 and 74–75.

22. *OH, 1916, II*, p. 561.

23. *Ibid.*, particularly pp. 551–579.

24. Edmonds, 'Preface' to *OH, 1916, II*, p. xvi.

25. Robin Prior and Trevor Wilson, *Command on the Western Front: The Military Career of Sir Henry Rawlinson, 1914–18*, Blackwell, Oxford, 1992, pp. 222–223; Haig to Rawlinson (OAD 123), 24 August 1916, Fourth Army papers, IWM, Volume 5; *OH, 1916, II*, p. 202.

26. *OH, 1916, II*, pp. 551–579.

27. David French, 'Sir James Edmonds and the Official History', in Bond, *The First World War and British Military History*, pp. 72, 85.

28. B.H. Liddell Hart, 'Impressions of the Great British Offensive on the Somme by a company commander who saw three and a half weeks of it', Autumn 1916, pp. 84, 95–96, Liddell Hart papers, Liddell Hart centre for Military Archives, King's College London (LHCMA/KCL), 7/1916/22; John J. Mearsheimer, *Liddell Hart and the Weight of History*, Cornell University Press and Brassey's, London, 1988, pp. 22–23; Brian Bond, 'Liddell Hart and the First World War', in Brian Bond et al., *Look to Your Front: Studies in the First World War by the British Commission for Military History*, Spellmount, Staplehurst, 1999, p. 14.

29. Liddell Hart, copy of 'Pocket Notebook with Jottings', 1917, Liddell Hart papers, LHCMA/ KCL, 7/1917/2.
30. Liddell Hart, 'Thoughts Jotted Down – to be Expanded', memorandum for the record, entry for 17 July 1936, Liddell Hart papers, LHCMA/KCL, 11/1936/2; see also his *Memoirs*, Cassell, London, 1965, Vol. 1, p. 26.
31. Liddell Hart, 'Thoughts Jotted Down – to be Expanded' and *Memoirs*, Vol. 1, p. 65.
32. B.H. Liddell Hart, *Reputations*, John Murray, London, 1928.
33. Sheffield and Todman, 'Command and Control in the British Army on the Western Front', in Sheffield and Todman (eds), *Command and Control on the Western Front*, p. 2.
34. Bond, 'Liddell Hart and the First World War', p. 18.
35. B.H. Liddell Hart, *The Real War, 1914–1918*, Faber, London, 1930 and *A History of the World War, 1914–1918*, Faber, London, 1934; Hew Strachan, 'The Real War: Liddell Hart, Cruttwell and Falls' in Bond (ed.), *The First World War and British Military History*, pp. 46–49; Bond, 'Liddell Hart and the First World War', pp. 19, 23.
36. Winston S. Churchill, *The World Crisis, 1911–1918*, 2 vols, Odhams, London, 1938, particularly pp. 946–947, 1070–1093, 1374–1375, 1384–1385; Bond, *The Unquiet Western Front*, pp. 44–45.
37. David French, 'Sir James Edmonds and the Official History', in Bond, *The First World War and British Military History*, p. 75.
38. Lloyd George to Hankey, 18 April 1934, Lloyd George papers, Parliamentary Archive, House of Lords, Box G/212; C. Cross (ed.), *Life with Lloyd George: The Diary of A.J. Sylvester, 1931–45*, Macmillan, London, 1975, pp. 111–112.
39. David Lloyd George, *War Memoirs*, 6 vols, Ivor Nicholson and Watson, London, 1933–1936, and abridged edition, 2 vols, Odhams, London, 1938, Foreword, pp. v–vi and p. 2011.
40. Bond, *The Unquiet Western Front*, p. 46.
41. Leon Wolff, *In Flanders Fields: The 1917 Campaign*, Longmans, London, 1959; Brian Bond, 'Passchendaele: Verdicts, Past and Present', in Peter H. Liddle (ed.), *Passchendaele in Perspective: The Third Battle of Ypres*, Leo Cooper, London, 1997, p. 481.
42. Alan Clark, *The Donkeys*, Hutchinson, London, 1961, pp. 180–186; Bond, *The Unquiet Western Front*, p. 60; Alex Danchev, '"Bunking" and Debunking: The Controversies of the 1960s', in Bond (ed.), *The First World War and British Military History*, p. 268; Michael Howard, review in the *Listener*, 3 August 1961.
43. Bond, *The Unquiet Western Front*, p. 65; Peter Simkins, 'Everyman at War: Recent Interpretations of the Front Line Experience' in Bond (ed.), *The First World War and British Military History*, pp. 289–313.
44. A.J.P. Taylor, *The First World War: An Illustrated History*, Hamish Hamilton, London, 1963, pp. 68–71, 99–105, 220, 287; Danchev, '"Bunking" and Debunking', in Bond (ed.), *The First World War and British Military History*, p. 273; Bond, *The Unquiet Western Front*, pp. 62–63.
45. Brian Gardner, *The Big Push: A Portrait of the Battle of the Somme*, Cassell, London, 1961.
46. A.H. Farrar-Hockley, *The Somme*, Batsford, London, 1964, see Pan Books edition, London, 1970, pp. 5, 182–187, 208, 219, 232, 246, 253.
47. John Terraine, *Douglas Haig: The Educated Soldier*, Cassell, London, 1963, p. 230.
48. John Terraine, *The Smoke and the Fire: Myths and Anti-Myths of War, 1861–1945*, Sidgwick and Jackson, London, 1980, p. 122.
49. Liddell Hart, '1964 Great War Series on Television', Liddell Hart papers, LHCMA/KCL, 13/62; Bond, *The Unquiet Western Front*, p. 69.
50. BBC Audience Research Reports, 11 September and 28 December 1964, BBC Written Archives Centre, VR/64/461 and 624; Danchev, '"Bunking" and Debunking', in Bond (ed.), *The First World War and British Military History*, pp. 280–281.
51. Danchev, '"Bunking" and Debunking', in Bond (ed.), *The First World War and British Military History*, p. 278.
52. Martin Middlebrook, *The First Day on the Somme: 1 July 1916*, Allen Lane/The Penguin Press, London, 1971; John Keegan, *The Face of Battle*, Penguin edition, London, 1976, p. 262.
53. Keegan, *The Face of Battle*, p. 277.
54. Malcolm Brown, *Tommy Goes to War*, Dent, London, 1978.
55. Alex Aiken, *Courage Past: A Duty Done*, published by the author, Glasgow, 1971.
56. Lyn Macdonald, *Somme*, Michael Joseph, London, 1983.
57. Robin Prior and Trevor Wilson, *The Somme*, Yale University Press, New Haven CT and London, 2005, p. 118.

58. Colin Hughes, *Mametz: Lloyd George's "Welsh Army" at the Battle of the Somme*, Orion Press, Garrards Cross, 1982. See Gliddon Books edition, Norwich, 1990, p. 148.
59. Philip Orr, *The Road to the Somme: Men of the Ulster Division Tell their Story*, Blackstaff Press, Belfast, 1987, pp. 200–201; Middlebrook, *The First Day on the Somme*, p. 280.
60. William Turner, *Accrington Pals: The 11th (Service) Battalion (Accrington) East Lancashire Regiment. A History of the Battalion Raised from Accrington, Blackburn, Burnley and Chorley in World War One*, Wharncliffe, Barnsley, 1987.
61. Rose E.B. Coombs, *Before Endeavours Fade: A Guide to the Battlefields of the First World War*, After the Battle, London, 1976; John Giles, 'Prologue' to *The Somme: Then and Now*, Bailey Brothers and Swinfen, Folkestone, 1977, p. 111.
62. Peter Dennis and Jeffrey Grey, 'Australian and New Zealand Writing on the First World War', in Jurgen Rohwer (ed.), *Neue Forschungen zum Ersten Weltkrieg*, Bernard und Graf Verlag, Coblenz, 1985, p. 2.
63. Peter Charlton, *Australians on the Somme: Pozières 1916*, Leo Cooper/Secker and Warburg, London, 1986, pp. 293, 311.
64. Christopher Pugsley, *The Anzac Experience: New Zealand, Australia and Empire in the First World War*, Reed, Auckland, 2004, p. 230.
65. Martin Samuels, *Doctrine and Dogma: German and British Infantry Tactics in the First World War*, Greenwood Press, Westport CT, 1992, pp. 137–148, and *Command or Control? Command, Training and Tactics in the British and German Armies, 1888–1918*, Frank Cass, London, 1995, pp. 94–157, 230–269.
66. Shelford Bidwell and Dominick Graham, *Fire-Power: British Army Weapons and Theories of War, 1904–1945*, Allen and Unwin, London, 1982; Andy Simpson, *Directing Operations: British Corps Command on the Western Front, 1914–18*, Spellmount, Stroud, 2006, p. xviii.
67. Bidwell and Graham, *Fire-Power*, p. 3.
68. General Sir Martin Farndale, *History of the Royal Regiment of Artillery: Western Front, 1914–18*, Royal Artillery Institution, London, 1986, pp. 141–157, 343–345, 349, 355–357.
69. John Bourne, 'Haig and the Historians', in Brian Bond and Nigel Cave (eds), *Haig: A Reappraisal 70 Years On*, Leo Cooper/Pen and Sword, Barnsley, 1999, p. 6.
70. Tim Travers, *The Killing Ground: The British Army, the Western Front and the Emergence of Modern Warfare, 1900–1918*, Allen and Unwin, London, 1987, pp. 3–27, 37–55, 62–78.
71. Travers, *The Killing Ground*, pp. 85–97 and particularly pp. 97, 104.
72. Simpson, *Directing Operations*, pp. xxii–xxiii.
73. Peter Simkins, 'Haig and the Army Commanders', in Bond and Cave (eds), *Haig: A Reappraisal 70 Years On*, pp. 78–97; GHQ to Fourth Army (OAD 123), 24 August 1916, Fourth Army papers, IWM, Vol. 5. See also Rawlinson Diary, Rawlinson papers, Churchill College, Cambridge (CCC) 1/5.
74. John Bourne, 'The BEF's Generals on 29 September 1918: An Empirical Portrait with some British and Australian Comparisons', in Peter Dennis and Jeffrey Grey (eds), *1918: Defining Victory*, Proceedings of the Chief of Army's History Conference, Canberra, 1998, Army History Unit, Canberra, 1999, p. 108.
75. Bill Rawling, *Surviving Trench Warfare: Technology and the Canadian Corps, 1914–1918*, University of Toronto Press, 1992, pp. 67–113.
76. Rawling, *Surviving Trench Warfare*, pp. 89–97; see also A.M.J. Hyatt, *General Sir Arthur Currie: A Military Biography*, University of Toronto Press, 1987, pp. 63–67; and Tim Cook, *Shock Troops: Canadians Fighting the Great War, 1917–1918*, Viking, Toronto, 2008, pp. 19–22. However, Mark Humphries notes that Currie went to Verdun 'with other British officers': see Mark Osborne Humphries, 'Old Wine in New Bottles: A Comparison of British and Canadian Preparations for the Battle of Arras', in Geoffrey Hayes, Andrew Iarocci and Mike Bechtold (eds), *Vimy Ridge: A Canadian Reassessment*, Wilfrid Laurier Press, Waterloo, Ontario, 2007, p. 67.
77. Rawling, *Surviving Trench Warfare*, pp. 148, 187.
78. Robin Prior and Trevor Wilson, *Command on the Western Front*, pp. 395–396.
79. *Ibid.*, pp. 305, 396–397.
80. Chris McCarthy, *The Somme: The Day-by-Day Account*, Arms and Armour Press, London, 1993.
81. Paddy Griffith, *Battle Tactics of the Western Front: The British Army's Art of Attack, 1916–18*, Yale University Press, New Haven CT and London, 1994, see in particular pp. 65–100, 120–134, 135–158, 179–186 and 192–200.

82. Paddy Griffith, 'The Extent of Tactical Reform in the British Army' and Jonathan Bailey, 'British Artillery in the Great War', in Griffith (ed.), *British Fighting Methods in the Great War,* Frank Cass, London, 1996, pp. 1–19, 23–43. See also Bailey, 'The First World War and the Birth of the Modern Style of Warfare', *The Occasional,* No. 22, Strategic and Combat Studies Institute, Camberley, 1996, pp. 3–21.

83. John Keegan, review of *Facing Armageddon: The First World War Experienced,* Leo Cooper/ Pen and Sword, 1996, quoted in Peter Simkins, 'The Events of the "Last Hundred Days", 1918', *RUSI Journal,* Vol. 143, No. 6, December 1998, pp. 81–82; Keegan, *The First World War,* Hutchinson, London, 1998, p. 315.

84. Ian Malcolm Brown, *British Logistics on the Western Front,* pp. 109–204, 231–239.

85. Peter Chasseaud, *Artillery's Astrologers: A History of British Survey and Mapping on the Western Front, 1914–1918,* Mapbooks, Lewes, 1999, *passim.*

86. 'Editors Foreword' in Brian Bond and Nigel Cave (eds), *Haig: A Reappraisal,* pp. xiii–xiv.

87. John Bourne, 'Haig and the Historians', in Brian Bond and Nigel Cave (eds), *Haig: A Reappraisal,* p. 5.

88. John Lee, 'Some Lessons of the Somme: The British Infantry in 1917' in Bond et al., *Look to Your Front,* pp. 79–87, and 'Command and Control in Battle: British Divisions on the Menin Road Ridge, 20 September 1917', in Sheffield and Todman (eds), *Command and Control on the Western Front,* pp. 119–139.

89. Gary Sheffield, *Forgotten Victory. The First World War: Myths and Realities,* Headline, London, 2001, p. 150; Everard Wyrall, *The History of the 19th Division, 1914–1918,* Edward Arnold and Humphries, Bradford, 1932, pp. 41–42; Report from GOC 99th Brigade, 29 July 1916, 99th Brigade War Diary (WD), The National Archives (TNA) WO 95/1368.

90. Sheffield, *Forgotten Victory,* pp. 150–151; and *The Somme,* Cassell, London, 2003, p. 159.

91. Sheffield, *Forgotten Victory,* pp. 151–154; *The Somme,* pp. 156–157, 160.

92. Gary Sheffield and John Bourne (eds), *Douglas Haig: War Diaries and Letters, 1914–1918,* Weidenfeld & Nicolson, London, 2005, pp. 30–34.

93. Andrew A. Wiest, *Haig: The Evolution of a Commander,* Potomac Press, Dulles, VA, 2005, pp. 63–65.

94. Walter Reid, *Architect of Victory: Douglas Haig,* Birlinn, Edinburgh, 2006, pp. 306–309; Sheffield, *Forgotten Victory,* p. 151.

95. Gary Mead, *The Good Soldier: The Biography of Douglas Haig,* Atlantic Books, London, 2007, pp. 231, 264–265, 342–344.

96. Simon Robbins, *British Generalship on the Western Front, 1914–1918: Defeat into Victory,* Frank Cass, London, 2005, pp. 94–95, 100, 107–110; Alfred Pollard VC, *Fire-Eater: The Memoirs of a VC,* Hutchinson, London, 1932, p. 249.

97. Alistair Geddes, 'Solly-Flood, GHQ and Tactical Training in the BEF, 1916–1918', MA dissertation, University of Birmingham, 2007, pp. 8, 26, 29–31; Andrew Whitmarsh, 'Tactical and Operational Practice in the British Expeditionary Force. A Divisional Study: The 12th (Eastern) Division, 1915–1918', MA dissertation, University of Leeds, 1995, pp. 22–23; Major-General J.F.C. Fuller, *Memoirs of an Unconventional Soldier,* Ivor Nicholson and Watson, London, 1936, p. 82; Memorandum (G 794) signed by Major-General J.S.M. Shea (30th Division), 28 November 1916, Fuller papers, LHCMA/KCL, 1/1/29; 'Notes on an exercise carried out near Chalons in the Fourth French Army to demonstrate the new training of Infantry Units introduced in 1916', accompanying Shea's memeorandum in the Fuller papers, LHCMA/KCL, 1/1/30; 'Note annexe provisoire à l'instruction du 8 Janvier 1916 sur le combat offensif des petites unités', 27 September 1916 (translated by GHQ and published as *SS 601* in December 1916.

98. Geddes, 'Solly-Flood, GHQ and Tactical Training', pp. 32–33; 7th Norfolks WD, entries for January 1917 and 2 February 1917, TNA WO 95/1853; 'Report on Operation by 29th Division, January 27th, 1917', by Major-General Beauvoir de Lisle, 30 January 1917, Montgomery-Massingberd papers, LHCMA/KCL, 7/32; Mark Humphries, 'Old Wine in New Bottles', in Hayes, Iarocci and Bechtold (eds), *Vimy Ridge,* p. 69. There is some evidence that Currie had recommended changes in organsiation *before* his visit to Verdun, for battalion commanders in the 2nd Canadian Brigade were apparently advised of such measures in late December 1916, 2nd Canadian Brigade WD, December 1916, Appendix III, 29 December 1916, TNA WO 95/3764.

99. Geddes, 'Solly-Flood, GHQ and Tactical Training in the BEF', pp. 33–34; Haig Diary, 2 and 3 February 1917, TNA WO 256/15; 7th Norfolks WD, 2 February 1917, TNA WO 95/1853.

100. Geddes, 'Solly-Flood, GHQ and Tactical Training in the BEF', pp. 59–60.

101. *Ibid.*, p. 35; Jim Beach (ed.), *The Military Papers of Lieutenant-Colonel Sir Cuthbert Headlam, 1910–1942*, History Press, Stroud, for the Army Records Society, 2010, pp. 85–87; see also Dave Molineux, 'The Effect of Platoon Structure on Tactical Development in the BEF, June to November 1918', MA dissertation, University of Birmingham, 2009.

102. The details of the composition of the party in question are taken from a photograph of the lid of a cigar box presented by the party to the officers of the Verdun garrison. This photograph may be found in the Alanbrooke papers, LHCMA/KCL, 2/1/10. At the time of writing, Trevor Harvey is working on a doctoral thesis at the University of Birmingham on the subject of brigade command at the Battle of Arras in 1917. I am immensely grateful to him for sharing these fruits of his research with me.

103. Andy Simpson, *Directing Operations*, pp. xvi–xvii, 4–7, 25–54 (particularly pp. 50–51), 61, 70; see also Albert Palazzo, *Seeking Victory on the Western Front: The British Army and Chemical Warfare in World War I*, University of Nebraska Press, Lincoln, Nebraska, and London, 2000. An earlier summary of Simpson's arguments can be found in his 'British Corps Command on the Western Front, 1914–1918' in Sheffield and Todman (eds), *Command and Control on the Western Front*, pp. 97–115.

104. Peter Hart, *The Somme*, Weidenfeld & Nicolson, London, 2005, pp. 533–534.

105. Prior and Wilson, *The Somme*, pp, 203–215.

106. *Ibid.*, pp. 303–304.

107. *Ibid.*, pp. 300–309.

108. Pugsley, *The Anzac Experience*, pp. 165–244, 278–299.

109. Sheffield and Todman (eds), *Command and Control on the Western Front*, *passim* (see, for example, pp. 8–9).

110. Jack Sheldon, *The German Army on the Somme, 1914–1916*, Pen and Sword, Barnsley, 2005, pp. 397–398.

111. Christopher Duffy, *Through German Eyes: The British and the Somme 1916*, Weidenfeld & Nicolson, London, 2006, pp. 167–169, 275, 323, 326–327.

112. J.P. Harris, *Douglas Haig and the First World War*, Cambridge University Press, 2008, pp. 270–273, 312–314, 539–540.

113. William Philpott, *Bloody Victory: The Sacrifice on the Somme and the Making of the Twentieth Century*, Little, Brown, London, 2009, pp. 51–2, 189–190, 264–6, 366–377, 428, 439–440.

114. *Ibid.*, pp. 11, 52, 55, 149.

115. *Ibid.*, pp. 67, 358, 607–608; see also Philpott, 'Sir Douglas Haig's Command? The Image of Alliance in Douglas Haig's Record of the War' (the Douglas Haig Fellowship Lecture, June 2011), in *Records: The Douglas Haig Fellowship's Journal*, No. 15, November 2011, pp. 3–13.

116. Philpott, *Bloody Victory*, pp. 177, 205–207, 241, 267, 281–282, 345–346, 363, 441–442, 606–607, 637.

117. Gary Sheffield, *The Chief: Douglas Haig and the British Army*, Aurum Press, London, 2011, pp. 197–198.

118. Sheffield, *The Chief*, p. 196; Nicholas Perry, *Major-General Oliver Nugent and the Ulster Division, 1915–1918*, Sutton Publishing, Stroud, for the Army Records Society, 2007, pp. 125–126; Nugent to his wife, 20 December 1916, Farren Connell (Nugent) papers, Public Record Office of Northern Ireland, D/3835/E/2/11.

119. Sanders Marble, *British Artillery on the Western Front in the First World War: The Infantry cannot do with a gun less*, Ashgate, Farnham, 2013, pp. 111–155; see also Paul Strong and Sanders Marble, *Artillery in the Great War*, Pen and Sword, Barnsley, 2001, pp. 78–125.

120. Brian Bond, 'Foreword' in *Look to Your Front*, p. vii.

121. John Bourne, 'A Personal Reflection on 1 July 1916', in *Firestep: The Magazine of the London Branch of the Western Front Association*, Vol. 5, No. 2, November 2004, p. 27.

Chapter 3

1. Brigadier-General Sir James Edmonds, *Military Operations: France and Belgium, 1916, Volume I*, Macmillan, London, 1932 (hereafter *OH, 1916, I*), p. 315.

2. Private George Morgan, 16th Battalion, West Yorkshire Regiment (1st Bradford Pals), quoted in Malcolm Brown, *The Imperial War Museum Book of the Somme*, Sidgwick and Jackson, London, 1996, p. 102.

3. Captain Wilfrid Miles, *Military Operations: France and Belgium, 1916, Volume II*, Macmillan, London, 1938 (hereafter *OH, 1916, II*), pp. 570–571.

4. Denis Winter, *Haig's Command: A Reassessment*, Viking, London, 1991, pp. 144, 150.

5. Bruce I. Gudmunsdsson, *Stormtroop Tactics: Innovation in the German Army, 1914–1918*, Praeger, New York, 1989, pp. 175–176.

6. Martin Samuels, *Doctrine and Dogma: German and British Infantry Tactics in the First World War*, Greenwood Press, Westport CT, 1992, p. 180, and *Command or Control?: Command, Training and Tactics in the British and German Armies, 1888–1918*, Frank Cass, London, 1995, pp. 148, 152, 156–157.

7. See Peter Simkins, 'Co-Stars or Supporting Cast? British Divisions in "The Hundred Days", 1918', in Paddy Griffith (ed.), *British Fighting Methods in the Great War*, Frank Cass, London, 1996, pp. 50–69.

8. This information relating to the length of service of various divisions on the Western Front prior to 1 July 1916 has been drawn mainly from a detailed examination of the relevant volumes of the British official history and particularly from Major A.F. Becke, *Order of Battle of Divisions: Part 3A, New Army Divisions (9–26)*, HMSO, London, 1938, and *Part 3B, New Army Divisions (30–41) and 63rd (R.N.) Division*, HMSO, London, 1945; see also Captain G.H.F. Nichols, *The 18th Division in the Great War*, Blackwood, Edinburgh and London, 1922, pp. 12–34.

9. Becke, *Order of Battle of Divisions, Parts 3A* and *3B*.

10. *Ibid.*

11. *OH, 1916, II*, p. 299, n. 2; and Christopher Pugsley, *On the Fringe of Hell: New Zealanders and Military Discipline in the First World War*, Hodder and Stoughton, Auckland, 1991, p. 122. Pugsley states that the New Zealanders remained in the line from 15 September until 2 October 1916, 'the longest unbroken spell of any division'. See also Lieutenant-Colonel J. Stewart and John Buchan, *The Fifteenth (Scottish) Division, 1914–1919*, Blackwood, Edinburgh and London, 1926, pp. 78–94.

12. 35th Division War Diary (WD), TNA WO 95/2468; 104th Brigade WD, TNA WO 95/2482; 105th Brigade WD, TNA WO 95/2485; 15th Sherwood Foresters WD, TNA WO 95/2488; 16th Cheshires WD, TNA WO 95/2487; 14th Gloucesters WD, TNA WO 95/2488; 17th Lancashire Fusiliers WD, TNA WO 95/2484; Diary of Major-General (Sir) Reginald Pinney, entries for 20, 22 and 25 August 1916, Pinney papers, IWM 66/257/1; *OH, 1916, II*, pp. 111–112, 199–201; Maurice Bacon and David Langley, *The Blast of War: A History of Nottingham's Bantams, 15th (S) Battalion, Sherwood Foresters*, Sherwood Press, Nottingham, 1986, pp. 25–29; Stephen McGreal, *Cheshire Bantams: 15th, 16th and 17th Battalions of the Cheshire Regiment*, Pen and Sword, Barnsley, 2006, pp. 116–117, 121–122; Lieutenant-Colonel H.M. Davson, *The History of the 35th Division in the Great War*, Sifton Praed, London, 1926, pp. 27–52. For a more detailed summary of the experiences of the division, see Peter Simkins, 'Each One a Pocket Hercules: The Bantam Experiment and the Case of the Thirty-Fifth Division', in Sanders Marble (ed.), *Scraping the Barrel: The Military Use of Substandard Manpower, 1860–1960*, Fordham University Press, New York, 2012, pp. 79–104.

13. *OH, 1916, I*, pp. 329–342, 346–368.

14. *Ibid.*, pp. 371–391; Martin Middlebrook, *The First Day on the Somme*, p. 267.

15. *OH, 1916, I*, pp. 394–421; Cyril Falls, *The History of the 36th (Ulster) Division*, M'Caw, Stevenson and Orr, Belfast and London, 1922, pp. 41–62.

16. *OH, 1916, I*, pp. 424–451.

17. Winter, *Haig's Command*, p. 148.

18. Becke, *Order of Battle of Divisions, Parts 3A, 3B*.

19. *OH, 1916, I*, pp. 375–376; Lieutenant-Colonel J. Shakespear, *The Thirty-Fourth Division, 1915–1919*, pp. 35–36; Robin Prior and Trevor Wilson, *The Somme*, p. 93.

20. Captain G.H.F. Nichols, *The 18th Division in the Great War*, pp. 38–39, 43–44; *OH, 1916, I*, p. 329.

21. Prior and Wilson, *The Somme*, pp. 112–118.

22. John Bourne, 'The BEF on the Somme: Some Career Aspects – Part 1, July 1916' in *Gun Fire: A Journal of First World War History*, No. 35, n.d., p. 12.

23. The other two were Major-General The Hon. E.J. Montagu–Stuart–Wortley of the 46th (North Midland) Division and Major-General Ivor Philipps of the 38th (Welsh) Division.

24. Bourne, 'The BEF on the Somme: Some Career Aspects', p. 10; see also Bourne, *Who's Who in World War One*, Routledge, London, 2001, pp. 49–50.

25. Bourne, 'The BEF on the Somme: Some Career Aspects', p. 10, and *Who's Who in World War One*, p. 37.

26. Bourne, 'The BEF on the Somme: Some Career Aspects', p. 11; Becke, *Parts 3A, 3B*; Frank Davies and Graham Maddocks, *Bloody Red Tabs: General Officer Casualties of the Great War*, Leo Cooper/Pen and Sword, London and Barnsley, 1995, pp. 65–66, 100–101, 123, 189.

27. Becke, *Part 3B*, pp. 31, 51, 71, 81.

28. John Bourne, 'The BEF on the Somme: Some Career Aspects, Part Two: 2 July –19 November 1916' in *Gun Fire*, No. 39, n.d., p. 15; Major G.P.L. Drake-Brockman to official historian, 7 February 1930, TNA CAB 45/189; Colin Hughes, *Mametz*, pp. 137–140.

29. Bourne, 'Some Career Aspects, Part Two', pp. 15–16, and p. 24, n. 18.

30. Frank Richards, *Old Soldiers Never Die*, Faber, London, 1933, p. 217; *The Times*, 20 February 1943; Haig Diary, 28 October 1916, TNA WO 256/13; Gary Sheffield and John Bourne (eds), *Douglas Haig: War Diaries and Letters, 1914–1918*, Weidenfeld & Nicolson, London, 2005, p. 249; Bourne, *Who's Who*, p. 234.

31. Bourne, 'Some Career Aspects: Part Two', pp. 17 and 24, n. 20; and *Who's Who*, pp. 166–167. Lawford's son, Peter, became a child actor and Hollywood star and was a leading member of Frank Sinatra's 'Rat Pack'. Sydney Lawford himself is known to have appeared in at least three movies, including *The Picture of Dorian Grey* (1945).

32. Hughes, *Mametz*, pp. 85–91; Wyn Griffith, *Up to Mametz*, Faber, London, 1931, pp. 205–206; Bourne, 'Some Career Aspects, Part Two', p. 19; Becke, *Part 3B*, p. 82.

33. Bourne, 'Some Career Aspects, Part Two', pp. 18–19; Becke, *Part 3A*, pp. 54, 88.

34. Becke, *Part 3A*, p. 128.

35. Becke, *Part 3A*, pp. 54, 96; Bourne, 'Some Career Aspects, Part Two', p. 19.

36. Bourne, 'Some Career Aspects, Part Two', pp. 19–20; Davies and Maddocks, *Bloody Red Tabs*, p. 152.

37. Tim Travers, *The Killing Ground*, p. 13.

38. Becke, *Part 3A*, p. 72.

39. Haig Diary, 8 July 1916, TNA WO 256/11; *OH, 1916, II*, pp. 93–94; Travers, *The Killing Ground*, pp. 169–170.

40. Malcolm Brown, *The Imperial War Museum Book of the Western Front*, Sidgwick and Jackson, London, 1993, pp. 125–130. The relevant papers can be found in the collections of the Imperial War Museum.

41. Major-General Ivor Maxse, *The 18th Division in the Battle of the Ancre*, printed report, December 1916, pp. 16–17. Copies of this report, also known as 'The Red Book', can be found in the Maxse papers in the Imperial War Museum, IWM 69/53/8.

42. Bourne, 'Some Career Aspects, Part Two', p. 20.

43. *Ibid.*, pp. 22–23.

44. Becke, *Part 3A*, pp. 96, 128, 136, and *Part 3B*, p. 92.

45. John Ewing, *The History of the 9th (Scottish) Division, 1914–1919*, John Murray, London, 1921, pp. 170–172; Becke, *Part 3A*, pp. 3,19; and *Part 3B*, p. 71.

46. Becke, *Part 3B*, p. 21.

47. *Ibid.*, p. 71; J.C. Dunn to Robert Graves, 27 October 1925, Dunn-Graves correspondence, Regimental Archives of the Royal Welch Fusiliers, cited in Keith Simpson's Introduction to the edition of Dunn's *The War The Infantry Knew, 1914–1919* published by Sphere Books, Lodnon, 1989, p. xi. During the war itself, the name 'Welsh' in the titles of the Royal Welsh Fusiliers and the Welsh Regiment was spelt with an 's'. The old alternative spelling 'Welch' was reinstated, at the request of the regiments, by Army Order 56 of 1920. I have therefore employed the spelling 'Welsh' in a wartime context and the spelling 'Welch' when referring to post-war publications etc.

48. *OH, 1916, I*, pp. 359–361; *OH, 1916, II*, pp. 15–16; 21st Division WD, TNA WO 95/2130; 62nd Brigade WD, TNA WO 95/2151; 64th Brigade WD, TNA WO 95/2159; 13th Northumberland Fusiliers WD, TNA WO 95/2155.

49. *OH, 1916, II*, pp. 52–53; 114th Brigade WD, TNA WO 95/2557, Appendix C, Report on operations of 10–11 July 1916 by Brigadier-General T.O. Marden, dated 16 July.

50. *OH, 1916, I*, pp. 376–377, 417–418.
51. Nichols, *18th Division*, pp. 59–69; Charlotte Maxwell (ed.), *Frank Maxwell: Brig.-General VC, CSI, DSO: A Memoir and Some Letters*, John Murray, London, 1921, pp. 152–159; *OH, 1916, II*, pp. 75–78.
52. Ewing, *9th (Scottish) Division*, pp. 106–107.
53. *OH, 1916, II*, p. 40; Hughes, *Mametz*, p. 95.
54. *OH, 1916, II*, pp. 139–140.
55. *Ibid.*, pp. 166.
56. Shakespear, *Thirty-Fourth Division*, pp. 72–73.
57. Ewing, *9th (Scottish) Division*, pp. 101–138, 403; *OH, 1916, II*, pp. 92, 104–105; Davies and Maddocks, *Bloody Red Tabs*, p. 65.
58. Middlebrook, *The First Day on the Somme*, Appendix D, 'Senior Officer Casualties', pp. 326–328.
59. *OH, 1916, II*, pp. 54, 321–323, 327–328; Hughes, *Mametz*, p. 109; 41st Division WD, TNA WO 95/2617; Trevor Pidgeon, *The Tanks at Flers: An Account of the First Use of Tanks in War at the Battle of Flers-Courcelette, The Somme, 15 September 1916*, Fairmile Books, Cobham, Surrey, 1995, Vol. I, pp. 163–175.
60. Jonathan Nicholls, *Cheerful Sacrifice: The Battle of Arras 1917*, Leo Cooper, London, 1990, p. 211.
61. Middlebrook, *The First Day on the Somme*, p. 268; also Martin and Mary Middlebrook, *The Somme Battlefields: A Comprehensive Guide from Crécy to the two World Wars*, Viking, London, 1991, p. 139.
62. Shakespear, *Thirty-Fourth Division*, p. 87; *War Establishment of New Armies*, London, 1915.
63. Ewing, *9th (Scottish) Division*, p. 409.
64. *OH, 1916, II*, p. 276, n. 1; Major-General Sir Arthur B. Scott and P. Middleton Brumwell, *History of the 12th (Eastern) Division in the Great War, 1914–1918*, Nisbet, London, 1923, p. 254.
65. *OH, 1916, II*, pp. 443, including n. 5.
66. Helen McCartney, *Citizen Soldiers: The Liverpool Territorials in the First World War*, Cambridge University Press, 2005, pp. 57–88; Shakespear, *Thirty-Fourth Division*, pp. 64–65.
67. Robert Cude, unpublished typed transcript of diary, entry for 17 January 1917, IWM CON/RC.
68. See 113th Brigade WD, TNA WO 95/2552, Appendix 15, Summary of the action at Mametz Wood by Brigadier-General L.A.E. Price-Davies, dated 14 July 1916; also Appendix 20, message dated 16 July 1916. The latter appears to have been submitted by the Brigade Major on behalf of Price-Davies. David Jones, the author of *In Parenthesis*, who also served in the 15th Royal Welsh Fusiliers and who witnessed the incident, was slightly more charitable than Price-Davies, recalling that the situation had developed 'if not into a panic, at least into a disorderly falling back' (letter to Colin Hughes, 24 March 1971, quoted in *Mametz*, p. 110).
69. Bacon and Langley, *The Blast of War*, p. 26; 15th Sherwood Foresters WD, TNA WO 95/2488; Judge Advocate General's Records: Proceedings of Field General Court Martial and associated papers, TNA WO 71/489; Register of Field General Courts Martial, TNA WO 213/10 and 213/11 (hereafter JAG FGCM Proceedings and Register); Cathryn Corns and John Hughes-Wilson, *Blindfold and Alone: British Military Executions in the Great War*, Cassell, London, 2001, pp. 151–153; Peter Simkins, 'Each One a Pocket Hercules: The Bantam Experiment and the Case of the Thirty-Fifth Division', p. 86.
70. Timothy Bowman, *The Irish Regiments in the Great War: Discipline and Morale*, Manchester University Press, 2003, pp. 127–129, 194–196, 202; Terence Denman, *Ireland's Unknown Soldiers: The 16th (Irish) Division in World War I*, Irish Academic Press, Dublin, 1992, p. 144; Jane Leonard, 'The Reaction of Irish Officers in the British Army to the Easter Rising of 1916', in Cecil and Liddle (eds), *Facing Armageddon: The First World War Experienced*, pp. 256–268.
71. Julian Putkowski and Julian Sykes, *Shot at Dawn: Ececutions in World War One by authority of the British Army Act*, Wharncliffe, Barnsley, 1989, p. 99.
72. These figures and calculations are drawn from a detailed analysis of the evidence presented in Gerard Oram, *Death Sentences Passed by Military Courts of the British Army, 1914–1924*, Francis Boutle, London, 2005 (rev. edn), pp. 39–46.
73. 35th Division WD, TNA WO 95/2468; 19th Durham Light In fantry WD, TNA WO 95/2490; JAG FGCM Proceedings and Register, TNA WO 71/534, 71/535 and 213/13. Detailed analyses and discussions of the events of the night of 25–26 November 1916 can be found in John Sheen, *Durham Pals: 18th, 19th and 22nd Battalions of the Durham Light Infantry. A History of*

Three Battalions Raised by Local Committee in County Durham, Pen and Sword, Barnsley, 2007, pp. 128–134, 273–294; Corns and Hughes-Wilson, *Blindfold and Alone*, pp. 157–175; Davson, *History of the 35th Division*, pp. 74–80; Bacon and Langley, *The Blast of War*, p. 41; Simkins, 'Each One a Pocket Hercules', pp. 90–94.

74. General Sir Aylmer Haldane, *A Soldier's Saga*, Blackwood, Edinburgh, 1948, pp. 335–336; Davson, *History of the 35th Division*, pp. 80–82; Sheen, *Durham Pals*, p. 132; Becke, *Part 3B*, p. 58; 35th Division WD, TNA WO 95/2468; Assistant Director of Medical Services, 35th Division, WD, TNA WO 95/2472; Simkins, 'Each One a Pocket Hercules', pp. 92–93.

75. 'Report on Complaints, Moral etc', November 1916, pp. 6–12, and 'Summaries of Censorship Reports on General Conditions in British Forces in France', M. Hardie papers, IWM 84/46/1, quoted in Gary Sheffield, *Leadership in the Trenches: Officer-Man Relations, Morale and Discipline in the British Army in the Era of the First World War*, Macmillan, London, 2000, Appendix I, 'The Morale of the British Army on the Western Front, 1914–18', p. 181.

76. *Aus Unterhaltungen mit im December 1916 eingebrachten englischen Gefangenen*, 1 January 1917, Bavarian Kriegsarchiv, Munich 14 ID, *Bund* 13, quoted in Chistopher Duffy, *Through German Eyes: The British and the Somme 1916*, p. 328.

77. See Gerald Gliddon (ed.), *VCs Handbook: The Western Front 1914–1918*, Sutton Publishing, Stroud, 2005, pp. 51–71.

Chapter 4

1. The most recent description of the 18th Division's memorial at Thiepval in relation to the site of the original Chateau is given in Michael Stedman's *Thiepval* in the Battleground Europe series, Leo Cooper/Pen and Sword, London and Barnsley, 1995, pp. 185–187. The 18th Division has two other memorials on the Western Front – one at Trones Wood on the Somme and the other at Clapham Junction, on the Menin Road, near Ypres.

2. See Captain G.H.F. Nichols, *The 18th Division in the Great War*; also Peter Simkins, 'The War Experience of a Typical Kitchener Division: The 18th Division, 1914–1918', in Hugh Cecil and Peter H. Liddle (eds), *Facing Armageddon: The First World War Experienced*, Leo Cooper/Pen and Sword, London and Barnsley, 1996, pp. 297–313; and Peter Simkins, *Kitchener's Army: The Raising of the New Armies, 1914–16*, Manchester University Press, 1988, pp. 26, 236, 252, 361, 293, 306 and 316–317.

3. The 18th Division's principal opponents at Thiepval were the Wurttembergers of the German 26th Reserve Division, who had been in the area since the autumn of 1914 and possessed an intimate knowledge of the sector. See Stedman, *Thiepval*, pp. 28, 35–41.

4. See Chapter 3.

5. Captain Wilfrid Miles, *Miltary Operations, France and Belgium, 1916, Volume II (OH, 1916, II)*, Macmillan, London, 1938, pp. 392–393.

6. Major-General F.I. Maxse, *The 18th Division in the Battle of the Ancre*, printed report, December 1916, pp. 3–4. Copies of this report, often referred to as 'The Red Book', can be found in the Maxse papers at the Imperial War Museum, IWM 69/53/8.

7. Nichols, *18th Division*, pp. 79–82; *OH, 1916, II*, p. 393 (including n. 3 and n. 4) and p. 394 (including n. 1); Maxse, *The 18th Division in the Battle of the Ancre*, pp. 4–5, also Appendix B 'Barrage Instructions', 18th Division G. 97, 25 September 1916; John Baynes, *Far from a Donkey: The Life of General Sir Ivor Maxse, KCB, GCVO, DSO*, Brassey's, London, 1995, p. 152; II Corps, General Staff War Diary (WD), TNA WO 95/639; II Corps, Commander Royal Artillery WD, TNA WO 95/651; II Corps, Commander Heavy Artillery WD, TNA WO 95/654; 18th Division, General Staff WD, TNA WO 95/2015.

8. Nichols, *18th Division*, p. 81; Baynes, *Far from a Donkey*, pp. 153–154.

9. Nichols, *18th Division*, pp. 82–85; *OH, 1916, II*, pp. 403–404; Maxse, *The 18th Division in the Battle of the Ancre*, pp. 6–7; Lieutenant-Colonel C.C.R. Murphy, *The History of the Suffolk Regiment, 1914–1927*, Hutchinson, London, 1928, pp. 168–169; Lieutenant-Colonel T.M. Banks and Captain R.A. Chell, *With the 10th Essex in France*, Burt and Sons, London, 1921, pp. 131–132; 18th Division WD, TNA WO 95/2015; 53rd Brigade WD, TNA WO 95/2034; 8th Suffolks WD, TNA WO 95/2039; 10th Essex WD, TNA WO 95/2038; see also Peter Simkins, '"Just as Much as is Humanly Possible": The 10th Essex at Thiepval, September 1916', in *The Eagle: Journal of the Essex Regiment Association*, Issue 67, Spring 2007, pp. 38–45.

10. Maxse, *The 18th Division in the Battle of the Ancre*, pp. 6–8; Nichols, *18th Division*, pp. 85–86; 'E.R.', *The 54th Infantry Brigade, 1914–1918: Some Records of Battle and Laughter in France*,

Gale and Polden, Aldershot, 1919, pp. 51–53; *OH, 1916, II*, pp. 404–405; 18th Division WD, TNA WO 95/2015; 54th Brigade WD, TNA WO 95/2041; 12th Middlesex WD, TNA WO 95/2044; 11th Royal Fusiliers WD, TNA WO 95/2045.

11. Nichols, *18th Division*, pp. 86–95; *OH, 1916, II*, pp. 405–407; 'E.R.', *54th Infantry Brigade*, pp. 53–55; Charlotte Maxwell (ed.), *Frank Maxwell, Brigadier-General, VC, CSI, DSO: A Memoir and Some Letters*, John Murray, London, 1921, pp. 175–178; 18th Division WD, TNA WO 95/2015; 54th Brigade WD, TNA WO 95/2041; 12th Middlesex WD, TNA WO 95/2044; 11th Royal Fusiliers WD, TNA WO 95/2045; 6th Northants WD, TNA WO 95/2044; Baynes, *Far from a Donkey*, pp. 156–157.

12. Maxse, *18th Division in the Battle of the Ancre*, pp. 10–12 and Appendix E, 'Casualties for Battle of Thiepval – 26th and 27th September, 1916'; Nichols, *18th Division*, pp. 101–106; 'E.R.', *54th Brigade*, pp. 61–67; Baynes, *Far from a Donkey*, p. 158; Charlotte Maxwell (ed.), *Frank Maxwell: A Memoir and Some Letters*, pp. 175–178; M.G. Deacon (ed.), *The Shiny Seventh: The 7th (Service) Battalion Bedfordshire Regiment at War, 1915–1918*, Bedfordshire Historical Record Society/ Boydell Press, Woodbridge, 2004, pp. 56–57, and also including pp. 119–120 (quoting the personal diary of Second-Lieutenant Henry J. Cartwright, 1916–1917) and pp. 185–189 'COs Report – Action at Thiepval and Schwaben Redoubt)'; 54th Brigade WD, TNA WO 95/2041; 18th Division WD, TNA WO 95/2015; 7th Bedfords WD, TNA WO 95/2043.

13. Maxse, *18th Division in the Battle of the Ancre*, pp. 13–14; Nichols, *18th Division*, pp. 111–114; Baynes, *Far from a Donkey*, pp. 158–160; 18th Division WD, TNA WO 95/2015; 53rd Brigade WD, TNA WO 95/2034; 54th Brigade WD, TNA WO 95/2041; 55th Brigade WD, TNA WO 95/2046; *OH, 1916, II*, p. 417.

14. Maxse, *18th Division in the Battle of the Ancre*, pp. 14–16; Nichols, *18th Division*, pp. 113–121; *OH, 1916, II*, pp. 418–420; 53rd Brigade WD, TNA WO 95/2034; 8th Suffolks WD, TNA WO 95/2039; Murphy, *The History of the Suffolk Regiment*, pp. 169–170; 54th Brigade WD, TNA WO 95/2041; 7th Queen's WD, TNA WO 95/2051; Colonel H.C. Wylly, *History of The Queen's Royal (West Surrey) Regiment in the Great War*, pp. 216–217; M.G. Deacon (ed.), *The Shiny Seventh*, pp. 120–121, 185–189; 7th Bedfords WD, TNA WO 95/2043; 'E.R.', *54th Brigade*, pp. 68–71.

15. Maxse, *18th Division in the Battle of the Ancre*, p. 16; Nichols, *18th Division*, pp. 121–122; *OH, 1916, II*, pp. 420–421; Baynes, *Far from a Donkey*, p. 161; 18th Division WD, TNA WO 95/2015.

16. Maxse, *18th Division in the Battle of the Ancre*, pp. 15–16; Nichols, *18th Division*, pp. 123–124; *OH, 1916, II*, pp. 422. 453; 18th Division WD, TNA WO 95/2015; 55th Brigade WD, TNA WO 95/2046; 8th East Surreys WD, TNA WO 95/2050; 7th Royal West Kents WD, TNA WO 95/2049; C.T. Atkinson, *The Queen's Own Royal West Kent Regiment, 1914–1919*, Simpkin, Marshall, Hamilton, Kent and Co. Ltd, London, 1924, pp. 213–217; 7th Buffs WD, TNA WO 95/2049; Colonel R.S.H. Moody, *Historical Records of The Buffs, East Kent Regiment, 1914–1919*, Medici Society, London, 1922, pp. 152–154.

17. Maxse, *18th Division in the Battle of the Ancre*, pp. 16–17; *OH, 1916, II*, pp. 453–454; Nichols, *18th Division*, pp. 124–128; 55th Brigade WD, TNA WO 95/2046; Colonel R.S.H. Moody, *Historical Records of The Buffs*, pp. 154–155.

18. Maxse, *18th Division in the Battle of the Ancre*, p. 17 and Appendix F, 'Casualties for Battle of Schwaben, 29th September, 1916, to 5th October, 1916'; Nichols, *18th Division*, p. 128; *OH, 1916, II*, p. 453, n. 5.

19. See Gary Sheffield and Dan Todman (eds), *Command and Control on the Western Front*.

20. See Andy Simpson, 'British Corps Command on the Western Front, 1914–1918', in Sheffield and Todman (eds), *Command and Control on the Western Front*, pp. 97–118, and *Directing Operations: British Corps Command on the Western Front, 1914–18*, Spellmount, Stroud, 2006, particularly the Introduction and Chapters 1 and 2.

21. John Bourne, 'The BEF on the Somme. Some Career Aspects, Part 2: 2 July–19 November 1916', in *Gun Fire: A Journal of First World War History*, No. 39, p. 14; see also Bourne, *Who's Who in World War One*, Routledge, London, 2001, p. 143.

22. General Sir Hubert Gough, *The Fifth Army*, Hodder and Stoughton, London, 1931, pp. 159–160.

23. Maxse, *18th Division in the Battle of the Ancre*, p. 4. Philip Howell was killed by a shell near Authuille on 7 October 1916.

24. Martin Middlebrook, *The First Day on the Somme*, p. 279; Paddy Griffith, *Battle Tactics of the Western Front: The British Army's Art of Attack, 1916–18*, Yale University Press, New Haven CT and London, 1994, p. 184; Baynes, *Far from a Donkey*, pp. 125, 223–224.

25. B.H. Liddell Hart, *Memoirs, Vol. I*, Cassell, London, 1965, p. 43.
26. Lieutenant-Colonel H.H. Hemming, unpublished account, IWM PP/MCR/155.
27. Gough, *The Fifth Army*, pp. 147–148.
28. Maxse, *18th Division in the Battle of the Ancre*, pp. 3–4.
29. T.M. Banks and R.A. Chell, *With the 10th Essex in France*, p. 128; 10th Essex WD, TNA WO 95/2038; Aimée Fox-Godden, 'One Long Loaf? Military Administration and the Role of the Brigade Staff in Operations on the Western Front', in *Records: The Douglas Haig Fellowship's Journal*, No. 16, November 2012 (actually published in 2013), p. 16.
30. Maxse, *18th Division in the Battle of the Ancre*, p. 5; Baynes, *Far from a Donkey*, p. 146; Nichols, *18th Division*, pp. 68–69.
31. Maxse, *18th Division in the Battle of the Ancre*, p. 6.
32. Jonathan Walker, *The Blood Tub: General Gough and the Battle of Bullecourt, 1917*, Spellmount, Staplehurst, 1998, pp. 61, 167–170; Hanway R. Cumming, *A Brigadier in France, 1917–1918*, Cape, London, 1922, pp. 44, 53, 56–57, 74–84.
33. Maxse, *18th Division in the Battle of the Ancre*, pp. 11–12, 16–17.
34. *Ibid.*, pp. 7–12; Nichols, *18th Division*, pp. 85–100; Baynes, *Far from a Donkey*, pp. 154–158; Charlotte Maxwell (ed.), *Frank Maxwell: A Memoir and Some Letters*, pp. 138–162; 'E.R.', *54th Brigade*, pp. 51–67.
35. Charlotte Maxwell, *Frank Maxwell: A Memoir and Some Letters*, p. 182.
36. Private C. Cooksey, pencilled note, 6 January 1917, in Colonel R.A. Chell papers, Liddle Collection, Brotherton Library, University of Leeds; Sergeant (?) Barrett, pencilled note, n.d., probably late 1916 or early 1917, also in Chell papers.
37. *London Gazette*, 24 November 1916; Gerald Gliddon, *VCs of the First World War: The Somme*, Sutton, Stroud, 1997, pp. 165–169; Maxse, *18th Division in the Battle of the Ancre*, p. 12.
38. Maxse, *18th Division in the Battle of the Ancre*, p. 15; Nichols, *18th Division*, pp. 114–115; 7th Queen's WD, TNA WO 95/2051.
39. Gudmundsson, *Stormtroop Tactics: Innovation in the German Army, 1914–1918*, p. 175.
40. Gliddon, *VCs of the First World War*, pp. 154–165; *London Gazette*, 25 November 1916.
41. *OH, 1916, II*, p. 407.
42. Helen McCartney, *Citizen Soldiers*, particularly Chapter 4, pp. 57–88.
43. *Soldiers Died in the Great War*, CD-Rom version, published by the Naval and Military Press; see also *OH, 1916, II*, p. 48 (n. 1 and n. 2).
44. The same conclusions might be drawn in the case of the 18th Division's sister formation – the 12th (Eastern) Division (see Chapter 8).
45. Various forms of machine-gun barrages had been fired – for example, at Pozières in July, at High Wood on 24 August and at Morval on 25 September 1916, see Paul Cornish, *Machine Guns and the Great War*, Pen and Sword, Barnsley, 2009, pp. 67–68.
46. Baynes, *Far from a Donkey*, p. 164; see also Maxse papers, IWM 69/53/7.
47. Oberstleutnant Alfred Bischler, quoted in Ian Passingham, *All the Kaiser's Men: The Life and Death of the German Army on the Western Front, 1914–1918*, Sutton, Stroud, 2003, p. 123; General B.E. Palat, *La Grand Guerre sur le Front Occidental*, 14 vols, Berger-Levrault, Paris, 1917–1929, Vol. IX, pp. 216–217.
48. Banks and Chell, *With the 10th Essex in France*, pp. 132–133.

Chapter 5

1. This essay was originally published, in a shorter form, in the *Imperial War Museum Review*, No. 9, 1994. It is reproduced here, in an updated and revised version, by kind permission of the Trustees of the Imperial War Museum.
2. The alternative spelling 'Frankfurt Trench' is also used in a variety of sources, and the small cemetery located near the scene of the 32nd Division's attack is called 'Frankfurt Trench British Cemetery'. However, in this essay I have employed the spelling 'Frankfort Trench' which is given in the British official history and the majority of contemporary documents.
3. 3.See n. 2 on pp. 522–523 of *OH, 1916, II*.
4. Gerard J. De Groot, *Douglas Haig, 1861–1928*, Unwin Hyman, London, 1988, pp. 260–263; Tim Travers, *The Killing Ground*, pp. 173–177; *OH, 1916, II*, pp. 174–175.
5. Prior and Wilson, *Command on the Western Front*, pp. 203–205.
6. Anthony Farrar-Hockley, *Goughie: The Life of General Sir Hubert Gough*, Hart-Davis, MacGibbon, London, 1975, p. 130.

7. 'The Commander-in-Chief's Instructions to the Fourth and Reserve Armies, 2nd August' (OAD 91), 2 August 1916, see *OH, 1916*, Maps and Appendices volume, Appendix 13, pp. 34–36.

8. General Headquarters (GHQ) to Fourth Army (OAD 123), 24 August 1916, Fourth Army papers, IWM, Vol. 5.

9. See, for instance, Travers, *The Killing Ground*, pp. 183–187, and De Groot, *Haig*, pp. 269–271.

10. Gary Sheffield, *The Chief: Douglas Haig and the British Army*, p. 193; Haig to King George V, 5 October 1916, see Sheffield and Bourne (eds), *Douglas Haig: War Diaries and Letters*, pp. 236–237.

11. Haig to Robertson, 'Present Situation' (OAD 173), 7 October 1916, TNA WO 158/21.

12. Prior and Wilson, *Command on the Western Front*, pp. 233–237, 249.

13. *OH, 1916, II*, pp. 391–393, 427–428.

14. *Ibid.*, p. 458.

15. *Ibid.*, pp. 458–459, 461–462.

16. *Ibid.*, p. 462.

17. *Ibid.*, p. 476.

18. Haig Diary, 12 November 1916, TNA WO 256/14.

19. Kiggell to Edmonds, 4 June 1938, TNA CAB 45/135.

20. Jeffreys to Edmonds, 23 October 1936, TNA CAB 45/135.

21. *OH, 1916, II*, Note II, p. 475.

22. *Ibid.*, p. 478, n. 1.

23. *Histories of Two Hundred and Fifty-One Divisions of the German Army Which Participated in the War (1914–1918)*, United States War Department, 1920, see London Stamp Exchange edition, 1989, pp. 211–214, 365–368, 702–704; also *OH, 1916, II*, p. 503.

24. One of those who fell on 14 November was Lance-Sergeant Hector Munro of the 22nd (Service) Battalion, Royal Fusiliers (Kensington). Munro was better known as the author and satirist 'Saki'. See Gary Sheffield and G.I.S. Inglis (eds), *From Vimy Ridge to the Rhine: The Great War Letters of Christopher Stone, DSO, MC*, Crowood Press, Marlborough, 1989, pp. 14, 19, 75; also A.J. Langguth, *Saki: A Life of Hector Hugh Munro*, Oxford University Press, 1981; *OH, 1916, II*, pp. 506–508.

25. Paul Fichel, *Geschichte des Infanterie-Regiments von Winterfeldt (2 Oberschlesisches) No. 23: Das Regiment im Weltkrieg*, Baden, 1929, pp. 150–163.

26. *OH, 1916, II*, pp. 507–508.

27. *Ibid.*, p. 511.

28. Jeffreys to Edmonds, 23 October 1936, TNA CAB 45/135; *OH, 1916, II*, pp. 511–512.

29. Thomas Chalmers (ed.), *An Epic of Glasgow: History of the 15th Battalion The Highland Light Infantry (City of Glasgow Regiment)*, McCallum, Glasgow, 1934, p. 2; also *A Saga of Scotland: History of the 16th Battalion The Highland Light Infantry*, McCallum, Glasgow, 1930, pp. 1–3; J.W. Arthur and I.S. Munro (eds), *The Seventeenth Highland Light Infantry (Glasgow Chamber of Commerce Battalion): Record of War Service, 1914–1918*, Clark, Glasgow, 1920, pp. 14–15.

30. Captain C.H. Cooke, *Historical Records of the 16th (Service) Battalion Northumberland Fusiliers*, Newcastle and Gateshead Chamber of Commerce, 1923, pp. 1–2; Sir C.A. Montague Barlow (ed.), *The Lancashire Fusiliers: The Roll of Honour of the Salford Brigade*, Sherratt and Hughes, Manchester, 1920. pp. 23–30.

31. 'V.M.', *Record of the XIth (Service) Battalion Border Regiment (Lonsdale) from September 1914 to July 1st 1916*, Whitehead, Appleby, n.d., p. 6; Hugh Cecil Lowther, the fifth Earl of Lonsdale, popularly known as the 'Yellow Earl', is perhaps best remembered for his association with the Lonsdale Belt awarded to boxing champions.

32. Becke, *Order of Battle of Divisions, Part 3B*, pp. 21–29.

33. This can be deduced by analysing the personal details contained in the appropriate parts of *Soldiers Died in the Great War* and in various casualty regsisters of the Commonwealth War Graves Commission.

34. 'GSO2' denoted 'General Staff Officer 2nd Grade' and 'GSO1' stood for 'General Staff Officer 1st Grade'. The 'G' Branch of the General Staff was concerned with such matters as operations, training and military intelligence; the 'A' (Adjutant-General's) Branch dealt with administration, personnel and discipline; and the 'Q' (Quartermaster-General's) Branch covered such duties as quartering, supply and transportation.

35. Girdwood to Edmonds, 30 June 1930, TNA CAB 45/134.

36. E.G. Wace to Edmonds, 30 October 1936, TNA CAB 45/138.

37. H.J.N. Davis to Edmonds, 10 November 1936, TNA CAB 45/133.

38. 32nd Division, General Staff War Diary (WD), File marked 'General Ryecroft [*sic*], Private Diary', entry for 11 November 1916, TNA WO 95/2368.

39. E.G. Wace to Edmonds, 30 October 1936, TNA CAB 45/138; H.J.N. Davis to Edmonds, 10 November 1936, TNA CAB 45/133.

40. R. Fitzmaurice to Edmonds, 7 November 1936, TNA CAB 45/133.

41. Leonard Kentish to Edmonds, 19 November 1936, TNA CAB 45/135; see also 17th HLI WD, TNA WO 95/2403; and Major-General R.W.R. Barnes (GOC 32nd Division from 22 November 1916 to 29 January 1917), 'Summary of Operations for week ending 24/11/16', TNA WO 95/2368.

42. N. Luxmoore to Edmonds, 2 November 1936, TNA CAB 45/135.

43. *OH, 1916, II*, p. 512; 32nd Division Operation Order No. 65, 17 November 1916, TNA WO 95/2368; Brigadier-General W.W. Seymour (GOC 14th Brigade, 24 November 1916 to 12 April 1917), Report on 'recent operations' to 32nd Division, 3 December 1916, TNA WO 95/2368; 16th HLI WD, TNA WO 95/2403; Chalmers, *A Saga of Scotland*, pp. 50–52.

44. 32nd Division General Staff WD, File marked 'General Ryecroft [*sic*], Note 'B', TNA WO 95/2368.

45. Wace to Edmonds, 30 October 1936, TNA CAB 45/138; *OH, 1916, II*, p. 521.

46. H.J.N. Davis to Edmonds, 10 November 1936, TNA CAB 45/133; 'Narrative of Operations carried out by 32nd Division, 18 November 1916', TNA WO 95/2368; *OH, 1916, II*, p. 522.

47. 32nd Division, 'Narrative of Operations', TNA WO 95/2368; Major-General W.H. Rycroft, Report to V Corps, 21 November 1916, TNA WO 95/2368; *OH, 1916, II*, p. 522; Kurt Mucke, *Das Grossherzoglich Badische Infanterie Regiment Nr. 185*, Berlin, 1922, pp. 38–42.

48. 17th HLI WD, TNA WO 95/2403; 32nd Division, 'Narrative of Operations', TNA WO 95/2358; Rycroft, Report to V Corps, TNA WO 95/2368.

49. 16th HLI WD, TNA WO 95/2403; 11th Border Regiment WD, TNA WO 95/2403; 32nd Division, 'Narrative of Operations', TNA WO 95/2368; Rycroft 'Private Diary', entries for 18 and 19 November 1916, and Report to V Corps, 21 November 1916, TNA WO 95/2368; R. Fitzmaurice to Edmonds, 7 November 1936, TNA CAB 45/133; Girdwood to Edmonds, n.d., probably 1936, TNA CAB 45/134; Chalmers, *A Saga of Scotland*, pp. 52–54.

50. H. Reymann, *Das 3 Oberschlesische Infanterie Regiment Nr. 62 im Kriege 1914–1918*, Zeulenrode, 1930, pp. 133–141; Rycroft, 'Private Diary', entry for 18 November 1916, TNA WO 95/2368.

51. 16th HLI WD, TNA WO 95/2403; Leonard Kentish to Edmonds, 19 November 1936, TNA CAB 45/135.

52. 'Lessons derived from the experiences of 32nd Division in the recent operations', November 1916, TNA WO 95/2368.

53. 'Report by Major [R] Rowan on the situation of a party of the 97th Infantry Brigade in the Frankfort Trench', 21 November 1916; 'Narrative of Operations'; and 'Report on Operations carried out by the 32nd Division from Nov.19th to 24th' – all in TNA WO 95/2368.

54. Chalmers, *A Saga of Scotland*, pp. 59–60.

55. *Ibid.*, p. 60.

56. Major Rowan, 'Report on the situation of a party of the 97th Inf, Bde.', 21 November 1916, TNA WO 95/2368.

57. Chalmers, *A Saga of Scotland*, pp. 62–64, 161.

58. 16th HLI WD, TNA WO 95/2403; 11th Border Regiment WD, TNA WO 95/2403; Haig Diary, 21 November 1916, TNA WO 256/14. Haig recorded that Gough was 'very pleased to have Barnes as Rycroft's successor'; Major-General R.W.R. Barnes to V Corps, 22 November 1916, 'Report on attempt to relieve a party in dugouts in Frankfort Trench ... Night of 21st/22nd November 1916', TNA WO 95/2368. See also 'Report on operations carried out by the 32nd Division from Nov.19th to 24th', TNA WO 95/2368.

59. Chalmers, *A Saga of Scotland*, pp. 64–65.

60. 'Report on attack carried out by 16th Lancs.Fus. and 2nd R.Innis.Fus. on 23.11.16 to relieve party in Frankfort Trench', forwarded by Major-General Barnes to V Corps hedadquarters with a covering note, TNA WO 95/2368; 'Report on Operations carried out by the 32nd Division from Nov.19th to 24th, TNA WO 95/2368.

61. *OH, 1916, II*, p. 523, n. 1.

62. Chalmers, *A Saga of Scotland*, pp. 65–67.

63. *Ibid.*, p. 67. Chalmers states tht the survivors were awarded one Distinguished Service Order, eleven Distinguished Conduct Medals and twenty-two Military Medals, although he does not make it clear whether these were just the decorations conferred upon members of the 16th HLI.

64. Girdwood to Edmonds, 30 June 1930, TNA CAB 45/134. Major-General C.D. Shute commanded the 32nd Division from February to May 1917 and again from June 1917 to April 1918. Lieutenant-Colonel A.E. McNamara was GSO1 from November 1916 to September 1918. Brigadier-General F.W. Lumsden, who won the Victoria Cross in April 1917, commanded the 14th Brigade from April 1917 until he was killed on 4 June 1918.

65. Simpson, *Directing Operations*, p. 48.

66. Travers, *The Killing Ground*, p. 187; Fifth Army, SG 72/90, TNA WO 95/518.

67. V Corps, GX 8325, 16 November 1916, TNA WO 95/747.

68. 'Report on Attack by 51st (Highland) Division on Munich and Frankfurt Trenches on November 15th, 1916', TNA WO 95/747.

69. 2nd Division, GS 1017/1/176, 17 November 1916, TNA WO 95/747.

70. V Corps, GX 8325, 21 November 1916, TNA WO 95/747.

71. Simpson, *Directing Operations*, p. 49.

Chapter 6

1. Monash papers, typescript of *War Letters of General Monash*, Vol. II, see under 4 April 1918, Australian War Memorial (AWM), 3DRL 2316.

2. *Ibid.*, see under 26 April.

3. Hobbs diary, 27 April 1918, quoted in Suzanne Welborn, *Lords of Death: A People, A Place, A Legend*, Fremantle Arts Centre Press, 1982, p. 139.

4. Typed copy of diary of Lieutenant S.R. Traill, entries for 9 and 29 April 1918, AWM 2DRL 0711.

5. Letter from Lieutenant J.W. Axtens to his parents, 2 May 1918, AWM 2DRL 0308.

6. A copy of this letter can be found in the papers of Brigadier-General H.E. 'Pompey' Elliott, AWM 2DRL 513, Item 16. There is also a copy in the Monash papers.

7. C.E.W. Bean, *The Official History of Australia in the War of 1914–1918, Vol. V: The Australian Imperial Force in France During the Main German Offensive, 1918* (hereafter Bean, *AOH V*), Angus and Robertson, Sydney, 1937, pp. 145–192, 236–297, 298–353, 499–643.

8. Brigadier-General Sir James Edmonds, *Military Operations: France and Belgium, 1918, Vol. II* (hereafter *OH, 1918, II*), Macmillan, London, 1937, pp. 121–128, 381–408.

9. Gregory Blaxland, *Amiens 1918*, Frederick Muller, London, 1968, pp. 98–106, 117–132; Peter Pedersen, *Villers-Bretonneux*, Battleground Europe Series, Pen and Sword, Barnsley, 2004, *passim*.

10. A.M. Henniker, *Transportation on the Western Front, 1914–1918*, Macmillan, London, 1937, pp. 232–233; Ian M. Brown, *British Logistics on the Western Front*, pp. 183–184; David T. Zabecki, *The German 1918 Offensives: A Case Study in the Operational Level of War*, Routledge, Abingdon, 2006, pp. 84–86.

11. Brigadier-General Sir James Edmonds, *Military Operations: France and Belgium, 1918, Vol. I* (hereafter *OH, 1918, I*), Macmillan, London, 1935, pp. 135–160; Zabecki, *The German 1918 Offensives*, pp. 97–112, 113–138.

12. *OH, 1918, I*, pp. 395–398; Zabecki, op. cit., pp. 143–148.

13. *OH, 1918, I*, pp. 494–5; Zabecki, *The German 1918 Offensives*, pp. 146–152.

14. *OH, 1918, II*, pp. 1–8, 12–16, 39–41, 43–44, 61–77; Zabecki, *The German 1918 Offensives*, pp. 152–155.

15. Bean, *AOH, V*, pp. 296–297; *OH, 1918, II*, pp. 84–86, 100–101.

16. Bean, *AOH, V*, pp. 123–124, 266–268.

17. *OH, 1918, I*, pp. 456–457; Captain G.H.F. Nichols, *The 18th Division in the Great* War, pp. 293–301; 18th Division War Diary (WD), January 1918–March 1919, TNA WO 95/2017; 54th Brigade WD, TNA WO 95/2042.

18. *OH, 1918, II*, pp. 4–8, 486.

19. *OH, 1918, I*, pp. 538–544; William Philpott, *Anglo-French Relations and Strategy on the Western Front, 1914–18*, Macmillan, London, 1996, pp. 150–160, and 'Marshal Ferdinand Foch and

Allied Victory' in Matthew Hughes and Matthew Seligmann (eds), *Leadership in Conflict, 1914–1918*, Leo Cooper/Pen and Sword, Barnsley, 2000, pp. 38–51.

20. *OH, 1918, II*, pp. 8, 83; Bean, *AOH, V*, pp. 288–295.
21. Lieutenant-Colonel J.H. Boraston and Captain Cyril E.O. Bax, *The Eighth Division in War, 1914–1918*, Medici Society, London, 1926, pp. 188–190; *OH, 1918, II*, pp. 19–28; 8th Division WD, January–June 1918, TNA WO 95/1678.
22. *OH, 1918, II*, pp. 12–40, 42–55.
23. *OH, 1918, II*, p. 27; Bean, *AOH, V*, p. 297.
24. Blaxland, *Amiens 1918*, p. 101; *OH, 1918, II*, p. 51, n. 1.
25. General Sir Hubert Gough, 'Troops in V Army', 27 March 1918, Rawlinson papers, National Army Museum (NAM), 5201/33/77; Table headed 'March 30th 1918', Rawlinson papers, Churchill College, Cambridge (CCC), 1/10; Blaxland, *Amiens 1918*, p. 98.
26. Rawlinson to Foch, 28 March 1918, Rawlinson papers, CCC, 1/10; *OH, 1918, II*, pp. 51–52.
27. *OH, 1918, II*, p. 15, n.1.
28. Nichols, *18th Division*, p. 303.
29. *Ibid.*, p.138.
30. *Ibid.*, p. 393; Bean, *AOH, V*, p. 335.
31. Robert Cude, unpublished transcript of diary, entries for 24–26 March 1918, IWM, CON/RC.
32. 'Report on the Operations of the III Corps from the 21st March, 1918, to the 1st April, 1918', p. 11, Butler papers, IWM, 69/10/1.
33. *Ibid.*, p. 24; Haig Diary, 29 March 1918, National Library of Scotland (NLS), Acc. 3155.
34. Bean, *AOH, V*, p. 300.
35. *OH, 1918, II*, pp. 88–91.
36. *Ibid.*, pp. 92–93; Bean, *AOH, V*, pp. 302–309; Pedersen, *Villers-Bretonneux*, pp. 30–34; 12th Lancers WD, TNA WO 95/1140; 33rd Battalion AIF, Counter-Attack Report, 31 March 1918, Appendix 19 to 9th Australian Brigade WD, AWM 4, 23/9/17; 33rd Battalion AIF WD, AWM 4, 23/50/17.
37. Bean, *AOH, V*, p. 309.
38. *OH, 1918, II*, pp. 93, 103, 110.
39. Nichols, *18th Division*, pp. 306–307; 54th Brigade WD, TNA WO 95/2042; 7th Bedfords WD, TNA WO 95/2043; 11th Royal Fusiliers WD, TNA WO 95/2045; 7th Royal West Kents WD, TNA WO 95/2040.
40. *OH, 1918, II*, p. 123.
41. 14th Division WD, April–July 1918, TNA WO 95/1875; 14th Division, 'Report on Operations during the period 21st March to 4th April, 1918', pp. 20–21, Butler papers, IWM, 69/10/1.
42. Bean, *AOH, V*, pp. 309–330; *OH, 1918, II*, pp. 123–124; Pedersen, *Villers-Bretonneux*, pp. 52–56; Nichols, *18th Division*, pp. 310–311; 9th Australian Brigade WD, April 1918, AWM 4, 23/9/18; 35th Battalion AIF WD, AWM 4, 23/52/10; 18th Division WD, TNA WO 95/2017; 55th Brigade WD, TNA WO 95/2048; 7th Buffs WD, TNA WO 95/2049; 7th Royal West Kents WD, TNA WO 95/2040; Colonel R.S.H. Moody, *Historical Records of The Buffs, East Kent Regiment, 1914–1919*, Medici Society, London, 1922, pp. 350–351; C.T. Atkinson, *The Queen's Own Royal West Kent Regiment, 1914–1919*, Simpkin, Marshall, Hamilton, Kent and Co. Ltd, London, 1924, pp. 380–381.
43. 14th Division WD, TNA WO 95/1875; 41st Brigade WD, TNA WO 95/1894; 42nd Brigade WD, TNA WO 95/1899; Pedersen, *Villers-Bretonneux*, pp. 49–52; Frank Davies and Graham Maddocks, *Bloody Red Tabs: General Officer Casualties of the Great War, 1914–1918*, Leo Cooper/Pen and Sword, London and Barnsley, 1995, pp. 61–62; 14th Division, 'Report on Operations', Butler papers, IWM, 69/10/1.
44. 9th Australian Brigade WD, AWM 4, 23/9/18; H.A. Goddard, 'Villers-Bretonneux, Mar.30 – Apr.6', undated account, AWM 3DRL, 2379; 'Report on Defensive Operations East of Villers-Bretonneux, Apr.4–5 1918', dated 6 April 1918, 33rd Battalion AIF WD, AWM 4, 23/50/18; 35th Battalion AIF WD, AWM 4, 23/52/10; 'Account of 55 Bde. Operations, 1–6 April 1918', 55th Brigade WD, TNA WO 95/2048; 7th Buffs WD, TNA WO 95/2049; 7th Royal West Kents WD, TNA WO 95/2040; Pedersen, *Villers-Bretonneux*, pp. 52–56; Bean, *AOH, V*, pp. 317–335; Nichols, *18th Division*, pp. 311–312.
45. Bean, *AOH, V*, pp. 330–336; *OH, 1918, II*, pp. 125–126; Pedersen, *Villers-Bretonneux*, pp. 56–58; Nichols, *18th Division*, pp. 312–315; 'Account of 55 Bde. Operations', 55th Brigade WD, TNA

WO 95/2048; 53rd Brigade WD, TNA WO 95/2036; 54th Brigade WD, TNA WO 95/2042; 8th East Surreys WD, TNA WO 95/2037; 6th Northants WD, TNA WO 95/2044; 7th Buffs WD, TNA WO 95/2049; 7th Royal West Kents WD, TNA WO 95/2040.

46. Bean, *AOH, V*, pp. 337–348; *OH, 1918, II*, pp. 126–127; Pedersen, *Villers-Bretonneux*, pp. 58–66; Nichols, *18th Division*, pp. 314–315; 7th Queen's WD, TNA WO 95/2051; 6th Londons WD, TNA WO 95/3005/3; 36th Battalion AIF WD, AWM 4, 23/53/18.

47. Nichols, *18th Division*, p. 315; *OH, 1918, II*, p. 129; 'E.R' (ed.), *The 54th Infantry Brigade, 1914–1918: Some Records of Battle and Laughter in France*, Gale and Polden, Aldershot, 1919, pp. 144–145.

48. Bean, *AOH, V*, pp. 327–328, 333; Ross A. McMullin, *Pompey Elliott*, Scribe, Melbourne, 2002, pp. 374–375.

49. Bean, *AOH, V*, pp. 499–500.

50. Rawlinson Diary, 5 April 1918, Rawlinson papers, CCC 1/9; Rawlinson to GHQ, 15 April 1918, TNA WO 158/252; Haig to Foch (OAD 821), 17 April 1918, TNA WO 158/252; see also Rawlinson, 'An Appreciation: 18/4/18', TNA WO 158/252; and Peter Simkins, 'For Better or For Worse: Sir Henry Rawlinson and his Allies in 1916 and 1918' in Hughes and Seligmann (eds), *Leadership in Conflict*, p. 23.

51. *OH, 1918, II*, pp. 114–117; GHQ to Byng and Rawlinson (OAD 806), 4 April 1918, TNA WO 158/252; Directive from Foch concerning the junction of the Franco-British Armies, 6 April 1918, TNA WO 158/252.

52. Copy of Agreement made on 8 April at midday between the Commander of the Reserve Group of Armies (GAR) and Rawlinson, TNA WO 158/252; Rawlinson Diary, 8 and 9 April 1918, CCC 1/9.

53. 'Report on the Operations of the III Corps from 5th April to 27th April, 1918', p. 4, Butler papers, IWM, 69/10/1; Bean, *AOH, V*, pp. 503–513; *London Gazette*, 7 June 1918; 19th Battalion AIF WD, AWM 4, 23/36/27; 20th Battalion AIF WD, AWM 4, 23/37/33.

54. Bean, *AOH, V*, pp. 513–516; *OH, 1918, II*, p. 382; III Corps, 'Report on Operations 5–27 April 1918', Butler papers, IWM, 60/10/1; Nichols, *18th Division*, pp. 319–320; 53rd Brigade WD, TNA WO 95/2036; 7th Royal West Kents WD, TNA WO 95/2040; 10th Essex WD, TNA WO 95/2038; Lieutenant-Colonel T.M. Banks and Captain R.A. Chell, *With the 10th Essex in France*, pp. 233–240.

55. Bean, *AOH, V*, pp. 516–520; *OH, 1918, II*, p. 382; 18th Battalion AIF WD, AWM 4, 23/35/33.

56. Bean, *AOH, V*, p. 521; *OH, 1918, II*, pp. 366, 382; Rawlinson Diary, 18 April 1918, CCC 1/9. Rawlinson described the attack as 'a small push'.

57. Bean, *AOH, V*, pp. 523–524.

58. *Ibid.*, pp. 527–532, 535; Rawlinson Diary, 14 April 1918, CCC, 1/9; McMullin, *Pompey Elliott*, pp. 388–389; Rawlinson to Wilson, 17 April 1918, Rawlinson papers, NAM.

59. Boraston and Bax, *Eighth Division*, p.199. The British official history gives slightly different overall casualty figures at 237 officers and 4, 632 other ranks (*OH, 1918, II*, p. 386). See also Alun Thomas, 'The British 8th Infantry Division on the Western Front, 1914–18', unpublished PhD thesis, University of Birmingham, 2010. I am most grateful to Dr Thomas for providing me with copies of the relevant chapters.

60. John Terraine (ed.), *General Jack's Diary 1914–1918: The Trench Diary of Brigadier-General J.L. Jack, DSO*, Eyre and Spottiswoode, London, 1964, p. 197; Hubert Essame, *The Battle for Europe 1918*, Batsford, London, 1972, p. 109; John Bourne, 'Major-General W.C.G. Heneker: A Divisional Commander of the Great War', in Gary Sheffield (ed.), *Leadership and Command: The Anglo-American Military Experience since 1861*, Brassey's, London, 1997, pp. 106–107; Beddington, 'My Life', pp. 119–120, Brigadier Sir Edward Beddington papers, LHCMA/KCL.

61. Nichols, *18th Division*, p. 321; Banks and Chell, *With the 10th Essex in France*, p. 243; Rawlinson to Wilson, 24 April 1918, Rawlinson papers, NAM, 5201/73/44.

62. McMullin, *Pompey Elliott*, pp. 388–391.

63. III Corps, 'Report on Operations, 5–27 April', Butler papers, IWM, 69/10/1; *OH, 1918, II*, pp. 383–388; Bean, *AOH, V*, pp. 533–9; Boraston and Bax, *Eighth Division*, pp. 200–202.

64. *OH, 1918, II*, pp. 355, 388.

65. McMullin, *Pompey Elliott*, pp. 389–390; Pedersen, *Villers-Bretonneux*, pp. 85–86; Bean, *AOH, V*, p. 541.

66. *OH, 1918, II*, pp. 381, 383–384, 406–408.
67. *Ibid.*, p. 389.
68. *Ibid.*, p. 389; Bean, *AOH, V*, p. 555; Fourth Army WD, 27 March–30 April 1918, 'Summary of Operations', 24 April 1918, Fourth Army papers, IWM, Vol. 41; 173rd Brigade WD, TNA WO 95/3000; 2/2nd Londons WD, TNA WO 95/3001/4; 3rd Londons WD, TNA WO 95/3001/5; 2/4th Londons WD, TNA WO 95/3001/9; 2/10th Londons WD, TNA WO 95/3009/5; III Corps, 'Report', pp. 9–10, Butler papers, IWM, 69/10/1; Major W.E. Grey, *The 2nd City of London Regiment (Royal Fusiliers) in the Great War (1914–19)*, published by the Headquarters of the Regiment, London, 1929, pp. 306–315.
69. Pedersen, *Villers-Bretonneux*, pp. 91–94; *OH, 1918, II*, pp. 390–391; Boraston and Bax, *Eighth Division*, pp. 203–206; III Corps, 'Report', p. 10, Butler papers, IWM, 69/10/1; 'Narrative of Operations, 22nd April to 28th April 1918, 8th Division WD, TNA WO 95/1678; 23rd Brigade WD, TNA WO 95/1711; 2nd Devons WD, TNA WO 95/1712; 2nd Middlesex WD, TNA WO 95/1713/2; 2nd West Yorkshires WD, TNA WO 95/1714.
70. Bean, *AOH, V*, pp. 543–545; *OH, 1918, II*, pp. 390–391; Boraston and Bax, *Eighth Division*, pp. 204–206; Pedersen, *Villers-Bretonneux*, pp. 94–97; Nichols, *18th Division*, pp. 322–323; 8th Division WD, 'Narrative of Operations', TNA WO 95/1678; 25th Brigade WD, TNA WO 95/1728; 2nd Royal Berkshires WD, TNA WO 95/1729/1; 2nd East Lancashires WD, TNA WO 95/1729/2; 2nd Rifle Brigade WD, TNA WO 95/1731.
71. III Corps, 'Report', Butler papers, IWM, 69/10/1; *OH, 1918, II*, pp. 391–392.
72. Bean, *AOH, V*, pp. 564–565; *OH, 1918, II*, pp. 392–393; Pedersen, *Villers-Bretonneux*, pp. 99–102; David Fletcher (ed.), *Tanks and Trenches: First Hand Accounts of Tank Warfare in the First World War*, Sutton, Stroud, 1994, pp. 95–116; B.H. Liddell Hart, *The Tanks*, Vol. 1, Cassell, London, 1959, pp. 167–168.
73. Bean, *AOH, V*, pp. 566–567; *OH, 1918, II*, pp. 392–439; Boraston and Bax, *Eighth Division*, p. 207; Pedersen, *Villers-Bretonneux*, p. 103; 1st Sherwood Foresters WD, TNA WO 95/1721.
74. III Corps, 'Report', p. 12, Butler papers, IWM, 69/10/1.
75. 15th Australian Brigade WD, AWM 4, 23/15/26, Part 2; 5th Australian Division WD, AWM 4, 1/50/26, Part 11; 13th Australian Brigade WD, AWM 4, 23/13/27, Part 1; Pedersen, *Villers-Bretonneux*, p. 104.
76. Pedersen, *Villers-Bretonneux*, pp. 104–105; McMullin, *Pompey Elliott*, pp. 392–396; Bean, *AOH, V*, pp. 549–551; 5th Australian Division WD, AWM 4, 1/50/26; Part 1; 15th Australian Brigade WD, AWM 4, 23/15/26, Part 2.
77. Bean, *AOH, V*, pp. 568–569; *OH, 1918, II*, p. 394; Pedersen, *Villers-Bretonneux*, p. 105; 13th Australian Brigade WD, AWM 4, 23/13/27, Part 1; 'Report on Operations near Villers-Bretonneux from 24th to 26th April 1918', 13th Australian Brigade WD, AWM 4, 23/13/27, Part 2; III Corps, 'Report', p. 11, Butler papers, IWM, 69/10/1.
78. Bean, *AOH, V*, pp, 563–564, 569; *OH, 1918, II*, p. 394; Pedersen, *Villers-Bretonneux*, p. 106; McMullin, *Pompey Elliott*, pp. 396–400; 5th Australian Division WD, AWM 4, 1/50/26, Parts 11 and 12.
79. III Corps, 'Report', p. 12, Butler papers, IWM, 69/10/1; Bean, *AOH, V*, pp. 569–570; *OH, 1918, II*, pp. 394–395.
80. Haig Diary, 24 April 1918, TNA WO 256/30; *OH, 1918, II*, pp. 395–396; III Corps, 'Report', pp. 12–13, Butler papers, IWM, 69/10/1; Haig to Foch, 6.30 p.m., 24 April 1918, TNA WO 158/252; Rawlinson Diary, 24 April 1918, Rawlinson papers, CCC, 1/9; Simkins, 'For Better or For Worse', pp. 24–25.
81. Pedersen, *Villers-Bretonneux*, p. 108; Bean, *AOH, V*, pp. 569–571; 5th Australian Division WD, AWM 4, 1/50/26, Part 12.
82. Bean, *AOH, V*, pp. 571–572; 13th Australian Brigade WD, 24 April 1918, AWM 4, 23/13/27, Part 1; 13th Australian Brigade, 'Report on Operations near Villers-Bretonneux', 13th Australian Brigade WD, AWM 4, 23/13/27, Part 2; McMullin, *Pompey Elliott*, p. 401.
83. 13th Australian Brigade, 'Report on Operations', 13th Australian Brigade WD, AWM 4, 23/13/27, Part 2; Bean, *AOH, V*, pp. 574–575.
84. III Corps G. 596, 5.30 p.m., 24 April 1918, III Corps WD, TNA WO 95/678; 8th Division, Order No. 287, 8 p.m., 24 April 1918, 8th Division WD, TNA WO 95/1678; 13th Australian Brigade, 'Report on Operations', 13th Australian Brigade WD, AWM 4, 23/13/27, Part 2; III Corps, 'Report', pp. 12–13, Butler papers, IWM, 69/10/1; *OH, 1918, II*, pp. 396–397.

85. Bean, *AOH, V*, pp. 577–578; Pedersen, *Villers-Bretonneux*, p. 110.
86. 13th Australian Brigade, 'Report on Operations', 13th Australian Brigade WD, AWM 4, 23/13/27, Part 2; 51st Battalion AIF WD, AWM 4, 23/68/26; 52nd Battalion AIF WD, AWM 4, 23/69/25, Parts 1–3; *OH, 1918, II*, pp. 398–399; Bean, *AOH, V*, pp. 579–598.
87. 15th Australian Brigade, 'brief summary' of operations of 24–25 April 1918, 15th Australian Brigade WD, AWM 4, 23/15/26, Part 2; 59th Battalion AIF WD, AWM 4, 23/76/27; Bean, *AOH, V*, pp. 598–624; *OH, 1918, II*, pp. 399–400.
88. 9th Londons WD, TNA WO 95/3009/1; 54th Brigade WD, TNA WO 95/2042; 7th Royal West Kents WD, TNA WO 95/2040; 7th Bedfords WD, TNA WO 95/2043; Nichols, *18th Division*, pp. 325–329; Atkinson, *The Queen's Own Royal West Kent Regiment*, pp. 384–385; M.G. Deacon (ed.), *The Shiny Seventh: The 7th (Service) Battalion Bedfordshire Regiment at War, 1915–1918*, Bedfordshire Historical Record Society, Bedford, 2004, pp. 92–93, 100; *OH, 1918, II*, pp. 397–398.
89. 8th Division WD, TNA WO 95/1678; 22nd DLI WD, TNA WO 95/1702/1; 2nd Northants WD, TNA WO 95/1722; III Corps, 'Report', p. 14, Butler papers, IWM, 69/10/1; Boraston and Bax, *Eighth Division*, pp. 210–212; 2nd Royal Berkshires WD, TNA WO 95/1729/1; Bean, *AOH, V*, pp. 613–629; *OH, 1918, II*, pp. 400–402.
90. *OH, 1918, II*, p. 403.
91. Bean, *AOH, V*, p. 630.
92. *Ibid.*, pp. 630–633; *OH, 1918, II*, pp. 404–405; Nichols, *18th Division*, pp. 329–332; Banks and Chell, *With the 10th Essex in France*, pp. 243–248; Colonel H.C. Wylly, *History of the Queen's Royal (West Surrey) Regiment in the Great War*, Gale and Polden, Aldershot, 1924, pp. 228–229.
93. Bean, *AOH, V*, p. 637; *OH, 1918, II*, p. 405, n. 1.
94. Boraston and Bax, *Eighth Division*, p. 215.
95. Bean, *AOH, V*, p. 639 and n. 2.
96. Rawlinson Diary, 25 April 1918, Rawlinson papers, CCC, 1/9; Fourth Army, 'Summary of Operations, 24–25 April 1918', Fourth Army WD, 27 March–30 April 1918, Fourth Army papers, IWM, Vol. 41.
97. *Reveille*, 1 August 1936, p. 8.
98. III Corps, 'Report', p. 18, Butler papers, IWM, 69/10/1.
99. Boraston and Bax, *Eighth Division*, p. 212; Bean, *AOH, V*, p. 548.
100. Haig Diary, 24 April 1918, TNA WO 256/30.
101. Bean, *AOH, V*, p. 639.
102. 'Report on the Operations of the III Corps from the 21st March, 1918, to the 1st April, 1918', dated 10 June 1918 (see also Appendix 'J'), Butler papers, IWM, 69/10/1.
103. Nichols, *18th Division*, p. 329.

Chapter 7

1. Brigadier-General Sir James Edmonds, *Military Operations: France and Belgium, 1918, Volume IV* (hereafter *OH, 1918, IV*), HMSO, London, 1947, p. 181.
2. Brigadier-General Sir James Edmonds, *Military Operations: France and Belgium, 1918, Volume I* (hereafter *OH, 1918, I*), Macmillan, London, 1935, pp. 480, 488, 490, 518, and *Volume II* (hereafter *OH, 1918, II*), Macmillan, London, 1937, pp. 29, 31, 33–35, 55–56, 104, 130, 132 and 135.
3. See, for instance, A. Hilliard Atteridge, *History of the 17th (Northern)Division*, Maclehose, for the Glasgow University Press, 1929, pp. 363–367; Lieutenant-Colonel H.M. Davson, *The History of the 35th Division in the Great War*, Sifton Praed, London, 1926, pp. 221–235; Lieutenant-Colonel J.E. Munby (ed.), *A History of the 38th (Welsh) Division: By the GSOs I of the Division*, Hugh Rees, London, 1920, pp. 40–47; Hanway R. Cumming, *A Brigadier in France, 1917–1918*, Cape, London, 1921, pp. 196–200; Captain J.C. Dunn, *The War the Infantry Knew, 1914–1919*, Sphere Books edition, London, 1989, pp. 461–502.
4. *OH, 1918, IV*, pp. 14, 27, 169; Atteridge, *History of the 17th Division*, p. 367; Cumming, *A Brigadier in France*, p. 201; Munby (ed.), *History of the 38th Division*, p. 48; C.H. Dudley Ward, *Regimental Records of the Royal Welch Fusiliers, Volume III, 1914–1918, France and Flanders*, Forster and Groom, London, 1928, p. 451.
5. Brigadier-General Sir James Edmonds, *Military Operations: France and Belgium, 1918, Volume III* (hereafter *OH, 1918, III*), Macmillan, London, 1939, pp. 312–13; Haig Diary, 16 July

1918, TNA WO 256/34; Gary Sheffield and John Bourne (eds), *Douglas Haig: War Diaries and Letters, 1914–1918*, Weidenfeld & Nicolson, London, 2005, p. 431.

6. GHQ to Third Army, 10 August 1918, TNA WO 158/227; *OH, 1918, IV*, pp. 132–136, see also Appendix XIV, 'GHQ Operation Order of 10th August, 1918' (OAD 900/22), pp. 579–580; Haig Diary, 10 August 1918, TNA WO 256/34; Sheffield and Bourne (eds), *Douglas Haig: War Diaries and Letters*, pp. 441–442; Jonathan Boff, *Winning and Losing on the Western Front: The British Third Army and the Defeat of Germany 1918*, Cambridge University Press, 2012, p. 24; William Philpott, 'Marshal Foch and Allied Victory', in Matthew Hughes and Matthew Seligmann (eds), *Leadership in Conflict, 1914–1918*, Leo Cooper/Pen and Sword, Barnsley, 2000, pp. 38–53.

7. Haig Diary, 11 and 12 August 1918, TNA WO 256/34; Sheffield and Bourne (eds), *Douglas Haig: War Diaries and Letters*, pp. 442–443; *OH, 1918, IV*, pp. 152–154, and Appendix XVII, 'Marshal Foch's Instruction of 12th August, 1918', pp. 583–584.

8. *OH, 1918, IV*, p. 167, and Appendix XVIII, 'GHQ Operation Order of 13th August, 1918' (OAD 907), pp. 584–585; GHQ to Third Army, 13 August 1918, TNA WO 158/227; Haig Diary, 12 and 13 August 1918, TNA WO 256/34; Sheffield and Bourne (eds), *Douglas Haig: War Diaries and Letters*, pp. 443–444.

9. *OH, 1918, IV*, p. 168 and n. 1; Third Army, General Staff WD, 1 August–31 August 1918, TNA WO 95/372.

10. Haig Diary, 14 August 1918, TNA WO 256/34; Rawlinson Diary, 14 August 1914, Rawlinson papers, CCC, 1/11; *OH, 1918, IV*, pp. 167–169; Haig to Foch, 14 August 1914 (OAD 900/25), TNA WO 256/34.

11. Haig Diary, 15 August 1918, TNA WO 256/34; *OH, 1918, IV*, p. 169, and Appendix XIX, 'GHQ Operation Order of 15th August, 1918' (OAD 907/2), pp. 585–586, and TNA WO 158/311.

12. *OH, 1918, IV*, pp. 169–170; Haig Diary, 15 August 1918, TNA WO 256/34; Sheffield and Bourne (eds), *Douglas Haig: War Diaries and Letters*, pp. 445–446; Rawlinson Diary, 15 August 1918, Rawlinson papers, CCC, 1/11; Robin Prior and Trevor Wilson, *Command on the Western Front: The Military Career of Sir Henry Rawlinson, 1914–1918*, Blackwell, Oxford, 1992, pp. 534–536; Ian Malcolm Brown, *British Logistics on the Western Front, 1914–1919*, Praeger, Westport CT and London, 1998, p. 237.

13. *OH, 1918, IV*, pp. 182–183; J.P. Harris and Niall Barr, *Amiens to the Armistice: The BEF in the Hundred Days Campaign, 8 August – 11 November 1918*, Brassey's, London, 1998, pp. 122–126; GHQ letter, 18 August 1918, (OAD 907/4), TNA WO 158/241; Third Army GS 73/1, Third Army WD, TNA WO 95/372; 'Notes for Operation G2 (Bucquoy-Moyenneville)', Third Army GS 73/5, 18 August 1918, Third Army WD, TNA WO 95/372; Third Army to Mullens, 18 August 1918, TNA WO 95/372; 'Summary of Operations of Third Army from 21st August to 30th September 1918', TNA WO 95/372; 'Previous Orders and Dispositions for the Army Offensive of the 21st August 1918', TNA WO 95/372.

14. Haig Diary, 19 August 1918, TNA WO 256/35; Sheffield and Bourne (eds), *Douglas Haig: War Diaries and Letters*, p. 447; *OH, 1918, IV*, p. 172; Harris and Barr, *Amiens to the Armistice*, p. 126.

15. Haig Diary, 19 August 1918, TNA WO 256/35; Harris and Barr, *Amiens to the Armistice*, p. 126.

16. Haig Diary, 19 August 1918, TNA WO 256/35; *OH, 1918, IV*, pp. 173, 479.

17. *OH, 1918, IV*, p. 173; General Erich Ludendorff, *My War Memories, 1914–18*, Hutchinson, London, n.d., p. 694.

18. Atteridge, *History of the 17th Division*, pp. 265–296, 298–349, 352–374; Major A.F. Becke, *Order of Battle of Divisions: Part 3A, New Army Divisions (9–26)*, HMSO, London, 1938, pp. 74–77; 17th Division, General Staff WD, 1 August 1918–28 February 1919, 'Narrative of Operations, 21 August–11 September 1918', TNA WO 95/1985.

19. 'Situation Prior to the General Offensive which commenced on August 21st 1918', 17th Division WD, TNA WO 95/1985.

20. Becke, *Order of Battle of Divisions: Part 3A*, pp. 106–109; Cumming, *A Brigadier in France*, pp. 202–203; D.V. Kelly, *39 Months with the 'Tigers', 1915–1918*, Ernest Benn, London, 1930, p. 134.

21. Munby, *History of the 38th Division*, pp. 34–48; Becke, *Order of Battle of Divisions: Part 3B, New Army Divisions (30–41) and 63rd (R.N.) Division*, HMSO, London, 1945, pp. 84–89; Dunn, *The War The Infantry Knew*, pp. 496–498.

22. Andy Simpson, *Directing Operations: British Corps Command on the Western Front, 1914–18*, Spellmount, Stroud, 2006, pp. 161–162; Third Army note of 20 August 1918 (GS 73/24), Third Army WD, TNA WO 95/372.

23. Simpson, *Directing Operations*, p. 162; Boff, *Winning and Losing on the Western Front*, p. 201; V Corps Order, No. 230, 19 August 1918, V Corps, General Staff WD, 1 June–31 August 1918, TNA WO 95/750; V Corps Artillery Instructions, No. 193, V Corps GOCRA WD, TNA WO 95/756; V Corps, GS 490/18, 20 August 1918, TNA WO 95/750.

24. John Bourne, *Who's Who in World War One*, Routledge, London, 2001, pp. 264–265; Major-General Sir Reginald Pinney, Diary, 29 September 1918, Pinney papers, IWM, 66/257/1; see also entries for 15 and 21 September, 2, 5, 12, 21, 23, 24 and 29 October.

25. Major-General David Campbell, Introduction to Hanway R. Cumming's *A Brigadier in France*, p. 11.

26. Bourne, *Who's Who in World War One*, p. 265; Becke, *Order of Battle of Divisions, Part 3B*, p. 21; Austin Girdwood to Edmonds, 30 June 1936, TNA CAB 45/134.

27. Becke, *Part 3A*, p. 71; J.C. Dunn to Robert Graves, 27 October 1925, Dunn-Graves correspondence, Regimental Archives of the Royal Welch Fusiliers.

28. See W.N. Nicholson, *Behind the Lines: An Account of Administrative Staffwork in the British Army 1914–18*, Cape, London, 1939, pp. 122–124.

29. Captain Cyril Falls, *Military Operations: France and Belgium, 1917, Volume I*, Macmillan, London, 1940, p. 378; Haig Diary, 12, 13 and 14 April 1917, TNA WO 95/256/17; Edmonds to A.B. Acheson (Cabinet Office), 19 July 1950, and Acheson to Edmonds, 18 and 27 July 1950, TNA CAB 103/113, Items 101–2, 111.

30. Dunn, *The War The Infantry Knew*, pp. 487, 491–492, 506, 546, 555–556; *The Times*, 22, 26, 27 and 29 May 1939. I am most grateful to Dr John Bourne for sharing his knowledge of Robertson and Cubitt with me.

31. Becke, *Part 3A*, p. 103.

32. Bourne, *Who's Who*, pp. 49–50.

33. Haig Diary, 25 August and 25 September 1918, TNA WO 256/35 and 256/36.

34. Cumming, *A Brigadier in France*, p. 95.

35. Bourne, *Who's Who*, p. 103; John Stephen Morse, *9th (Service) Battalion The Sherwood Foresters (Notts and Derby Regiment)*, Tommies Guides, Eastbourne, 2007, pp. 34, 54; *The Times*, 15 January 1963; Becke, *Part 3A*, p. 104; Nigel Wood, 'A Very Local Hero', *Westender*, Vol. 7, No. 1, pp. 5–6; *The Wykehamist*, No. 1110, 12 February 1963, p. 100.

36. Cumming, *A Brigadier in France*, p. 96. The report on Gater by Campbell is cited in a record of Gater's military service that appears to have been compiled by Gater himself or by his family. I am most grateful to Steve Broomfield and Andy Lonergan for passing a copy of this on to me. After the war Gater had a distinguished career as an administrator and civil servant, becoming Clerk to the London County Council in the 1930s and then serving with various government departments, including the Colonial Office, the Ministry of Supply and the Ministry of Home Security. He died in 1963.

37. Once again I am indebted to John Bourne for sharing much of this information on McCulloch with me. See also Derek Clayton, *From Pontefract to Picardy: The 9th King's Own Yorkshire Light Infantry in the First World War*, Tempus, Stroud, 2004, p. 130.

38. Cumming, *A Brigadier in France*, pp. 12–13 (Introduction by David Campbell), 82–84, 88–90; Bourne, *Who's Who*, pp. 65–66; Haig to Military Secretary, 18 May 1917, Officers' Personal Files, TNA WO 374/17191; see also entry on Cumming by Peter Simkins in the *Oxford Dictionary of National Biography*, Oxford University Press, online edition, 2009 (revised 2013). Cumming was killed in an IRA ambush at Clonbanin, Co. Cork, in March 1921, when serving as Military Governor of Kerry.

39. *OH, 1918, I*, pp. 509, 514–515; *OH, 1918, II*, pp. 29, 32, 421–423; *OH, 1918, III*, p. 130.

40. *OH, 1918, IV*, p. 192; Atteridge, *History of the 17th Division*, pp. 375–377; R.H. Kiernan, *Little Brother Goes Soldiering*, Constable, London, 1930, p. 109.

41. *OH, 1918, IV*, p. 192; 21st Division, General Staff WD, September 1918–March 1919, 'Report on Operations, August 21st to September 3rd, 1918', G.748, TNA WO 95/2134; 17th Division WD, 'Narrative of Operations', 21 August–11 September 1918, TNA WO 95/1985.

42. *OH, 1918, IV*, pp. 192–193; Harris and Barr, *Amiens to the Armistice*, p. 130; 21st Division, 'Report on Operations', 21st Division WD, TNA WO 95/2134; 62nd Brigade WD, January 1918–April 1919, TNA WO 95/2153; 2nd Lincolnshires WD, TNA WO 95/2154; 1st

Lincolnshires WD, TNA WO 95/2154. The 62nd Brigade war diary states that Beaucourt was captured as early as 6.15 a.m.

43. 62nd Brigade WD, TNA WO 95/2153; 21st Division WD, January–August 1918, TNA WO 95/2133; *OH, 1918, IV*, p. 193; 12th/13th Northumberland Fusiliers WD, TNA WO 95/2155. Edmonds and the 62nd Brigade war diary both state that the Northumberland Fusiliers crossed the Ancre by 3.30 p.m., whereas the divisional war diary suggests that this took place in mid-evening.

44. *OH, 1918, IV*, p. 193; Matthew Richardson, *The Tigers: 6th, 7th, 8th and 9th (Service) Battalions of the Leicestershire Regiment*, Leo Cooper/Pen and Sword, Barnsley, 2000, p. 251; Kiernan, *Little Brother Goes Soldiering*, p. 113; Cumming, *A Brigadier in France*, p. 204; 6th Leicesters WD, TNA WO 95/2164; 110th Brigade WD, July 1916–June 1919, TNA WO 95/2163.

45. *OH, 1918, IV*, p. 193; 38th Division, General Staff WD, 1 August 1916–28 February 1919, TNA WO 95/2540; 114th Brigade WD, 1 January 1917–31 May 1919, TNA WO 95/2558; 115th Brigade WD, 1 December 1915–30 April 1919, TNA WO 95/2558; 14th Welsh Regiment WD, TNA WO 95/2559/3; Major-General Sir Thomas Marden, *The History of the Welch Regiment: Part II, 1914–1918*, Western Mail and Echo, Cardiff, 1932, p. 464; Cumming, *A Brigadier in France*, pp. 204–205.

46. *OH, 1918, IV*, pp. 185–192, 193–194; Harris and Barr, *Amiens to the Armistice*, pp. 125–130; Third Army WD, 21 August 1918 and Third Army 'Summary of Operations from 21st August 1918 to 30th September 1918', TNA WO 95/372.

47. *OH, 1918, IV*, pp. 193–194; Harris and Barr, *Amiens to the Armistice*, pp. 131–133; Third Army Order GS 73/40, 21 August 1918, Third Army WD, TNA WO 95/372 'Appendix 2 to 'Summary of Operations', Third Army WD, TNA WO 95/372; Haig Diary, 21 August 1918, TNA WO 256/35.

48. *OH, 1918, IV*, pp. 220–221; Harris and Barr, *Amiens to the Armistice*, pp. 135–136; Third Army Order GS 73/46, 22 August 1918, Third Army WD, TNA WO 95/372; see also Third Army Operations, TNA WO 158/227; handwritten note sent from Third Army to V Corps at 11.45 a.m. on 22 August and received at 12.05 p.m., modifying GS 73/46, TNA WO 95/372.

49. GHQ to Third Army (OAD 907/10), 22 August 1918, Third Army Operations, TNA WO 158/227; Haig Diary, 22 August 1918, TNA WO 256/35. Edmonds (in *OH, 1918, IV*, p. 220) suggests that Byng revised his plans for the next day during the *afternoon* of 22 August, in response to instructions from Haig, but the last relevant orders emanating from Third Army were issued by midday.

50. *OH, 1918, IV*, pp. 204–205, 209–210; Harris and Barr, *Amiens to the Armistice*, p. 142.

51. *OH, 1918, IV*, p. 205; 21st Division WD, TNA WO 95/2133; 21st Division, 'Report on Operations', TNA WO 95/2134; 62nd Brigade WD, TNA WO 95/2153; 110th Brigade WD, TNA WO 95/2163.

52. Captain G.H.F. Nichols, *The 18th Division in the Great War*, Blackwood, Edinburgh and London, 1922, pp. 136–138.

53. Nichols, *18th Division*, pp. 362–363; Mark Connelly, *Steady the Buffs! A Regiment, a Region, and the Great War*, Oxford University Press, 2006, p. 188; 18th Division WD, TNA WO 95/2017; 55th Brigade WD, TN A WO 95/2048; 8th East Surreys WD, TNA WO 95/2050; 7th Buffs WD, TNA WO 95/2049.

54. *OH, 1918, IV*, pp. 208–209; Nichols, *18th Division*, p. 367; Connelly, *Steady the Buffs!*, pp. 188–189; 55th Brigade WD, TNA WO 95/2048; 7th Buffs WD, TNA WO 95/2049; Major-General Sir Archibald Montgomery, *The Story of the Fourth Army in the Battles of the Hundred Days: August 8th to November 11th, 1918*, Hodder and Stoughton, London, 1919, p. 83.

55. Munby, *38th Division*, p. 49; 114th Brigade WD, TNA WO 95/2558; 14th Welsh Regiment WD, TNA WO 95/2559/3.

56. Haig to Army commanders, 11.30 p.m., 22 August 1918 (OAD 911), see *OH, 1918, IV*, Appendix XX, 'Commander-in-Chief's Telegram of 22nd August, 1918', pp. 587–588.

57. Harris and Barr, *Amiens to the Armistice*, pp. 137–143; *OH, 1918, IV*, pp. 220–232; Third Army, 'Summary of Operations from 21st August to 30th September 1918', TNA WO 95/372.

58. *OH, 1918, IV*, p. 233; Munby, *38th Division*, pp. 49–50; Nichols, *18th Division*, pp. 329, 367.

59. *OH, 1918, IV*, p. 233; Munby, *38th Division*, p. 50; Nichols, *18th Division*, pp. 368–369; Ward, *Royal Welch Fusiliers, III*, p. 454; 53rd Brigade WD, TNA WO 95/2036; 113th Brigade WD, TNA WO 95/2554; 13th Royal Welsh Fusiliers WD, TNA WO 95/2555/1.

60. *OH, 1918, IV*, p. 233; Munby, *38th Division*, p. 50; Dunn, *The War the Infantry Knew*, pp. 510–512; 115th Brigade WD, TNA WO 95/2560; 2nd Royal Welsh Fusiliers WD, TNA WO 95/2561/1.

61. Ward, *Royal Welch Fusiliers, III*, p. 454; *OH, 1918, IV*, p. 233.

62. 17th Division WD, 'Narrative of Operations – Aug. 21st to Sept. 12th', TNA WO 95/1985; Atteridge, *17th Division*, pp. 378–379.

63. *OH, 1918, IV*, pp. 238–239; 21st Division WD, including Divisional Order No. 210 (3.15 p.m., 23 August), TNA WO 95/2133, and 'Report on Operations', TNA WO 95/2134.

64. *OH, 1918, IV*, pp. 242–243; V Corps WD, TNA WO 95/750; Clayton, *From Pontefract to Picardy*, pp. 186–188.

65. 21st Division, 'Order No. 210' (3.15 p.m., 23 August), including Appendix III, 'Machine Gun Arrangements', 21st Division WD, TNA WO 95/2133; Cumming, *A Brigadier in France*, p. 205.

66. Brigadier-General A.J. McCulloch, 'Report on Night Attack, 23rd–24th August 1918', 64th Brigade WD, TNA WO 95/2160; *OH, 1918, IV*, pp. 243–244.

67. McCulloch, 'Report on Night Attack', 64th Brigade WD, TNA WO 95/2160; 21st Division, Telegram, 8.50 p.m., 23 August 1918, confirming amendments to Order No. 210, 21st Division WD, TNA WO 95/2133; *OH, 1918, IV*, p. 244.

68. McCulloch, 'Report on Night Attack', 64th Brigade WD, TNA WO 95/2160; 21st Division, 'Report on Operations', 21 August –3 September 1918, 21st Division WD, TNA WO 95/2134; *OH, 1918, IV*, pp. 244–245.

69. McCulloch, 'Report', TNA WO 95/2160; 9th King's Own Yorkshire Light Infantry WD, TNA WO 95/2162; 1st East Yorkshires WD, TNA WO 95/2161; 15th Durham Light Infantry WD, TNA WO 95/2161; Clayton, *From Pontefract to Picardy*, p. 189; *OH, 1918, IV*, p. 245.

70. *OH, 1918, IV*, pp. 245–246; Clayton, *From Pontefract to Picardy*, p. 190; McCulloch, 'Report', TNA WO 95/2160; 15th DLI WD, TNA WO 95/2161; 1st East Yorkshires WD, TNA WO 95/2161; 9th KOYLI WD, TNA WO 95/2162.

71. Cumming, *A Brigadier in France*, pp. 206–208; Kiernan, *Little Brother Goes Soldiering*, p. 116.

72. 110th Brigade WD, TNA WO 95/2163; Cumming, *A Brigadier in France*, pp. 208–211; 21st Division, 'Report on Operations', 21st Division WD, TNA WO 95/2134; *OH, 1918, IV*, p. 246.

73. 7th Leicesters WD, TNA WO 95/2164; Cumming, *A Brigadier in France*, pp. 211–212; Richardson, *The Tigers*, p. 253.

74. *OH, 1918, IV*, pp. 247–248; Atteridge, *17th Division*, pp. 380–385; 17th Division, 'Notes on the Advance' and 'Narrative of Operations – Aug. 21st to Sept. 12th' (1918), 17th Division WD, TNA WO 95/1985; 50th Brigade WD, September 1917–March 1919, TNA WO 95/1999.

75. *OH, 1918, IV*, pp. 248–249; Munby, *38th Division*, pp. 5–51; Ward, *Royal Welch Fusiliers, III*, pp. 454–455; 38th Division WD, TNA WO 95/2540; 114th Brigade WD, January 1917–May 1919, TNA WO 95/ 2558.

76. 38th Division WD, TNA WO 95/2540; 113th Brigade WD, January 1918–April 1919, TNA WO 95/2554; 115th Brigade WD, December 1915 – April 1919, TNA WO 95/2560; *OH, 1918, IV*, p. 249; Ward, *Royal Welch Fusiliers, III*, pp. 454–456; Dunn, *The War the Infantry Knew*, pp. 512–515; Nichols, *18th Division*, pp. 370–372.

77. 38th Division WD, TNA WO 95/2540; 115th Brigade WD, TNA WO 95/2560; *OH, 1918, IV*, pp. 249–250; Munby, *38th Division*, p. 51; Ward, *Royal Welch Fusiliers, III*, pp. 456–457.

78. *OH, 1918, IV*, pp. 250–251, 269.

79. Atteridge, *History of the 17th Division*, p. 384.

80. Clayton, *From Pontefract to Picardy*, p. 191.

81. 17th Division, 'Situation Prior to the General Offensive which commenced on August 21st 1918' and 'Narrative of Operations – Aug. 21st to Sept. 12th', 17th Division WD, TNA WO 95/1985.

82. McCulloch, 'Report on Night Attack', 64th Brigade WD, TNA WO 95/2160.

83. Boff, *Winning and Losing on the Western Front*, pp. 134–135.

84. Harris and Barr, *Amiens to the Armistice*, pp. 142–143.

85. Jonathan Boff, 'Command Culture and Complexity: Third Army during the Hundred Days, August–November 1918', in Gary Sheffield and Peter Gray (eds), *Changing War: The British Army, the Hundred Days Campaign and the Birth of the Royal Air Force, 1918*, Bloomsbury, London, 2013, pp. 27, 31.

86. Peter Simkins, 'Somme Reprise: Reflections on the Fighting for Albert and Bapaume, August 1918', in Brian Bond et al., *Look to Your Front: Studies in the First World War by the British Commission for Military History*, Spellmount, Staplehurst, 1999, p. 159.

Chapter 8

1. See Chapter 3.
2. For a general assessment of the performance of British divisions in the final offensive, see Peter Simkins, 'Co-Stars or Supporting Cast?: British Divisions in the "Hundred Days", 1918', in Paddy Griffith (ed.), *British Fighting Methods in the Great War*, Frank Cass, London, 1996, pp. 50–69.
3. Major-General Sir Arthur B. Scott and P. Middleton Brumwell, *History of the 12th (Eastern) Division in the Great War, 1914–1918*, Nisbet, London, 1923, pp. 163, 180, 254; Major A.F. Becke, *Order of Battle of Divisions: Part 3A, New Army Divisions (9–26)*, HMSO, London, 1938, pp. 27–33; Lieutenant-Colonel C.C.R. Murphy, *The History of the Suffolk Regiment, 1914–1927*, Hutchinson, London, 1928, pp. 277, 352–353; Brigadier-General E. Riddell and Colonel M.C. Clayton, *The Cambridgeshires, 1914 to 1919*, Bowes and Bowes, Cambridge, 1934, pp. 176–179.
4. Becke, *Order of Battle of Divisions: Part 3A*, p. 31.
5. These sample statistics have been compiled from a detailed analysis of casualties named in *Soldiers Died in the Great War* (CD-Rom version published by the Naval and Military Press).
6. 12th Division, General Staff War Diary (WD), August 1918–June 1919, TNA WO 95/1827; Scott and Brumwell, *12th Division*, pp. 190–230, 254.
7. 7th Royal Sussex WD, TNA WO 95/1856/3; 9th Royal Fusiliers WD, TNA WO 95/1857/2; 5th Royal Berkshires WD, TNA WO 95/1856/1; 6th Queen's WD, TNA WO 95/1863/1; 6th Royal West Kents WD, TNA WO 95/1861.
8. Brigadier-General Sir James Edmonds, *Military Operations: France and Belgium, 1918, Volume IV*, HMSO, London, 1947 (hereafter *OH, 1918, IV*), pp. 333, 486–488; Scott and Brumwell, *12th Division*, pp. 199–200, 206–212; 12th Division WD, TNA WO 95/1827; 9th Royal Fusiliers WD, TNA WO 95/1857/2.
9. Brigadier-General Sir James Edmonds, *Military Operations: France and Belgium, 1918, Volume V* (hereafter *OH, 1918, V*), HMSO, London, 1947, pp. 248–249, 370, 383; Scott and Brumwell, *12th Division*, pp. 221–223; Mark Connelly, *Steady The Buffs!: A Regiment, A Region and the Great War*, Oxford University Press, 2006, p. 205; 12th Division WD, TNA WO 95/1827; 6th Buffs WD, TNA WO 95/1860; 37th Brigade WD, July 1917–March 1919, TNA WO 95/1859.
10. *OH, 1918, IV*, pp. 75–76, 351–352, 486–488.
11. Owen Rutter (ed.), *The History of the Seventh (Service) Battalion, The Royal Sussex Regiment, 1914–1919*, The Times Publishing Company, London, 1934, pp. 246–247.
12. For a more detailed summary of Higginson's military service see Peter Simkins. 'The Very Model of a Modern Major-General: Major-General H.W. Higginson, CB, DSO and Bar, Royal Dublin Fusiliers', in *The Blue Cap: Journal of the Royal Dublin Fusiliers Association*, Vol. 14, December 2007, pp. 18–22.
13. Trevor Pidgeon, *Boom Ravine*, Battleground Europe series, Leo Cooper/Pen and Sword, Barnsley, 1998, pp. 107–123; Captain G.H.F. Nichols, *The 18th Division in the Great War*, Blackwood, London and Edinburgh, 1922, pp. 139–153; 53rd Brigade WD, January–December 1917, TNA WO 95/2035.
14. Nichols, *18th Division in the Great War*, pp. 157–158; 53rd Brigade WD, TNA WO 95/2035.
15. Nichols, *18th Division in the Great War*, pp. 194–230, 232–246; 18th Division WD, January–December 1917, TNA WO 95/2016; 53rd Brigade WD, TNA WO 95/2035; Brigadier-General Sir James Edmonds, *Military Operations, France and Belgium, 1917, Volume II*, HMSO, London, 1948, pp. 153–155, 186–188, 343–344.
16. Nichols, *18th Division in the Great War*, p. 312; 53rd Brigade WD, January 1918–March 1919, TNA WO 95/2036.
17. Nichols, *18th Division in the Great War*, p. 323.
18. 'Report for V Corps on Operations made in support of 18 Division, 30 June–3 July 1918', dated 13 July 1918, 12th Division WD, January–July 1918, TNA WO 95/1826; 6th Buffs WD, TNA WO 95/1860; Mark Connelly, *Steady The Buffs!*, pp. 184–186.
19. Higginson, having been awarded a CB in 1919, finally retired in 1932, by which time he had been in the army for thirty-eight years. Remarkably, unlike other divisional commanders and

even one of his own subordinates (Berkeley Vincent), he never received a knighthood –surely something of an injustice given his long, distinguished and often brilliant service. He died in October 1954, aged 80.

20. Frank Davies and Graham Maddocks, *Bloody Red Tabs: General Officer Casualties of the Great War, 1914–1918*, Leo Cooper/Pen and Sword, Barnsley, 1995, pp. 199–200. I am also indebted to Dr John Bourne and to Berkeley Vincent's grandson (also named Berkeley Vincent) for further information about Vincent's early career.
21. 12th Division WD, September 1916–June 1917, TNA WO 95/1824; 35th Brigade WD, January–December 1917, TNA WO 95/1848; Captain Cyril Falls, *Military Operations: France and Belgium, 1917, Volume I*, Macmillan, London, 1940, pp. 217–220, 248–249; Jonathan Nicholls, *Cheerful Sacrifice: The Battle of Arras, 1917*, Leo Cooper, London, 1990, pp. 110–113; Scott and Brumwell, *12th Division*, pp. 99–104.
22. 12th Division WD, July–December 1917, TNA WO 95/1825; 35th Brigade WD, TNA WO 95/1848; Captain Wilfrid Miles, *Military Operations: France and Belgium, 1917, Volume III*, HMSO, London, 1948, pp. 51, 171, 185–186, 188–190, 192, 194, 196, 200, 227, 237, 256; Scott and Brumwell, *12th Division*, pp. 135–136, 138, 141–142, 143–160.
23. Davies and Maddocks, *Bloody Red Tabs*, p. 199.
24. Riddell and Clayton, *The Cambridgeshires*, pp. 180–244.
25. Davies and Maddocks, *Bloody Red Tabs*, p. 112; letter from Lieutenant-Colonel L.M. Dyson to official historian, [?] July 1931, TNA CAB 45/122; *London Gazette*, 3 June 1916.
26. Alan Thomas, *A Life Apart*, Gollancz, London, 1968, p. 56. Once again I am grateful to John Bourne for additional information about Owen's military service.
27. Note by GOC 37th Brigade, [?] July 1918, 12th Division WD, August 1918–June 1919, TNA WO 95/1827; Connelly, *Steady The Buffs!*, p. 185.
28. See Peter Simkins, 'Building Blocks: Aspects of Command and Control at Brigade Level in the BEF's Offensive Operations, 1916–1918', in Gary Sheffield and Dan Todman (eds), *Command and Control on the Western Front: The British Army's Experience, 1914–1918*, Spellmount, Staplehurst, 2004, p. 155; also John Bourne, 'The BEF's Generals on 29 September 1918: An Empirical Portrait with some British and Australian Comparisons', in Peter Dennis and Jeffrey Grey (eds), *1918: Defining Victory*, Army History Unit, Department of Defence, Canberra, 1999, p. 108, and 'British Generals in the First World War', in Gary Sheffield (ed.), *Leadership and Command: The Anglo-American Military Experience since 1861*, Brassey's, London, 1997, pp. 96, 111.
29. Scott and Brumwell, *12th Division*, pp. 240–245; C.T. Atkinson, *The Queen's Own Royal West Kent Regiment, 1914–1919*, Simpkin, Marshall, Hamilton, Kent and Co., London, 1924, pp. 231, 626; Riddell and Clayton, *The Cambridgeshires*, p. 150; Rutter, *Seventh Battalion, The Royal Sussex Regiment*, pp. 116, 218, 320; John W. Burrows, *The Essex Regiment: 9th, 10th, 11th, 13th and 15th Battalions*, John H. Burrows and Sons, Southend, 1935, p. 102. Grateful thanks are also due to Peter Hodgkinson for additional information about Dawson, Smeltzer and Scarlett.
30. Burrows, *The Essex Regiment: 9th, 10th, 11th, 13th and 15th Battalions*, pp. 115, 125–126.
31. Riddell and Clayton, *The Cambridgeshires*, pp. 210, 213–214.
32. C.T. Atkinson, *The Queen's Own Royal West Kent Regiment, 1914–1919*, pp. 445–446, 470; Scott and Brumwell, *12th Division*, p. 222; Thomas, *A Life Apart*, pp. 156–157.
33. Scott and Brumwell, *12th Division*, pp. 226, 241; Colin Fox et al. (eds), *Their Duty Done: The Kitchener Battalions of the Royal Berkshire Regiment, 1918*, Centre for Continuing Education, University of Reading, 1998, pp. 18, 55.
34. Riddell and Clayton, *The Cambridgeshires*, pp. xviii, 7, 11, 213–214.
35. John W. Burrows, *The Essex Regiment: Essex Territorial Infantry Brigade (4th, 5th, 6th and 7th Battalions)*, Burrows, Southend, 1932, pp. 65–66; also *The Essex Regiment: 9th, 10th, 11th, 13th and 15th Battalions*, pp. 9, 10, 13, 73–74; Scott and Brumwell, *12th Division*, p. 241.
36. Fox et al. (eds), *Their Duty Done*, p. 31. Curiously, neither the regimental history nor the war diary of the 5th Royal Berkshires make any mention of the battalion's involvement in *action* on 8 August 1918 or of any casualties on that day. See also Scott amd Brumwell, *12th Division*, p. 241.
37. Scott and Brumwell, *12th Division*, p. 222; Thomas, *A Life Apart*, pp. 57–61, 99–100.
38. Colonel R.H.S. Moody, *Historical Records of The Buffs, East Kent Regiment, 1914–1919*, Medici Society, London, 1922, pp. 139, 235, 270, 373; Connelly, *Steady The Buffs!*, pp. 19, 21–22, 71,

82, 133; Scott and Brumwell, *12th Division*, pp. 139, 153–154, 170, 173, 192, 211, 223, 227, 244; Thomas, *A Life Apart*, p. 139. Peter Hodgkinson kindly provided additional information on Smeltzer's career.

39. 6th Buffs WD, TN A WO 95/1860; Connelly, *Steady The Buffs!*, p. 193.
40. 6th Buffs WD, TNA WO 95/1860; 37th Brigade WD, TNA WO 95/1859; Connelly, *Steady The Buffs!*, p. 199.
41. Scott and Brumwell, *12th Division*, p. 211; Connelly, *Steady The Buffs!*, p. 200; 6th Buffs WD, TNA WO 95/1860; 37th Brigade WD, TNA WO 95/1859; 12th Division WD, August 1918–June 1919, TNA WO 95/ 1827.
42. Scott and Brumwell, *12th Division*, pp. 222–223; Connelly, *Steady The Buffs!*, p. 205; 37th Brigade WD, TNA WO 95/1859; 6th Buffs WD, TNA WO 95/1960.
43. Riddell and Clayton, *The Cambridgeshires*, pp. 127, 218–229, 235–246; 1/1st Cambridgeshires WD, May 1918–March 1919, TNA WO 95/1850/2.
44. Burrows, *Essex Regiment: 9th, 10th, 11th, 13th and 15th Battalions*, pp. 125–126; 35th Brigade WD, January 1918–May 1919, TNA WO 95/1849; 9th Essex WD, TNA WO 95/1851.
45. Scott and Brumwell, *12th Division*, pp. 208–209.
46. *Ibid.*, p. 193.
47. Burrows, *Essex Regiment: 9th, 10th, 11th, 13th and 15th Battalions*, p. 117.
48. Riddell and Clayton, *The Cambridgeshires*, pp. 245, 250, 267.
49. Burrows, *Essex Regiment: 9th, 10th, 11th, 13th and 15th Battalions*, pp. 114–115, 118; 9th Essex WD, TNA WO 95/1851.
50. Riddell and Clayton, *The Cambridgeshires*, pp. 213, 215–216; 1/1st Cambridgeshires WD, TNA WO 95/1850/2.
51. Rutter, *Seventh Royal Sussex Regiment*, see particularly Appendix F, pp. 313–321.
52. Scott and Brumwell, *12th Division*, Appendix IV, p. 254.
53. Riddell and Clayton, *The Cambridgeshires*, p. 215.
54. Rutter, *Seventh Royal Sussex Regiment*, p. 247.
55. See, for example, *OH, 1918, IV*, pp. 82, 183, 192, 515; Paddy Griffith, *Battle Tactics of the Western Front: The British Army's Art of Attack, 1916–18*, Yale University Press, New Haven and London, 1994, p. 22. See also Peter Simkins, 'Co-Stars or Supporting Cast?', p. 65.
56. Scott and Brumwell, *12th Division*, pp. 200, 211; 6th Buffs WD, TNA WO 95/1860; 37th Brigade WD, TNA WO 95/1859.
57. Riddell and Clayton, *The Cambridgeshires*, pp. 252–253; 1/1st Cambridgeshires WD, TNA WO 95/1850/2; 35th Brigade WD, January 1918–May 1919, TNA WO 95/1849.
58. Burrows, *Essex Regiment: 9th, 10th, 11th, 13th and 15th Battalions*, p. 121.
59. Riddell and Clayton, *The Cambridgeshires*, pp. 236–241.
60. C.T. Atkinson, *The Queen's Own Royal West Kent Regiment, 1914–1919*, p. 406; Scott and Brumwell, *12th Division*, pp. 193, 253; 6th Royal West Kents WD, TNA WO 95/1861.
61. Riddell and Clayton, *The Cambridgeshires*, pp. 164, 191–192, 200–202; Scott and Brumwell, *12th Division*, p. 194; 1/1st Cambridgeshires WD, TNA WO 95/1850/2.
62. Rutter, *Seventh Royal Sussex Regiment*, pp. 203, 228–229, 251, 306, 309; Scott and Brumwell, *12th Division*, p. 196; 7th Royal Sussex WD, TNA WO 95/1856/3.
63. Scott and Brumwell, *12th Division*, p. 218; 7th Norfolks WD, June 1915–May 1919, TNA WO 95/1853/1; 35th Brigade WD, January 1918–May 1919, TNA WO 95/1849.
64. Rutter, *Seventh Royal Sussex Regiment*, p. 233; 7th Royal Sussex WD, TNA WO 95/1856/3.
65. Scott and Brumwell, *12th Division*, p. 254.
66. Rutter, *Seventh Royal Sussex Regiment*, pp. 234, 244, 251.
67. Burrows, *Essex Regiment: 9th, 10th, 11th, 13th and 15th Batalions*, pp. 117–118.
68. Riddell and Clayton, *The Cambridgeshires*, p. 207.
69. *Ibid.*, pp. 217.
70. *Ibid.*, pp. 220, 228–229.
71. See, for example, Robin Prior and Trevor Wilson, 'Winning the War', in Dennis and Grey (eds), *1918: Defining Victory*, p. 41 ('no advance could be pushed beyond the protection of the covering artillery'). See also Tim Travers, *How The War Was Won: Command and Technology in the British Army on the Western Front, 1917–1918*, Routledge, London, 1992.
72. Scott and Brumwell, *12th Division*, pp. 191–192; *OH, 1918, IV*, p. 83; 35th Brigade WD, TNA WO 95/1849.

73. Colonel H.C. Wylly, *History of the Queen's Royal (West Surrey) Regiment in the Great War*, Gale and Polden, Aldershot, 1924, p. 207; 37th Brigade WD, TNA WO 95/1859; 6th Queen's WD, TNA WO 95/1863/1; Riddell and Clayton, *The Cambridgeshires*, pp. 190–191; 35th Brigade WD, TNA WO 95/1849; 1/1st Cambridgeshires WD, TNA WO 95/1850/2; *OH, 1918, IV*, p. 113.

74. Scott and Brumwell, *12th Division*, p. 196; *OH, 1918, IV*, pp. 200–201; 35th Brigade WD, TNA WO 95/1849; 5th Royal Berkshires WD, February 1918–May 1919, TNA WO 95/1856/1; 36th Brigade WD, January 1918–June 1919, TNA WO 95/1855; 9th Essex WD, TNA WO 95/1851.

75. *OH, 1918, IV*, p. 241; Scott and Brumwell, *12th Division*, p. 197; Atkinson, *The Queen's Own Royal West Kent Regiment*, p. 414; 37th Brigade WD, TNA WO 95/1859; 6th Royal West Kents WD, TNA WO 95/1861.

76. Rutter, *Seventh Royal Sussex Regiment*, pp. 245–246; 7th Royal Sussex WD, TNA WO 95/1856/3; Scott and Brumwell, *12th Division*, p. 212; 6th Buffs WD, TNA WO 95/1860.

77. *OH, 1918, IV*, pp. 82–83; 12th Division WD, August 1918–June 1919, TNA WO 95/1827; 35th Brigade WD, TNA WO 95/1849; Riddell and Clayton, *The Cambridgeshires*, pp. 186–190.

78. Rutter, *Seventh Royal Sussex Regiment*, p. 226; 12th Division WD, TNA WO 95/1827; 36th Brigade WD, January 1918–June 1919, TNA WO 95/1855; 7th Royal Sussex WD, TNA WO 95/1856/3; Riddell and Clayton, *The Cambridgeshires*, p. 253; 35th Brigade WD, TNA WO 95/1849; 1/1st Cambridgeshires WD, TNA WO 95/1850/2.

79. Riddell and Clayton, *The Cambridgeshires*, pp. 222–223.

80. Scott and Brumwell, *12th Division*, p. 204; 63rd Brigade Royal Field Artillery WD, January 1915–April 1919, TNA WO 95/1838/1; 6th Buffs WD, TNA WO 95/1860.

81. Riddell and Clayton, *The Cambridgeshires*, pp. 241–242, 244; 62nd Brigade Royal Field Artillery WD, TNA WO 95/1836/3; 1/1st Cambridgeshires WD, TNA WO 95/1850/2.

82. *OH, 1918, IV*, pp. 200, 333.

Sources and Bibliography

Unpublished Official Records

The National Archives, Kew, London

OFFICIAL HISTORIES: CORRESPONDENCE

CAB 45/122 Lys, 1918
CAB 45/133 Somme, 1916 (D–F)
CAB 45/134 Somme, 1916 (G–H)
CAB 45/135 Somme, 1916 (I–L)
CAB 45/138 Somme, 1916 (T–Y)

CAB 45/139 Vimy Ridge
CAB 45/189 Fourth Army Operations (G–L)
CAB 103/113 Cabinet Office Historical
  Section, 1946–1953

WAR DIARIES

WO 95/372 Third Army
WO 95/518 Fifth (Reserve) Army
WO 95/639 II Corps
WO 95/651 II Corps, BGRA
WO 95/654 II Corps, Commander Heavy
  Artillery
WO 95/678 III Corps
WO 95/750 V Corps
WO 95/756 V Corps, BGRA
WO 95/1140 12th Lancers
WO 95/1368 99th Brigade
WO 95/1678 8th Division
WO 95/1702/1 22nd Durham Light Infantry
WO 95/1711 23rd Brigade
WO 95/1712 2nd Devonshire
WO 95/1713/2 2nd Middlesex
WO 95/1714 2nd West Yorkshire
WO 95/1721 1st Sherwood Foresters
WO 95/1722 2nd Northamptonshire
WO 95/1728 25th Brigade
WO 95/1729/1 2nd Royal Berkshire
WO 95/1729/2 2nd East Lancashire
WO 95/1824–7 12th Division
WO 95/1848–9 35th Brigade
WO 95/1836/3 62nd Brigade, RFA
WO 95/1838/1 63rd Brigade, RFA
WO 95/1850/2 1/1st Cambridgeshire
WO 95/1851 9th Essex
WO 95/1853 7th Norfolk
WO 95/1855 36th Brigade
WO 95/1856/1 5th Royal Berkshire
WO 95/1856/3 7th Royal Sussex
WO 95/1857/2 9th Royal Fusiliers
WO 95/1859 37th Brigade
WO 95/1860 7th Buffs

WO 95/1861 6th Royal West Kent
WO 95/1863/1 6th Queen's
WO 95/1875 14th (Light) Division
WO 95/1894 41st Brigade
WO 95/1899 42nd Brigade
WO 95/1985 17th (Northern) Division
WO 95/1999 50th Brigade
WO 95/2015–7 18th (Eastern) Division
WO 95/2034–6 53rd Brigade
WO 95/2037 8th Royal Berkshire
WO 95/2038 10th Essex
WO 95/2039 8th Suffolk
WO 95/2040 7th Royal West Kent
WO 95/2041–2 54th Brigade
WO 95/2042 7th Bedfordshire
WO 94/2044 6th Northamptonshire
WO 95/2045 11th Royal Fusiliers
WO 95/2046–8 55th Brigade
WO 95/2049 7th Royal West Kent
WO 95/2049 7th Buffs
WO 95/2050 8th East Surrey
WO 95/2051 7th Queen's
WO 95/2133–4 21st Division
WO 95/2151–3 62nd Brigade
WO 95/2154 1st Lincolnshire
WO 95/2154 2nd Lincolnshire
WO 95/2155 12th/13th Northumberland
  Fusiliers
WO 95/2159–60 64th Brigade
WO 95/2161 1st East Yorkshire
WO 95/2161 15th Durham Light Infantry
WO 95/2162 9th King's Own Yorkshire Light
  Infantry
WO 95/2163 110th Brigade
WO 95/2164 6th Leicestershire

WO 95/2164 7th Leicestershire
WO 95/2368 32nd Division
WO 95/2403 16th Highland Light Infantry
WO 95/2403 17th Highland Light Infantry
WO 95/2403 11th Border
WO 95/2468 35th (Bantam) Division
WO 95/2472 35th Division, ADMS
WO 95/2482 104th Brigade
WO 95/2484 17th Lancashire Fusiliers
WO 95/2485 105th Brigade
WO 95/2487 16th Cheshire
WO 95/2488 14th Gloucestershire
WO 95/2488 15th Sherwood Foresters
WO 95/2490 19th Durham Light Infantry
WO 95/2540 38th (Welsh) Division

WO 95/2552-4 113th Brigade
WO 95/2555/1 13th Royal Welsh Fusiliers
WO 95/2557-8 114th Brigade
WO 95/2559/3 14th Welsh
WO 95/2560 115th Brigade
WO 95/2561/1 2nd Royal Welsh Fusiliers
WO 95/2617 41st Division
WO 95/3000 173rd Brigade
WO 95/3001/4 2/2nd London
WO 95/3001/5 3rd London
WO 95/3001/9 2/4th London
WO 95/3005/3 6th London
WO 95/3009/5 2/10th London
WO 95/3764 2nd Canadian Brigade

JUDGE ADVOCATE GENERAL'S OFFICE: COURTS MARTIAL PROCEEDINGS
WO 71/534 Field General Court Martial (Lance-Corporal P. Goggins)
WO 71/535 Field General Court Martial (Lance-Sergeant J.W. Stones)
WO 213/10 Register of Field General Courts Martial, July 1916–September 1916
WO 213/11 Register of Field General Courts Martial, September 1916–September 1917
WO 213/13 Register of Field General Courts Martial, January 1917–March 1917

MILITARY HEADQUARTERS PAPERS
WO 158/21 GHQ Correspondence with CIGS and Secretary of State for War, 1915–1916
WO 158/227 Third Army Operations, July–September 1918
WO 158/241 Fourth Army Operations, July–August 1918
WO 158/247 Fifth Army Operations, November 1916–March 1917
WO 158/252 Fifth Army Operations, November 1917–July 1918

OFFICERS' FILES
WO 374/17191 Officer's Personal File (H.R. Cumming)

Australian War Memorial, Canberra

WAR DIARIES
AWM 4, 1/53/26 5th Australian Division
AWM 4, 23/13/27 13th Australian Brigade
AWM 4, 23/15/26 15th Australian Brigade
AWM 4, 23/35/33 18th Battalion, AIF
AWM 4, 23/36/27 19th Battalion, AIF
AWM 4, 23/37/33 20th Battalion, AIF
AWM 4, 23/50/17 33rd Battalion, AIF

AWM 4, 23/50/18 33rd Battalion, AIF
AWM 4, 23/52/10 35th Battalion, AIF
AWM 4, 23/53/18 36th Battalion, AIF
AWM 4, 23/68/26 51st Battalion, AIF
AWM 4, 23/69/25 52nd Battalion. AIF
AWM 4, 23/76/27 59th Battalion, AIF

Imperial War Museum, London
Fourth Army papers

Unpublished Private Records

The National Archives, Kew, London
Field-Marshal Earl Haig (Diaries: WO 256/11–256/36)

Australian War Memorial, Canberra
Lieutenant J.W. Axtens
C.E.W. Bean
Brigadier-General H.E. Elliott

Major-General Sir John Gellibrand
Lieutenant-Colonel H.A. Goddard
General Sir John Monash
Lieutenant S.R. Traill

Brotherton Library, University of Leeds
Colonel R.A. Chell

Churchill Archive Centre, Churchill College, Cambridge
General Lord Rawlinson

Imperial War Museum, London
Lieutenant-General Sir Richard Butler
Private Robert Cude
M. Hardie
Lieutenant-Colonel H.H. Hemming
General Sir Ivor Maxse
Major-General Sir Reginald Pinney

Liddell Hart Centre for Military Archives, King's College, London
Field-Marshal Viscount Alanbrooke
Brigadier Sir Edward Beddington
Major-General J.F.C. Fuller
Captain Sir Basil Liddell Hart
Field-Marshal Sir Archibald Montgomery-Massingberd

National Army Museum, London
General Lord Rawlinson

National Library of Scotland, Edinburgh
Field-Marshal Earl Haig

Parliamentary Archive, House of Lords
David (Earl) Lloyd George

Public Record Office of Northern Ireland, Belfast
Major-General Sir Oliver Nugent (Farren Connell papers)

Published Sources

Official Histories
Edmonds, Brigadier-General Sir James, *Military Operations: France and Belgium, 1916, Volume I*, Macmillan, London, 1932
Miles, Captain Wilfrid, *Military Operations: France and Belgium, 1916, Volume II*, Macmillan, London, 1938
Falls, Captain Cyril, *Military Operations: France and Belgium, 1917, Volume I*, Macmillan, London, 1940
Edmonds, Brigadier-General Sir James, *Military Operations: France and Belgium, 1917, Volume II*, HMSO, London, 1948
Miles, Captain Wilfrid, *Military Operations: France and Belgium, 1917, Volume III*, HMSO, London, 1948
Edmonds, Brigadier-General Sir James, *Military Operations: France and Belgium, 1918, Volume I*, Macmillan, London, 1935
——, *Military Operations: France and Belgium, 1918, Volume II*, Macmillan, London, 1937
——, *Military Operations: France and Belgium, 1918, Volume III*, Macmillan, London, 1939
——, *Military Operations: France and Belgium, 1918, Volume IV*, HMSO, London, 1947

——, *Military Operations: France and Belgium, 1918, Volume V*, HMSO, London, 1947

Becke, Major A.F., *Order of Battle of Divisions: Part 3A, New Army Divisions (9–26)*, HMSO, London, 1938

——, *Order of Battle of Divisions: Part 3B, New Army Divisions (30–41) and 63rd (R.N.) Division*, HMSO, London, 1945

Henniker, Colonel A.M., *Transportation on the Western Front, 1914–1918*, HMSO, London, 1937

Bean, C.E.W., *The Official History of Australia in the War of 1914–1918: Volume III, The Australian Imperial Force in France, 1916*, Angus and Robertson, Sydney, 1929

——, *Volume IV, The Australian Imperial Force in France, 1917*, Angus and Robertson, Sydney, 1939

——, *Volume V, The Australian Imperial Force in France during the Main German Offensive, 1918*, Angus and Robertson, Sydney, 1937

——, *Volume VI, The Australian Imperial Force in France during the Allied Offensive, 1918*, Angus and Robertson, Sydney, 1942

Official Publications and GHQ/Stationery Service Pamphlets

Field Service Regulations, Part I: Operations (1909)

Maxse, Major-General F.I., *The 18th Division in the Battle of the Ancre*, printed report, December 1916

SS 135: Instructions for the Training of Divisions for Offensive Action (December 1916)

SS 139/3: Artillery Notes, No. 3: Counter-Battery Work (March 1917)

SS 143: Instructions for the Training of Platoons for Offensive Action (February 1917)

SS 144: The Normal Formation for the Attack (February 1917)

SS 152: Instructions for the Training of the British Armies in France (June 1917)

Biographies, Memoirs and Personal Experience Accounts

Baynes, John, *Far from a Donkey: The Life of General Sir Ivor Maxse, KCB, CVO, DSO*, Brassey's, London, 1995

Beach, Jim (ed.), *The Military Papers of Lieutenant-Colonel Sir Cuthbert Headlam, 1910–1942*, History Press, Stroud, for the Army Records Society, 2010

Bourne, John and Bushaway, Bob (eds), *Joffrey's War: A Sherwood Forester in the Great War (Geoffrey Ratcliff Husbands)*, Salient Books, Nottingham, 2011

Churchill, Winston S., *The World Crisis, 1911–1918*, 2 vols, Odhams, London, 1938

Cross C. (ed.), *Life with Lloyd George: The Diary of A.J. Sylvester, 1931–45*, Macmillan, London, 1975

Cumming, Hanway R., *A Brigadier in France, 1917–1918*, Cape, London, 1921

De Groot, Gerard, *Douglas Haig, 1861–1928*, Unwin Hyman, London, 1988

Dunn, Captain J.C., *The War the Infantry Knew, 1914–1918*, Sphere Books edition, London, 1989

Edmonds, Charles (Charles Carrington), *A Subaltern's War*, Anthony Mott edition, London, 1984

Farrar-Hockley, Anthony, *Goughie: The Life of General Sir Hubert Gough*, Hart-Davis, MacGibbon, London, 1975

Fuller, Major-General J.F.C., *Memoirs of an Unconventional Soldier*, Ivor Nicholson and Watson, London, 1936

Griffith, Wyn, *Up to Mametz*, Faber, London, 1931

Haldane, General Sir Aylmer, *A Soldier's Saga*, Blackwood, Edinburgh, 1948

Harris, J.P., *Douglas Haig and the First World War*, Cambridge University Press, 2008

Hyatt, A.M.J., *General Sir Arthur Currie: A Military Biography*, Toronto University Press, 1987

Kelly, D.V., *39 Months with the 'Tigers'*, Ernest Benn, London, 1930

Kiernan, R.H., *Little Brother Goes Soldiering*, Constable, London, 1930

Langguth, A.J., *Saki: A Life of Hector Hugh Munro*, Oxford University Press, 1981

Liddell Hart, B.H., *Memoirs, Volume I*, Cassell, London, 1965

Lloyd George, David, *War Memoirs*, 6 vols, Ivor Nicholson and Watson, London, 1933–1936 and abridged edn, 2 vols, Odhams, London, 1938

Ludendorff, General Erich, *My War Memories, 1914–18*, 2 vols, Hutchinson, London, n.d.

McMullin, Ross, *Pompey Elliott*, Scribe, Melbourne, 2002

Maxwell, Charlotte (ed.), *Frank Maxwell, Brig.-General VC, CSI, DSO: A Memoir and Some Letters*, John Murray, London, 1921

Mead, Gary, *The Good Soldier: The Biography of Douglas Haig*, Atlantic Books, London, 2007

Mearsheimer, John J., *Liddell Hart and the Weight of History*, Cornell University Press and Brassey's, London, 1988

Perry, Nicholas (ed.), *Major-General Oliver Nugent and the Ulster Division, 1915–1918*, Sutton, Stroud, for the Army Records Society, 2007

Pollard, Alfred, *Fire-Eater: The Memoirs of a VC*, Hutchinson, London, 1932

Prior, Robin and Wilson, Trevor, *Command on the Western Front: The Military Career of Sir Henry Rawlinson, 1914–18*, Blackwell, Oxford, 1992

Reid, Walter, *Architect of Victory: Douglas Haig*, Birlinn, Edinburgh, 2006

Richards, Frank, *Old Soldiers Never Die*, Faber, London, 1933

Sheffield, Gary, *The Chief: Douglas Haig and the British Army*, Aurum Press, London, 2011

—— and Bourne, John (eds), *Douglas Haig: War Diaries and Letters, 1914–1918*, Weidenfeld & Nicolson, London, 2005

—— and Inglis, G.I.S. (eds), *From Vimy Ridge to the Rhine: The Great War Letters of Christopher Stone, DSO, MC*, Crowood Press, Marlborough, 1989

Terraine, John (ed.), *General Jack's Diary: The Trench Diary of Brigadier-General J.L. Jack, DSO*, Eyre and Spottiswoode, London, 1964

——, *Douglas Haig: The Educated Soldier*, Cassell, London, 1963

Thomas, Alan, *A Life Apart*, Gollancz, London, 1968

Wiest, Andrew A., *Haig: The Evolution of a Commander*, Potomac Books, Dulles VA, 2005

Unit Histories

Aiken, Alex, *Courage Past: A Duty Done* (1/9th Highland Light Infantry), published by the author, Glasgow, 1971

Alexander, Jack, *McRae's Battalion: The Story of the 16th Royal Scots*, Mainstream, Edinburgh, 2003

Arthur, J.W. and Munro, I.S. (eds), *The Seventeenth Highland Light Infantry (Glasgow Chamber of Commerce Battalion): Record of War Service, 1914–1918*, Clark, Glasgow, 1920

Atkinson, C.T., *The Queen's Own Royal West Kent Regiment, 1914–1919*, Simpkin, Marshall, Hamilton, Kent and Co., London, 1924

Atteridge, A. Hilliard, *History of the 17th (Northern) Division*, Maclehose, for the Glasgow University Press, 1929

Bacon, Maurice, and Langley, David, *The Blast of War: A History of Nottingham's Bantams, 15th (S) Battalion, Sherwood Foresters*, Sherwood Press, Nottingham, 1986

Banks, Lieutenant-Colonel T.M. and Chell, Captain R.A., *With the 10th Essex in France*, Burt and Sons, London, 1921

Barlow, Sir C.A. Montague, *The Lancashire Fusiliers: The Roll of Honour of the Salford Brigade*, Sherratt and Hughes, Manchester, 1920

Bird, Derek, *The Spirit of the Troops is Excellent: The 6th (Morayshire) Battalion, Seaforth Highlanders, in the Great War, 1914–1919*, Birdbrain Books, Moray, 2008

Blair, Dale, *Dinkum Diggers: An Australian Battalion at War* (1st Battalion AIF), Melbourne University Press, 2001

Boraston, Lieutenant-Colonel J.H. and Bax, Captain Cyril E.O., *The Eighth Division in War, 1914–1918*, Medici Society, London, 1922

Burrows, John W., *The Essex Regiment: 9th, 10th, 11th, 13th and 15th Battalions*, John H. Burrows and Sons, Southend, 1935

——, *The Essex Regiment: Essex Territorial Infantry Brigade (4th, 5th, 6th and 7th Battalions)*, John H. Burrows and Sons, Southend, 1932

Chalmers, Thomas (ed.), *An Epic of Glasgow: History of the 15th Battalion The Highland Light Infantry (City of Glasgow Regiment)*, McCallum, Glasgow, 1934

——, *A Saga of Scotland: History of the 16th Battalion The Highland Light Infantry*, McCallum, Glasgow, 1930

Clayton, Derek, *From Pontefract to Picardy: The 9th King's Own Yorkshire Light Infantry in the First World War*, Tempus, Stroud, 2004

Connelly, Mark, *Steady the Buffs!: A Regiment, A Region and the Great War*, Oxford University Press, 2006

Cooke, Captain C.H., *Historical Records of the 16th (Service) Battalion Northumberland Fusiliers*, Newcastle and Gateshead Chamber of Commerce, 1923

Davson, Lieutenant-Colonel H.M., *The History of the 35th Division in the Great War*, Sifton Praed, London, 1926

Deacon, M.G. (ed.), *The Shiny Seventh: The 7th (Service) Battalion Bedfordshire Regiment at War, 1915–1918*, Bedfordshire Historical Record Society/Boydell Press, Woodbridge, 2004

Denman, Terence, *Ireland's Unknown Soldiers: The 16th (Irish) Division in World War I*, Irish Academic Press, Dublin, 1992

Ellis, Captain A.D., *The Story of the Fifth Australian Division: Being an Authoritative Account of the Division's Doings in Egypt, France and Belgium*, Hodder and Stoughton, London, 1920

'E.R.', *The 54th Infantry Brigade, 1914–1918: Some Records of Battle and Laughter in France*, Gale and Polden, Aldershot, 1919

Ewing, John, *The History of the 9th (Scottish) Division, 1914–1919*, John Murrary, London, 1921

Falls, Cyril, *The History of the 36th (Ulster) Division*, M'Caw, Stevenson and Orr, Belfast and London, 1922

Farndale, General Sir Martin, *History of the Royal Regiment of Artillery: Western Front 1914–18*, Royal Artillery Institution, Woolwich, 1986

Fox, Colin, et al. (eds), *Their Duty Done: The Kitchener Battalions of the Royal Berkshire Regiment, 1918*, Centre for Continuing Education, University of Reading, 1998

Gough, General Sir Hubert, *The Fifth Army*, Hodder and Stoughton, London, 1931

Grey, Major W.E., *The 2nd City of London Regiment (Royal Fusiliers) in the Great War, 1914–1919*, Regimental Headquarters, London, 1929

Hughes, Colin, *Mametz: Lloyd George's 'Welsh Army' at the Battle of the Somme*, Orion Press, Gerrards Cross, 1982 and Gliddon Books edn, Norwich, 1990

Hussey, Brigadier-General A.H. and Inman, Major D.S., *The Fifth Division in the Great War*, Nisbet, London, 1921

Kincaid-Smith, Lieutenant-Colonel M., *The 25th Division in France and Flanders*, Harrison, London, 1919

Knight, Jill, *The Civil Service Rifles in the Great War: 'All Bloody Gentlemen'*, Pen and Sword, Barnsley, 2004

McCartney, Helen B., *Citizen Soldiers: The Liverpool Territorials in the First World War*, Cambridge University Press, 2005

McGreal, Stephen, *Cheshire Bantams: 15th, 16th and 17th Battalions of the Cheshire Regiment*, Pen and Sword, Barnsley, 2006

Marden, Major-General Sir Thomas, *The History of the Welch Regiment: Part II, 1914–1918*, Western Mail and Echo, Cardiff, 1932

Mitchinson, K.W., *Gentlemen and Officers: The Impact and Experience of War on a Territorial Regiment* (London Rifle Brigade)*, 1914–1918*, Imperial War Museum, London, 1995

—— and McInnes, Ian, *Cotton Town Comrades: The Story of the Oldham Pals Battalion, 1914–1919*, Bayonet Publications, 1993

Montgomery, Major-General Sir Archibald, *The Story of the Fourth Army in the Battles of the Hundred Days, August 8th to November 11th, 1918*, Hodder and Stoughton, London, 1919

Moody, Colonel R.S.H., *Historical Records of The Buffs, East Kent Regiment, 1914–1919*, Medici Society, London, 1922

Morse, John Stephen, *9th (Service) Battalion The Sherwood Foresters (Notts and Derby Regiment)*, Tommies Guides, Eastbourne, 2007

Munby, Lieutenant-Colonel J.E. (ed.), *A History of the 38th (Welsh) Division: By the G.S.O.'s I of the Division*, Hugh Rees, London, 1920

Murphy, Lieutenant-Colonel C.C.R., *The History of the Suffolk Regiment, 1914–1927*, Hutchinson, London, 1928

Nichols, Captain G.H.F., *The 18th Division in the Great War*, Blackwood, Edinburgh and London, 1922

Orr, Philip, *The Road to the Somme: Men of the Ulster Division Tell Their Story*, Blackstaff Press, Belfast, 1987

Osborne, Wayne, *The 10th Notts and Derbys in the Great War: Dorset 1914 to Ypres 1915*, Salient Books, Nottingham, 2009

Radley, Kenneth, *We Lead, Others Follow: First Canadian Division, 1914–1918*, Vanwell, St Catherine's, 2006

Richardson, Matthew, *The Tigers: 6th, 7th, 8th and 9th (Service) Battalions of the Leicestershire Regiment*, Leo Cooper/Pen and Sword, Barnsley, 2000

Riddell, Brigadier-General E. and Clayton, Colonel M.C., *The Cambridgeshires, 1914 to 1919*, Bowes and Bowes, Cambridge, 1934

Rutter, Owen (ed.), *The History of the Seventh (Service) Battalion, The Royal Sussex Regiment, 1914–1919*, The Times Publishing Company, London, 1934

Scott, Major-General Sir Arthur B. and Brumwell, P. Middleton, *History of the 12th (Eastern) Division in the Great War, 1914–1918*, Nisbet, London, 1923

Sellers, Leonard, *The Hood Battalion*, Leo Cooper/Pen and Sword, Barnsley, 2005

Shakespear, Lieutenant-Colonel J., *The Thirty-Fourth Division, 1915–1919: The Story of its Career from Ripon to the Rhine*, Witherby, London, 1921

Sheen, John, *Durham Pals: 18th, 19th and 22nd Battalions of the Durham Light Infantry. A History of Three Battalions Raised by Local Committee in County Durham*, Pen and Sword, Barnsley, 2007

Smith, Leonard V., *Between Mutiny and Obedience: The Case of the French Fifth Infantry Division during World War I*, Princeton University Press, New Jersey, 1994

Stanley, Peter, *Men of Mont St. Quentin: Between Victory and Death* (21st Battalion AIF), Scribe, Melbourne, 2009

Stewart, Lieutenant-Colonel J. and Buchan, John, *The Fifteenth (Scottish) Division, 1914–1919*, Blackwood, Edinburgh and London, 1926

Turner, William, *Accrington Pals: The 11th (Service) Battalion (Accrington) East Lancashire Regiment. A History of the Battalion raised from Accrington, Blackburn, Burnley and Chorley in World War One*, Wharncliffe, Barnsley, 1987

United States War Department, *Histories of Two Hundred and Fifty-One Divisions of the German Army Which Participated in the War (1914–1918)*, originally published 1920; London Stamp Exchange edition, 1989

'V.M.', *Record of the XIth (Service) Battalion Border Regiment (Lonsdale) from September 1914 to July 1st 1916*, Whitehead, Appleby, n.d.

Ward, C.H. Dudley, *Regimental Records of the Royal Welch Fusiliers: Volume III, 1914–1918, France and Flanders*, Forster and Groom, London, 1928

——, *The 56th Division (1st London Territorial Division)*, John Murray, London, 1921

Weir, Alec, *Come on Highlanders! Glasgow Territorials in the Great War*, Sutton, Stroud, 2005

Wylly, Colonel H.C., *History of the Queen's Royal (West Surrey) Regiment in the Great War*, Gale and Polden, Aldershot, 1924

Wyrall, Everard, *The History of the 19th Division, 1914–1918*, Edward Arnold and Humphries, Bradford, 1932

General Works

Bailey, Jonathan, 'The First World War and the Birth of the Modern Style of Warfare', *The Occasional*, No. 21, Strategic and Combat Studies Institute, Camberley, 1996

Baker, Chris, *The Battle for Flanders: German Defeat on the Lys, 1918*, Pen and Sword, Barnsley, 2011

Bennett, Scott, *Pozières: The Anzac Story*, Scribe, Melbourne, 2011

Bidwell, Shelford and Graham, Dominick, *Fire-Power: British Army Weapons and Theories of War, 1904–1945*, Allen and Unwin, London, 1982

Blair, Dale, *The Battle of Bellicourt Tunnel: Tommies, Diggers and Doughboys on the Hindenburg Line, 1918*, Frontline Books (Pen and Sword), London, 2011

Blaxland, Gregory, *Amiens 1918*, Frederick Muller, London, 1968

Boff, Jonathan, *Winning and Losing on the Western Front: The British Third Army and the Defeat of Germany 1918*, Cambridge University Press, 2012

Bond, Brian, *The Unquiet Western Front: Britain's Role in Literature and Politics*, Cambridge University Press, 2002

—— and Cave, Nigel (eds), *Haig: A Reappraisal 70 Years On*, Leo Cooper/Pen and Sword, Barnsley, 1999

—— et al., *Look to Your Front: Studies in the First World War by the British Commission for Military History*, Spellmount, Staplehurst, 1999

—— (ed.), *The First World War and British Military History*, Clarendon Press, Oxford, 1991

Bourne, John, *Who's Who in World War One*, Routledge, London, 2001

Bowman, Timothy, *The Irish Regiments in the Great War: Discipline and Morale*, Manchester University Press, 2003

Brown, Ian M., *British Logistics on the Western Front, 1914–1919*, Praeger, Westport CT and London, 1998

Brown, Malcolm, *The Imperial War Museum Book of 1918: Year of Victory*, Sidgwick and Jackson, London, 1998

——, *The Imperial War Museum Book of the Somme*, Sidgwick and Jackson, London, 1996

——, *The Imperial War Museum Book of the Western Front*, Sidgwick and Jackson, London, 1993

——, *Tommy Goes to War*, Dent, London, 1978

Charlton, Peter, *Australians on the Somme: Pozières 1916*, Leo Cooper/Secker and Warburg, London, 1986

Chasseaud, Peter, *Artillery's Astrologers: A History of British Survey and Mapping on the Western Front, 1914–1918*, Mapbooks, Lewes, 1999

Clark, Alan, *The Donkeys*, Hutchinson, London, 1961

Cobb, Paul, *Fromelles 1916*, Tempus, Stroud, 2007

Cook, Tim, *Shock Troops: Canadians Fighting the Great War, 1917–1918*, Viking, Toronto, 2008

——, *At the Sharp End: Canadians Fighting the Great War, 1914–1916*, Viking, Toronto, 2007

Cornish, Paul, *Machine Guns and the Great War*, Pen and Sword, Barnsley, 2009

Corns, Cathryn and Hughes-Wilson, John, *Blindfold and Alone: British Military Executions in the Great War*, Cassell, London, 2001

Davies, Frank and Maddocks, Graham, *Bloody Red Tabs: General Officer Casualties of the Great War, 1914–1918*, Leo Cooper/Pen and Sword, London and Barnsley, 1995

Dennis, Peter and Grey, Jeffrey (eds), *1918: Defining Victory*, Proceedings of the Chief of Army's History Conference, Canberra, 1998, Army History Unit, Canberra, 1999

Duffy, Christopher, *Through German Eyes: The British and the Somme 1916*, Weidenfeld & Nicolson, London, 2006

Essame, Hubert, *The Battle for Europe 1918*, Batsford, London, 1972

Farrar-Hockley, Anthony, *The Somme*, Batsford, London, 1964 and Pan Books edn, London, 1970

Fletcher, David (ed.), *Tanks and Trenches: First-Hand Accounts of Tank Warfare in the First World War*, Sutton, Stroud, 1994

Gardner, Brian, *The Big Push: A Portrait of the Battle of the Somme*, Cassell, London, 1961

Gliddon, Gerald, *VCs Handbook: The Western Front 1914–1918*, Sutton, Stroud, 2005

——, *VCs of the First World War: The Somme*, Sutton, Stroud, 1997

Griffith, Paddy (ed.), *British Fighting Methods in the Great War*, Frank Cass, London, 1996

——, *Battle Tactics of the Western Front: The British Army's Art of Attack, 1916–18*, Yale University Press, New Haven and London, 1994

Grotelueschen, Mark Ethan, *The AEF Way of War: The American Army and Combat in World War I*, Cambridge University Press, 2007

Gudmundsson, Bruce I., *Stormtroop Tactics: Innovation in the German Army, 1914–1918*, Praeger, New York, 1989

Hammond, Bryn, *Cambrai 1917: The Myth of the First Great Tank Battle*, Weidenfeld & Nicolson, London, 2008

Harper, Glyn, *Dark Journey: Three Key New Zealand Battles of the Western Front*, Harper Collins, Auckland, 2007

Harris, J.P. and Barr, Niall, *Amiens to the Armistice: The BEF in the Hundred Days Campaign, 8 August–11 November 1918*, Brassey's, London, 1998

Hart, Peter, *1918: A Very British Victory*, Weidenfeld & Nicolson, London, 2008

——, *The Somme*, Weidenfeld & Nicolson, London, 2005

Hayes, Geoffrey, Iarocci, Andrew and Bechtold, Mike (eds), *Vimy Ridge: A Canadian Reassessment*, Wilfrid Laurier University Press, Waterloo, Ontario, 2007

Holmes, Richard, *Tommy: The British Soldier on the Western Front, 1914–1918*, Harper Collins, London, 2004

Hughes, Matthew and Seligmann, Matthew (eds), *Leadership in Conflict, 1914–1918*, Leo Cooper/Pen and Sword, Barnsley, 2000

Keegan, John, *The First World War*, Hutchinson, London, 1998

——, *The Face of Battle*, Penguin edn, London, 1976

Kendall, Paul, *Bullecourt 1917: Breaching the Hindenburg Line*, Spellmount, Stroud, 2010

Lewis-Stempel, John, *Six Weeks: The Short and Gallant Life of the British Officer in the First World War*, Weidenfeld & Nicolson, London, 2010

Liddell Hart, B.H., *The Tanks, Volume I*, Cassell, London, 1959
——, *A History of the World War, 1914–1918*, Faber, London, 1934
——, *The Real War 1914–1918*, Faber, London, 1930
——, *Reputations*, John Murray, London, 1928
Liddle, Peter H. (ed.), *Passchendaele in Perspective: The Third Battle of Ypres*, Leo Cooper, London, 1997
Liddle, Peter H. and Hugh Cecil (eds), *Facing Armageddon: The First World War Experienced*, Leo Cooper/Pen and Sword, London and Barnsley, 1996
McCarthy, Chris, *The Somme: The Day-by-Day Account*, Arms and Armour Press, London, 1993
Macdonald, Lyn, *Somme*, Michael Joseph, London, 1983
Marble, Sanders, *British Artillery on the Western Front in the First World War: The Infantry cannot do with a gun less*, Ashgate, Farnham, 2013
—— (ed.), *Scraping the Barrel: The Military Use of Substandard Manpower, 1860–1960*, Fordham University Press, New York, 2012
Messenger, Charles, *The Day We Won The War: Turning Point at Amiens, 8 August 1918*, Weidenfeld & Nicolson, London, 2008
Middlebrook, Martin, *The First Day on the Somme: 1 July 1916*, Allen Lane/The Penguin Press, London, 1971
Millman, Brock, *Pessimism and British War Policy, 1916–18*, Frank Cass, London, 2001
Moore-Bick, Christopher, *Playing the Game: The British Junior Infantry Officer on the Western Front 1914–18*, Helion, Solihull, 2011
Morton, Desmond, *When Your Number's Up: The Canadian Soldier in the First World War*, Random House, Toronto, 1993
Nicholls, Jonathan, *Cheerful Sacrifice: The Battle of Arras 1917*, Leo Cooper, London, 1990
Nicholson, W.N., *Behind the Lines: An Account of Administrative Staffwork in the British Army, 1914–18*, Cape, London, 1939
Oram, Gerard, *Death Sentences Passed by Military Courts of the British Army 1914–1924*, Francis Boutle, London, 2005
Palat, Général Barthélemy E., *La Grande Guerre sur le Front Occidental*, 14 vols, Berger-Levrault, Paris, 1917–1929
Palazzo, Albert, *Seeking Victory on the Western Front: The British Army and Chemical Warfare in World War I*, University of Nebraska Press, Lincoln NE and London, 2000
Passingham, Ian, *All the Kaiser's Men: The Life and Death of the German Army on the Western Front, 1914–1918*, Sutton, Stroud, 2003
——, *Pillars of Fire: The Battle of Messines Ridge, June 1917*, Sutton, Stroud, 1998
Pedersen, Peter, *The Anzacs: Gallipoli to the Western Front*, Viking, Camberwell, Vic., 2007
——, *Villers-Bretonneux*, Battleground Europe series, Pen and Sword, Barnsley, 2004
Philpott, William, *Bloody Victory: The Sacrifice on the Somme and the Making of the Twentieth Century*, Little, Brown, London, 2009
——, *Anglo-French Relations and Strategy on the Western Front, 1914–18*, Macmillan, London, 1996
Pidgeon, Trevor, *Boom Ravine*, Battleground Europe series, Leo Cooper/Pen and Sword, Barnsley, 1998
——, *The Tanks at Flers: An Account of the First Use of Tanks in War at the Battle of Flers-Courcelette, The Somme, 15 September 1916*, Fairmile Books, Cobham, Surrey, 1995
Prior, Robin and Wilson, Trevor, *The Somme*, Yale University Press, New Haven CT and London, 2005
Pugsley, Christopher, *The Anzac Experience: New Zealand, Australia and Empire in the First World War*, Reid, Auckland, 2004
——, *On the Fringe of Hell: New Zealanders and Military Discipline in the First World War*, Hodder and Stoughton, Auckland, 1991
Putkowski, Julian and Sykes, Julian, *Shot at Dawn: Executions in World War One by authority of the Brirtish Army Act*, Wharncliffe, Barnsley, 1989
Rawling, Bill, *Surviving Trench Warfare: Technology and the Canadian Corps, 1914–1918*, University of Toronto Press, 1987
Robbins, Simon, *British Generalship on the Western Front, 1914–18: Defeat into Victory*, Frank Cass, London, 2005
Samuels, Martin, *Command or Control?: Command, Training and Tactics in the British and German Armies, 1888–1918*, Frank Cass, London, 1995

——, *Doctrine and Dogma: German and British Infantry Tactics in the First World War*, Greenwood Press, Westport CT, 1992

Sheffield, Gary, *The Somme*, Cassell, London, 2003

——, *Forgotten Victory. The First World War: Myths and Realities*, Headline, London, 2001

——, *Leadership in the Trenches: Officer-Man Relations, Morale and Discipline in the British Army in the Era of the First World War*, Macmillan, London, 2000

——, *Leadership and Command: The Anglo-American Military Experience since 1861*, Brassey's London, 1997

——, and Peter Gray (eds), *Changing War: The British Army, the Hundred Days Campaign and the Birth of the Royal Air Force, 1918*, Bloomsbury, London, 2013

——, and Todman, Dan (eds), *Command and Control on the Western Front: The British Army's Experience, 1914–1918*, Spellmount, Staplehurst, 2004

Sheldon, Jack, *The German Army on the Western Front, 1915*, Pen and Sword, Barnsley, 2012

——, *The German Army at Ypres 1914 and the Battle for Flanders*, Pen and Sword, Barnsley, 2010

——, *The German Army at Cambrai*, Pen and Sword, Barnsley, 2009

——, *The German Army on Vimy Ridge, 1914–1917*, Pen and Sword, Barnsley, 2008

——, *The German Army at Passchendaele*, Pen and Sword, Barnsley, 2007

——, *The German Army on the Somme, 1914–1916*, Pen and Sword, Barnsley, 2006

Simkins, Peter, *Kitchener's Army: The Raising of the New Armies, 1914–16*, Manchester University Press, 1988

Simpson, Andy, *Directing Operations: British Corps Command on the Western Front 1914–18*, Spellmount, Stroud, 2006

Stedman, Michael, *Thiepval*, Battleground Europe series, Leo Cooper/Pen and Sword, London and Barnsley, 1995

Stephen, Martin, *The Price of Pity: Poetry, History and Myth in the Great War*, Leo Cooper, London, 1996

Strong, Paul and Marble, Sanders, *Artillery in the Great War*, Pen and Sword, Barnsley, 2011

Taylor, A.J.P., *The First World War: An Illustrated History*, Hamish Hamilton, London, 1963

Terraine, John, *The Smoke and the Fire: Myths and Anti-Myths of War, 1861–1945*, Sidgwick and Jackson, London, 1980

Travers, Tim, *How the War was Won: Command and Technology in the British Army on the Western Front, 1917–1918*, Routledge, London, 1992

——, *The Killing Ground: The British Army, the Western Front and the Emergence of Modern Warfare, 1900–1918*, Allen and Unwin, London, 1987

Walker, Jonathan, *The Blood Tub: General Gough and the Battle of Bullecourt, 1917*, Spellmount, Staplehurst, 1998

Watson, Alexander, *Enduring the Great War: Combat, Morale and Collapse in the German and British Armies, 1914–1918*, Cambridge University Press, 2008

Welborn, Suzanne, *Lords of Death: A People, A Place, A Legend*, Fremantle Arts Centre Press, 1982

Winter, Denis, *Haig's Command: A Reassessment*, Viking, London, 1991

Wolff, Leon, *In Flanders Fields: The 1917 Campaign*, Longmans, London, 1959

Yockelson, Mitchell A., *Borrowed Soldiers: Americans Under British Command, 1918*, University of Oklahoma Press, 2008

Zabecki, David T., *The German 1918 Offensives: A Case Study in the Operational Level of War*, Routledge, Abingdon, 2006

Chapters, Essays and Journal Articles

Bailey, Jonathan, 'British Artillery in the Great War', in Paddy Griffith (ed.), *British Fighting Methods in the Great War*, Frank Cass, London, 1996

Bond, Brian, 'Liddell Hart and the First World War', in *Look to Your Front: Studies in the First World War by the British Commission for Military* History, Spellmount, Staplehurst, 1999

——, 'Passchendaele: Verdicts, Past and Present', in Peter H. Liddle (ed.), *Passchendaele in Perspective: The Third Battle of Ypres*, Leo Cooper, London, 1997

Boff, Jonathan, 'Command Culture and Complexity: Third Army during the Hundred Days, August–November 1918', in Gary Sheffield and Peter Gray (eds), *Changing War: The British Army, the Hundred Days Campaign and the Birth of the Royal Air Force, 1918*, Bloomsbury, London, 2013

Bourne, John, 'The BEF on the Somme: Some Career Aspects – Part I, July 1916', in *Gun Fire: A Journal of First World War History*, No. 35

——, 'The BEF on the Somme: Some Career Aspects – Part Two: 2 July–19 November 1916', in *Gun Fire*, No. 39

——, 'A Personal Reflection on 1 July 1916', in *Firestep: The Magazine of the Western Front Association's London Branch*, Vol. 5, No. 2, November 2004

——, 'Major–General W.C.G. Heneker: A Divisional Commander of the Great War', in Matthew Hughes and Matthew Seligmann (eds), *Leadership in Conflict, 1914–1918*, Leo Cooper/Pen and Sword, Barnsley, 2000

——, 'Haig and the Historians', in Brian Bond and Nigel Cave (eds), *Haig: A Reappraisal 70 Years On*, Leo Cooper/Pen and Sword, Barnsley, 1999

——, 'The BEF's Generals on 29 September 1918: An Empirical Portrait with some British and Australian Comparisons', in Peter Dennis and Jeffrey Grey (eds), *1918: Defining Victory*, Army History Unit, Canberra, 1999

——, 'British Generals in the First World War', in Gary Sheffield (ed.), *Leadership and Command: The Anglo-American Military Experience since 1861*, Brassey's London, 1997

Danchev, Alex, '"Bunking and Debunking": The Controversies of the 1960s', in Brian Bond (ed.), *The First World War and British Military History*, Clarendon Press, Oxford, 1991

French, David, 'Sir James Edmonds and the Official History: France and Belgium', in Brian Bond (ed.), *The First World War and British Military History*, Clarendon Press, Oxford, 1991

Griffith, Paddy, 'The Extent of Tactical Reform in the British Army', in Paddy Griffith (ed.), *British Fighting Methods in the Great War*, Frank Cass, London, 1996

Humphries, Mark Osborne, 'Old Wine in New Bottles: A Comparison of British and Canadian Preparations for the Battle of Arras', in Geoffrey Hayes, Andrew Iarocci and Mike Bechtold (eds), *Vimy Ridge: A Canadian Reassessment*, Wilfrid Laurier University Press, Waterloo, Ontario, 2007

Lee, John, 'Command and Control in Battle: British Divisions on the Menin Road Ridge, 20 September 1917', in Gary Sheffield and Dan Todman (eds), *Command and Control on the Western Front: The British Army's Experience, 1914–1918*, Spellmount, Staplehurst, 2004

——, 'Some Lessons of the Somme: The British Infantry in 1917', in *Look to Your Front: Studies in the First World War by the British Commission for Military History*, Spellmount, Staplehurst, 1999

Leonard, Jane, 'The Reaction of Irish Officers in the British Army to the Easter Rising of 1916', in Peter H. Liddle and Hugh Cecil (eds), *Facing Armageddon: The First World War Experienced*, Leo Cooper/Pen and Sword, London and Barnsley, 1996

Peaty, John, 'Capital Courts-Martial during the Great War', in *Look to Your Front: Studies in the First World War by the British Commission for Military History*, Spellmount, Staplehurst, 1999

Philpott, William, 'Marshal Ferdinand Foch and Allied Victory', in Matthew Hughes and Matthew Seligmann (eds), *Leadership in Conflict, 1914–1918*, Leo Cooper/Pen and Sword, Barnsley, 2000

Prior, Robin and Wilson, Trevor, 'Winning the War', in Peter Dennis and Jeffrey Grey (eds), *1918: Defining Victory*, Army History Unit, Canberra, 1999

Sheffield, Gary and Todman, Dan, 'Command and Control in the British Army on the Western Front', in Gary Sheffield and Dan Todman (eds), *Command and Control on the Western Front: The British Army's Experience, 1914–1918*, Spellmount, Staplehurst, 2004

Simkins, Peter, 'Each One a Pocket Hercules: The Bantam Experiment and the Case of the Thirty-Fifth Division', in Sanders Marble (ed.), *Scraping the Barrel: The Military Use of Substandard Manpower, 1860–1960*, Fordham University Press, New York, 2012

——, '"Just as Much as is Humanly Possible": The 10th Essex at Thiepval, September 1916', *The Eagle: Journal of the Essex Regiment Association*, Issue 57, Spring 2007

——, 'The Very Model of a Modern Major-General: Major-General H.W. Higginson, CB, DSO and Bar, Royal Dublin Fusiliers', *The Blue Cap: Journal of the Royal Dublin Fusiliers Association*, Vol. 14, December 2007

——, '"The Black Man", "The Brat" and Londoners on the Somme: Some Reflections on the Capture of Thiepval, September 1916', *Firestep: The Magazine of the Western Front Association's London Branch*, Vol. 5, No. 2, November 2004

——, '"Building Blocks": Aspects of Command and Control at Brigade Level in the BEF's Offensive Operations, 1916–1918', in Gary Sheffield and Dan Todman (eds), *Command and Control on the Western Front: The British Army's Experience, 1914–1918*, Spellmount, Staplehurst, 2004

——, 'For Better or For Worse: Sir Henry Rawlinson and his Allies in 1916 and 1918', in Matthew Hughes and Matthew Seligmann (eds), *Leadership in Conflict, 1914–1918*, Leo Cooper/Pen and Sword, Barnsley, 2000

——, 'Somme Reprise: Reflections on the Fighting for Albert and Bapaume, August 1918', in *Look to Your Front: Studies in the First World War by the British Commission for Military History*, Spellmount, Staplehurst, 1999

——, 'Haig and the Army Commanders', in Brian Bond and Nigel Cave (eds), *Haig: A Reappraisal 70 Years On*, Leo Cooper/Pen and Sword, Barnsley, 1999

——, 'The Events of the "Last Hundred Days", 1918', *Royal United Services Institute Journal*, Vol. 143, No. 6, December 1998

——, 'The War Experience of a Typical Kitchener Division: The 18th Division, 1914–1918', in Peter H. Liddle and Hugh Cecil (eds), *Facing Armageddon: The First World War Experienced*, Leo Cooper/Pen and Sword, London and Barnsley, 1996

——, 'Co-Stars or Supporting Cast?: British Divisions in the "Hundred Days", 1918', in Paddy Griffith (ed.), *British Fighting Methods in the Great War*, Frank Cass, London, 1996

——, 'Everyman at War: Recent Interpretations of the Front Line Experience', in Brian Bond (ed.), *The First World War and British Military History*, Clarendon Press, Oxford, 1991

Simpson, Andy, 'British Corps Command on the Western Front, 1914–1918', in Gary Sheffield and Dan Todman (eds), *Command and Control on the Western Front: The British Army's Experience, 1914–1918*, Spellmount, Staplehurst, 2004

Battlefield Guides

Coombs, Rose E.B., *Before Endeavours Fade: A Guide to the Battlefields of the First World War*, After the Battle, London, 1976

Giles, John, *The Somme: Then and Now*, Bailey Brothers and Swinfen, Folkestone, 1977

Middlebrook, Martin and Mary, *The Somme Battlefields: A Comprehensive Guide From Crécy to the Two World Wars*, Viking, London, 1991

Theses and Dissertations

Geddes, Alistair, 'Solly-Flood, GHQ and Tactical Training in the BEF, 1916–1918', MA Dissertation, University of Birmingham, 2007

Molineux, Dave, 'The Effect of Platoon Structure on Tactical Development in the BEF, June to November 1918', MA Dissertation, University of Birmingham, 2009

Thomas, Alun, 'The British 8th Infantry Division on the Western Front, 1914–18', PhD Thesis, University of Birmingham, 2010

Whitmarsh, Andrew, 'Tactical and Operational Practice in the British Expeditionary Force. A Divisional Study: The 12th (Eastern) Division, 1915–1918', MA Dissertation, University of Leeds, 1995

Index

Index to Formations and Units